Complete BASIC Programming

Complete BASIC Programming

Steven L. Mandell

West Publishing Company

St. Paul New York San Francisco Los Angeles

Copy Editor: Mary Berry
Cover Art: © James T. Hoffman 1980
Text Design: Bruce Kortebien, The Design Office
Composition: TriStar Graphics
Color Airbrush Artwork: Dave Pauly Graphics
Technical Artwork: Editing, Design & Production

Library of Congress Cataloging in Publication Data

Mandell, Steven L.
Complete BASIC programming.

Bibliography: p.
Includes index.
1. Basic (Computer program language) 2. Microcomputers —Programming. I. Title. II. Title: Complete B.A.S.I.C. programming.
QA76.73.B3M35 1984 001.64'24 83-23500
ISBN 0-314-77921-3
2nd Reprint—1984

Photo Credits

Opposite Title Page: Courtesy of Paradyne Corporation. **Chapter 1:** Courtesy of Cal Arts, photo by Dennis Gilbert. **Chapter 2:** Courtesy of Bell Laboratories. **Chapter 3:** Courtesy of Comshare Incorporated. **Chapter 4:** Courtesy of DATAPRODUCTS CORP. **Chapter 5:** © Copyright Phillip A. Harrington. **Chapter 6:** Courtesy of the Naval Photographic Center, Naval District Washington, Washington, D.C. **Chapter 7:** Courtesy of IBM. **Chapter 8:** Courtesy of Sperry-Univac Corporation. **Chapter 9:** © Copyright Phillip A. Harrington. **Chapter 10:** Courtesy of Bell Laboratories. **Chapter 11:** Courtesy of Auto-trol Technology Corporation. **307:** Courtesy of Digital Corporation. **311:** Courtesy of Apple Computers. **315:** Courtesy of IBM. **319:** Courtesy of Radio Shack. **323:** Courtesy of Commodore. **329:** Courtesy of Bell Laboratories.

Contents

Chapter 6

Chapter 7

Preface

BASIC has traditionally been accepted as the most effective programming language for instructional purposes. In recent years, business and computer manufacturers have recognized the vast potential for the BASIC language beyond education. Therefore, the availability and usage of BASIC has increased dramatically. Today most small business computer systems and home computer systems rely heavily on BASIC programming support.

One major problem associated with such tremendous growth has been the lack of controls on the implementation of the language. Although there is a national standard (ANSI) version of BASIC, it is normally not followed by computer designers. Thus there are differences in the BASIC language found on various computers. The material in this book not only presents BASIC found on a typical large time-shared computer system (Digital Equipment Corp.), but also includes coverage of microcomputer implementations (Apple, IBM, PET/Commodore 64, TRS-80). Whenever a BASIC instruction deviates from the national standard, it is highlighted.

Color coding has been used extensively throughout the material to assist the reader. The following legend should prove valuable:

Blue	Computer Output
Brown shading	Highlighted Statements
Red	User Response
Grey shading	Nonstandard BASIC

Several special features have been included in the text to assist the student to better grasp the material. Learning Checks with answers are included as a means of self testing before proceeding to a subsequent section. A Comprehensive Programming Problem permits the student to bring all of the key chapter material together. An extensive set of Review Questions, Debugging Exercises, and Programming Problems provide a wide selection of feedback material for comprehension.

A criticism of many BASIC textbooks is a lack of examples depicting how instructions are actually utilized. This text has focused on these concerns. Throughout the material, every effort has been made to teach the student through showing rather than telling. In this manner the instructions become concrete rather than visual abstractions. Flowcharts are also widely spaced throughout the text to provide a graphical exploration of the programming segments.

A special note of appreciation to Terrye Gregory, Dr. Stephen Gregory, Bob Szymanski, and Karen McKee for their herculean efforts on this project. Every program has been both class tested and run on the various computer systems. I would also like to thank the following reviewers whose insight greatly improved the manuscript: George A. Bohlen, University of Dayton, and David A. Kay, Moorpark College, California. Our primary goal has been to develop a student-oriented BASIC text that is both logical and consistent in its presentation. I would appreciate receiving any suggestions that might improve the material.

STEVEN L. MANDELL

Complete BASIC Programming

1 Introduction to BASIC

Outline

Objectives

After reading this chapter, the student should be able to do the following:

- Give a general overview of what a computer system is and how it functions.
- Understand and define the stored-program concept.
- Understand and define the operational capabilities of a computer system—input, output, arithmetic, and logical operations.
- Understand and define the five steps of the programming process.
- Understand system and editing commands.

Background

BASIC was developed in the mid-1960s at Dartmouth College by Professors John G. Kemeny and Thomas E. Kurtz and has become one of the most popular programming languages. BASIC, short for Beginner's All-purpose Symbolic Instruction Code, is easy to learn, can be used for a wide variety of useful tasks, and is well suited for classroom teaching.

BASIC, like any language, includes rules for spelling, syntax, grammar, and punctuation. Just as the rules in English help us understand one another, so the rules in BASIC help the computer understand what we want it to do. In BASIC, the rules link abstract algebraic expressions with easy-to-understand English words like LET, GOTO, FOR/NEXT, INPUT, PRINT, and END.

BASIC was originally developed for use in a large, interactive computer environment: one or more BASIC users could communicate with the computer *during* processing and feel as though they had the computer all to themselves. As the demand for minicomputers and microcomputers increased, manufacturers of such computers felt pressure to develop simple but effective languages for them. Rather than create entirely new languages, most opted to offer BASIC because of its interactive capability—where the user can communicate directly with the computer in a conversational fashion. Many altered the original BASIC, however, to suit their equipment. The result is that, although the BASIC language has a universally accepted set of standard rules called **ANSI BASIC,** each manufacturer adds its "quirks" to this standard to make use of special features of its machines.

This book discusses BASIC commands common to most computer systems but will note the language variations among vendors. Most programming examples have been executed on five different computers: a DECSYSTEM 20 to represent the major time-sharing systems; and the Apple, IBM Personal Computer, TRS-80, and PET/Commodore 64 to represent popular microcomputer systems. Most other microcomputers are capable of using a dialect called BASIC-80 from Microsoft Consumer Products and an operating system called CP/M produced by Digital Research. Since the IBM's BASIC and operating systems were also designed by Microsoft, they are similar to BASIC-80 and CP/M. Therefore references for those systems will parallel the IBM instructions. The programming examples will run on the DECSYSTEM 20 computer, but important changes required to execute them on the other computers are noted. Although there are a variety of models and languages for the Apple and TRS-80 computers, this book discusses only one of each—the Apple II computer with the Applesoft language and the TRS-80 Model III computer with Model III language (essentially the same as level II BASIC for Model I).

Computers and the Stored-Program Concept

A computer system consists of three primary units—input units, the processor unit, and output units—that perform the following functions, respectively: accept data (input), process data by performing comparisons and calculations, and output the results. Computers perform operations through the use of electronic currents. They are fast, accurate, inexhaustible, and require no human intervention.

Data are facts, numbers, and characters that often are entered into the computer via a typewriter–like keyboard. Many other types of input devices also can be used to enter data (light pens, scanners, tapes, and so on).

The processor unit is divided into two main parts: the central processing unit (CPU) and main computer storage (main memory). The actual processing takes place in the CPU. Each numeric, alphabetic, and special character of data is stored in the main computer memory when it is entered.

The contents of main memory can be transferred to auxiliary storage devices such as magnetic tape and disks. This allows us to bring in new data to main memory while preserving the previous contents. The data on the auxiliary storage devices later can be loaded into main memory and used again without the user's having to retype it. Main memory also stores the instructions (processing steps) that tell the CPU what to do with the data. This ability to store all necessary instructions and data to execute a program is referred to as the **stored-program concept.** In the early days of computers, before the stored-program concept was realized, human operators had to manually enter the instructions and data needed to run a program as it was running, thus slowing down the processing considerably.

After the data has been processed, the results of processing are output in the form of useful information. Output units such as video screens and printers make the results accessible for use by people. Figure 1–1 illustrates a typical basic computer system.

Computer Processing: Arithmetic and Logical Operations

Once the data has been entered and stored in main memory, it can be processed. Basic arithmetic operations such as addition, subtraction, multiplication, and division can be performed on numeric data. The results of arithmetic operations can be used for further operations or as output. Computer systems also have the ability to perform logical operations. Numbers, letters, and special characters can be compared to see if they are equal to, less than, or greater than one another. The computer then can determine what steps to take according to the results of these comparisons.

Interpreters and Compilers

A programmer writes the instructions, or processing steps, in a programming language such as FORTRAN, COBOL, and Pascal. This book will

Figure 1–1 BASIC COMPUTER SYSTEM

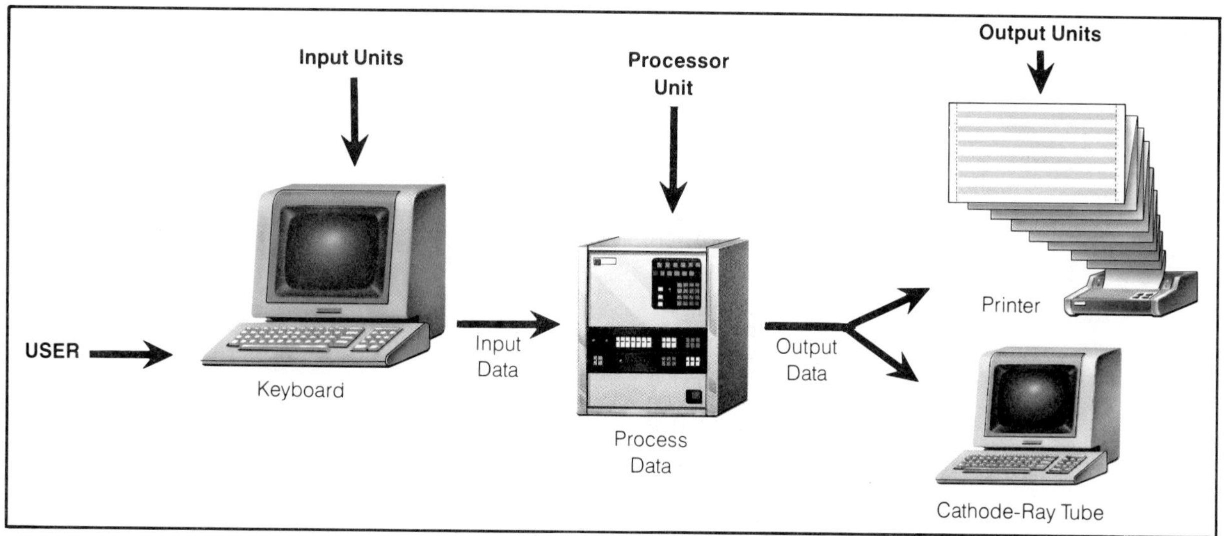

teach you how to write programs using the BASIC programming language. These languages are high-level languages, which are fairly easy for people to understand. However, the CPU cannot interpret these languages. The CPU, which executes the instructions, can understand only machine language (the code of 0's and 1's that designates the proper electrical states in the computer). Microcomputer systems require an interpreter or compiler to translate the high-level language to machine language. Interpreters and compilers are programs that are either loaded into the computer from disk each time the system is turned on or stored permanently inside the computer in memory.

Most microcomputers use an interpreter for BASIC, whereas larger systems often use a compiler to translate languages. This is because a compiler typically requires much more storage space than an interpreter. The difference between an interpreter and a compiler is that the compiler creates an object program (the entire program in machine language format) and then loads the entire object program into main memory. The CPU then directly executes the object program. An interpreter passes only one line of machine language at a time to the CPU. Programs that have been compiled into an object program normally execute faster than those translated by an interpreter.

Introduction to Computer Programming

Computer programs (also called software) are step-by-step instructions to solve a problem. Since the computer must be able to read and interpret each instruction, it must be precisely written. To know what instructions are required to solve a problem, the programmer follows five steps, commonly called the **programming process:**

1. Define and document the problem.
2. Design and document a solution.
3. Write and document a program.
4. Submit the program to the computer.
5. Test and debug the program, and revise the documentation if necessary.

To show how these steps are used in the programming process, let us take a sample data-processing problem: calculating our metric weight from our weight in pounds.

The first step is to define and document the problem. To do so, we analyze it by using the basic flow of all data processing—**input, processing, output**—but with a twist. It is often easier to determine what processing is needed by working backward. First, determine what output is required, and then see what input is available for the program. The gap between the available input and the required output will be the processing needed in the program.

Determining the output required for the problem is quite simple—we need to know our weight in kilograms. The input available is our weight in pounds. We now need to develop a series of steps, called an **algorithm,** that will enable us to produce the desired output from the available input. We need some conversion factor that translates the weight in pounds to kilograms. One kilogram equals 2.2 pounds; hence, the algorithm to calculate our metric weight is metric weight = weight ÷ 2.2 pounds. We have now defined the problem.

The second step, designing and documenting a solution, requires developing a logical sequence of instructions, or statements, to solve the problem. Remember, good documentation can help avoid future problems or make them easier to solve when they do come about. Documentation consists of all written descriptions and explanations necessary for later modification or updating of the program. A great tool to use at this point is the flowchart. **Flowcharts** are a form of documentation and are composed of symbols that stand for program statements. For example, the symbol for a processing step is this:

The following is the symbol for a step that involves either input from the terminal or output to the terminal or printer:

This symbol shows where the program starts or stops:

To create a flowchart for our example, we only need these three symbols. Some additional symbols that we will use later in this book include the following:

1. The symbol that shows where a comparison (decision) is to be made and where alternative processing is to occur based upon the results of the comparison is this:

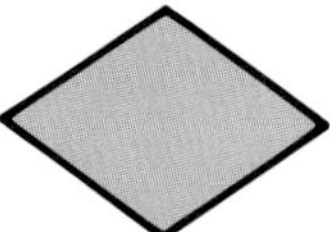

2. To indicate an entry from or an exit to another part of the program flowchart, use this symbol:

3. The following symbol represents a preparation step, such as defining the dimensions of an array (discussed in Section 9):

Figure 1–2 shows a flowchart depicting the steps of the programming example. Notice how the symbols are shown in logical order, top down, connected by arrows. The first symbol shows the start of the program. It may correspond to one or more remarks at the beginning of the program. The second symbol shows an input step—we enter our weight. The third shows the processing done by the program—conversion of weight in pounds to metric weight. After that, we want to see the result, so we output the converted weight to the terminal. Finally, another start/stop symbol signifies the end of the program. The flowchart makes it easy to see the input, processing, and output steps of the program.

If the solution has been designed carefully, the third step—writing and documenting the program—should be relatively easy. All that is required is to translate the flowchart into BASIC statements. Figure 1–3 shows this program written in BASIC. As you can see, many BASIC words, such as

Figure 1-2 FLOWCHART EXAMPLE

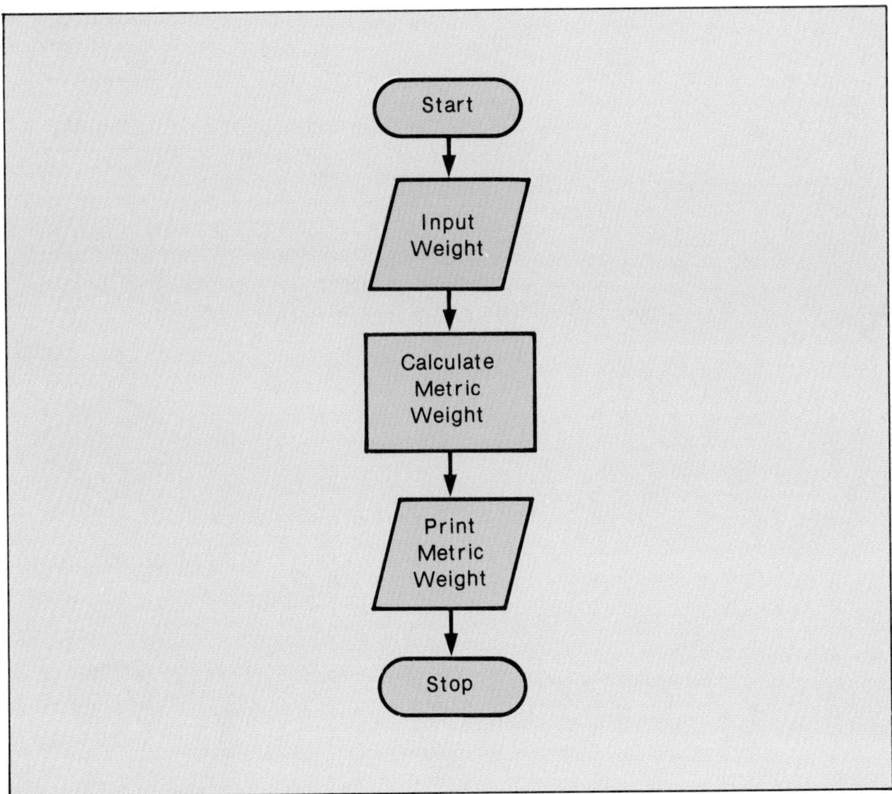

INPUT and PRINT, are easy to interpret. The symbol / means "divide." The REM statement is used to document the program. Compare the coded BASIC statements in Figure 1-3 to the flowchart in Figure 1-2; the correspondence between the two is obvious.

In the program in Figure 1-3, each statement starts with a **line number.** Line numbers tell the computer the order in which to execute statements.

ANSI Standards

The purpose of a programming standard is to make it possible for a program to have **transportability.** In other words, if you write a program whose syntax lies completely within the BASIC standard, this program will run correctly on *any* brand of computer that claims its BASIC meets the standards.

The American National Standards Institute, Inc. (ANSI), 1430 Broadway, New York, NY 10018, has published the ANSI Standard for Minimal BASIC. It is one of the standards least adhered to, with extremely few manufacturers' designing their machines around it. As the title of the document suggests, the standard does not include many features implemented by computer manufacturers.

Figure 1–3 METRIC WEIGHT PROGRAM

```
00100 REM *** THIS PROGRAM CALCULATES METRIC WEIGHT ***
00105 INPUT "ENTER YOUR WEIGHT IN POUNDS";W
00110 LET M = W / 2.2
00115 PRINT "YOUR METRIC WEIGHT IS";M;"KILOGRAMS"
00999 END
```

Line 100 is a comment describing the program. The computer ignores all such comment statements; they are for documentation purposes. Line 105 tells the computer to print out a statement (shown in quotes)—your cue to enter your weight—and then to accept the input after you type it in. Line 110 is an example of an assignment statement, which assigns values on the right side of the equal sign to special variables on the left (this is discussed in Chapter 3). Line 115 instructs the computer to print out first a heading (shown in quotes) and then the computed metric weight. Finally, line 999 tells the computer to stop processing. Again, you can see how each statement follows the flow of input, processing, and output.

The fourth step involves sitting down at the terminal and typing the program, line for line, into the computer. Many interactive BASIC interpreters and compilers check for syntax errors as each statement is typed in. **Syntax** refers to the way instructions have to be written (rules must be followed, just as grammatical rules must be followed in English). A syntax check can save considerable debugging time. Figure 1–4 shows an interactive session with syntax checking.

In the first example, the word PRINT was misspelled. After entering line 10, the computer performed a syntax check. Upon discovering that the keyword PRINT was misspelled, the user is informed of the error. In this case, the computer reprinted the line in error followed by the error message: ? STATEMENT NOT RECOGNIZED. In the second example, an arithmetic expression was found on the left side of an equal (=) sign. In BASIC, only a single variable name can be on the left side of an equal sign. The computer informs the user of the syntax error by reprinting the line in error followed by the error message: ? FOUND "+" WHEN EXPECTING "="

After all syntax errors have been eliminated, the program can be tested with sample data (the fifth step). During this stage, the logic of the program is checked for correctness; for instance, were the correct statements used to determine the metric weight? Figure 1–5 shows the execution of the metric weight program.

During each of these five steps, it is important that adequate documentation be written and maintained. During the last step, any revisions to the documentation that may be required should be made.

This example is relatively simple, but it shows each of the steps required to complete a program. Although other problems may be more com-

Figure 1–4 SYNTAX CHECKING

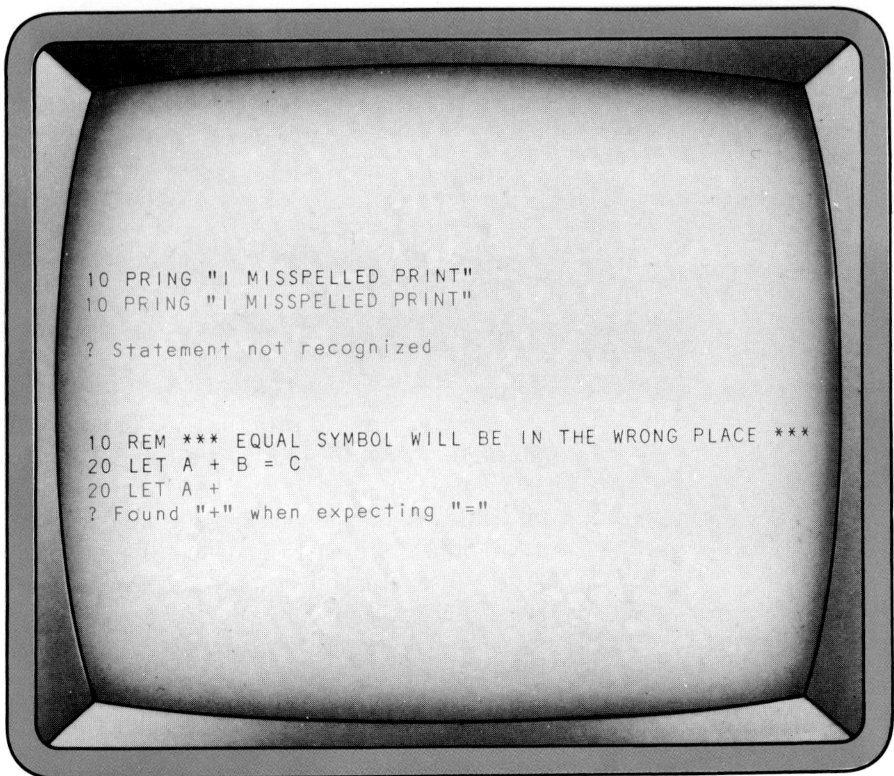

plex, the steps involved are the same. Successful programming can only come about through diligent application of the five steps in the programming process.

10 PRING "I MISSPELLED PRINT"
10 PRING "I MISSPELLED PRINT"
? Statement not recognized
10 REM *** EQUAL SYMBOL WILL BE IN THE WRONG PLACE ***
20 LET A + B = C
20 LET A +
? Found "+" when expecting "="

Figure 1–5
EXECUTION OF METRIC WEIGHT PROGRAM

RUNNH
ENTER YOUR WEIGHT IN POUNDS ? 150
YOUR METRIC WEIGHT IS 68.18182 KILOGRAMS

LEARNING CHECK

1. A computer system consists of three primary units: ________, ________, and ________.
2. ________ are facts, numbers, and characters that are entered into the computer.
3. The processor unit is divided into two main parts: the ________ and the ________.
4. The ________ refers to the ability to store internally all necessary instructions and data to execute a program.
5. A(n) ________ or a(n) ________ translates a high-level language to machine language.
6. The following is the correct sequence of steps for the programming process: Define and document the problem; design and document a solution; write and document a program; submit the program to the computer; test and debug the program, and revise the documentation. TRUE FALSE (Circle the correct answer.)

Interacting with the Computer

An important step in BASIC programming is learning to control the computer. Although this book cannot present the full operational details for each computer, it can discuss the principles of how to turn the computer on, use the BASIC programming language, retrieve a program from auxiliary storage, display the program, alter the program, and save the program for future reference.

Basic System and Editing Commands

BASIC programming requires the use of several types of commands. Some of the commands, such as GOTO, LET, and READ, are program language statements. They are assembled into programs to solve specific business, scientific, engineering, and mathematical problems. The remaining chapters of this book describe their characteristics and how they are used.

There are also **system commands** and **editing commands** used by the programmer to communicate with the operating system of the computer to perform functions like saving programs for future reference and making changes in programs. Table 1–1 summarizes common system and editing commands. Some commands, such as LIST, RUN, and DELETE, are almost universally used but are not covered by ANSI standards. Appendixes A through E describe such commands as they relate to the five computer systems used in the programming examples in this book.

Answers

1. input units; processor unit; output units
2. Data
3. CPU; main computer storage
4. stored-program concept
5. interpreter; compiler
6. True

Table 1–1 COMMON SYSTEM AND EDITING COMMANDS

	DEC	Apple	PET/Commodore 64
POWERSWITCH LOCATION	Left rear of terminal	Left rear of terminal	Right side panel (rear)
SIGN-ON PROCEDURES			
User	Control-C	No response	No response
Computer response	TOPS-20 MONITOR	APPLE II	***COMMODORE 64 BASIC V2***
User	LOG ACCT. # PASSWORD	No response	No response
STARTING BASIC			
User	BASIC	Comes up in BASIC	Comes up in BASIC
Computer response	READY	Flashing cursor	READY (Flashing block)
User	NEW	Begin typing program	Begin typing program
Computer response	NEW FILENAME--		
User	Enter name of program; begin typing program		
SYSTEM COMMANDS			
List	LIST	LIST	LIST
Execute a program	RUN	RUN	RUN
Delete a line	DELETE line #	Type line #, then RETURN	Type line #, then RETURN
Store program on disk	SAVE	SAVE name	SAVE "name",8
Store program on tape	Does not apply	SAVE	SAVE "name"
Retrieve program from disk	OLD OLD FILENAME--	LOAD name or RUN name8	LOAD "name",
Retrieve program from tape	Does not apply	LOAD	LOAD "name"
SIGN-OFF PROCEDURES			
User	GOODBYE or BYE	No response	No response
Computer response	KILLED JOB	No response	No response
User	Power off	Power off	Power off

The system and editing commands are **immediate-mode commands;** that is, they are executed as soon as the carriage control key (RETURN, ENTER) is pressed. They differ from BASIC language commands, which are not executed until the program is run. The most commonly used system commands are discussed in the following sections.

System Commands

NEW The NEW command tells the computer to erase any program currently in active memory. After typing this command, you can start entering a new program.

	TRS-80	IBM/Cassette BASIC	IBM/Disk BASIC
POWERSWITCH LOCATION	Right front under keyboard	Right rear of computer	Right rear of computer
SIGN-ON PROCEDURES			
User	No response	No response	No response
Computer response	CASS? MEMORY SIZE? RADIO SHACK MODEL III BASIC (C) 80 TANDY	IBM Personal Computer BASIC Version C1.00 Copyright IBM Corp. 1981 61404 Bytes Free OK	Enter today's date (m-d-y): time The IBM Personal Computer DOS Version 1.10 (C) Copyright IBM Corp. 1981, 1982 A >
User	Respond to CASS? and MEMORY SIZE? Queries	No response	Respond to date query
STARTING BASIC			
User	Comes up In BASIC	Comes up in BASIC	Type BASIC or BASICA (For Advanced BASIC) after computer types A >
Computer response	READY	OK	OK
User	Begin typing program	Begin typing program	Begin typing program
Computer response			
User			
SYSTEM COMMANDS			
List	LIST	LIST	LIST
Execute a program	RUN	RUN	RUN
Delete a line	DELETE line #	DELETE line #	DELETE line #
Store program on disk	SAVE "name"	----------	SAVE "name"
Store program on tape	SAVE "name"	SAVE "name"	Does not apply
Retrieve program from disk	LOAD "name"	----------	LOAD "name"
Retrieve program from tape	CLOAD "name"	LOAD "name"	Does not apply
SIGN-OFF PROCEDURES			
User	No response	No response	No response
Computer response	No response	No response	No response
User	Power off	Power off	Power off

LIST After typing in a long program, you may want to admire the finished product. Type LIST to see the program commands displayed at the terminal. If you have a very short program, LIST can display the whole program on the screen. However, if the program has more lines than the screen does, only the last part of the program will remain on the screen.

Some screens permit only twenty-four lines to be displayed. You can display portions of programs by specifying the lines to be listed—LIST 250-400, for example. Most computers also allow you to suppress scrolling, that is, to freeze the listing temporarily (see "Controlling the Scroll" later in this section).

SAVE After you have typed many program lines, you will want to avoid losing them when the computer is turned off. To do this, you have to move a program from main memory to an auxiliary storage medium such as a cassette tape or disk. This move is accomplished by the SAVE command. There are generally several options to this command; for example, you may supply a name that distinguishes this particular program from all others. The discussions of each computer in Appendixes A through E summarize the most elementary forms of the SAVE command.

LOAD This command moves the designated program from auxilary storage to main computer memory. Before moving the program. LOAD closes all open files and deletes all variables and program lines currently residing in memory.

Controlling the Scroll If your program's output consists of forty lines of information but your screen only has a twenty-four–line capacity, how will you see all your output? The forty lines will be displayed so quickly that you will not be able to read them until the listing is finished. By then, however, the first sixteen lines will be gone—scrolled off the top of the screen.

Most computers have a means of controlling the scroll of the screen. The programmer can simply push one or two keys to freeze the display and then press the same keys to resume listing when desired. This method also can be used to freeze the output listing of a program during execution.

The next box in this chapter summarizes the method of scroll freezing, as well as the type of editor (discussed below) used on each of the five computers.

Editing Commands

Everyone makes typing mistakes. You should quickly learn how to correct yours. You may find a mistake before you press the RETURN key, or you may find it later. These two conditions call for different methods of correction.

Before RETURN Has Been Pressed Suppose you type LOST when you wish to LIST a program. If you notice the error before pressing RETURN, you can move the computer's cursor back to the O in LOST by pressing the DELETE key (on the DEC), the ← key (on the Apple, IBM, and TRS-80), or the INST DEL key (on the PET/Commodore 64). Then you can retype LIST correctly.

After RETURN Has Been Pressed If you notice an error after RETURN has been pressed, the simplest correction, in principle, is to retype the

Type of Editor and Scroll Control

Computer	Screen Editor?	Line Editor?	Scroll Stop/Start
DECSYSTEM 20	X	X	NO SCROLL[1]
Apple	X		CTRL-S[2]
IBM/Microsoft	X		CTRL-NUMLOCK[3]
TRS-80		X	SHIFT-@[4]
PET/Commodore 64	X		None[5]

Notes:

1. NO SCROLL is a separate single key.
2. CTRL-S means hold down the CONTROL key and the S key at the same time.
3. CTRL-NUMLOCK means hold down the control key and the NUMLOCK key at the same time.
4. SHIFT-@ means hold down the SHIFT key and the @ key at the same time.
5. There is no scroll stop/start keys; however, pressing the shift key slows down the scroll to one line at a time.

whole line. This may get tiresome for long lines, however—especially if you need to change only one character. Each computer has a means of correcting mistakes within a given line. There is not enough space here for a full explanation of these methods, but there are two general kinds—the screen editor and the line editor.

To use the screen editor, list the portion of the program containing the error. Then move the cursor to the position of the error—typically by pressing four keys with arrows that move the cursor up, down, left, or right. The incorrect characters then can be typed over or deleted, or new characters can be inserted between existing characters.

The line editor works on individual lines. The user specifies the line containing the error and uses commands such as REPLACE, INSERT, and DELETE instead of moving the cursor to the error.

LEARNING CHECK

1. Commands used by the programmer to communicate with the operating system of the computer are called ________.
2. System and editing commands are ________ commands; that is, they are executed as soon as the carriage control key is pressed.
3. The ________ command tells the computer to erase any program currently in memory.
4. The ________ command is used to move a program from internal memory to an external storage medium such as a cassette tape or disk.
5. Two general types of editors are the ________ and the ________.

Answers

1. system commands
2. immediate-mode
3. NEW
4. SAVE
5. screen editor; line editor

Summary

- BASIC (Beginner's All-purpose Symbolic Instruction Code) was developed in the mid-1960s by Professors John G. Kemeny and Thomas E. Kurtz.
- BASIC has rules of grammar (syntax) to which programmers must adhere.
- A computer system consists of three primary units: input units, the processor unit, and output units.
- Computers can perform the following functions: accept data (input), process data, and output results.
- The processor unit is made up of two main parts: the CPU and main computer storage.
- The stored-program concept refers to the ability to store all necessary instructions and data to execute a program.
- The CPU uses arithmetic and logical operations to manipulate data to obtain the desired results.
- Interpreters and compilers are programs that translate high-level languages into machine languages.
- The following are the five steps in the programming process: (1) define and document the problem; (2) design and document a solution; (3) write and document a program; (4) enter it into the computer; and (5) test and debug the program, and revise the documentation if necessary.
- System commands are used by the programmer to communicate with the operating system of the computer. Some commonly used ones are NEW, LIST, and SAVE.
- Editing commands help the programmer correct mistakes.
- Table 1–1 summarizes start-up procedures and common system and editing commands.

Review Questions

1. What is BASIC?
2. What three primary units are required on a computer system?
3. What three functions are required of a computer system?
4. The processor unit is divided into what two parts?
5. What is data, and where is it stored when entered into the computer?
6. Where is data processed?

7. How are the results of processing made accessible for use by people?
8. What is the stored-program concept?
9. What is the purpose of interpreters and compilers?
10. Computers can process data using what two general types of operations?
11. Name the five steps of the programming process.
12. What is documentation, and why is it important?
13. What is the basic flow of all data processing?
14. What tool is useful in designing a solution (Step 2 of the five steps)?
15. Which of the following symbols represents a processing step?

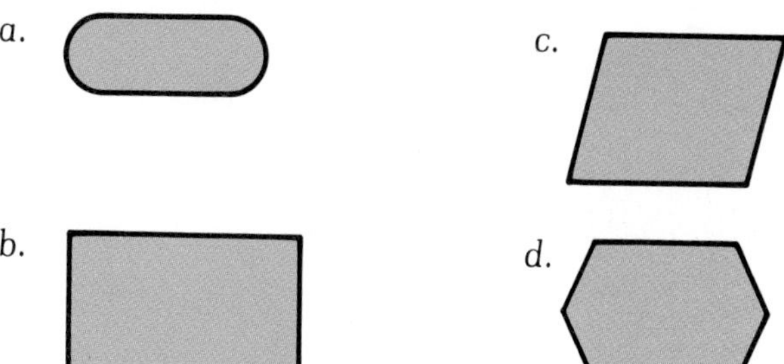

16. What is a syntax error?
17. The commands used by the programmer to communicate with the operating system are referred to as ______.
18. Explain the function of the system command NEW.
19. Explain the function of the system command LIST.
20. Explain the function of the system command SAVE.

JKL
5
6
PRS
7
OPER
0
*

2 BASIC Fundamentals

Outline

Objectives

After reading this chapter the student should be able to do the following:

- Understand what a BASIC program is.
- Recognize a BASIC instruction.
- Understand the function of line numbers.
- Recognize and understand the use of numeric and character string constants.
- Recognize and understand the use of numeric and string variables.

Overview

One of the best ways to learn any programming language is to examine sample programs. This and the remaining sections in this text will intersperse discussions of the language's general characteristics with program examples and practice problems to promote the learning process.

This chapter discusses some BASIC fundamentals: line numbers, BASIC statements, constants, character strings, and variables. All are demonstrated so that you can use them properly when you write programs.

Fundamentals of the BASIC Language

A BASIC program is a sequence of instructions that tells the computer how to solve a problem. Figure 2–1 is an example. This program calculates the gross pay of an employee who worked thirty hours at a rate of pay of $4.50.

Notice that each instruction contains a line number and a BASIC **statement.** BASIC statements are composed of special programming commands, numeric or character string constants, numeric or string variables, and formulas (also called **expressions**). Line 120 from the sample program is a typical BASIC statement. It tells the computer to multiply two values together and place the result in a location called G. G is the location in memory where the gross pay is stored.

On the DECSYSTEM 20 there are two commands, RUN and RUNNH, that can be used to execute (run) a program. If RUN is used, as in Figure 2–1, the computer will print a header giving the name of your program, the date, and the time as well as the output of the program. The RUNNH (Run No Header) command will eliminate the header and print only the output of the program. Throughout the remainder of this book we will use the RUNNH format. (See box "Important Keys and Commands.")

Line Numbers

The line number must be an integer between 1 and 99999. The upper limit for line numbers may vary according to the system being used. Program

Important Keys and Commands

Computer	Execution Command	Carriage Control Key	Comments
DECSYSTEM 20	RUN or RUNNH	RETURN	RUNNH means "RUN No Header." When RUN alone is pressed, the computer prints out the date and a system-identifying label.
Apple	RUN	RETURN	
IBM/Microsoft	RUN	↵	Although there is no lettering on the key, we will refer to it as *carriage return.*
TRS-80	RUN	ENTER	The ENTER key is located on the right side of the keyboard. This is the location of the RETURN key on the other computers. The two keys serve the same purpose.
PET/Commodore 64	RUN	RETURN	

Figure 2–1 GROSS PAY PROGRAM

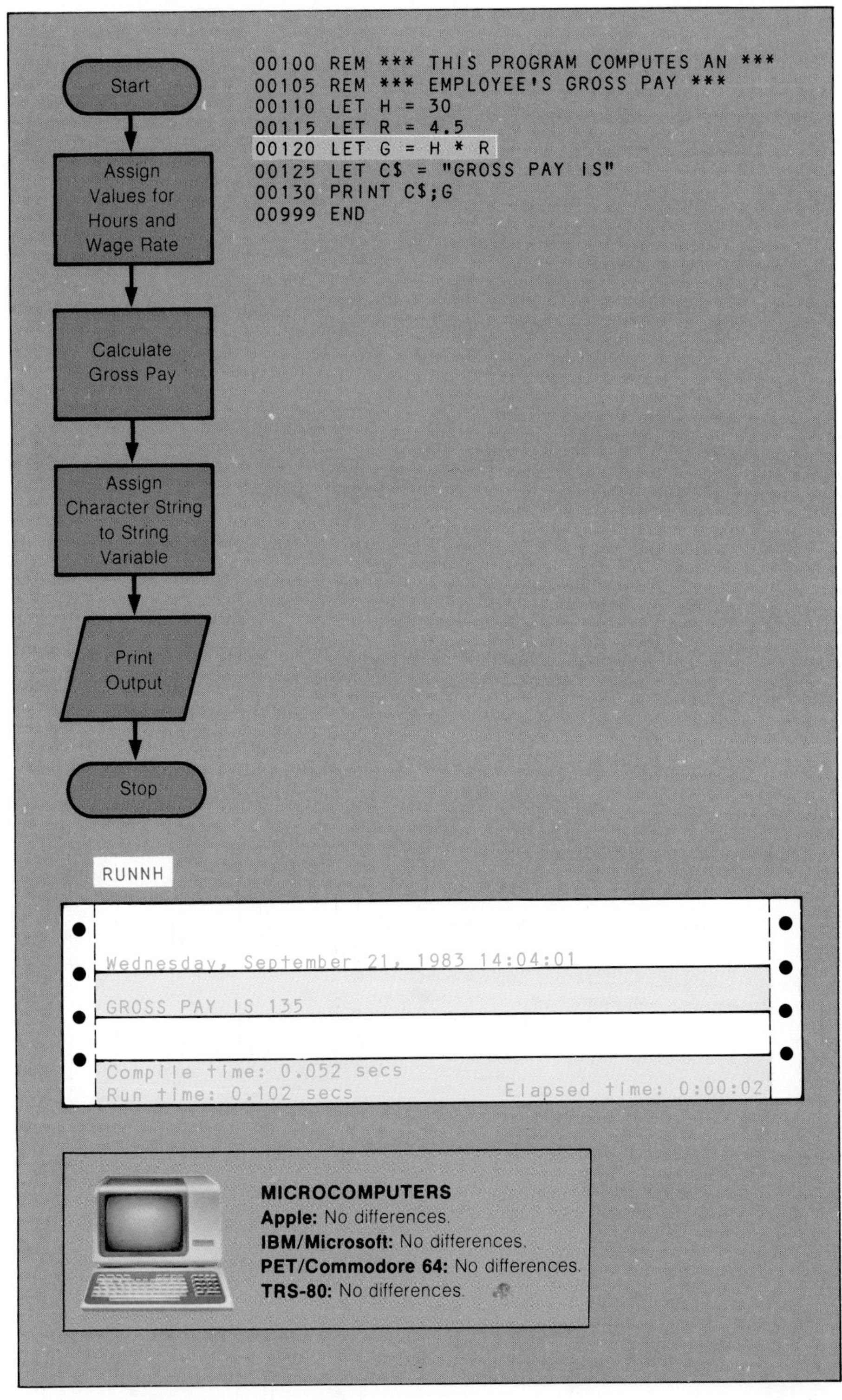
Start
Assign Values for Hours and Wage Rate
Calculate Gross Pay
Assign Character String to String Variable
Print Output
Stop
00100 REM *** THIS PROGRAM COMPUTES AN ***
00105 REM *** EMPLOYEE'S GROSS PAY ***
00110 LET H = 30
00115 LET R = 4.5
00120 LET G = H * R
00125 LET C$ = "GROSS PAY IS"
00130 PRINT C$;G
00999 END
RUNNH
Wednesday, September 21, 1983 14:04:01
GROSS PAY IS 135
Compile time: 0.052 secs
Run time: 0.102 secs
Elapsed time: 0:00:02
MICROCOMPUTERS
Apple: No differences.
IBM/Microsoft: No differences.
PET/Commodore 64: No differences.
TRS-80: No differences.

statements are executed by the computer in the sequence in which they are numbered. (Later we will explain how this sequence can be altered.) Line numbers also can be used as labels to refer to specific statements in the program.

Line numbers do not have to be specified in increments of 1. Using increments of 5, for example, makes it easier to insert new statements between existing lines at a later time without renumbering all the old statements in the program. For example, if we wanted to insert a new statement in the sample program between statements 115 and 120, we could number the new statement 117 without disturbing the order or numbering of the existing statements (see Figure 2–2). The BASIC interpreter or compiler arranges all the program statements in ascending order according to line number, even though the lines actually may have been entered in some other order.

Another advantage of BASIC line numbers is that they permit changes to be made to the program as it is being entered. For example, if two lines

Figure 2–2 GROSS PAY PROGRAM WITH INSERTED LINE

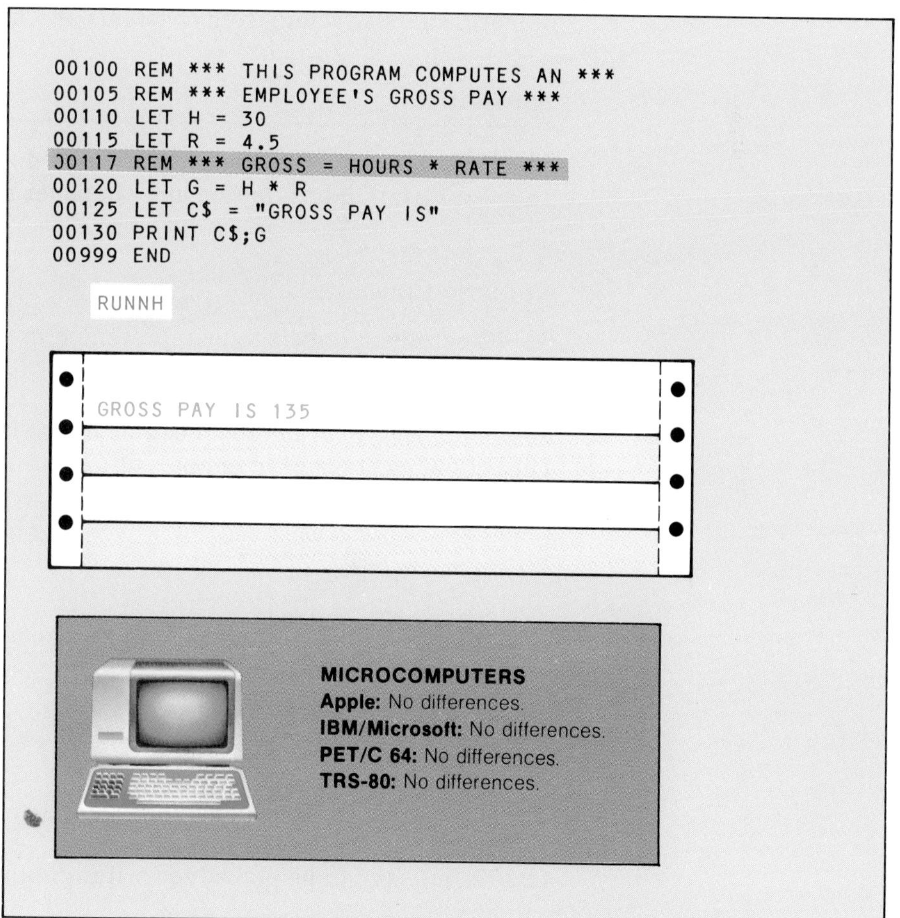

```
00100 REM *** THIS PROGRAM COMPUTES AN ***
00105 REM *** EMPLOYEE'S GROSS PAY ***
00110 LET H = 30
00115 LET R = 4.5
00117 REM *** GROSS = HOURS * RATE ***
00120 LET G = H * R
00125 LET C$ = "GROSS PAY IS"
00130 PRINT C$;G
00999 END

RUNNH

GROSS PAY IS 135
```

MICROCOMPUTERS
Apple: No differences.
IBM/Microsoft: No differences.
PET/C 64: No differences.
TRS-80: No differences.

are typed in with the same line number, the computer will accept the last one entered as the correct one. Thus, if we make a mistake in a statement, we can simply type in the same line number and the correct statement. Suppose that in the gross pay example, we gave H the wrong number of hours; it should have been 40, not 30. All we have to do to correct this is type the line number of the line to be changed and then retype the instruction with the correct number of hours:

```
00110 LET H = 40
```

The line we just entered will be put into computer memory where line 110 in the program was stored. The first instruction with line 110 is erased from the computer's memory.

BASIC Statement Components

In the remaining portion of this chapter, we will take a closer look at numeric and character string constants and numeric and string variables.

Constants

Constants are values that do not change during a program's execution. There are two kinds: numeric and character string.

Numeric Constants

BASIC permits numbers to be represented in two ways: as real numbers or in exponential notation.

Real Numbers **Real numbers** can be either integers or decimal fractions. The following are some examples of real numbers:

Real

↙ ↘

Decimals	Integers
0.58	−72456
6.782	+56
−7.234	5000

There are some rules to remember when using numbers in BASIC:

1. No commas can be embedded within numbers:

   3751 (valid) 7,892 (invalid)

BASIC interprets the invalid example not as the number seven thousand eight hundred ninety-two, but as the number seven and the number eight hundred ninety-two.

2. If the number is negative, it must be preceded by a minus sign:

   −0.145 (valid)   0.145− (invalid)

3. If no sign is included, the number is assumed to be positive:

   4096 is the same as +4096

Exponential Notation **Exponential notation** (scientific notation) usually is used for very large or very small numbers. Some examples follow:

2.783019E+09   3.724E−06

The E represents base 10, and the signed number following the E is the **power** to which 10 is raised. The number preceding the E is called the **mantissa** and in most systems lies between 1.000 and 9.999. A plus sign (+) by the power indicates that the decimal point is to be shifted to the right that number of places, whereas a minus sign (−) indicates that the decimal point should be shifted left the power number of places (see Figure 2–3).

The following are examples of exponential notation:

Decimal	Power Equivalent	Exponential Notation
5278	5.278×10^3	5.278E+03
0.0000021	2.1×10^{-6}	2.1E−06
−923180	-9.2318×10^5	−9.2318E+05

Figure 2–3 EXPONENTIAL NOTATION

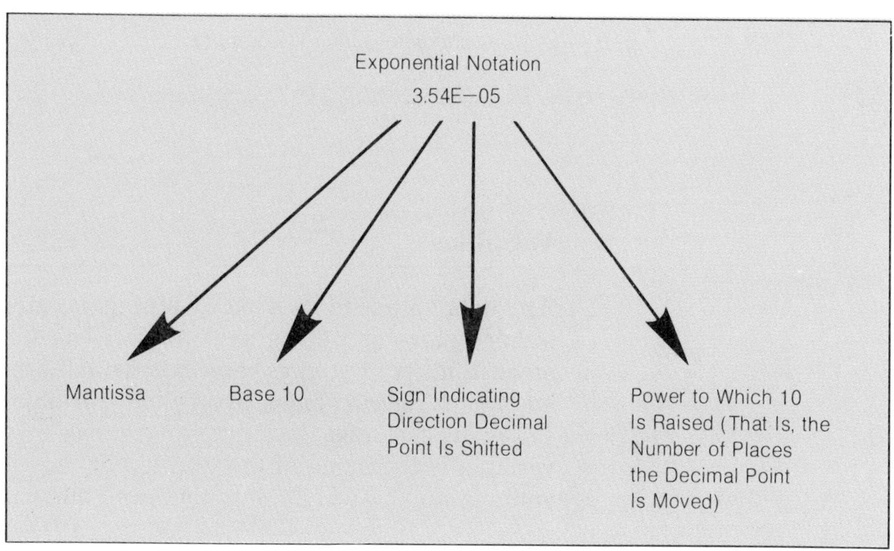

Character String Constants

The other type of constant is the **character string.** Character strings are composed of **alphanumeric data**—a sequence of letters, numbers, and/or special characters enclosed in quotation marks. The maximum number of characters allowed in a character string varies from system to system. On some systems it is not necessary to enclose character strings within quotation marks in data statements unless commas and semicolons are to be included within the character string. It is generally considered good practice to use the quotes, however. The following are examples of character strings:

```
"MIKE"
"281-77-6625"
"310 LAREDO DR."
```

The program in Figure 2–1 contains a character string in line 125:

```
00125 LET C$ = "GROSS PAY IS"
```

LEARNING CHECK

1. A sequence of instructions that tells the computer how to solve a problem is a(n) ________.
2. A BASIC instruction is composed of a(n) ________ and a(n) ________.
3. Line numbers ________.
   a. must be in increments of 1
   b. dictate the sequence of execution of BASIC statements
   c. must be real numbers
   d. all of the above
4. BASIC permits numbers to be represented as ________ or in ________.
5. A character string is composed of ________.

Answers

1. program
2. line number; BASIC statement
3. b
4. real numbers; exponential notation
5. alphanumeric data

Variables

Any data values to be used by a program must be stored in the computer either before or during execution of the program. The computer has a great number of storage locations, which are assigned names by the programmer. These names are called **variable names,** because the value stored in a storage location can change as the program is executed. A variable is the name of the location or the address in memory where the value is stored and can only represent one value at a time. Memory works something like post office boxes. The Variable is the P.O. box number, the memory cell is the actual box itself, and the value that is stored in memory is like the mail; however, in a computer memory "box" there can only be one piece of "mail" at a time. Each time a new piece of "mail" is put in the memory "box," the old one is taken out.

There are two types of variables: numeric and string. In our examples, H, R, and G are numeric variables, and C$ is a string variable.

Numeric Variables

A numeric variable name represents a number that is either supplied to the computer by the programmer or internally calculated by the computer during execution of the program. A numeric variable name can be either one letter alone or one letter followed by one numeric digit. (Almost all BASICs permit the use of two letters, and many computer systems permit more descriptive variable names—see box.) The following examples show valid and invalid numeric variable names:

Valid	Invalid and Why	
X	33	(must begin with a letter)
B4	*C	(must begin with a letter)
A	6	(cannot be a single digit)

Note lines 110, 115, and 120 in the program in Figure 2–2:

```
00110 LET H = 30
00115 LET R = 4.5
00120 LET G = H * R
```

H contains the hours worked—30. R holds the rate of pay, and the location of G has the result of hours multiplied by rate.

Numeric Variable Names

Microcomputer	Number of Unique Characters Recognized	Additional Characters Permitted
DECSYSTEM 20	35	No
Apple	2	Yes
IBM/Microsoft	40	No
TRS-80	2	Yes
PET/Commodore 64	2	Yes

String Variables

A string variable name can represent the value of a character string—for example, a name, an address, or a Social Security number. String variable names are distinguished from numeric variable names by the use of the dollar sign ($) following a single alphabetic character. The following are examples of valid and invalid string variable names:

Valid	Invalid and Why	
H$	6$	(first character must be alphabetic)
	$	
T$	X	(last character must be $)
	R1	

Many computer systems permit the use of more descriptive string variable names. However, all systems require that the first character be alphabetic and the last character be $. See the box for description of names permitted by other systems.

Typical examples of the proper use of string variables can be seen in lines 125 and 130 of the sample program:

```
00125 LET C$ = "GROSS PAY IS"
00130 PRINT C$;G
```

The character string "GROSS PAY IS" is assigned to the string variable name C$. In line 130, the values of C$ and G are printed out. This is the output:

```
RUNNH
GROSS PAY IS 135
```

String Variable Names

Microcomputer	Number of Unique Characters Recognized	Additional Characters Permitted
DECSYSTEM 20	34 (plus $)	No
Apple	2 (plus $)	Yes[1]
IBM/Microsoft	40 (plus $)	No
TRS-80	2 (plus $)	Yes[1]
PET/Commodore 64	2 (plus $)	Yes[1]

[1] When additional characters are used, the last character must be a dollar sign ($).

Common DECSYSTEM 20 Reserved Words

ABS	CALL	CHR	COS
DATA	DEF	DEL	DELETE
DIM	ELSE	END	EXP
FOR	GET	GO	GOSUB
GOTO	IF	INPUT	INT
LEFT$	LET	LOG	MAT
MID$	NEXT	NOT	ON
OPEN	OR	PRINT	PUT
READ	REM	RESTORE	RETURN
RIGHT	RND	SGN	SIN
SQR	SQRT	STEP	STOP
STR$	SYS	TAB	TAN
THEN	TO	UNTIL	VAL
WHILE			

Reserved Words

Reserved words are words that have a special meaning to the translator program (the interpreter or compiler) of the computer. These words cannot be used as variable names. The "Common DECSYSTEM 20 Reserved Words" box shows some of the most commonly used reserved words for the DECSYSTEM 20. Refer to your system's manual for additional reserved words or any differences in your system.

LEARNING CHECK

1. A(n) ______ allows the value stored in a storage location to change as the program is executed.
2. Variables can be one of two types: ______ or ______.
3. Which of the following are valid numeric variable names?
   - *a.* 3B
   - *b.* $X
   - *c.* Q
   - *d.* T2
4. A string variable name is identified by the use of the ______ character following a single alphabetic character.

Answers

1. variable
2. numeric; string
3. c and d
4. $ (dollar sign)

Summary

- A BASIC program is a series of instructions. Each one is composed of a line number and a BASIC statement.

- The line numbers serve (1) as labels by which statements can be referenced and (2) as instructions to specify the order of execution of the program.
- Using line numbers in increments of 5 or 10 permits easy insertion of new statements.
- BASIC statements contain special reserved words (programming commands), numeric or character string constants, numeric or string variables, and formulas.
- Constants are values that do not change. A valid numeric constant is any real number expressed as an integer, decimal fraction, or in exponential notation. Character strings are alphanumeric data enclosed in quotation marks.
- Variable names are programmer-supplied names that specify locations in storage where data values may be stored. Numeric variable names represent numbers. String variables contain alphanumeric values and their names are distinguished from numeric variable names by the symbol $.

Review Questions

1. What is a BASIC program?
2. What are the two components of a BASIC instruction?
3. What are the two main uses for line numbers?
4. What is the advantage of incrementing line numbers by 5 or 10 or more?
5. How would you correct the spelling error in this instruction (assume the ENTER key has been pressed.)?

   20 LET H$ = "GROS PAY IS"

6. How would you correct this instruction so M = A + B (assume the ENTER key has been pressed.)?

   170 LET M = A = B

7. Which of these are illegal real numbers in BASIC? Why?
   a. 56−
   b. +0.246
   c. 3,102
   d. 57981
8. How does BASIC interpret these numbers?
   a. 78,436
   b. −4,529
9. Convert these numbers to exponential notation using the BASIC format:

a. 459.2
b. 0.000297
c. −8251.7
d. 4.47 X 10^{-3}

10. Convert these numbers from exponential notation to decimals:
    a. 7.24396E+03
    b. 1.99E−02
    c. 4.972 E+05
    d. 8.05 E−04
11. Give the exponential power equivalent to these numbers using standard notation:
    a. 90206
    b. 23.785
    c. −275210
    d. .00321
12. What is a constant? Name two types.
13. Which of these are invalid numeric constants?
    a. 0.73
    b. 1072−
    c. 2.9171E−02
    d. 5.346+05
    e. 7,942
    f. +6029
14. Which of these are invalid character string constants in an expression?
    a. BOWLING GREEN, OHIO
    b. "APPLE"
    c. "7747"
    d. "PICKLE, DILL"
15. What is a variable? Name two types, and explain how they differ.
16. Give the computer memory equivalent to these P.O. box components:
    a. P.O. box number
    b. box
    c. mail
17. How many values can a memory location hold at one time?
18. Which of the following are illegal variable names, and why?

a. 7$	f. R
b. D	g. Z9
c. 5B	h. W*
d. H$	i. 25
e. M$	j. $F

19. When is it not necessary to enclose character strings within quotes?
20. Which of these is an illegal character string?
    a. "353-1070"
    b. "APARTMENT #4"
    c. BANDY, NICK J.

3 Getting Started with BASIC Programming

Outline

Objectives

After reading this chapter, the student should be able to do the following:

- Use and understand the value of the REM statement.
- Understand and use the LET statement.
- Evaluate arithmetic expressions according to the hierarchy of operations.
- Understand and use the PRINT statement.
- Understand and use the END statement.
- Understand how to place multiple statements on the same physical line.
- Differentiate between syntax errors and logic errors and be able to debug simple program examples.

Overview

This chapter describes four elementary BASIC statements—REM, LET, PRINT, and END. The LET statement is used to input, or assign, data to variables and to perform arithmetic calculations. The PRINT statement allows the programmer to see the results of processing. Processing is stopped with the END statement. The REM statement is presented here to underscore the importance of program documentation. The chapter also will discuss how to place multiple statements on the same physical line and introduce the debugging process.

The REM Statement

The remark (REM) statement provides information for the programmer or anyone else reading the program; it provides no information to the computer. The REM statement is used to **document** the program; the programmer generally uses it to explain program segments, to define variables used within the program, or to note any special instructions. These statements can be placed anywhere throughout the program.

The general format of the REM statement is this:

line# REM comment

Some example REM statements that could be used to document or explain a program follow:

```
00010 REM *** CALCULATE THE AVERAGE OF TWO NUMBERS ***
```

This example illustrates the use of a REM statement to explain the purpose of a program. A REM statement such as this could be used anywhere in a program to explain the purpose of individual program segments. Notice the asterisks that surround the descriptive statement. Many programmers will use the asterisks (although any character could be used) to set off the REM statement from the other statements in a program. This technique allows the REM statements to be easily identified when the programmer is looking through long program listings.

The following example illustrates the use of a REM statement to define a variable used within the program:

```
00030 REM *** N = NET PAY ***
```

It is a good practice to define the variables used in a program, especially if other people will be using it.

It is possible to have a REM statement with no comment following it:

```
00040 REM
```

In this case, the REM statement could be used to set off comments from executable statements and thus improve the readability of the program.

Note that each of the previous comments included the reserved word REM. Until recently, this was the only way a comment could be included in a program. However, some new versions of BASIC (TRS-80 and Microsoft) now allow the use of the apostrophe to make the rest of the line a comment:

```
00010 LET X = 0 ' X IS AN ACCUMULATOR
00020 LET D = 1.2 ' D EQUALS DISTANCE IN MILES
```

The LET Statement

The purpose of the LET, or assignment, statement is to assign values to variables. It can be used to enter data into a program, as well as to process it.

The general format of the LET statement is this:

line# LET variable = expression

The **expression** may be a constant, arithmetic formula or a variable. The following are examples:

Statement	Expression	Type
00010 LET X = 10	10	Numeric constant
00020 LET N$ = "BOB"	"BOB"	Character string constant
00030 LET P = T	T	Numeric variable
00040 LET A$ = B$	B$	String variable
00050 LET X = 3 * Y	3 * Y	Arithmetic formula

The LET statement can be used to assign values to numeric or string variables directly or to assign the result of a calculation to a numeric variable. In either case, the value or calculated result of an expression on the right side of the equal sign is assigned to the variable on the left side. It is important to note that the statement is not evaluated in the same way as an algebraic expression.

When BASIC assigns a value to a variable on the left side of the equation, it really is putting that value in a storage location in memory labeled by that variable name. Since a storage location can only be represented by a variable name, only a variable can be on the left.

The following examples of LET statements are presented along with a short description of how they are executed.

LET Statement	Computer Execution
00010 LET X = 1	The numeric value 1 is assigned to the location called X.
00040 LET C = A + B	The values in A and B are added together and assigned to C.
00085 LET N$ = "JOHN HENRY"	The character string enclosed in quotes is placed into the string variable N$ (the quotes are not).
00100 LET M = M + 1	1 is added to the current value of M, and the result is assigned to M. This result replaces whatever was in M previously.

LET Statement *(continued)*	Computer Execution
`100 LET M = M + 1`	Notice that this procedure effectively counts how many times line 100 is executed.
`00200 LET A = X / (M * 4)`	The arithmetic expression to the right of the equal sign is evaluated and assigned to A.

The reserved word LET identifies a statement in BASIC as an assignment statement. However, some compilers and interpreters do not require it. These versions accept the statement without the reserved word LET as follows:

```
00010 X = 2.5
```

This shorthand method can save both time and memory space.

Arithmetic Expressions

In BASIC, arithmetic expressions are composed of constants, numeric variables, and arithmetic operators. The arithmetic operators that can be used are the following:

BASIC Arithmetic Operation Symbol	Operation	Arithmetic Example	BASIC Arithmetic Expression
+	Addition	$A + B$	A + B
−	Subtraction	$A - B$	A − B
*	Multiplication	$A \times B$	A * B
/	Division	$A \div B$	A / B
∧ or ** or ↑ or [	Exponentiation	A^B	A ∧ B or A ** B or A ↑ B or A [B

Some examples of valid expressions in LET statements follow:

```
00010 LET M = 5 + 4
00020 LET T = N1 + N2 + N3 + N4
00030 LET J = A - B
00040 LET X = 3 * C
00050 LET Y = (P * D) * C
00060 LET Q = N ^ 5
00070 LET C = 6.4 + P / X
```

Again, some compilers and interpreters do not require the LET statement. If such is the case, all these statements could be written without using LET.

In an addition operation such as

```
00010 LET X = A + B
```

the value in the memory location identified by the variable A is added to the value in the memory location identified by the variable B. The result then is placed in the memory location identified by the variable X. For example, if A equals 5 and B equals 3, the computer would add 5 + 3 and place the result, 8, into the storage location identified by X.

For the example X = A − B, the same steps occur except that the value stored in B is subtracted from the value stored in A.

The multiplication operator (*) is used in multiplying two values. For example,

```
X = A * B
```

multiplies the value in the memory location identified by A by the value in the memory location identified by B and places the product in the memory location identified by X.

The division operator (/) is used in dividing two values. For example,

```
X = A / B
```

divides the value in the storage location A by the value in the storage location B and places the result in the storage location identified by X.

The result or product of an arithmetic operation can be used in subsequent calculations; for example,

```
00050 LET X = M + N
00060 LET Y = X * 6
00070 PRINT X,Y
```

Decimal points within numbers are automatically aligned by the BASIC interpreter before an arithmetic operation takes place.

The last arithmetic operation we will talk about here is **exponentiation,** or raising a number to a power. For example, A^3 is the same as A * A * A. The ∧ operator is used in exponentiation; however, some systems may use the operators **, ↑, or [instead. In the statement

```
00050 LET Y = X ^ 3
```

X would be cubed (X * X * X), and the result would be stored in the storage location identified by Y.

Examples using the operators **, ↑, and [follow:

```
00050 LET Y = X ** 3
00060 LET Y = X ↑ 3
00070 LET Y = X [ 3
```

In the examples above you will notice that we have left a space on each side of the operational symbol. This spacing is not necessary, however it greatly improves the readability of the program.

Hierarchy of Operations

When more than one operation is to be performed within an arithmetic expression, the computer follows a **hierarchy,** or priority, of operations. When parentheses are present in an expression, the operation within the parentheses is performed first. If parentheses are nested, the operation in the innermost set of parentheses is performed first. Thus, in the expression

```
(5 * (Y + 2) / 3.12) + 10
```

the first operation to be performed is to add 2 to the value in Y.

Parentheses aside, operations are performed according to the following rules of priority:

Priority	**Operation**	**Symbol**
First	Exponentiation	∧ or ** or ↑ or [
Second	Multiplication or division	* or /
Third	Addition or subtraction	+ or −

Operations with high priority are performed before operations with lower priority (subject to our discussion on parentheses). If more than one operation is to be performed at the same level, for example,

```
4 ^ 2 ^ 3
```

the computer evaluates them from left to right. In this example, the 4 would be raised to the second power and then the result, 16, raised to the third power. The answer is 4,096.

The following are examples of these hierarchical rules:

Expression	**Computer Evaluation**
Expression 1	
2 * 5 + 1	
First: 2 * 5 = 10	Multiplication has a higher priority than addition, so it is done first.
Second: 10 + 1 = 11	Then the addition is done. The result is 11.
Expression 2	
2 * (5 + 1)	
First: (5 + 1) = 6	In this case, the addition must be done first, because it is enclosed in parentheses.
Second: 2 * 6 = 12	The result is multiplied by 2. Compare this result with the result in Expression 1.

(Continued on next page)

Expression *(continued)*	Computer Evaluation
Expression 3 2 ∧ 3 / 4 − 2 *First:* 2 ∧ 3 = 8	The priority order tells the computer to start with exponentiation.
Second: 8 / 4 = 2	Next is division.
Third: 2 − 2 = 0	Last, the subtraction is done. The result is 0.
Expression 4 4 * 5 + 1 / 7 * 21 *First:* 4 * 5 = 20 *Second:* 1 / 7 = 0.142857 *Third:* 0.142857 * 21 = 3 *Fourth:* 20 + 3 = 23	There are three operations at the same level: *, /, and *. They are performed from left to right. Last, the addition is done, the result is 23.
Expression 5 4 * 6 / (2 ∧ 3) *First:* (2 ∧ 3) = 8	The exponentiation is done first, because it is enclosed in parentheses.
Second: 4 * 6 = 24	Next, the priority order tells the computer to do the multiplication.
Third: 24 / 8 = 3	Last, the division is done. The result is 3.

Assigning Character Strings

The LET statement also can be used to assign a character string value to a string name. A character string is composed of alphanumeric data enclosed in quotes. For example,

```
00010 LET T$ = "TOTAL SALES ="
00020 LET X$ = T$
```

The following examples show valid and invalid LET statements:

Valid	Invalid and Why	
`00010 LET T = P * Q`	`00010 LET P * Q = T`	(only a variable can appear on the left side of the equal sign)
`00020 LET N$ = "BOB"`	`00020 LET N = "BOB"`	(a character string must be assigned to a string variable)
`00030 LET X = 5 * P2`	`00030 LET X = 5 * P$`	(a string variable cannot be part of an arithmetic expression)

Figure 3–1, which calculates average monthly utility bills, illustrates several uses of the LET statement. The logic in this program is straightforward: First, enter the total amount spent on utilities for the year; second, calculate the monthly average; and third, print the results.

Line 110 is a LET statement used to enter the total amount spent on utilities for the year, $1,536.36, into the numeric variable T. The expression in line 115 calculates the monthly average—that is, the total amount spent on utilities for the year divided by 12, the number of months in a year. Line 120 assigns a character string to the string variable name B$. The character string and the results of the calculation are printed by line 125.

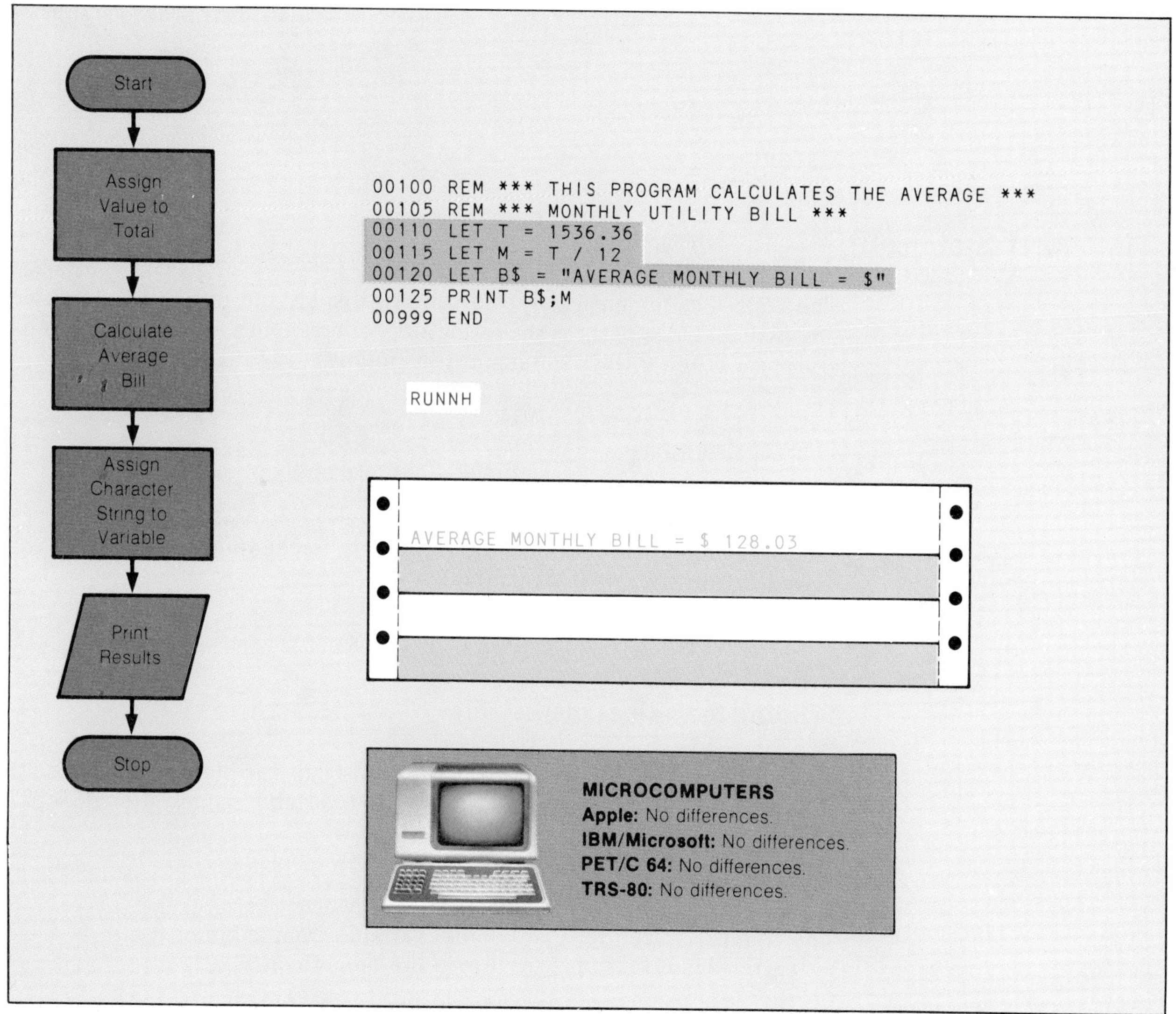

Figure 3–1 AVERAGE MONTHLY UTILITY BILL PROGRAM

LEARNING CHECK

1. The statement that is used to document a program is called the ________ statement.
2. A REM statement can be used anywhere in a program. TRUE FALSE (Circle the correct answer.)
3. The ________ statement assigns values to variables.
4. Which of the following is the correct hierarchy of operations?
   a. Exponentiation, parentheses, multiplication or division, addition or subtraction.
   b. Parentheses, multiplication or division, exponentiation, addition or subtraction.
   c. Parentheses, exponentiation, division or multiplication, addition or subtraction.
   d. None of the above.
5. A(n) ________ is composed of alphanumeric data enclosed within quotation marks.

Answers

1. REM
2. True
3. LET
4. c
5. character string

The PRINT Statement

The PRINT statement is used to print or display the results of computer processing. It also permits the formatting, or arranging, of output. The general form of the PRINT statement is as follows:

line# PRINT { Variables / Literals / Arithmetic expressions / Combination of above }

PRINT statements can take several forms, depending on the output required. Let us look at some examples.

Printing the Values of Variables

We can tell the computer to print values assigned to storage locations by simply using the keyword PRINT with the variable names after it, separated by commas:

```
00160 PRINT P,I,T
```

The comma is used to separate one variable from another; it also is used for carriage control (more on this in the next chapter).

Printing has no effect on the contents of storage. The PRINT statement is a simple reading of the value of a variable that allows the user to see what the contents are. Normally, each time the computer encounters a PRINT statement, it begins printing output on a new line. Exceptions to this are discussed in chapter 4.

Some systems, such as the TRS-80, allow the use of a question mark (?) as a shorthand notation for the PRINT command. For example, the statement

```
00010 PRINT X
```

would be written

```
10 ? X
```

Printing Literals

A **literal** is an expression consisting of alphabetic, numeric, or special characters or a combination of all three. The following are examples of literals:

X	3	T3
Y	126.78	B$

Character Strings

A character string literal is a group of letters, numbers, or special characters that you want printed on the output page. To have that done, enclose the group in quotation marks ("). Whatever is inside the quotation marks is printed exactly as it is; for example,

```
00030 PRINT "@#$%&SAMPLE"
```

would appear on the output page as

```
@#$%&SAMPLE
```

To print column headings, put each heading in quotes and separate each group by a comma. The comma instructs the printer to skip to the next print zone (more on this in Chapter 4). An example follows:

```
00040 PRINT "NAME","RANK","SERIAL NO."
```

When line 40 is executed, the character strings are printed out exactly as typed except that the quotation marks do not appear:

```
NAME              RANK              SERIAL NO.
```

Numeric Literals

Numeric literals do not have to be enclosed in quotation marks to be printed. For example, the statement

```
00200 PRINT 67
```

will print the following result:

```
67
```

Printing the Values of Expressions

The computer can print not only the values of literals and the values of variables, but also the values of arithmetic expressions:

```
00010 LET X = 4
00020 LET Y = 247
00030 PRINT X / Y * 100
```

First, the computer evaluates the highlighted expression according to the rules of priority. The result is printed as follows:

```
1.619433
```

If the value of the expression is extremely large or extremely small, the computer may print it in exponential notation.

Figure 3–2 deals with expressions in both decimal and exponential forms. When the PRINT statement in line 25 is executed, the three expressions are evaluated and their values printed. Notice that the first two numbers are too large to be printed conventionally and are printed instead in exponential notation.

Printing Blank Lines

A PRINT statement with nothing typed after it will provide a blank line of output. For example,

```
00100 PRINT
```

To skip more than one line, simply include more than one of these PRINT statements:

```
00110 PRINT
00115 PRINT
```

Some systems may require the use of " " to print a blank line. For example,

```
00100 PRINT " "
```

Figure 3-2 NUMERIC OUTPUT

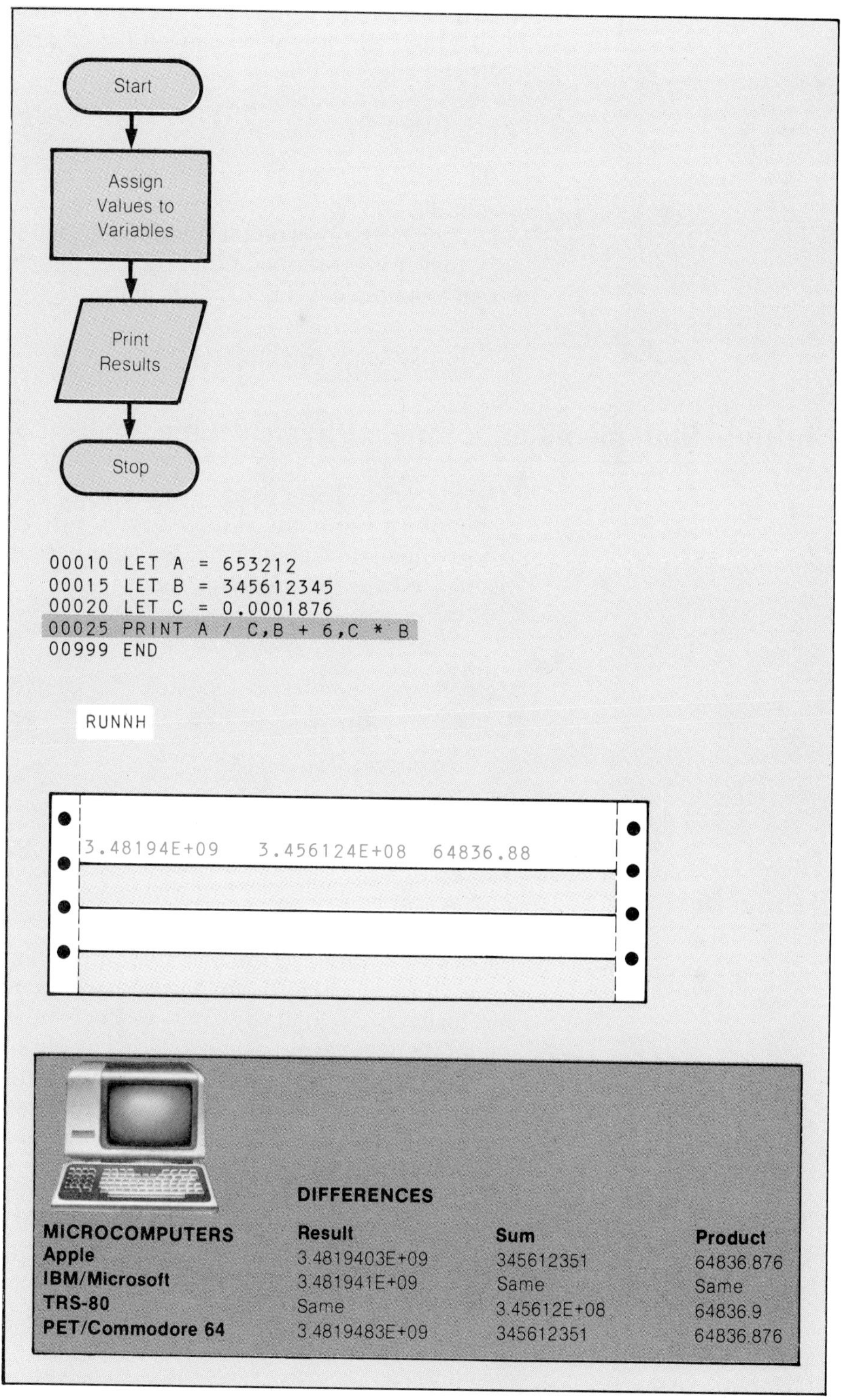

Start
Assign Values to Variables
Print Results
Stop
00010 LET A = 653212
00015 LET B = 345612345
00020 LET C = 0.0001876
00025 PRINT A / C,B + 6,C * B
00999 END
RUNNH
3.48194E+09 3.456124E+08 64836.88

DIFFERENCES

MICROCOMPUTERS	Result	Sum	Product
Apple	3.4819403E+09	345612351	64836.876
IBM/Microsoft	3.481941E+09	Same	Same
TRS-80	Same	3.45612E+08	64836.9
PET/Commodore 64	3.4819483E+09	345612351	64836.876

The END Statement

The END statement indicates the end of the program and so must be assigned the highest line number in the program. The general format of the END statement is this:

```
line# END
```

The use of an all-9s number for the END statement is a common programming practice, although it is not required. This convention serves as a reminder to the programmer to include the END statement and helps insure that it is positioned properly. See line 999 in the utility bill program for an example of an END statement.

Multiple Statements on a Single Physical Line

Most systems allow multiple statements on a single physical line. For example, if we wanted to skip two lines, instead of using two physical lines as was illustrated previously, we could accomplish the same result more efficiently with the following line:

```
00110 PRINT \ PRINT
```

Many microcomputer systems use the colon (:) instead of the backslash (\) to place multiple logical lines on the same physical lines. For example,

```
00110 PRINT : PRINT
```

Debugging

Debugging is the process of determining the specific errors in your program and correcting them. Two types of errors can occur: syntax errors and logic errors. Syntax errors are the results of improper use of the programming language. Logic errors occur because the logic that was designated would not process the data in the desired manner. Syntax errors are easy to find , because the interpreter or compiler does this for you. Logic errors, in contrast, can be very difficult to find or even identify. As a note of caution, remember that a program with a logic error may run and give results that appear to be correct but are not. Programs should be thoroughly tested to insure that the logic is correct. Detailed documentation should be included in the program to assist in any debugging that may be necessary.

Debugging exercises will be included after this and each subsequent chapter to help you learn to recognize and correct any errors you may encounter.

LEARNING CHECK

1. A(n) ______ statement is used to print or display the results of computer processing.
2. When a PRINT statement is executed, the contents of memory are changed. TRUE FALSE (Circle the correct answer.)
3. A(n) ______ is an expression consisting of alphabetic, numeric, or special characters or a combination of all three.
4. Which of the following are valid PRINT statements?
   a. 10 PRINT 25
   b. 100 PRINT "ANYTHING"
   c. 30 PRINT A * B + C
   d. 50 PRINT TOTAL PRICE
   e. none of the above
5. The ______ statement indicates the end of a program.

Answers
1. PRINT
2. False
3. literal
4. a, b, and c
5. END

A Programming Problem

Problem Definition

A local stereo shop was advertising the following discounts:

- 5 percent off the purchase of a receiver and a pair of speakers
- 20 percent off the purchase of a receiver, pair of speakers, and a turntable
- 40 percent off the purchase of a receiver, pair of speakers, turntable, and cassette deck

Being a small shop, it only carries one model of each item. The price for each is as follows:

Item	Price
Receiver	$423.00
Pair of speakers	$300.00
Turntable	$185.00
Cassette deck	$210.00

Before going to the stereo shop, you decide to write a program to tell you the discounted price of each of the advertised options (see Figure 3–3).

Figure 3–3 STEREO DISCOUNT PROGRAM AND FLOWCHART

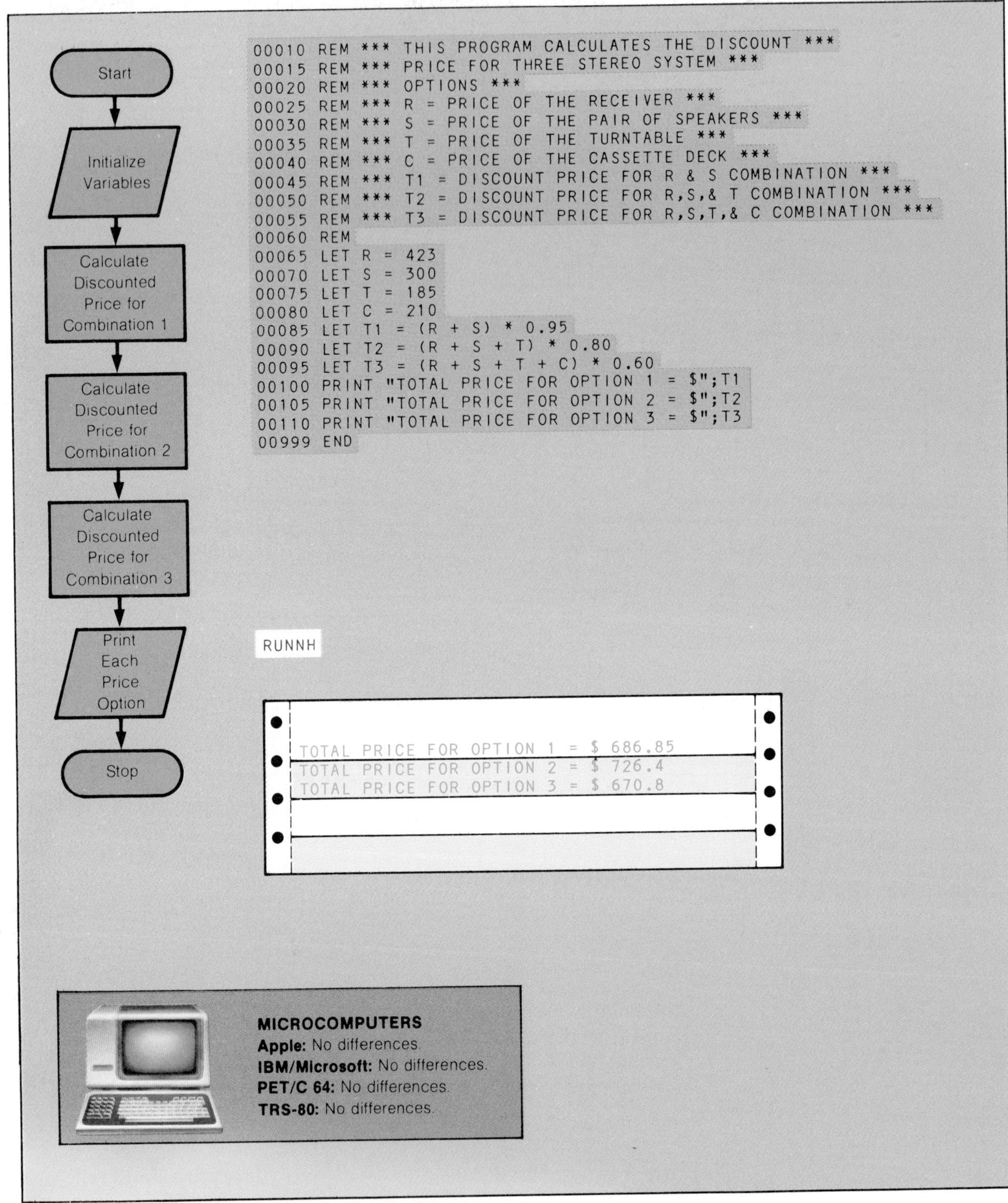


```
00010 REM *** THIS PROGRAM CALCULATES THE DISCOUNT ***
00015 REM *** PRICE FOR THREE STEREO SYSTEM ***
00020 REM *** OPTIONS ***
00025 REM *** R = PRICE OF THE RECEIVER ***
00030 REM *** S = PRICE OF THE PAIR OF SPEAKERS ***
00035 REM *** T = PRICE OF THE TURNTABLE ***
00040 REM *** C = PRICE OF THE CASSETTE DECK ***
00045 REM *** T1 = DISCOUNT PRICE FOR R & S COMBINATION ***
00050 REM *** T2 = DISCOUNT PRICE FOR R,S,& T COMBINATION ***
00055 REM *** T3 = DISCOUNT PRICE FOR R,S,T,& C COMBINATION ***
00060 REM
00065 LET R = 423
00070 LET S = 300
00075 LET T = 185
00080 LET C = 210
00085 LET T1 = (R + S) * 0.95
00090 LET T2 = (R + S + T) * 0.80
00095 LET T3 = (R + S + T + C) * 0.60
00100 PRINT "TOTAL PRICE FOR OPTION 1 = $";T1
00105 PRINT "TOTAL PRICE FOR OPTION 2 = $";T2
00110 PRINT "TOTAL PRICE FOR OPTION 3 = $";T3
00999 END
```

```
RUNNH
```

```
TOTAL PRICE FOR OPTION 1 = $ 686.85
TOTAL PRICE FOR OPTION 2 = $ 726.4
TOTAL PRICE FOR OPTION 3 = $ 670.8
```

MICROCOMPUTERS
Apple: No differences.
IBM/Microsoft: No differences.
PET/C 64: No differences.
TRS-80: No differences.

Solution Design

The first step in the program is to enter the price of each component. Next, determine the discount price for each option by adding the total price of the items in an option and multiplying by the appropriate discount factor. You will notice we multiplied by 0.95, 0.8, and 0.6 for the respective options instead of 0.05 0.20, and 0.40. This is because we are interested in what we have to pay rather than the discount amount itself. Finally, we print out the results.

The Program

Figure 3–3 shows a listing and output of the program, as well as a flowchart. The REM statements in lines 10 through 55 document the purpose of the program and the meanings of the variables. The REM statement in line 60 is used to set off the remarks from the executable statements. Lines 65 through 80 use LET statements to enter the price of each stereo component. Lines 85 through 95 calculate the discounted price for each option. The results are printed out in lines 100 through 110.

Summary

- REM statements are used to document a program; they are not executed by the computer.
- The purpose of the LET statement is to assign values to variables; LET is an optional keyword in some BASIC implementations.
- The LET statement is not evaluated as an algebraic equation. The computer first evaluates the expression on the right side of the equal sign and then assigns that result to the variable on the left side of the equal sign.
- Arithmetic expressions are evaluated according to the following hierarchy of operations: (1) operations in parentheses, (2) exponentiation, (3) multiplication or division, and (4) addition or subtraction. Multiple operations at the same level are evaluated left to right.
- The PRINT statement is used to print or display the results of processing.
- The END statement indicates the physical end of a program and stops execution.
- Multiple statements may be placed on the same physical line by separating them with the backslash (\) character.

- The two types of errors that can occur in a program are syntax errors (improper use of the programming language) and logic errors (program logic that does not process data in the desired manner).
- Debugging is the process of finding and correcting errors in a program.

Review Questions

1. What is the purpose of the REM statement?
2. Why is it important to document your program using REM statements?
3. What is the purpose of the LET statement?
4. Explain how a LET statement is evaluated by the computer.
5. In a LET statement, what are the three forms that the expression on the right side of the equal sign may take?
6. List the arithmetic operators used in BASIC, giving an example statement for each one.
7. What hierarchy, or priority, of arithmetic operations does BASIC follow?
8. Evaluate the expression 10 LET X = A / B * C ∧ Y / 2 where A = 24, B = 3, C = 2, and Y = 3.
9. Evaluate the expression 10 LET M = (X + B * (2 ∧ 5) − B * (4 + X)) / 2 where X = 8 and B = 2.
10. In a LET statement, why can only a variable name be on the left side of the equal sign?
11. Evaluate the expression 10 LET A = 2.5 + (X * (Y ∧ 2) / C) * (8 + X) where X = 2, Y = 4, and C = 8.
12. Identify which of the following are valid LET statements:
    a. 10 LET X = "STACY"
    b. 10 LET A / C = B
    c. 10 LET T = P * Q
    d. 10 LET Y = "X + Z"
    e. 10 LET M = X + (Y * Z)
13. What is the purpose of the PRINT statement?
14. What effect does the PRINT statement have on the contents of memory?
15. Define a literal, and give three examples.
16. Define a character string, and give three examples.
17. How can a blank line be added to an output? More than one?
18. What is the output of the following program segment?

```
10 LET X = 952
20 LET Y = 56
30 PRINT 5.3 + X / (Y * 10)
```

19. What is the purpose of the END statement?

20. Identify which of the following statements are invalid, and tell why:
    a. 10 LET P = 5 * (A + B)
    b. 10 PRINT TOTAL PRICE =
    c. 10 LET N = "NAN"
    d. 10 LET N = N + M
    e. 10 LET X = 5 + P$

Debugging Exercises

Identify the following programs or program segments that contain errors, and debug them.

1.
```
00010 REM *** THIS PROGRAM PRINTS ***
00015 A NAME AND AGE OF A PERSON ***
00020 REM
00025 LET A = 21
00030 LET N$ = "STACY"
00035 PRINT N$,A
00999 END
```

2.
```
00040 LET X = 15.5
00045 LET K = "DISTANCE IN KILOMETERS ="
00050 LET Y = 15.5 * 1.6
00055 LET M = "DISTANCE IN MILES ="
```

3.
```
00030 LET A = 3 + I
00035 LET X + Y = B
00040 LET N$ = 54
00045 PRINT N$,A,B
```

4.
```
00010 LET A = 2
00015 LET B = 4
00020 PRINT A * B / 2
00099 END
```

5.
```
00010 REM *** THIS PROGRAM CALCULATES ***
00015 REM *** AN AVERAGE OF TWO NUMBERS ***
00020 LET 10 = A
00025 LET 20 = B
00030 LET X = A + B / 2
00035 PRINT X
00999 END
```

6.
```
00100 REM *** THIS PROGRAM FINDS ***
00105 REM *** THE CUBE OF A NUMBER ***
00110 REM
00115 LET X = 5
00120 LET C$ = X ^ 3
00125 PRINT C$
00999 END
```

7.
```
00050 LET N$ = NANCY
00055 LET L$ = LINDA
00060 PRINT N$,L$
00099 END
```

8.
```
00010 THIS PROGRAM PRINTS
00015 THE HEADING FOR A REPORT
00020 PRINT PROJECTED 1984 BUDGET
00025 PRINT FOR ACME PRODUCTS INC.
00999 END
```

9.
```
00020 REM *** THIS PROGRAM CALCULATES ***
00025 REM *** BATTING AVERAGES ***
00030 REM *** B = TIMES AT BAT ***
00035 REM *** H = # OF HITS ***
00040 REM *** A = BATTING AVERAGE ***
00045 LET B = 160
00050 LET H$ = "41"
00055 LET A = B / H$ * 1000
00060 PRINT BATTING AVG =,A
00999 END
```

10.
```
00015 PRINT 62
00020 LET X = A * 3
00025 LET N$ = B + X
00030 PRINT N$
00999 END
```

Additional Programming Problems

1. Using the formula C = 5/9(F − 32), where C equals the degrees centigrade and F equals the degrees Fahrenheit, write a program that will convert 85° F to its centigrade equivalent. Include REM statements to document your program.
2. You own a house with fifteen identically shaped rooms that need carpeting. Each room has a length of twelve feet and a width of nine feet. The carpeting you choose is $9.50 a square foot. Write a program that will calculate the amount of carpeting needed, as well as the total cost of the carpeting. Your output should include both figures. The area of a room is equal to the length of the room multiplied by the width of the room. Document your program using REM statements.
3. Write a program that will print out the name and telephone number of the following persons:

   Linda Zadel 888–1111
   Anne Tate 223–3165
   Corky Strong 444–6537

Use the LET statement to enter the data. The output should have the following format:

```
NAME    TELEPHONE #

XXXX     XXX-XXXX
 .          .
 .          .
 .          .
```

4. The list price of a record you want is $8.98. A sign in the window says that all $8.98 LPs are on sale for 15 percent off the list price. Write a program that will calculate the sale price of the record using the list price of $8.98 and the 15 percent discount.
5. Billy Boy Brandon wants to know how much gas it would cost him to drive to Fort Lauderdale, Florida, and back home. Fort Lauderdale is 2,340 miles from his home. His car gets twenty-eight miles per gallon, and he figures that gas would cost $1.21 per gallon. Your output from this program should have the following format:

```
DISTANCE    TOTAL COST
XXXX        $XXX.XX
```

6. You have been asked to prepare a report listing the names and scores for the finalists in the annual Acapulco Cliff Diving Championship as well as the average for each diver. Each participant made three dives and was scored on a ten-point scale. The input data follows. The average score is calculated by adding the three scores and dividing by three. The report should contain report and column headings and use REM statements to document it.

DIVER	**Dive #1**	**Dive #2**	**Dive #3**
Vic Flynn	9.5	9.6	9.3
Karen McKee	8.3	8.5	9.0

4 Input and Output

Outline

Objectives

After reading this chapter, the student should be able to do the following:

- Understand and use the INPUT statement to enter data into a program.
- Understand and use the READ and DATA statements to enter data into a program.
- Understand and use commas and semicolons to control the spacing of output.
- Understand and use the TAB statement for controlling output.
- Understand and use the PRINT USING statement to format output.

Overview

This chapter will introduce new ways of entering data into a program. Although the LET statement can be used to enter small amounts of data, the INPUT statement and the READ/DATA statements are the most commonly used methods. The INPUT statement allows the user to put data into the computer as the program is running. The program can be written to ask the user for the data it needs. The READ/DATA statements are much more efficient than the LET statement when working with large amounts of data or data that may change frequently.

When programming, it is often necessary to have organized and formatted output. This yields a better appearance and readability. We will show you how to produce output with headings, columns, and appropriate spacing.

Figure 4–1 is a sample of the type of output you will be able to produce with the tools in this chapter. It also makes use of the INPUT statement.

Figure 4–1 FORMATTED OUTPUT

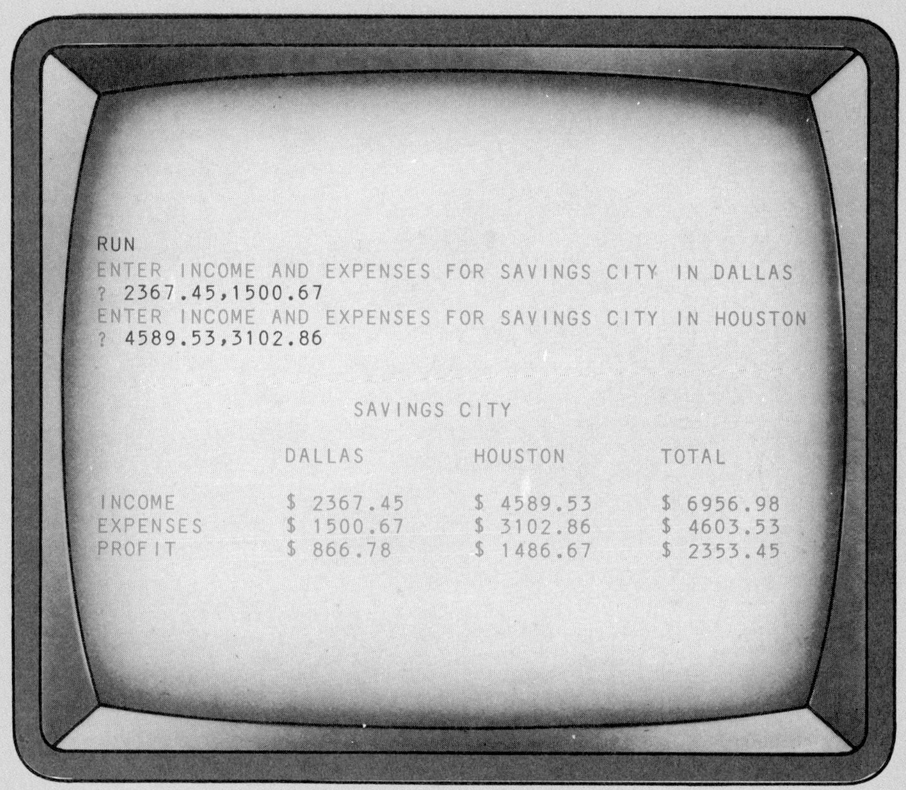

RUN
ENTER INCOME AND EXPENSES FOR SAVINGS CITY IN DALLAS
? 2367.45,1500.67
ENTER INCOME AND EXPENSES FOR SAVINGS CITY IN HOUSTON
? 4589.53,3102.86
SAVINGS CITY
DALLAS HOUSTON TOTAL
INCOME $ 2367.45 $ 4589.53 $ 6956.98
EXPENSES $ 1500.67 $ 3102.86 $ 4603.53
PROFIT $ 866.78 $ 1486.67 $ 2353.45

The INPUT Statement

The INPUT statement is used for inquiry and response when a user application calls for a question-and-answer environment. The last chapter explained how the LET statement can be used to enter data values into a program. The INPUT statement differs from the LET statement in that it allows the user to enter data at the terminal while the program is running.

The general format of the INPUT statement is as follows:

line# INPUT variable list

For example,

```
00140 INPUT L,W,H
00145 INPUT C$,H$
```

These also could be combined into one line as follows:

```
00140 INPUT L,W,H,C$,H$
```

or they could be on separate lines:

```
00140 INPUT L
00145 INPUT W
00150 INPUT H
00155 INPUT C$
00160 INPUT H$
```

The variables listed in the INPUT statements may be string or numeric. Just be sure to enter the correct value to be assigned to each variable. In other words, the type of data must be the same as that designated by the variable.

INPUT statements are placed where data values are needed in a program. This is determined by the logic of the program. After the program has been keyed in, the user types the execution command RUNNH on the DECSYSTEM 20; the computer then starts to execute the program. Whenever the computer reaches an INPUT statement, it stops, prints a question mark at the terminal, and waits for the user to enter data. After typing in the data, the user presses the RETURN key. The computer then assigns the data value to the variable indicated in the INPUT statement and resumes processing. More than one variable can be listed in the INPUT statement; the user must know how many values to enter. When there are not enough data entered, an error message is printed, telling the user there is insufficient data. For example, when line 140 is executed with only one value entered, the result would look like this:

```
00140 INPUT L,W,H
RUNNH
 ? 28.5

? 59  Insufficient data at line 00140 of MAIN PROGRAM
 ?
```

If the user knew what entries to make and how many, the output would look like this:

```
RUNNH
 ? 28.5,25,10
```

The variable L would have the value 28.5, W would be assigned the value 25, and H would contain 10. As you can see, the INPUT statement offers a great deal of flexibility. Each time the program is executed, new values can be entered without changing any program statements.

Prompts

The INPUT statement is usually preceded by a PRINT statement. This PRINT statement is referred to as a **prompt.** Since the INPUT statement signals the need for data with only a question mark, it is good programming to precede each INPUT statement with a PRINT statement that explains to the user what data is to be entered. This practice is particularly important in a BASIC program that contains numerous INPUT statements; otherwise, when users see only a question mark requesting data, they may not know what data values are to be entered and in what order.

Figure 4–2 is a program with a prompt that calculates the volume of a swimming pool. Line 135 and 140 cause the program to be executed in a question-and-answer mode (also called **inquiry-and-response,** or **conversational mode**). When the program is run, line 135 causes the computer to print a message at the terminal that says, "ENTER, LENGTH, WIDTH, AND DEPTH". A question mark then appears to signal the user that the data values are to be entered. At this point, the user types in the requested data values, separating them with commas, and then presses the RETURN key to continue execution of the program:

```
RUNNH
ENTER LENGHT,WIDTH,AND DEPTH  ←Program Prompt
 ? 28.5,25,10                 ←Computer Prompt (?), User Data Entry
VOLUME = 7125                 ←Computer Continues Execution after User
                                Pushes RETURN
```

Most computers permit the prompt to be an integral part of the INPUT statement. For example, the following line could be substituted for lines 135 and 140 in the volume program:

```
00135 INPUT "ENTER LENGHT,WIDTH,AND DEPTH";L,W,D
```

When the program is run with this new line, the question mark appears immediately after the prompt, and no separate PRINT statement for the prompt is needed:

```
RUNNH
ENTER LENGHT,WIDTH,AND DEPTH ? 20,18,6
VOLUME = 2160
```

Figure 4-2 SWIMMING POOL VOLUME PROGRAM USING A PROMPT AND AN INPUT STATEMENT

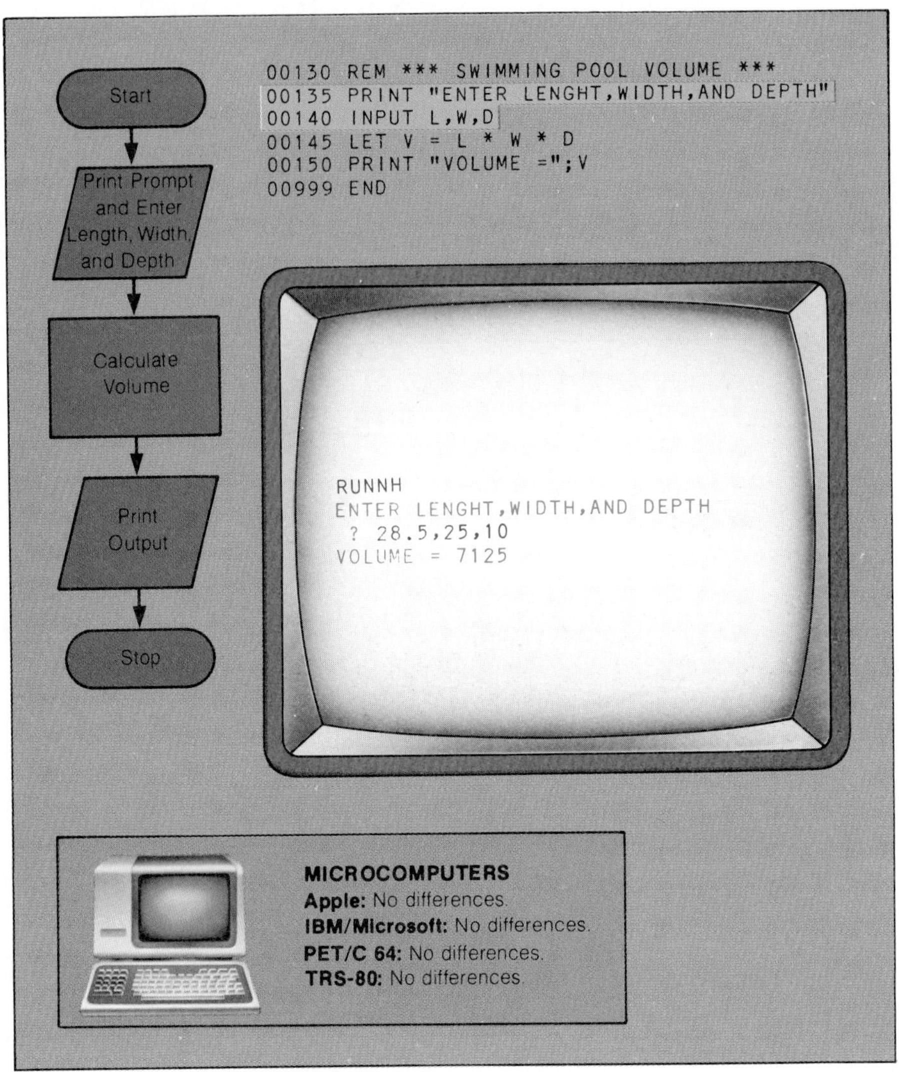

Start
Print Prompt and Enter Length, Width, and Depth
Calculate Volume
Print Output
Stop
00130 REM *** SWIMMING POOL VOLUME ***
00135 PRINT "ENTER LENGHT,WIDTH,AND DEPTH"
00140 INPUT L,W,D
00145 LET V = L * W * D
00150 PRINT "VOLUME =";V
00999 END
RUNNH
ENTER LENGHT,WIDTH,AND DEPTH
? 28.5,25,10
VOLUME = 7125
MICROCOMPUTERS
Apple: No differences.
IBM/Microsoft: No differences.
PET/C 64: No differences.
TRS-80: No differences.

The READ and DATA Statements

The READ and DATA statements provide another way to enter data into a BASIC program. These two statements always work together. Values contained in the DATA statements are assigned to variables listed in the READ statements.

The general format of the READ and DATA statements is this:

line# READ variable list
line# DATA variable list

Here are some examples of READ and DATA statements:

```
00100 READ X,Y
00200 READ N$,J$,Z
00500 DATA 76,81,"JILL","PROGRAMMER"
00510 DATA 1072
```

This method of entering data into a program works a little differently than the INPUT statement. The READ statement tells the computer to search through the BASIC program until it finds the first DATA statement. The computer then assigns the data values consecutively to the variables in the READ statement. Each READ statement causes as many values to be taken from the data list as there are variables in the READ variable list. Figure 4–3 illustrates this process of assigning values from the data list to variables.

Statement 10 says to the computer: "Take the value from the top of the data list and put it in the storage location named X. (Anything that was

Figure 4–3 READ/DATA EXAMPLE

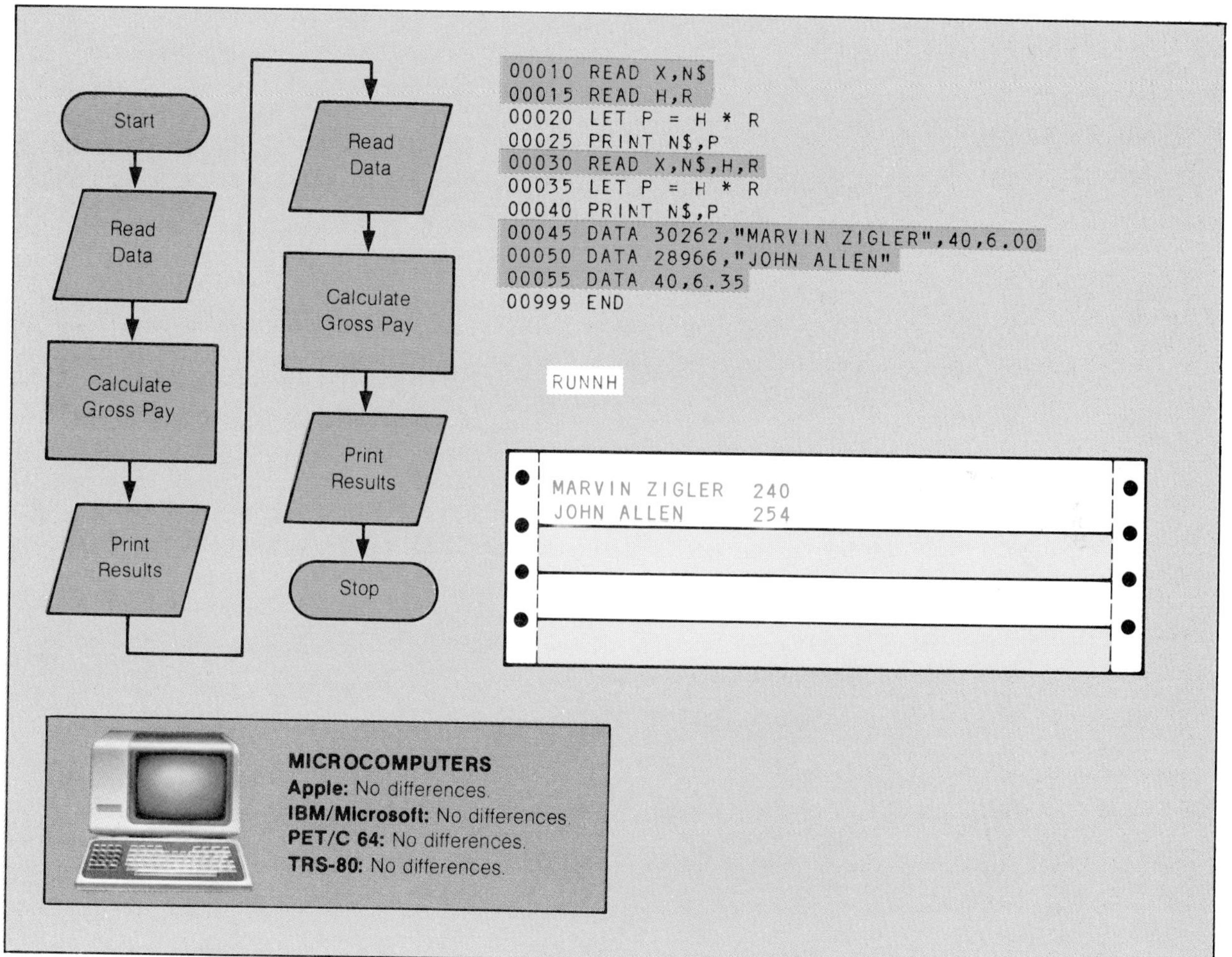
Start
Read Data
Calculate Gross Pay
Print Results
Read Data
Calculate Gross Pay
Print Results
Stop
00010 READ X,N$
00015 READ H,R
00020 LET P = H * R
00025 PRINT N$,P
00030 READ X,N$,H,R
00035 LET P = H * R
00040 PRINT N$,P
00045 DATA 30262,"MARVIN ZIGLER",40,6.00
00050 DATA 28966,"JOHN ALLEN"
00055 DATA 40,6.35
00999 END
RUNNH
MARVIN ZIGLER 240
JOHN ALLEN 254
MICROCOMPUTERS
Apple: No differences.
IBM/Microsoft: No differences.
PET/C 64: No differences.
TRS-80: No differences.

previously in storage location X is destroyed when the new information is put in X.) Then take the next value from the data list and assign it to variable N$ (which also destroys anything that was previously in location N$)." After statement 10 has been executed, the number 30262 is in storage location X, and the character string MARVIN ZIGLER is in storage location N$. This leaves the number 40 at the top of the data list.

The same process occurs when the computer encounters statement 15. The data from the top of the list (40) is placed in storage location H. The number 6.00 is assigned to R.

When statement 30 is executed, the number at the top of the data list (28966) is assigned to the variable X. The number 30262, which was assigned to X by statement 10, is replaced by the new value. In the same manner, the character string JOHN ALLEN is assigned to the variable N$; the number 40 is assigned to the variable H; and the number 6.35 is assigned to R. When these values are assigned, the values previously stored in the variables are destroyed.

This process illustrates the basic concept of nondestructive read, destructive write. Once the data items have been assigned to storage locations, they remain there until new data items are recorded over them. Thus, all four variables represent more than one value during execution, but never more than one at a time.

If a READ statement is attempted after the data list has been exhausted, a message is produced to indicate that the end of the data list has been reached. The message points out the line number of the READ statement in error; for example, if line 30 were such a READ statement, the computer would print the following:

```
? 57  End of DATA found at line 00030 of MAIN PROGRAM
```

READ statements, like INPUT, are located wherever the logic of the program indicates the need for data. DATA statements, however, are nonexecutable and may be located anywhere in the program. Although DATA statements may be anywhere in a program, it is common practice to group them together either at the beginning or the end of a program. This makes debugging easier. The BASIC interpreter or compiler simply takes all the data items in all the DATA statements and forms one combined data list, ordering the DATA statements from lowest line number to highest and then using the data from left to right. For example, the following three program segments look different, but the data lists they produce are alike:

DATA Statements	DATA List
00010 DATA "JIM",27 00020 DATA "JOANN",23 OR 00010 DATA "JIM",27,"JOANN",23 OR 00010 DATA "JIM" 00020 DATA 27 00030 DATA "JOANN" 00040 DATA 23	JIM 27 JOANN 23

Note that when two or more data values occupy a line, they are separated by commas. Character strings may or may not be enclosed in quotation marks in DATA statements. However, if the character strings are to contain leading or trailing blanks, commas, and/or semicolons, they must be enclosed in quotation marks.

We would assign the previous data items in the following manner:

```
00050 READ N$
00060 READ A
00070 READ M$
00080 READ B
          OR
00050 READ N$,A
00060 READ M$,B
          OR
00050 READ N$,A,M$,B
```

It does not matter in this example how many READ or DATA statements are used. However, the order of the variables and values is important. Make sure that the arrangement of values in the DATA statements correspond to the data required in the READ statements—that is, that character strings are assigned to string variables and numeric constants, to numeric variables.

Let us return to the swimming pool volume program and change it to use READ/DATA (see Figure 4–4). Lines 135 and 140 perform the same function as the INPUT statement did previously. With INPUT, the data values are assigned by the user as the program is running. With READ/DATA, on the other hand, the length, width, and depth values already are contained in program line 135, the DATA statement. If we wanted to run this program again using different data, we would have to change the DATA statement.

Comparison of the Three Methods of Data Entry

LET, INPUT, and READ/DATA all can be used to enter data into BASIC programs. You may wonder, then, which command is best to use. That depends on the particular application. Here are some general guidelines:

1. When the data to be used by a program are constant, use the LET statement. The LET statement is often used to assign a beginning value to a variable; this is called **initialization.** For example;

   ```
   LET X = 0
   LET I = 1
   ```

2. The INPUT statement is used when a question-and-answer mode is desired. It is also a good method to use when data values are likely to change frequently. A good application for the use of the INPUT statement might be entering data about hospital patients—a situation

Figure 4–4 SWIMMING POOL VOLUME PROGRAM USING READ/DATA STATEMENTS

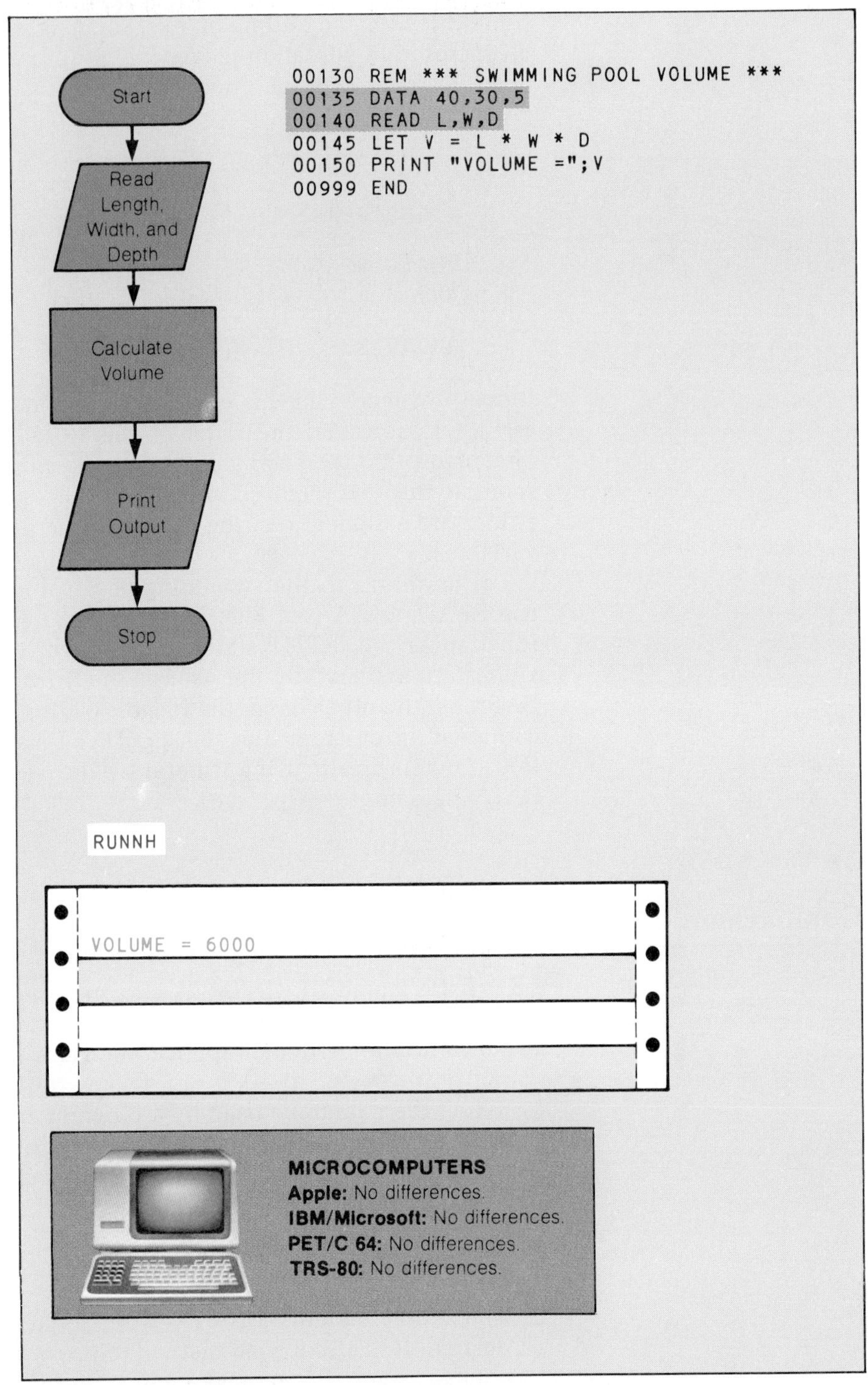

Start
Read Length, Width, and Depth
Calculate Volume
Print Output
Stop
00130 REM *** SWIMMING POOL VOLUME ***
00135 DATA 40,30,5
00140 READ L,W,D
00145 LET V = L * W * D
00150 PRINT "VOLUME =";V
00999 END
RUNNH
VOLUME = 6000
MICROCOMPUTERS
Apple: No differences.
IBM/Microsoft: No differences.
PET/C 64: No differences.
TRS-80: No differences.

in which people are checking in and out every day, and data about a particular patient changes frequently.

3. When many data values must be entered, READ/DATA statements are a good option. These statements often are used to read data into arrays (to be discussed in Chapter 9).

LEARNING CHECK

1. The ________ statement allows the user to enter data at the terminal while the program is running.
2. Only one variable can be listed in the INPUT statement. TRUE FALSE (Circle the correct answer.)
3. A PRINT statement that explains to the user what data is to be entered into the program is called a(n) ________.
4. Values contained in ________ statements are assigned to variables listed in ________ statements.
5. Using the following program, what values will be printed for N$, Z?

```
10 READ N$,X,Y
15 READ N$
20 LET Z = X + 4
25 READ X,Z
30 PRINT N$,Z
35 DATA "DANIEL",4,7,"JERRY",9,100
40 DATA "DEBBIE"
45 DATA 47,3
999 END
```

Answers

1. INPUT
2. False
3. prompt
4. DATA; READ
5. JERRY, 100

Printing Punctuation

Chapter 3 explained that the PRINT statement lets us get the results of processing printed. When more than one item is to be printed on a line, commas and semicolons can be used to control the spacing of the output.

Print Zones and Commas

The number of characters that can be printed on a line varies with the system used. On some terminals, such as the DEC VT-100 used with the DECSYSTEM 20 computer, each output line consists of eighty print positions. The line is divided into five print zones, each fourteen characters wide. The beginning columns of the five print zones are shown here:

ZONE 1	ZONE 2	ZONE 3	ZONE 4	ZONE 5
COL	COL	COL	COL	COL
1	15	29	43	57

When the computer encounters the PRINT statement in this program segment:

```
00010 READ A,M$,L$
00015 PRINT A,M$,L$
00020 DATA 20,"PINK","GRAPEFRUIT"
```

the value in A, which is 20, will be printed starting in the first print zone. Since 20 is a positive number, most computers will leave a blank before the number for the sign. Of course, if the value in A were negative, the minus sign would be printed starting in column 1. The comma between A and M$ tells the computer to space over to the next zone and print the value contained in M$. After PINK is printed, the comma directs the computer to space over to the third print zone and print the value in L$. The output is as follows:

Zone 1	Zone 2	Zone 3
RUNNH		
20	PINK	GRAPEFRUIT

If there are more items listed in a PRINT statement than there are print zones, the computer starts printing in the first zone of the next line. If the value to be printed exceeds the width of the print zone, the computer will completely print out the value, even though part of it goes into the next print zone. The comma then directs printing to start in the following print zone. Take a look at the following example and note where the value of P$ (49) is printed:

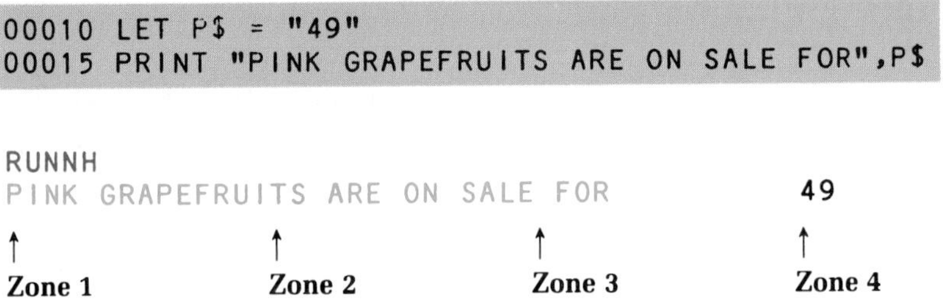

```
00010 LET P$ = "49"
00015 PRINT "PINK GRAPEFRUITS ARE ON SALE FOR",P$
```

```
RUNNH
PINK GRAPEFRUITS ARE ON SALE FOR                    49
↑               ↑               ↑               ↑
Zone 1          Zone 2          Zone 3          Zone 4
```

Table 4–1 presents the formatting differences among our five computers. The first column identifies the computer. Columns 2 and 3 give the number of columns and rows on the CRT screen. Columns 4 and 5 give the number of print zones (when commas are used as spacing control in

Table 4–1 COMPUTER DISPLAY CHARACTERISTICS

Computer	Screen Width (Characters)	Screen Height (Lines)	Number of Print Zones	Zone Width	Space for Sign?	Space Following?	Number of Digits Printed, Single Precision
DECSYSTEM 20	*80/132	*24/16	*5/9	14	Yes	Yes	7
Apple	40	24	2.5	16	No	No	9
IBM/Microsoft	80	24	5	14	Yes	Yes	7
TRS-80	*64/32	15	*4/2	16	Yes	Yes	6
PET/Commodore 64	40	25	4	10	Yes	Yes	9
					See example below		

*(Slash indicates both options are available to user.)

Example: With the Apple computer, the statement

10 PRINT −2;−1;0;1;2

would print

−2−1012 (no spaces)

With the DECSYSTEM 20, IBM/Microsoft, TRS-80, and PET/Commodore 64 computers, the same statement would print

−2 −1 0 1 2

PRINT statements) and print zone widths. Columns 6 and 7 indicate whether a space is always left in front of a number for a positive or negative sign and whether a space follows a number for ease in reading. Finally, column 8 gives the maximum number of digits output to the screen. If the number to be printed contains more characters than that listed, all remaining characters will be truncated—the number will not be rounded. (The DECSYSTEM 20, IBM Personal Computer, and TRS-80 have provisions for double precision; however, caution must be used, because the BASIC internal functions might not be any more accurate with double precision than with single precision—see your manual.)

Skipping Print Zones

A print zone can be skipped by the use of a technique that involves enclosing a space (the character blank) in quotation marks. This causes the entire zone to appear empty:

```
00010 PRINT "COURSE"," ","COURSE NUMBER"
```

Most computers (all five of ours) also allow the user to skip a zone by typing two consecutive commas:

```
00010 PRINT "COURSE",,"COURSE NUMBER"
```

Both of these techniques cause the literal "COURSE" to be printed in zone 1, the second zone to be blank, and the literal "COURSE NUMBER" to be printed in the third zone:

Zone 1	**Zone 3**
RUNNH	
COURSE	COURSE NUMBER

Ending with a Comma

As mentioned earlier, output generated by a PRINT statement normally begins in the first zone of a new line. However, if the previously executed PRINT statement ends with a comma, the output of a PRINT statement starts in the next available zone. Thus, the statements

```
00010 DATA 20,"PINK","GRAPEFRUIT","PLEASE"
00015 READ N,F$,M$,L$
00020 PRINT N,F$,
00025 PRINT M$,L$
00999 END
```

produce the following output:

```
RUNNH
 20             PINK              GRAPEFRUIT      PLEASE
```

Using Semicolons

Using a semicolon instead of a comma causes output to be packed more closely on a line. This alternative gives the programmer greater flexibility in formatting output. In the following examples, notice the difference in spacing when semicolons are used instead of commas:

Using Commas

```
00010 PRINT 100,-200,300
RUNNH
 100            -200              300
```

Using Semicolons

```
00010 PRINT 100;-200;300
RUNNH
 100 -200  300
```

The semicolon between the items tells the computer to skip to the next **column** to print the next item—not to the next print zone, as with the comma. Generally, when the number is positive, a space is left in front of the number for the sign.

Semicolons and Character Strings

The following example shows what happens when semicolons are used with character strings:

```
00060 PRINT "JASON";"JACKSON"
RUNNH
JASONJACKSON
```

Since letters do not have signs, they are run together. The best way to avoid this problem is to enclose a space within the quotes:

```
00060 PRINT "JASON ";"JACKSON"
RUNNH
JASON JACKSON
```

When printing character strings after numbers, it may also be necessary to enclose a leading space within quotes:

```
00060 PRINT 495207;" JASON";" JACKSON"
RUNNH
 495207   JASON JACKSON
```

Ending with a Semicolon

If the semicolon is the last character of the PRINT statement, carriage control is not advanced when the printing of the statement is completed; therefore, the output generated by the next PRINT statement continues on the same line, for example,

```
00060 PRINT 495207;
00070 PRINT " JASON";" JACKSON"
RUNNH
 495207   JASON JACKSON
```

Line 60 causes 495207 to be printed out. The semicolon after this number keeps the printer on the same line; then, when line 70 is encountered, JASON JACKSON is printed on the same line.

The comma causes the results of processing to be printed according to predefined print zones. The semicolon causes them to start printing in the next position on the output line. Both are easy to use, and many reports can be formatted in this fashion. However, there are times when a report should be structured differently.

The TAB function allows output to be printed in any column in an output line, providing the programmer greater flexibility to format printed output.

The general format of the TAB function is this:

TAB(expression)

The expression in parentheses may be a numeric constant, variable, or arithmetic expression; it tells the computer the column in which printing is to occur. The TAB function (as used in a PRINT statement) must immediately precede the variable or literal to be printed out. For example, the statement

```
00060 PRINT TAB(10);A$;TAB(25);B
```

causes the printer to be spaced to column 10 (indicated in parentheses) and to print the value stored in A$. The printer then spaces over to column 25, as indicated in the next parentheses, and prints the value in B. On many computers, such as the DECSYSTEM 20, IBM/Microsoft, and TRS-80, the value in A$ in this example would begin in column 11 and B, in column 26. In other words, the computer tabs to the tenth column and the semicolon instructs it to begin printing in the next column (column 11) (check your systems manual for your specific system). The program in Figure 4–5 illustrates the use of the TAB function.

Note that we have used the semicolon as the punctuation mark with the TAB function. The semicolon separates the expression from the values to be printed. If commas were used instead, the printer would default and use the predefined print zones, ignoring the columns specified in parentheses. For example, if line 120 of the program in Figure 4–5 had been

```
00120 PRINT TAB(5),"ITEM",TAB(25),"QUANTITY"
```

the output would have been

```
RUNNH
              INVENTORY REPORT

                    ITEM                                     QUANTITY

          PENCILS                 1000
          ERASERS                 200
          PAPER                   500
```

Figure 4–5 INVENTORY PROGRAM

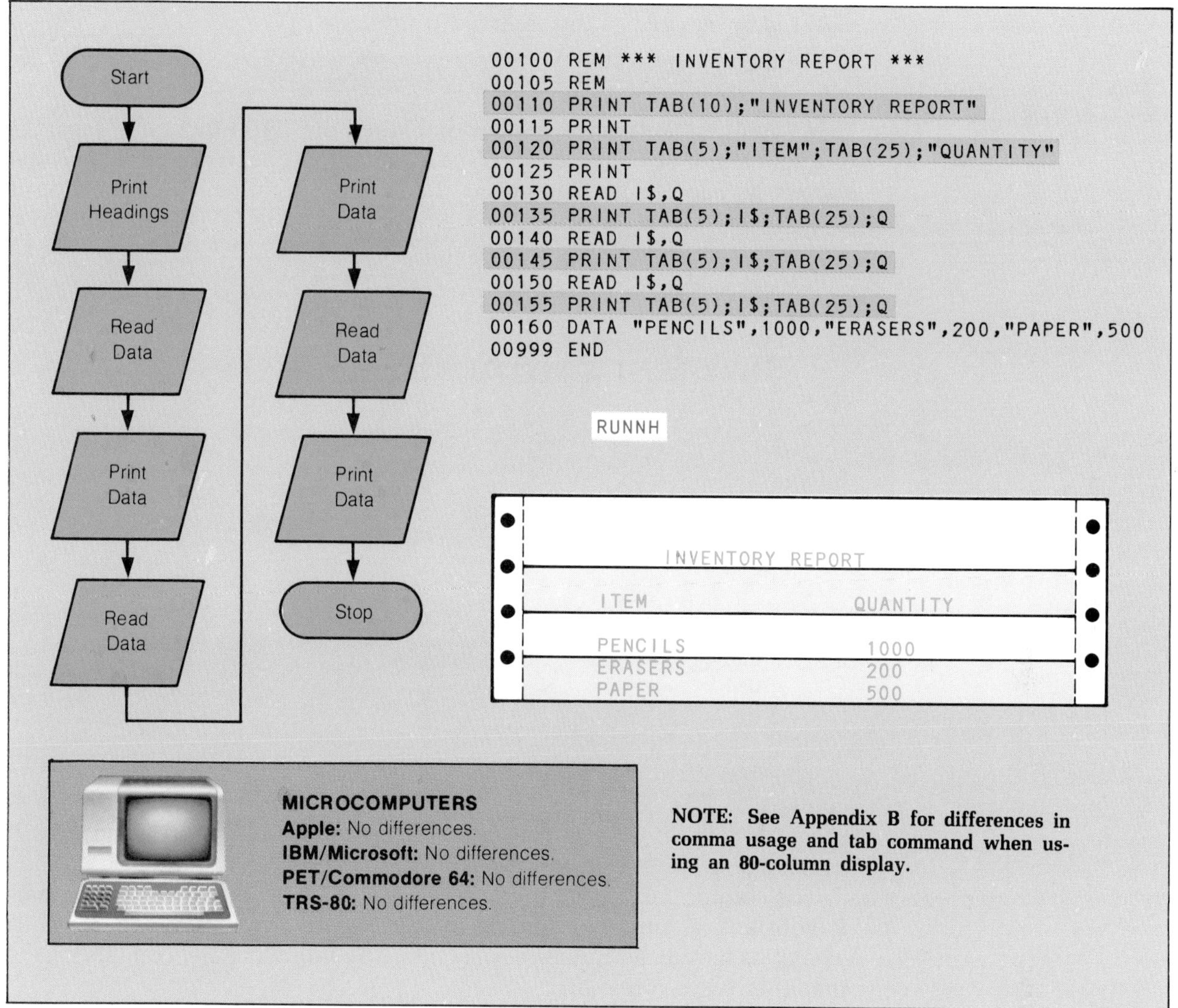

Start
Print Headings
Read Data
Print Data
Read Data
Print Data
Read Data
Print Data
Stop
00100 REM *** INVENTORY REPORT ***
00105 REM
00110 PRINT TAB(10);"INVENTORY REPORT"
00115 PRINT
00120 PRINT TAB(5);"ITEM";TAB(25);"QUANTITY"
00125 PRINT
00130 READ I$,Q
00135 PRINT TAB(5);I$;TAB(25);Q
00140 READ I$,Q
00145 PRINT TAB(5);I$;TAB(25);Q
00150 READ I$,Q
00155 PRINT TAB(5);I$;TAB(25);Q
00160 DATA "PENCILS",1000,"ERASERS",200,"PAPER",500
00999 END
RUNNH
INVENTORY REPORT
ITEM QUANTITY
PENCILS 1000
ERASERS 200
PAPER 500
MICROCOMPUTERS
Apple: No differences.
IBM/Microsoft: No differences.
PET/Commodore 64: No differences.
TRS-80: No differences.
NOTE: See Appendix B for differences in comma usage and tab command when using an 80-column display.

The computer spaced over the five columns indicated by the first TAB function, but when it saw the comma following the parentheses, it skipped over to the next predefined print zone to print ITEM. The same thing happens again with QUANTITY. Use semicolons rather than commas in PRINT statements containing the TAB function.

When using the TAB function, it is important to be aware of spacing. On the DECSYSTEM 20, there can be a space between the word TAB and the left parenthesis, because the DEC recognizes the reserved word TAB. On some systems—for example, IBM/Microsoft—there cannot be a space between TAB and the left parenthesis. This is because the reserved word that is recognized is TAB(. Without the opening parenthesis, TAB is taken as a variable with TA as its significant characters, and the value in parentheses is taken as an array position. The following would be invalid where TAB(is recognized as the reserved word:

```
00120 PRINT TAB (5);"ITEM";TAB (25);"QUANTITY"
```

As another caution, remember that when the TAB function is used, the printer cannot be backspaced. Once a column has been passed, the printer cannot go back to it. This means that if more than one TAB function is used in a PRINT statement, the column numbers in parentheses must increase from left to right. For example,

Valid:

```
00020 PRINT TAB(5);3;TAB(15);4;TAB(25);5
RUNNH
        3            4            5
```

Invalid:

```
00020 PRINT TAB(25);5;TAB(15);4;TAB(5);3
RUNNH
                                  5  4  3
```

```
00020 PRINT TAB(15);4;TAB(5);3;TAB(25);5
RUNNH
                     4  3         5
```

The first invalid example tells the computer to print the number 5 in column 25. The computer does this, but because the printer cannot backspace to column 15 and column 5, it prints the numbers 4 and 3 as it normally would using semicolons.

The column number of the TAB function may be expressed as a numeric constant, a numeric variable, or a numeric expression. All previous examples have used numeric constants. The following are examples using the other two expressions:

```
00010 LET Y = 25
00015 LET X = 10
00020 PRINT TAB(X);7;TAB(Y);"SUEANN"

RUNNH
             7                  SUEANN
```

```
00100 LET Y = 20
00105 LET X = 15
00110 PRINT TAB(X - 5);7;TAB(Y + 5);"SUEANN"

RUNNH
             7                  SUEANN
```

Notice that both of these have the same output, but the first one uses numeric variables and the second uses numeric expressions.

The PRINT USING Statement

Another convenient feature for controlling output is the PRINT USING statement; with it, the programmer can avoid print zone restrictions and can "dress up" the output. PRINT USING is an extension of the ANSI standards—not part of the standards. Its syntax is quite varied among different brands of computers. This section briefly describes its use on the DECSYSTEM 20 computer; the principles should be similar for other computers with this feature. Many microcomputers do not have a PRINT USING capability: The Apple and PET/Commodore 64 do not; the IBM/Microsoft and TRS-80 do. The general format of the PRINT USING statement is as follows:

line# PRINT USING image statement line#, expression-list

The PRINT USING statement tells which statement in the program has the print line image and what values are to be used in that print line. The expression list consists of a sequence of variables or expressions separated by commas; it is similar to the expression list in any PRINT statement. The line number of the image statement is the number of the BASIC statement that tells the computer how to print the items in the expression list.

The image statement is denoted by a colon (:) following the line number:

line#: format control characters

It is a nonexecutable statement, like DATA, and it can be placed anywhere in the program. The PRINT USING command, however, is placed where the logic demands. A single image statement can be referred to by several PRINT USING statements. Special format control characters are used in the image statement to describe the output image and to control spacing.

The major DECSYSTEM 20 formal control characters are listed in the following table. (a **mask** specifies the maximum number of characters to be printed in one field):

Format Control Character	Control Image for	Example
#	Numeric data; used in a mask; one symbol for each number to be printed; pads zeros to the left of the decimal point	###
$	Dollar sign; printed exactly as is	$###
$$	Causes dollar sign to be printed immediately before first digit	$$##.##
**	Leading asterisks; printed in place of blanks or spaces	**###.#

(Table continued next page)

Format Control Character	Control Image for	Example
	Decimal point; printed exactly as is	$##.##
E	Alphanumeric data; preceded by apostrophe ('); permits overflow to be printed to the right; left justifies; pads with blanks	'E
L	Alphanumeric data; preceded by apostrophe ('); used as a mask; left justifies; pads with blanks	'LLLLLL
R	Alphanumeric data; preceded by apostrophe ('); used as a mask; right justifies; pads with blanks	'RRRRRR
C	Alphanumeric data; preceded by apostrophe ('); used as a mask; centers in the field; pads with blanks	'CCCCCCC

Format Control Characters for IBM and TRS-80

IBM	TRS-80	Explanation
#	#	Same as DECSYSTEM 20.
.	.	Same as DECSYSTEM 20.
	$	Same as DECSYSTEM 20.
$$	$$	Two dollar signs cause the dollar sign to be floating, meaning that it will be in the first position before the number.
**$	**$	Vacant positions will be filled with asterisks, and the dollar sign will be in the first position to the left of the number.
+	+	When a + sign is placed at the beginning or end of a number, it causes a + sign to be printed if the number is positive and a − sign to be printed if the number is negative.
−	−	When a − sign is placed at the end of a number, negative numbers will have a negative sign, and for positive numbers it will appear as a space after the number.
∧∧∧∧	↑↑↑↑ or [[[[	This causes the number to be printed in exponential format.
\spaces\	%space%	This specifies a string field to be two plus the number of spaces between the characters.
!	!	This causes the computer to print only the first string character.
&		This specifies a variable-length field. The string is output exactly as it is entered.
_		Underscore causes the next character in the format string to be printed out. The character itself may be underscored by preceding it with two underscores (__).
%		If the number to be printed is larger than the specified field, a percent sign will appear before the number. If rounding caused the number to exceed the field, the percent sign will be printed in front of the rounded number.

Figure 4–6 PRINT USING STATEMENT ON DECSYSTEM 20

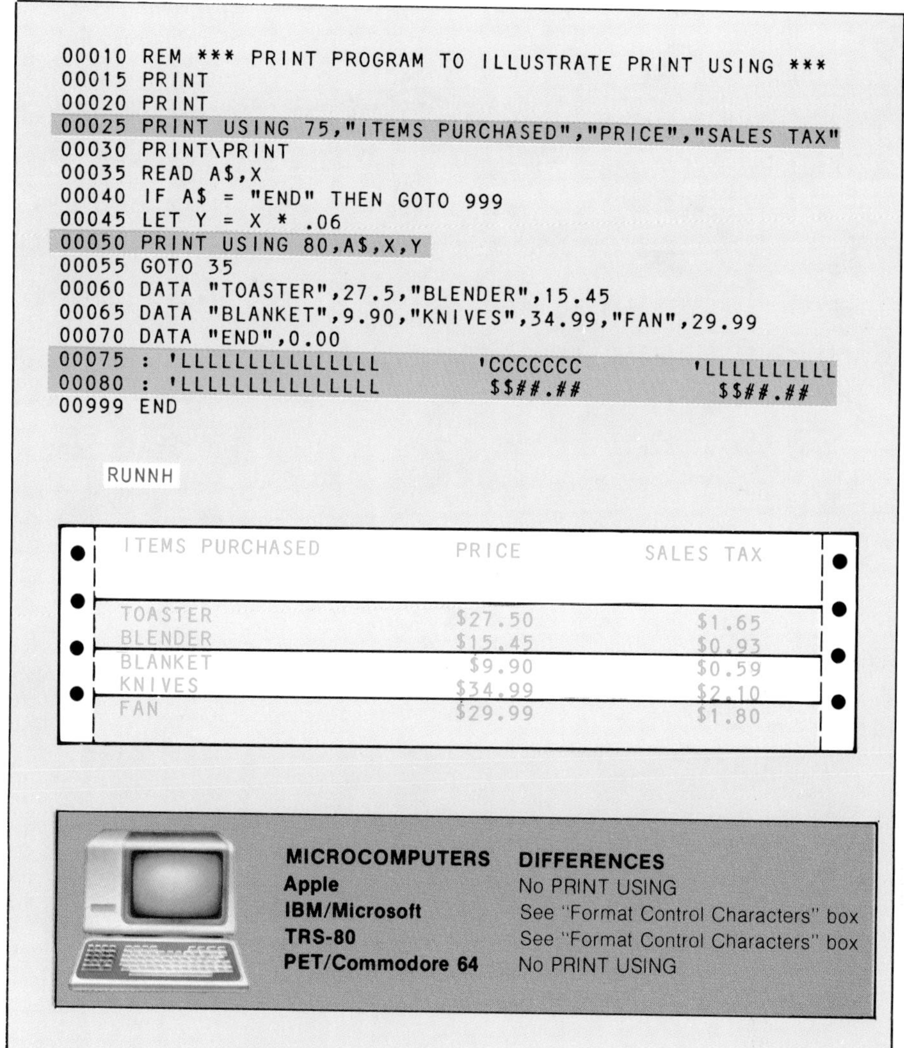

```
00010 REM *** PRINT PROGRAM TO ILLUSTRATE PRINT USING ***
00015 PRINT
00020 PRINT
00025 PRINT USING 75,"ITEMS PURCHASED","PRICE","SALES TAX"
00030 PRINT\PRINT
00035 READ A$,X
00040 IF A$ = "END" THEN GOTO 999
00045 LET Y = X * .06
00050 PRINT USING 80,A$,X,Y
00055 GOTO 35
00060 DATA "TOASTER",27.5,"BLENDER",15.45
00065 DATA "BLANKET",9.90,"KNIVES",34.99,"FAN",29.99
00070 DATA "END",0.00
00075 : 'LLLLLLLLLLLLLLL          'CCCCCCC          'LLLLLLLLLL
00080 : 'LLLLLLLLLLLLLLL           $$##.##            $$##.##
00999 END

RUNNH

ITEMS PURCHASED          PRICE          SALES TAX

TOASTER                  $27.50         $1.65
BLENDER                  $15.45         $0.93
BLANKET                   $9.90         $0.59
KNIVES                   $34.99         $2.10
FAN                      $29.99         $1.80
```

MICROCOMPUTERS	DIFFERENCES
Apple	No PRINT USING
IBM/Microsoft	See "Format Control Characters" box
TRS-80	See "Format Control Characters" box
PET/Commodore 64	No PRINT USING

The program in Figure 4–6 illustrates some of these control characters on the DECSYSTEM 20.

The IBM/Microsoft and TRS-80 PRINT USING statements are somewhat different. The general format for both of these systems looks like this:

line# PRINT USING "format";expression-list

For a list of the control characters for both IBM and TRS-80, see box.

Figure 4–7 shows examples of the PRINT USING statement on the IBM Personal Computer. Differences for the TRS-80 also are given.

Figure 4–7 PRINT USING STATEMENT ON IBM PERSONAL COMPUTER AND TRS-80

Statement	Output
`PRINT USING "###.##   ";12.67,345.986,3.1`	`12.67   345.99    3.10`
`PRINT USING "+##.##   ";-63.24,5.70,72.132`	`-63.24    +5.70  +72.13`
`PRINT USING "##.##-   ";-63.24,5.74,-38.22`	`63.24-     5.74   38.22-`
`PRINT USING "**###.## ";123.56,86.2`	`**123.56 ***86.20`
`PRINT USING "$$###.## ";123.56,86.2`	`$123.56   $86.20`
`PRINT USING "**$###.## ";549.26,44.2`	`**$549.26 ***$44.20`
`PRINT USING "#####,.##";3967.44`	`3,967.44`
`PRINT USING "##.##^^^^";26.843`	`2.68E+01`
`PRINT USING "###.#^^^^-";66642`	`666.4E+02`
`PRINT USING "_$##.##_$";12.34`	`$12.34`
`PRINT USING "##.##";876.34`	`%876.43`

```
10 LET A$ = "GOOD"
20 LET B$ = "BYE"
30 PRINT USING "!";A$;B$
40 PRINT USING "\  \";A$;B$
```

```
GB
GOODBYE
```

```
10 LET A$ = "GOOD"
20 LET B$ = "BYE"
30 PRINT USING "!";A$
40 PRINT USING "&";B$
```

```
G
BYE
```

DIFFERENCES for TRS-80

[1]Substitute [for

[2]There is no _

[3]There is no % for overflow.

[4]Substitute % for

[5]There is no &.

LEARNING CHECK

1. When printing more than one item on a line, a(n) ______ tells the computer to space over to the next print zone and print the value.
2. A print zone may be skipped by which of the following?
   a. Using two consecutive commas.
   b. Using two consecutive semicolons.
   c. Enclosing a space in quotation marks.
   d. Using a semicolon.
3. When a PRINT statement ends with a comma or semicolon, the next PRINT will begin ______.
   a. on the next line
   b. on the next page
   c. on the same line
4. A semicolon between the items tells the computer to skip to the next ______ to print the next item.
   a. line
   b. column
   c. print zone
5. The ______ function allows output to be printed in any column in an output line.
6. The ______ statement tells which statement in the program has the print image and what values are to be used in the print line.

Answers

1. comma
2. a and c
3. c
4. b
5. TAB
6. PRINT USING

A Programming Problem

Problem Definition

Savings City has two stores—one in Dallas and the other in Houston. It needs a program to list its income, expenses, and profits for each store, as well as the totals for both stores. It should be formatted as follows:

```
                    SAVINGS CITY

               DALLAS          HOUSTON          TOTAL


INCOME
EXPENSES
PROFIT
```

Solution Design

To produce the desired output, we need to ask the user to enter the income and expenses for each store. To find the profits for each, all we need to do is subtract expenses from income. To find the total income, expenses, and profit, just add the income, expenses, and profits from each store:

Income 1 + Income 2 = Total income.
Expenses 1 + Expenses 2 = Total expenses.
Profits 1 + Profits 2 = Total profits.

The Program

The program in Figure 4–8 documents the major variables used in lines 105 through 115. Lines 125 through 140 request the user to enter data. Lines 125 and 135 are prompts telling the user what values to enter. After the data have been entered, program execution continues. The headings are printed in lines 145 through 170. Notice how line 155 uses TAB to center the heading. Total income, I3, is figured in line 175; total expenses, E3, are computed in line 180, lines 185 and 190 figure the profits for each store, P1 for the Dallas's store profit and P2 for the Houston store's profit; and line 195 computes the total profit, P3. Lines 200 through 210 print the results in the desired format.

Summary

- The INPUT statement is used to enter data into a program in a question-and-answer mode.
- Another way of entering data into a program is to use READ and DATA statements. The READ statement causes values contained in the DATA statements to be assigned to variables.
- READ and INPUT statements are located where the logic of the program indicates. DATA statements are nonexecutable and may be located anywhere in the program.
- When more than one item is to be printed on a line of output, the spacing can be indicated by the use of commas and semicolons.
- Each line of output can be divided into a predetermined number of print zones. The comma is used to cause results to be printed in the print zones.
- Using a semicolon instead of comma to separate printed items causes output to be packed more closely on a line.
- Using the TAB function in a PRINT statement permits results to be printed anywhere on an output line.
- The PRINT USING feature provides a flexible method of producing output. The format control characteristics in the image statement define how the output will look.

Figure 4–8 INCOME, EXPENSE, AND PROFIT REPORT AND FLOWCHART

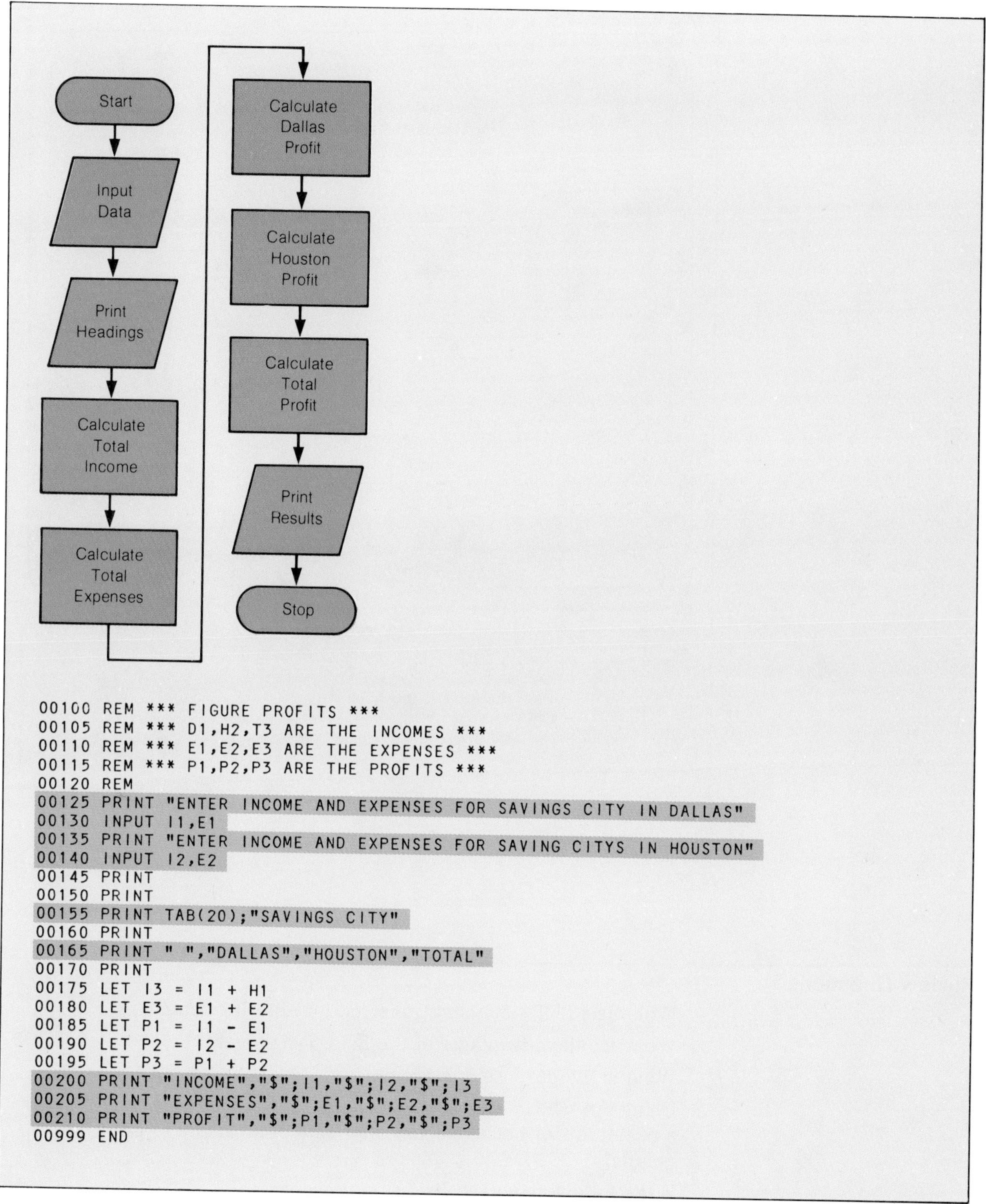


```
00100 REM *** FIGURE PROFITS ***
00105 REM *** D1,H2,T3 ARE THE INCOMES ***
00110 REM *** E1,E2,E3 ARE THE EXPENSES ***
00115 REM *** P1,P2,P3 ARE THE PROFITS ***
00120 REM
00125 PRINT "ENTER INCOME AND EXPENSES FOR SAVINGS CITY IN DALLAS"
00130 INPUT I1,E1
00135 PRINT "ENTER INCOME AND EXPENSES FOR SAVING CITYS IN HOUSTON"
00140 INPUT I2,E2
00145 PRINT
00150 PRINT
00155 PRINT TAB(20);"SAVINGS CITY"
00160 PRINT
00165 PRINT " ","DALLAS","HOUSTON","TOTAL"
00170 PRINT
00175 LET I3 = I1 + H1
00180 LET E3 = E1 + E2
00185 LET P1 = I1 - E1
00190 LET P2 = I2 - E2
00195 LET P3 = P1 + P2
00200 PRINT "INCOME","$";I1,"$";I2,"$";I3
00205 PRINT "EXPENSES","$";E1,"$";E2,"$";E3
00210 PRINT "PROFIT","$";P1,"$";P2,"$";P3
00999 END
```

(Figure continued next page)

Figure 4-8 *(continued)*

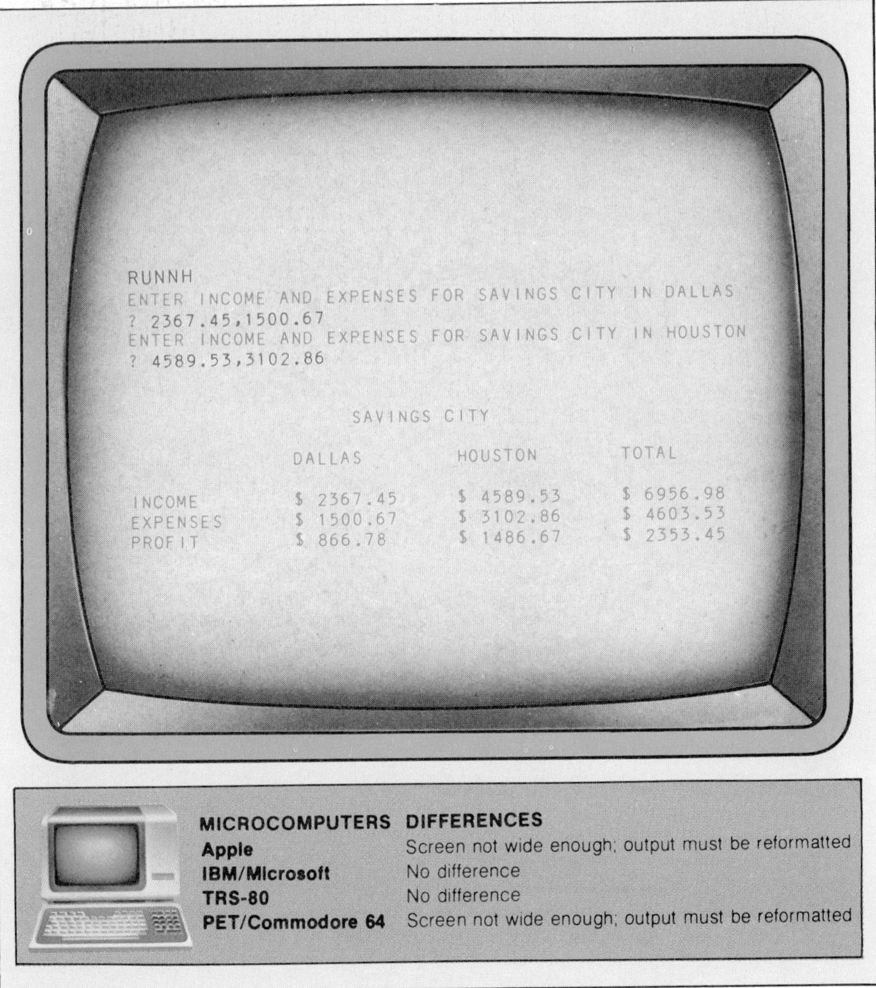
RUNNH
ENTER INCOME AND EXPENSES FOR SAVINGS CITY IN DALLAS
? 2367.45,1500.67
ENTER INCOME AND EXPENSES FOR SAVINGS CITY IN HOUSTON
? 4589.53,3102.86
SAVINGS CITY
DALLAS HOUSTON TOTAL
INCOME $ 2367.45 $ 4589.53 $ 6956.98
EXPENSES $ 1500.67 $ 3102.86 $ 4603.53
PROFIT $ 866.78 $ 1486.67 $ 2353.45

MICROCOMPUTERS	DIFFERENCES
Apple	Screen not wide enough; output must be reformatted
IBM/Microsoft	No difference
TRS-80	No difference
PET/Commodore 64	Screen not wide enough; output must be reformatted

Review Questions

1. When is a LET statement preferred for entering data?
2. What are the advantages of the INPUT statement?
3. What is the purpose of a prompt?
4. Using the INPUT statement, how would you set up a program to ask a person his or her name, age, and date of birth and to print the results?
5. Is the following a valid INPUT statement?
   10 INPUT "THE NAME OF YOUR DOG";N

6. When are READ/DATA statements best used?
7. Where should DATA statements be placed in a program?
8. Is the following a valid READ statement?

```
20 READ N$ B6 A
```

9. After the following READ/DATA statements were executed, what would be the value of each variable?

```
10 DATA 256,49
20 DATA "TAMPA BAY"
30 DATA "FLORIDA",40421
40 READ A,B,C$
50 READ S$,X
```

10. What happens when a PRINT statement ends with a comma?
11. What happens when a PRINT statement ends with a semicolon?
12. In which print zones would the following variables be printed?

```
300 PRINT C,X;" ",T
310 PRINT A," ",D,F
```

13. What would the output of this PRINT statement look like if A$ = DOG and B$ = HOUSE?

```
400 PRINT A$;B$
```

14. In what print zone would you find each of the following variables?

```
475 PRINT V,S,T,N,P,R,W
```

15. How would you print KIM YOUNG starting in column 12?
16. Using the TAB function, what would the PRINT statement look like that prints out NAME starting in column 1, CITY in column 20, and STATE in column 35?
17. Is the following a valid PRINT USING statement?

```
300 PRINT USING 20 Q,R,S,T
```

18. Why is the following image statement invalid?

```
250 'LLLLL $##.## 'RRRRR
```

19. What would the output from this PRINT statement look like if N$ = JOE and A = 1475.59?

```
130 PRINT USING 140,N$,A
140: 'LLLLLLL b̸b̸b̸b̸ $####.##
```

20. Give the output from the PRINT USING statement in Question 19 using the following image statement:

```
140: 'RRRRRRR b̸b̸b̸b̸ $#####.##
```

Debugging Exercises

1. Debug this program:

```
00010 DATA "MR. LEWIS",57,63,"MRS. WOODEND"
00015 READ N1$,A1
00020 READ N2$,A2
00999 END
```

2. How should these PRINT statements be corrected to match their output if X = 2, Y = 365, Z = 900, R = 52, A$ = YEARS, and B$ = WEEKS'?

Output

	Z1	**Z2**	**Z3**	**Z4**	**Z5**
a.			TIM TUCKER		
b.	2	365	900	52	
c.	2	356	YEAR		

```
a. 00060 PRINT "TIM";"TUCKER"
b. 00090 PRINT X,Y,Z;R
c. 00010 PRINT X,Y
   00020 PRINT A$
```

3. Correct these instructions so they are in proper format:

```
a. 00100 PRINT TAB(10),B$
b. 00110 PRINT TAB(47);X,TAB(55);Y
c. 00120 PRINT TAB(75);A$;TAB(20);X
d. 00130 PRINT TAB(10);T$;TAB(30);"HELLO"
```

4. Which of these READ statements are invalid? Correct them.

```
00010 READ A$,B,2
00100 READ B2,C$.X
00110 READ 7$,C
```

5. This program statement wants a person's name and age. Correct it so that the user knows what to enter (prompt):

```
00050 INPUT N$,A
```

6. Correct the following statement:

```
00010 INPUT "ENTER CITY,STATE,AND ZIP CODE";X,Y,Z$
```

7. How would you change this so that the heading is centered on an eighty-character line?

```
00100  PRINT "REPORT HEADING"
```

8. Correct this PRINT USING instruction:

```
00010 PRINT USING NAME,2563
```

9. Correct this image statement:

```
00100   'LLLLL      ##.##
```

10. Correct this READ statement:

```
00010 DATA 10,ABC,20
00020 READ X$,C,D
```

Additional Programming Problems

1. Write a program that asks for the name and weight of an object and computes the weight in kilograms (1 pound = 0.453592 kilograms). The program should print out the name of the object, weight in pounds, and weight in kilograms, each in three different zones.
2. Write a program that asks for four numbers, computes their average, and then prints the numbers and their average each in a separate zone.
3. Mr. Leady wants to know how much it would cost him to replant the grass in his backyard, which measures 150 by 200 feet. Grass seed costs $0.93 per pound, and one pound covers 50 square feet. He also needs to know how much it would cost if he used Special Blend Grass Seed, which is $0.99 per pound, and one pound also covers 50 square feet. The program should output the cost of using each and the cost difference between the two.
4. Write a program using READ/DATA statements to read in prices of four items and compute the tax. (Tax is 6 percent on a dollar.) List the four items, the tax, and the total, making use of the PRINT USING statement. Label the tax and total. Use this data: 12.79, 9.99, 4.57, 30.02. The output should look like this:

```
         12.79
          9.99
          4.57
         30.02
Tax      XX.XX
       -------
Total   $XX.XX
```

5. Write a program to read in the following data and print it out with the headings NAME, AREA CODE, and TELEPHONE #, using the TAB function:

   BOB HOAX, 491, 535-0101, JANICE FREZE, 982, 453-0748

6. Print out these holidays, with the date on the first line and the holiday on the next followed by two blank lines; then print the next date and holiday:

December 25	Christmas
January 1	New Year's Day

5 Control Statements

Outline

Objectives

After reading this chapter, the student should be able to do the following:

- Understand and use the unconditional transfer statement GOTO.
- Understand and use the conditional transfer statements IF/THEN and IF/THEN/ELSE.
- Be familiar with the logic of nested IF/THEN/ELSE statements.
- Understand and use the conditional transfer statement ON/GOTO.
- Understand the purpose of a menu.
- Set up loops using trailer values and counters.

Overview

The programs described to this point contained instructions that were always executed one right after the other—from the lowest line number to the highest. This chapter will discuss ways of transferring control to program statements out of sequence by using the GOTO, IF/THEN, and ON/GOTO statements. One of the most valuable programming techniques, looping, will also be discussed.

In the previous chapters, we have been able to run only one set of data without having to repeat a program segment multiple times or rerun the program. For example, if we had a program that computed an individual's bowling average for three games, chances are that we probably would want to calculate the average of more than just one person. Without the control statements discussed in this chapter, we would have to rerun the program for each set of data or rewrite the program segment that calculates the average as many times as we had bowlers. Using one of these control statements, however, allows us to process multiple sets of data more efficiently. We might want, for example, the output of the bowling average program to appear as follows:

```
NAME            AVERAGE
F. FLINTSTONE   163
B. RUBBLE       159
T. TIME         168
```

In this chapter we will see how these control statements allow us to obtain this output.

The GOTO Statement: Unconditional Transfer

All BASIC programs consist of a series of statements that normally are executed in sequential order. Sometimes, however, it is desirable to alter the flow of execution. This is called **branching,** and the programmer can use the GOTO statement to do it. The general format of the GOTO statement is as follows:

line# GOTO transfer line#

The programming command GOTO can be written as one word or as two words, GO TO.

The GOTO statement is called an **unconditional transfer statement,** because the flow of execution is altered to the transfer line number every time the statement is encountered.

A typical GOTO statement follows:

```
00100 GOTO 60
```

This statement tells the computer that the next statement to be executed is line 60. If line 60 is an executable statement, that statement and those following are executed. If it is a nonexecutable statement, execution proceeds at the first executable statement encountered after line 60.

Let us see how the GOTO statement might be used in an application by first looking at Figure 5–1, which calculates the bowling averages for three individuals and prints the results without using a GOTO statement. What we really have here is a single process (adding three numbers together and dividing by 3) repeated three times. The programmer typed in the following three lines as many times as was necessary:

```
READ N$,S1,S2,S3
LET A = (S1 + S2 + S3) / 3
PRINT N$,A
```

Although this is not a very difficult task with a small, uncomplicated problem, imagine how time consuming and inefficient it would be to do it for a hundred sets of data!

The same result can be achieved much more simply by using a GOTO statement. In Figure 5–2, the GOTO statement in line 30 directs the computer back to statement 15. A loop is formed. In this example, the error message "End of DATA found at line 00015 of MAIN PROGRAM" was printed because an attempt was made to read data after the data list had been exhausted. The execution of the program was terminated.

Note how the loop is indicated in the flowchart. A flow line is drawn from the process step immediately preceding the GOTO statement to the process step indicated by the transfer line number.

Figure 5–1 BOWLING AVERAGE PROGRAM

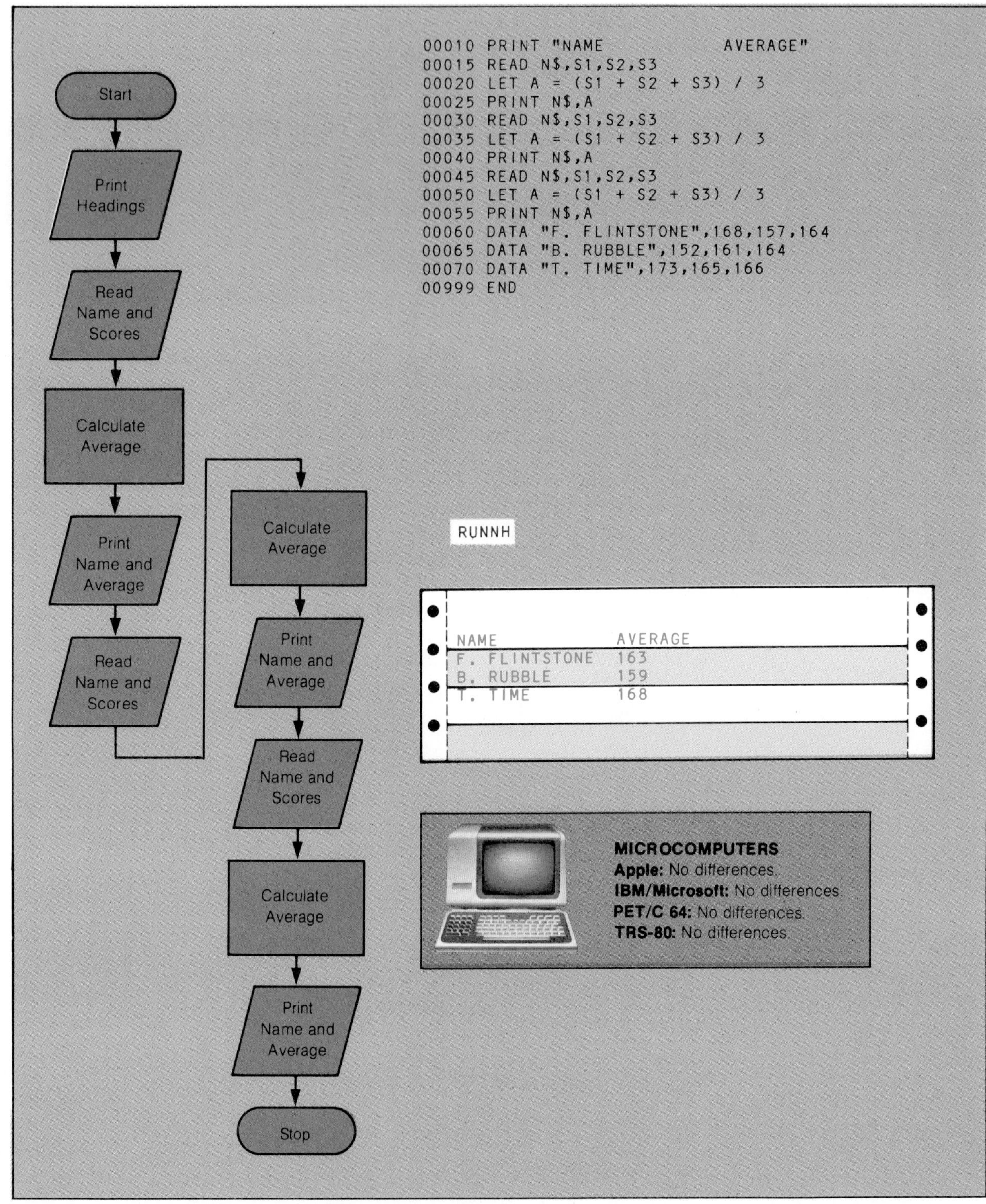


```
00010 PRINT "NAME            AVERAGE"
00015 READ N$,S1,S2,S3
00020 LET A = (S1 + S2 + S3) / 3
00025 PRINT N$,A
00030 READ N$,S1,S2,S3
00035 LET A = (S1 + S2 + S3) / 3
00040 PRINT N$,A
00045 READ N$,S1,S2,S3
00050 LET A = (S1 + S2 + S3) / 3
00055 PRINT N$,A
00060 DATA "F. FLINTSTONE",168,157,164
00065 DATA "B. RUBBLE",152,161,164
00070 DATA "T. TIME",173,165,166
00999 END
```

```
RUNNH
```

```
NAME              AVERAGE
F. FLINTSTONE     163
B. RUBBLE         159
T. TIME           168
```

MICROCOMPUTERS
Apple: No differences.
IBM/Microsoft: No differences.
PET/C 64: No differences.
TRS-80: No differences.

Figure 5–2 BOWLING AVERAGE PROGRAM WITH GOTO STATEMENT

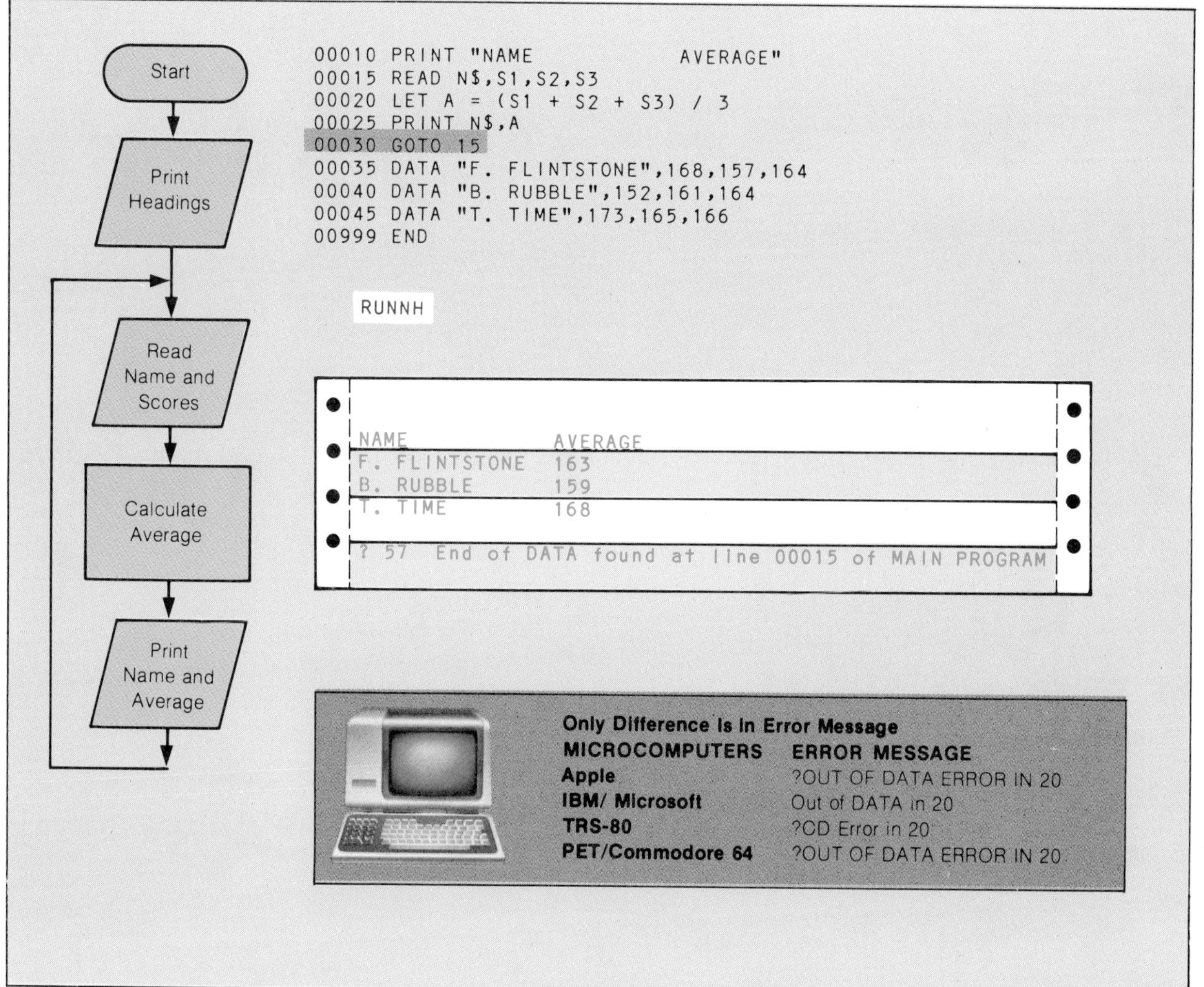

The INPUT statement could have been used in Figures 5–1 and 5–2 instead of the READ/DATA statements. Figure 5–3 shows the results of using an INPUT statement with the GOTO statement. Notice the computer response "^C at line 00010 of MAIN PROGRAM" at the end of the output. This appears because when we use the INPUT statement in conjunction with the GOTO statements, as we did in Figure 5–3, an infinite loop is formed. The program will keep asking us for input until we manually interrupt it. This can be done by pressing the control key (CTRL) and the C key simultaneously (CTRL and BREAK on some systems), which results in the message "^C at line 00010 of MAIN PROGRAM" (or something similar such as "Break in 10") to be printed.

Figure 5–3 BOWLING AVERAGE PROGRAM USING INPUT AND GOTO STATEMENTS

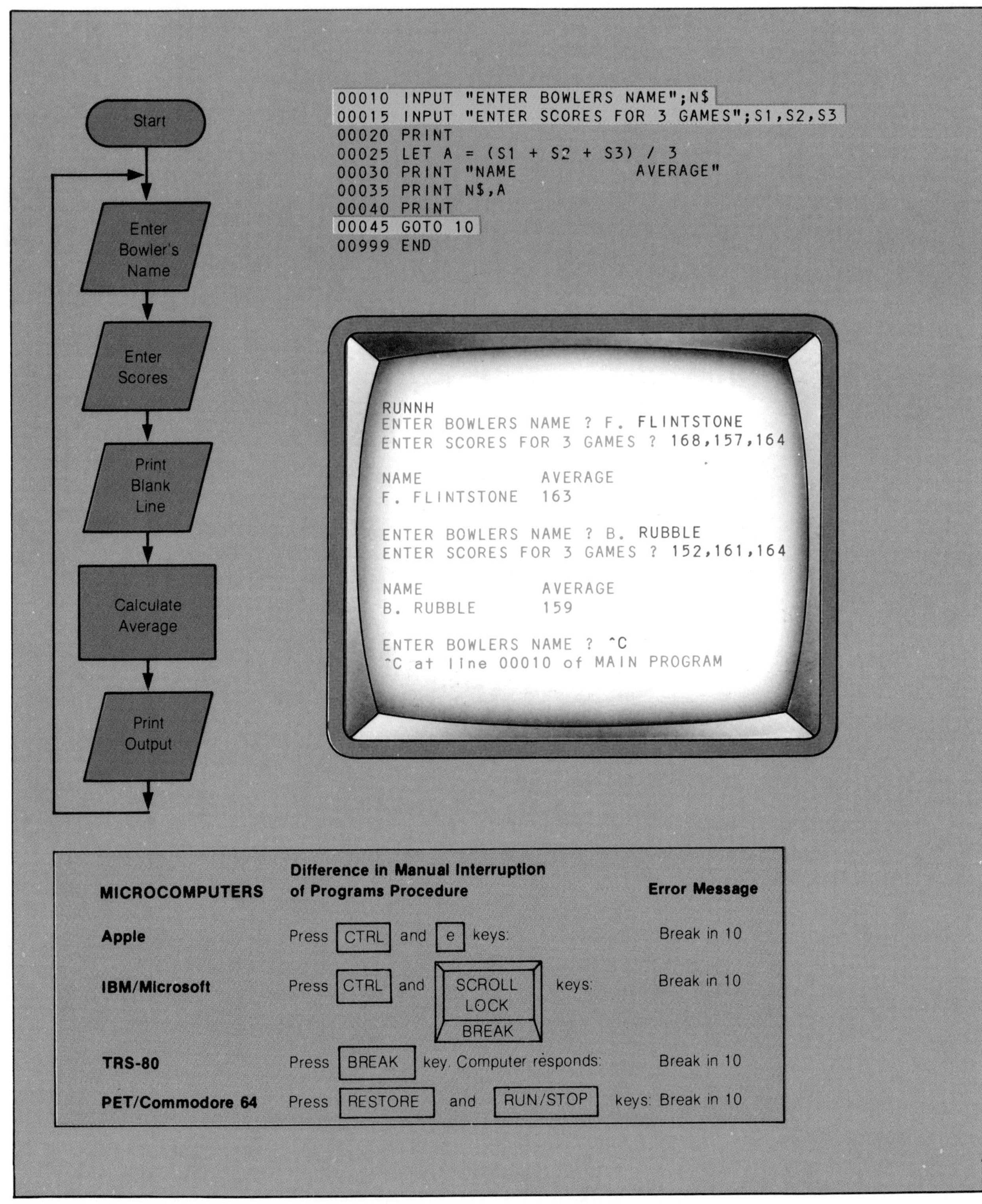


```
00010 INPUT "ENTER BOWLERS NAME";N$
00015 INPUT "ENTER SCORES FOR 3 GAMES";S1,S2,S3
00020 PRINT
00025 LET A = (S1 + S2 + S3) / 3
00030 PRINT "NAME                AVERAGE"
00035 PRINT N$,A
00040 PRINT
00045 GOTO 10
00999 END
```

```
RUNNH
ENTER BOWLERS NAME ? F. FLINTSTONE
ENTER SCORES FOR 3 GAMES ? 168,157,164

NAME            AVERAGE
F. FLINTSTONE   163

ENTER BOWLERS NAME ? B. RUBBLE
ENTER SCORES FOR 3 GAMES ? 152,161,164

NAME            AVERAGE
B. RUBBLE       159

ENTER BOWLERS NAME ? ^C
^C at line 00010 of MAIN PROGRAM
```

MICROCOMPUTERS	Difference in Manual Interruption of Programs Procedure	Error Message
Apple	Press [CTRL] and [e] keys:	Break in 10
IBM/Microsoft	Press [CTRL] and [SCROLL LOCK / BREAK] keys:	Break in 10
TRS-80	Press [BREAK] key. Computer responds:	Break in 10
PET/Commodore 64	Press [RESTORE] and [RUN/STOP] keys:	Break in 10

Later, this chapter will show how to control the number of times a loop is repeated (eliminating any error messages and the need to manually interrupt the program).

The IF/THEN Statement: Conditional Transfer

The GOTO statement always transfers control. Often, however, it is necessary to transfer control only when a specified condition exists. The IF/THEN statement is used to test for such a condition. If the condition does not exist, the next statement in the program is executed. The general format of the IF/THEN statement is this:

line# IF condition THEN line#

A condition has the following general format:

expression	relational symbol	expression

For example, in the statement "110 If X < Y + 1 THEN 230," X < Y + 1 is the condition.

Conditions tested can involve either numeric or character string data. **Relational symbols** that can be used include the following:

Symbol	**Meaning**	**Examples**
<	Less than	A < B
< = or ≤	Less than or equal to	X < = Y
>	Greater than	J > 1
> = or ≥	Greater than or equal to	A > = B
=	Equal to	X = T N$ = "NONE"
<> or ><	Not equal to	R <> Q "APPLE" <> R$

Some examples of valid IF/THEN statements follow:

Statement	**Computer Execution**

`00010 IF X >= 6 THEN 30`
`00020 LET A = A + X`
`00030 PRINT X`
	If the value contained in X is greater than or equal to 6, the computer branches to line 30. If not, the computer executes the next sequential instruction, line 20.

`00010 IF K <> N * 40 THEN 50` `00020 LET K = N * 40`	If K is not equal to N * 40, the computer transfers to statement 50. Otherwise, it executes the next statement, line 20.

(Table continued next page)

Statement *(continued)*	**Computer Execution**

`00040 IF A$ = "NO" THEN 60`
`00050 LET X = X + 1`
`00060 PRINT X`
	If the value contained in A$ is NO, control is passed to line 60. If A$ contains anything else, control goes to line 50.

The program in Figure 5–4 uses both numeric and character string comparisons to search voter registration records to find all registered Republicans in District 3 so they can be placed on a mailing list. The program reads the name, district in which registered, and party affiliation for each registered voter. A numeric comparison is made to determine if the voter resides in District 3:

Figure 5–4 MAILING LIST PROGRAM

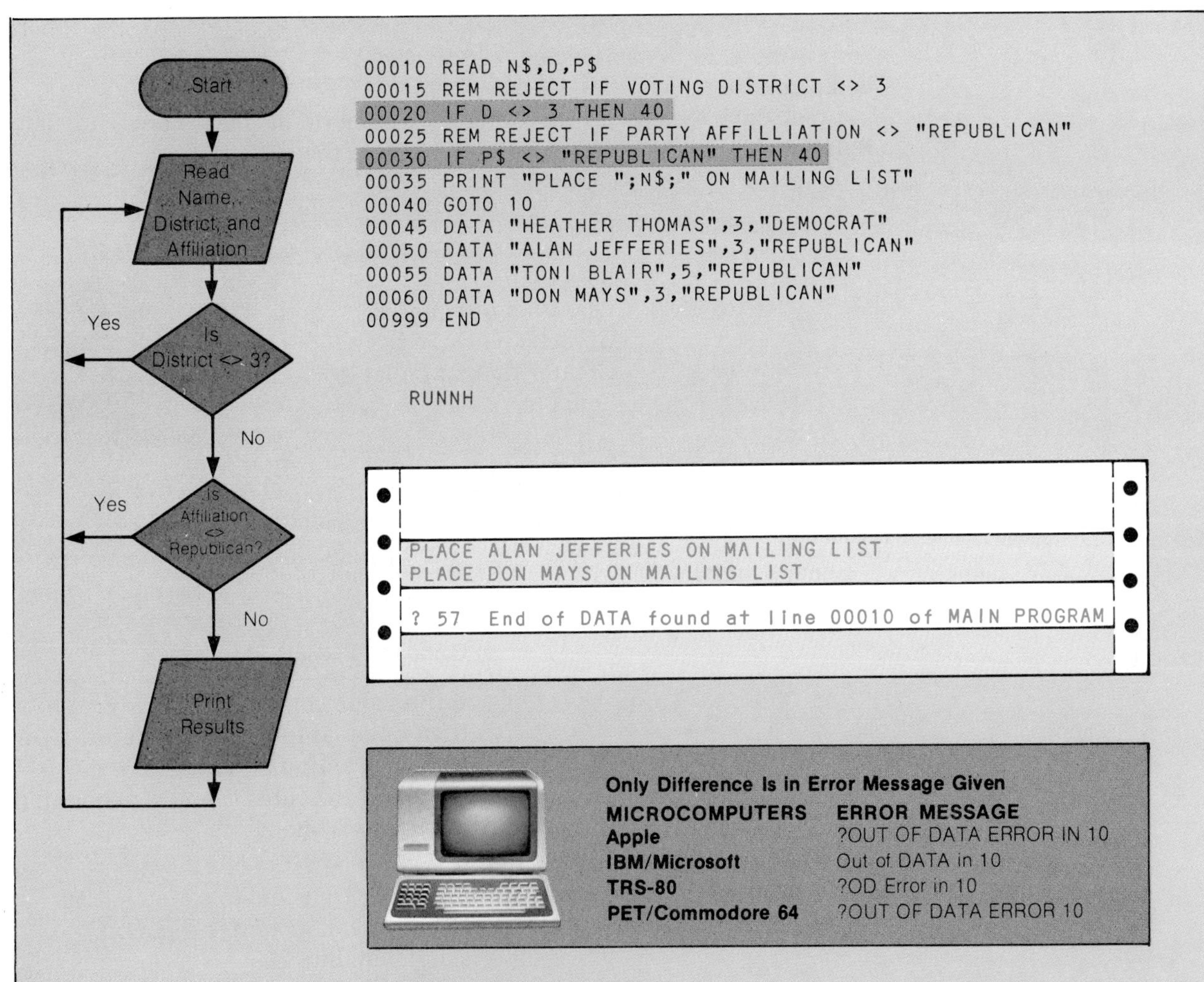

Start
Read Name, District, and Affiliation
Yes
Is District <> 3?
No
Yes
Is Affiliation <> Republican?
No
Print Results
00010 READ N$,D,P$
00015 REM REJECT IF VOTING DISTRICT <> 3
00020 IF D <> 3 THEN 40
00025 REM REJECT IF PARTY AFFILLIATION <> "REPUBLICAN"
00030 IF P$ <> "REPUBLICAN" THEN 40
00035 PRINT "PLACE ";N$;" ON MAILING LIST"
00040 GOTO 10
00045 DATA "HEATHER THOMAS",3,"DEMOCRAT"
00050 DATA "ALAN JEFFERIES",3,"REPUBLICAN"
00055 DATA "TONI BLAIR",5,"REPUBLICAN"
00060 DATA "DON MAYS",3,"REPUBLICAN"
00999 END
RUNNH
PLACE ALAN JEFFERIES ON MAILING LIST
PLACE DON MAYS ON MAILING LIST
? 57 End of DATA found at line 00010 of MAIN PROGRAM
Only Difference Is in Error Message Given
MICROCOMPUTERS ERROR MESSAGE
Apple ?OUT OF DATA ERROR IN 10
IBM/Microsoft Out of DATA in 10
TRS-80 ?OD Error in 10
PET/Commodore 64 ?OUT OF DATA ERROR 10

```
00020 IF D <> 3 THEN 40
```

The test is stated in such a way that only if the candidate resides in District 3 will the program continue to evaluate his or her record. Otherwise, control is transferred to line 40.

The other qualification for the mailing list is that the voter be a registered Republican. A comparison of character strings is made to determine this requirement:

```
00030 IF P$ <> "REPUBLICAN" THEN 40
```

If the person is not a Republican, control is transferred to line 40.

Any person who satisfies both conditions is placed on the mailing list. The program output indicates that only two people, Alan Jefferies and Don Mays, should be placed on the mailing list.

Note the diamond-shaped symbol in the flowchart in Figure 5–4. It is a **decision block** representing the IF/THEN test. The outcome of the test determines which flow line (path of program logic) will be followed.

Many BASIC implementations allow other, more general forms of the IF statement. One of these is the following:

line# IF condition THEN statement

The statement following THEN can be a BASIC statement or statements. Some examples follow:

```
00010 IF X < Y THEN LET A = A + 1\PRINT A
00050 IF M = N * P THEN PRINT M
```

Figure 5–5 uses this form of the IF statement to indicate whether the result of an arithmetic operation is positive, negative, or 0.

IF/THEN/ELSE Statements

Another useful form of the IF statement is the IF/THEN/ELSE statement. The general format of the IF/THEN/ELSE statement is this:

line# IF condition THEN clause ELSE clause

The clause can be a BASIC statement or statements or a line number to branch to.

If the condition being tested is true, the clause following the THEN statement is executed. If the condition is false, the THEN clause is bypassed, and the clause following ELSE is executed.

Some examples of valid IF/THEN/ELSE statements are given here:

```
00010 IF X = Y THEN PRINT "EQUAL" ELSE PRINT "NOT EQUAL"
00020 IF C = A * B THEN LET X = 1 ELSE LET X = 0
00030 IF M < R THEN 110 ELSE 150
```

Figure 5–5 SIGN OF NUMBER PROGRAM

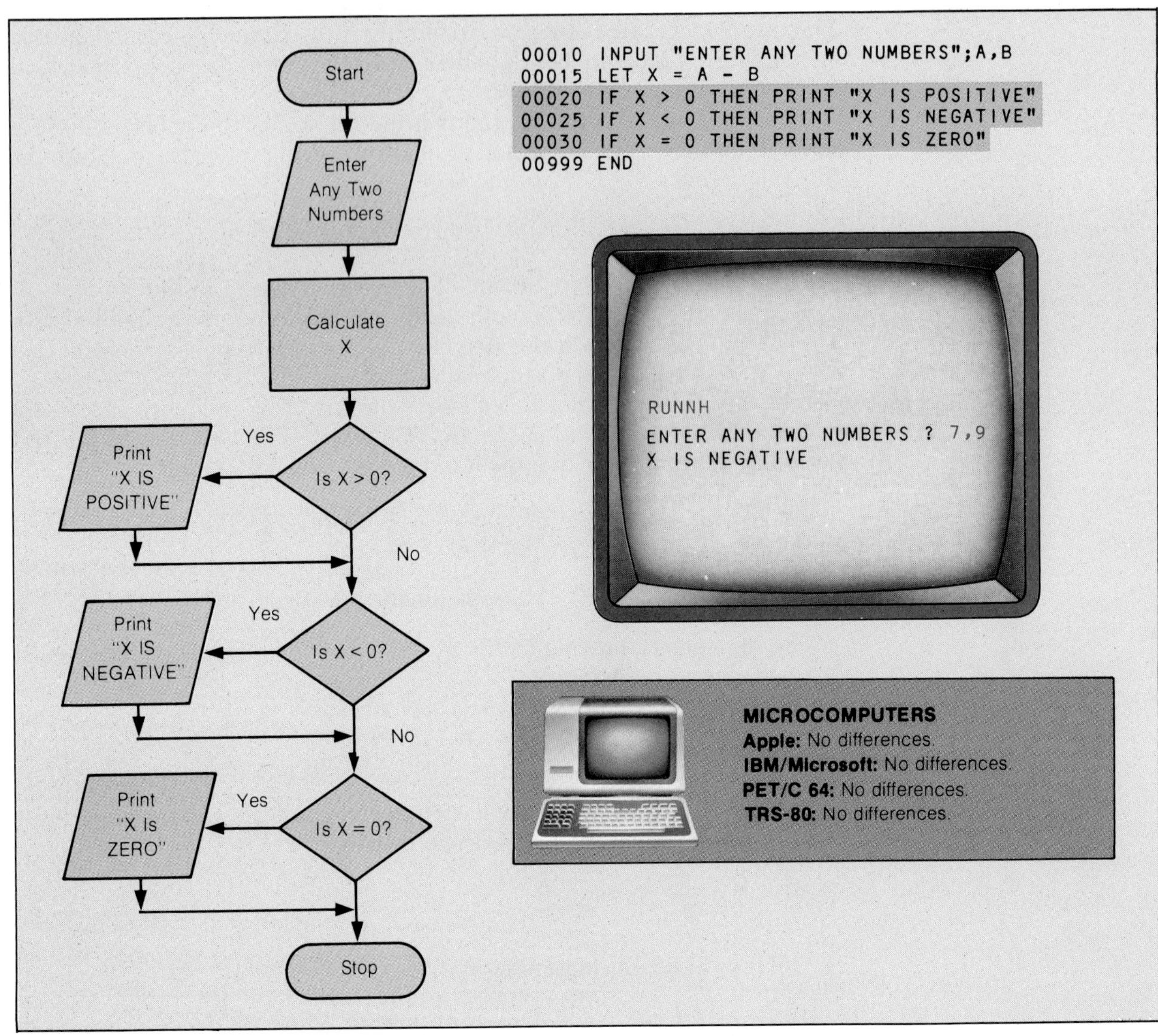

Figure 5–6 illustrates the use of an IF/THEN/ELSE statement.

Nested IF/THEN/ELSE Statements

Some systems allow IF/THEN/ELSE statements to be nested, for example,

```
00010 IF A > B THEN PRINT "GREATER" ELSE IF A < B
       THEN PRINT "LESS THAN" ELSE PRINT "EQUAL"
```

Figure 5-6 IF/THEN/ELSE STATEMENT

```
00010 PRINT
00015 PRINT "THIS PROGRAM CALCULATES THE"
00020 PRINT "AVERAGE OF TWO NUMBERS"
00025 PRINT "DO YOU WISH TO CONTINUE"
00030 INPUT "ENTER YES OR NO";A$
00035 IF A$ = "YES" THEN 40 ELSE 70
00040 PRINT
00045 PRINT "ENTER TWO NUMBERS"
00050 INPUT X,Y
00055 LET A = (X + Y) / 2
00060 PRINT "THE AVERAGE OF ";X;"AND ";Y;"IS ";A
00065 GOTO 10
00070 PRINT
00075 PRINT "BYE"
00999 END
```

```
RUNNH

THIS PROGRAM CALCULATES THE
AVERAGE OF TWO NUMBERS
DO YOU WISH TO CONTINUE
ENTER YES OR NO ? YES

ENTER TWO NUMBERS
 ? 7,9
THE AVERAGE OF  7 AND  9 IS  8

THIS PROGRAM CALCULATES THE
AVERAGE OF TWO NUMBERS
DO YOU WISH TO CONTINUE
ENTER YES OR NO ? N

BYE
```

MICROCOMPUTERS	DIFFERENCES
Apple	No IF/THEN/ELSE statement
IBM/Microsoft	No difference
TRS-80	No difference
PET/Commodore 64	No IF/THEN/ELSE statement

Figure 5–7 NESTED IF/THEN/ELSE STATEMENTS

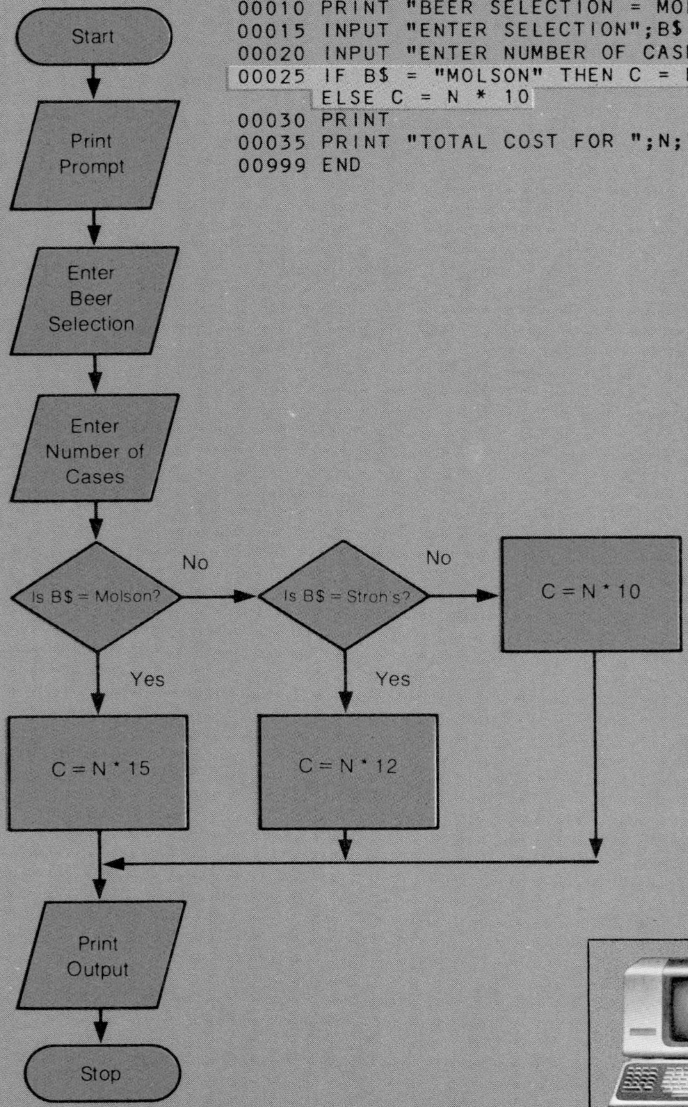

```
00010 PRINT "BEER SELECTION = MOLSON,STROH'S,AND BUD"
00015 INPUT "ENTER SELECTION";B$
00020 INPUT "ENTER NUMBER OF CASES";N
00025 IF B$ = "MOLSON" THEN C = N * 15 ELSE IF B$ = "STROH'S" THEN C = N * 12
      ELSE C = N * 10
00030 PRINT
00035 PRINT "TOTAL COST FOR ";N;" CASES OF ";B$;" = $";C
00999 END
```

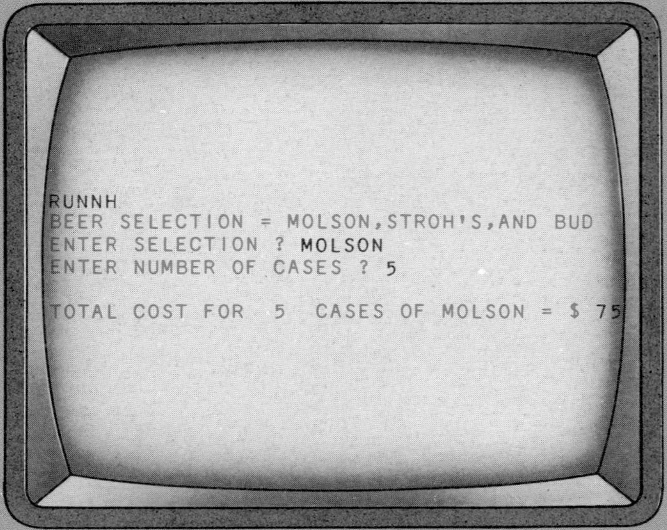

```
RUNNH
BEER SELECTION = MOLSON,STROH'S,AND BUD
ENTER SELECTION ? MOLSON
ENTER NUMBER OF CASES ? 5

TOTAL COST FOR  5  CASES OF MOLSON = $ 75
```

MICROCOMPUTERS	DIFFERENCES
Apple	No IF/THEN/ELSE statement
IBM/Microsoft	No difference
TRS-80	Same
PET/Commodore 64	No IF/THEN/ELSE statement

If a statement does not contain the same number of ELSE and THEN clauses, each ELSE is matched with the closest unmatched THEN. For example,

```
00010 IF X = Y THEN IF Y = Z THEN PRINT "X = Z" ELSE PRINT "X <> Z"
```

will not print "X <> Z" when X is not equal to Y.

Figure 5-7 illustrates the use of nested IF/THEN/ELSE statements to calculate the price of beer ordered.

LEARNING CHECK

1. In a BASIC program, the term ________ refers to altering the flow of execution.
2. The GOTO statement is called a(n) ________ transfer statement, because the flow of execution is altered every time the statement is encountered.
3. The ________ statement *always* transfers control.
4. The IF/THEN statement ________.
   a. always transfers control
   b. transfers control only when a specific condition exists
   c. never transfers control
   d. none of the above
5. Is the following a valid nested IF/THEN/ELSE statement?

```
IF X < 100 THEN Y = 1 ELSE IF X > 100 THEN Y = 2 ELSE Y = 0
```

Answers

1. branching
2. unconditional
3. GOTO
4. b
5. Yes

The ON/GOTO Statement: Conditional Transfer

The ON/GOTO, or computed GOTO, statement transfers control to other statements in the program based on the evaluation of a mathematical expression. The computed GOTO often operates as would multiple IF/THEN statements; any one of several transfers can occur, depending on the result computed for the expression. Since transfers depend on the expression, the computed GOTO is another **conditional transfer statement.** Its general formal is this:

line# ON expression GOTO line#1,line#2,line#3, . . . ,line#n

The arithmetic expression always is evaluated to an integer, and the line numbers following GOTO must identify statements in the program.

The general execution of the ON/GOTO statement proceeds as follows:

1. If the value of the expression is 1, control is transferred to the first line number indicated.

2. If the value of the expression is 2, control is transferred to the second line number indicated.

. . .

. . .

. . .

n. If the value of the expression is n, control is transferred to the nth line number indicated.

Several examples are presented here to illustrate the operation of this statement:

Statement	Computer Execution
`00010 ON X GOTO 50,80,100`	IF X = 1, control goes to line 50. IF X = 2, control goes to line 80. IF X = 3, control goes to line 100.
`00030 ON N / 50 GOTO 90,100`	IF N/50 = 1, control goes to line 90. IF N/50 = 2, control goes to line 100.

If the computed expression in an ON/GOTO statement does not evaluate to an integer, the value is either rounded or truncated (digits to the right of the decimal are ignored), depending on the BASIC implementation. For example,

Statement	Value of Variable	Action
`00040 ON N / 3 GOTO 60,80`	N = 7	7 ÷ 3 = 2.33. The expression is evaluated as 2.33. The remainder is truncated, and the result becomes the integer 2. Control passes to statement 80.

If the expression evaluates to an integer less than 1 or larger than the number of statements indicated, either the program will terminate with an error message or the ON/GOTO statement will be bypassed. For example,

Statement	Value of Variable	Action
`00060 ON X GOTO 100,140,170` `00070 LET X = X + 1`	X = 4	The value of X exceeds the number of line numbers in the GOTO list. Control passes to statement 70.

The box "ON/GOTO Errors" illustrates how various BASIC implementations respond to these conditions.

ON/GOTO Errors

Computer	Action If Number Evaluated Is Greater Than Number of Line Numbers	Action If Number Evaluated Is Less Than 1 or Greater Than Maximum Allowed
DECSYSTEM 20	Execution stops/Error message displayed	"ON STMT OUT OF RANGE" error
Apple	ON/GOTO bypassed	"ILLEGAL QUANTITY" error
IBM/Microsoft	ON/GOTO bypassed	"ILLEGAL FUNCTION CALL" or "OVERFLOW" error
TRS-80	ON/GOTO bypassed	"?FC" error
PET/Commodore 64	ON/GOTO bypassed	"ILLEGAL QUANTITY" error

Menus

A **menu** is a listing that displays the functions that can be performed by a program. The desired function is chosen by entering a code (typically a simple numeric or alphabetic character) from the terminal keyboard. A computer menu is like a menu in a restaurant. The user (diner) reads a group of possible selections on the screen (menu) and then enters a selection into the computer (describes the desired meal to the waiter or waitress).

The calculator menu program (Figure 5–8) illustrates a common use of the ON/GOTO statement in making a menu selection. The user tells the computer whether to add, subtract, multiply, or divide two numbers by entering either 1, 2, 3, or 4. Line 170 transfers the program execution to the appropriate operation.

In the example, after entering the values for A and B, the user indicates that division is the desired operation by typing in the number 4, which is assigned to the variable C. Line 170, an ON/GOTO statement, causes program execution to branch to the fourth line number, 205. The operation is then performed, and the result is printed.

Looping Procedures

There are several things to consider in setting up a loop. The programmer must decide not only what instructions are to be repeated, but also how many times the loop is to be executed. There are three techniques for loop

Figure 5–8 ON/GOTO EXAMPLE USING A MENU

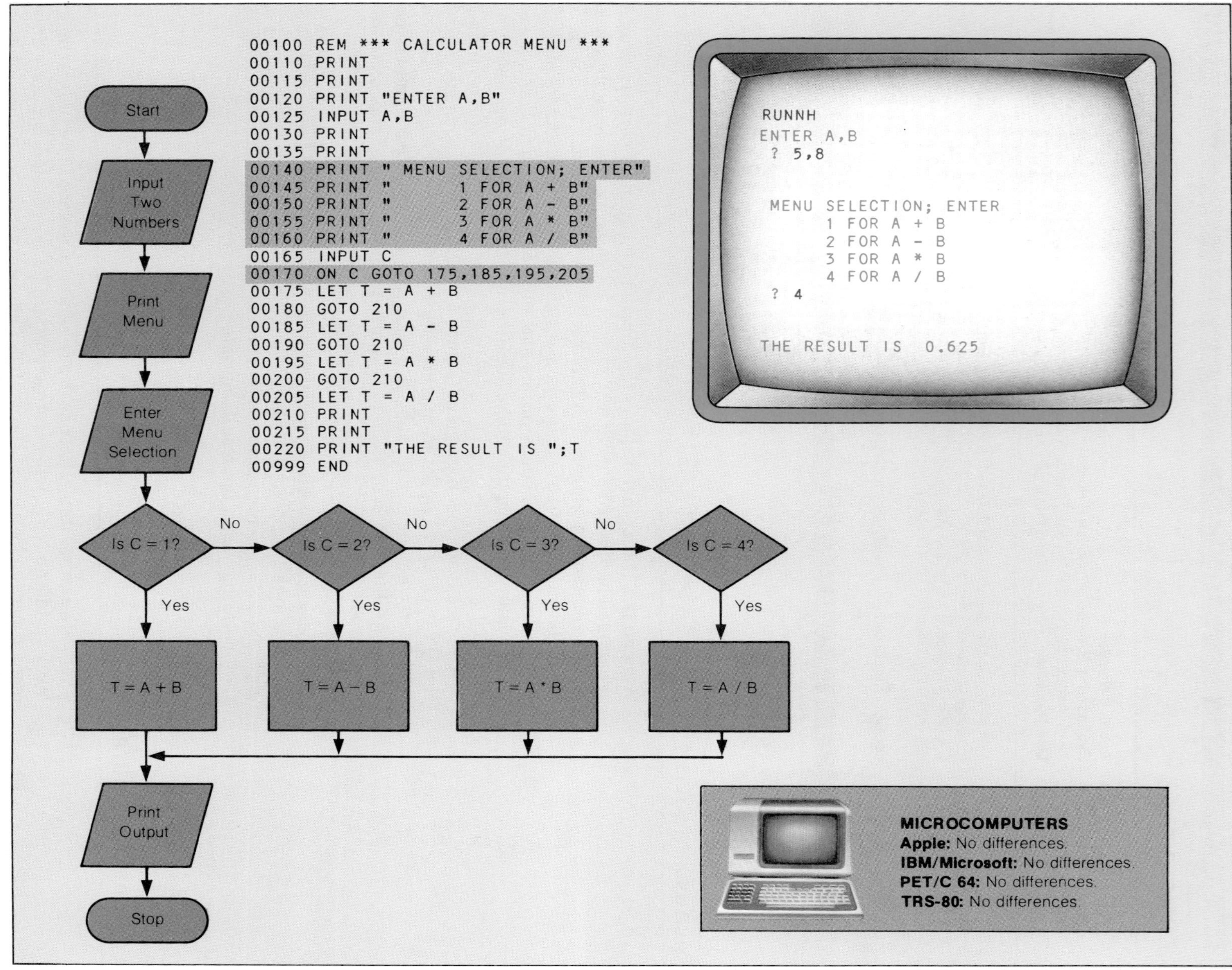
Start
Input Two Numbers
Print Menu
Enter Menu Selection
Is C = 1?
No
Yes
T = A + B
Is C = 2?
No
Yes
T = A − B
Is C = 3?
No
Yes
T = A * B
Is C = 4?
Yes
T = A / B
Print Output
Stop
00100 REM *** CALCULATOR MENU ***
00110 PRINT
00115 PRINT
00120 PRINT "ENTER A,B"
00125 INPUT A,B
00130 PRINT
00135 PRINT
00140 PRINT " MENU SELECTION; ENTER"
00145 PRINT "   1 FOR A + B"
00150 PRINT "   2 FOR A - B"
00155 PRINT "   3 FOR A * B"
00160 PRINT "   4 FOR A / B"
00165 INPUT C
00170 ON C GOTO 175,185,195,205
00175 LET T = A + B
00180 GOTO 210
00185 LET T = A - B
00190 GOTO 210
00195 LET T = A * B
00200 GOTO 210
00205 LET T = A / B
00210 PRINT
00215 PRINT
00220 PRINT "THE RESULT IS ";T
00999 END
RUNNH
ENTER A,B
? 5,8
MENU SELECTION; ENTER
1 FOR A + B
2 FOR A - B
3 FOR A * B
4 FOR A / B
? 4
THE RESULT IS 0.625
MICROCOMPUTERS
Apple: No differences.
IBM/Microsoft: No differences.
PET/C 64: No differences.
TRS-80: No differences.

control. This section covers trailer values and counters. Chapter 6 will discuss the other method, FOR and NEXT statements.

Trailer Value

A loop controlled by a **trailer value** contains an IF/THEN statement that checks for the end of the data. The last data item is a dummy value that is not part of the data to be processed. Either numeric or alphanumeric data can be used as a trailer value. However, the programmer must always select a trailer value that will not be confused with real data. For example, a customer account number is never 0, which implies that zero may be safely used as a dummy value.

Here is how it works. An IF/THEN statement is placed within the set of instructions to be repeated, usually at the beginning of the loop. One of the variables to which data is entered is tested. If it contains the dummy value, control is transferred out of the loop. If the variable contains valid data (does not equal the trailer value), looping continues.

Figure 5–9 contains a loop pattern controlled by a trailer value. The program calculates the commission on sales made by several employees of the Rich Rugs Company. Statement 135 tests the value N$ for the dummy value:

```
00135 IF N$ = "LAST" THEN 210
```

If the condition is true, the flow of processing drops out of the loop to line 170. If the condition is false, processing continues to the next line in sequence, line 140. Note that since we used the INPUT statement to enter the data, it is necessary to tell the user how to end the looping process. This is done in line 120. The user has to enter two dummy values, LAST and 0, because the INPUT statement expects two values to be entered.

Counter

A second method of controlling a loop requires the programmer to create a **counter**—a numeric variable that is incremented each time the loop is executed. Normally, the increment is 1. A counter is effective only if the programmer notifies the computer how many times a loop should be repeated. The following steps are involved in setting up a counter for loop control:

1. Initialize the counter to give it a beginning value.
2. Increment the counter each time the loop is executed.
3. Test the counter to determine if the loop has been executed the desired number of times.

Figure 5–9 SALES COMMISSION PROGRAM USING TRAILER VALUE

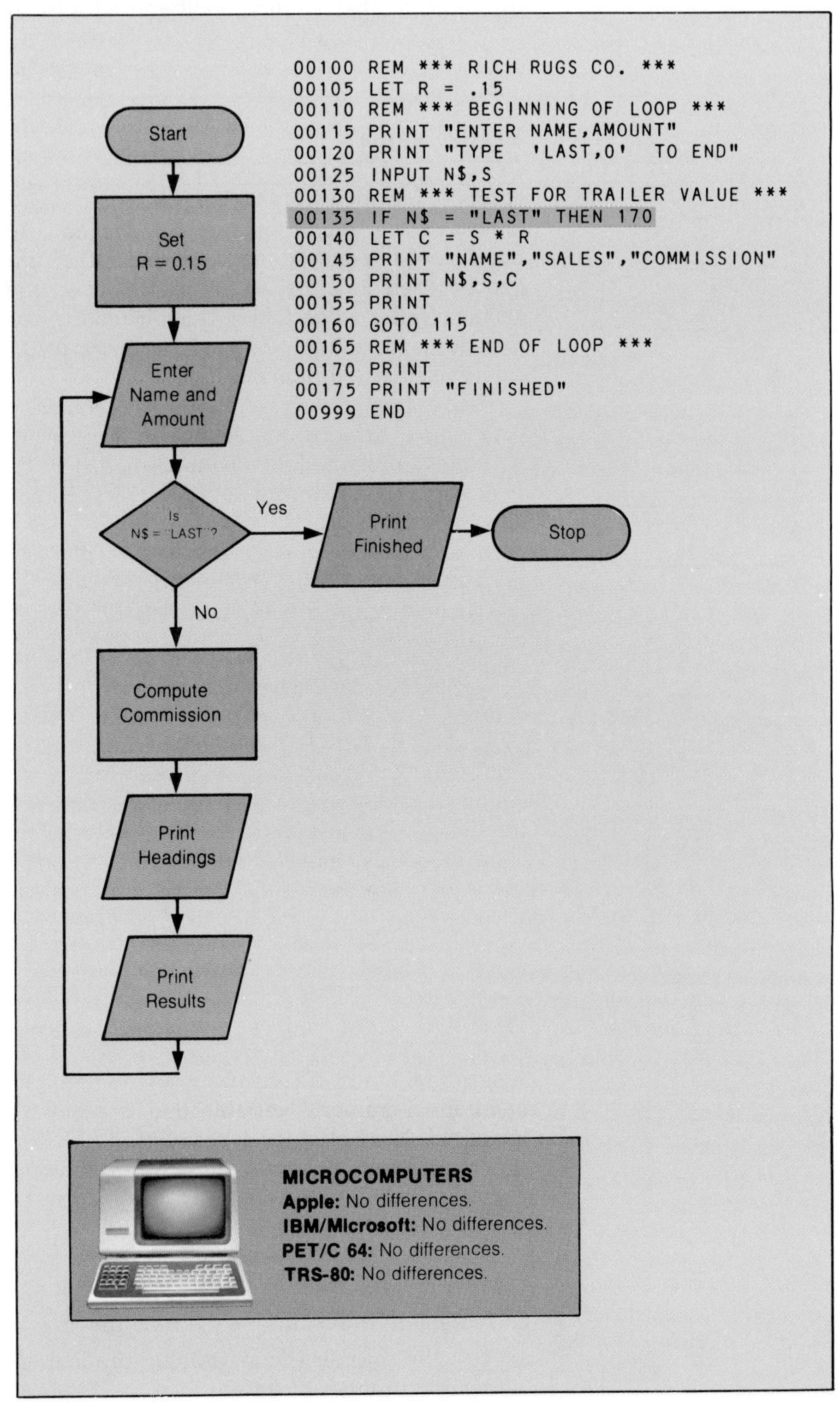

00100 REM *** RICH RUGS CO. ***
00105 LET R = .15
00110 REM *** BEGINNING OF LOOP ***
00115 PRINT "ENTER NAME,AMOUNT"
00120 PRINT "TYPE 'LAST,0' TO END"
00125 INPUT N$,S
00130 REM *** TEST FOR TRAILER VALUE ***
00135 IF N$ = "LAST" THEN 170
00140 LET C = S * R
00145 PRINT "NAME","SALES","COMMISSION"
00150 PRINT N$,S,C
00155 PRINT
00160 GOTO 115
00165 REM *** END OF LOOP ***
00170 PRINT
00175 PRINT "FINISHED"
00999 END
Start
Set R = 0.15
Enter Name and Amount
Is N$ = "LAST"?
Yes
Print Finished
Stop
No
Compute Commission
Print Headings
Print Results
MICROCOMPUTERS
Apple: No differences.
IBM/Microsoft: No differences.
PET/C 64: No differences.
TRS-80: No differences.

Figure 5–9 OUTPUT *(continued)*

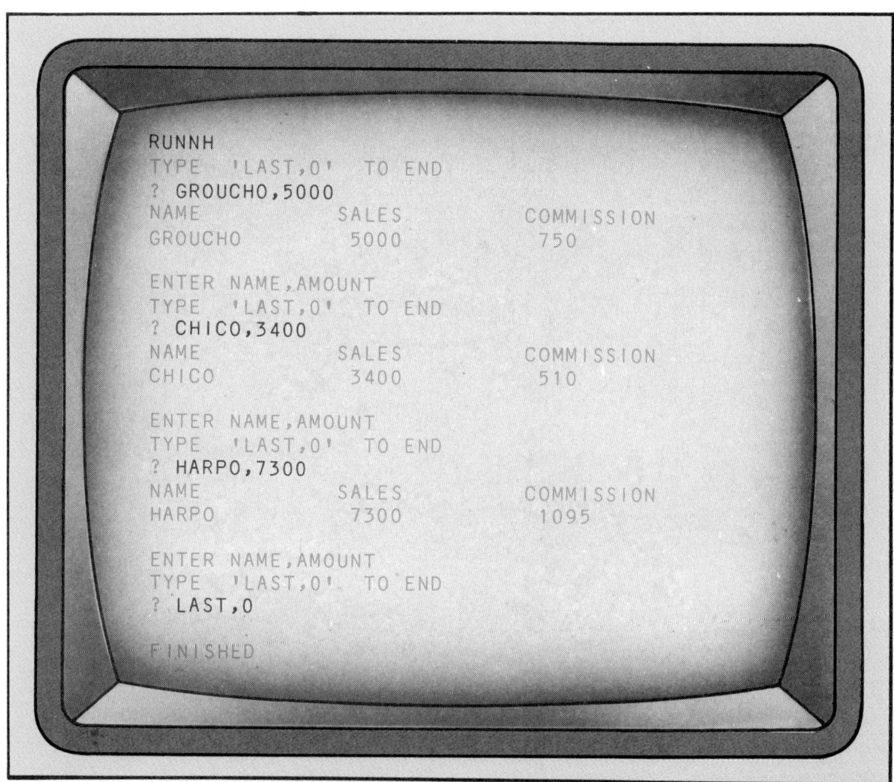

RUNNH
TYPE 'LAST,0' TO END
? GROUCHO,5000
NAME SALES COMMISSION
GROUCHO 5000 750
ENTER NAME,AMOUNT
TYPE 'LAST,0' TO END
? CHICO,3400
NAME SALES COMMISSION
CHICO 3400 510
ENTER NAME,AMOUNT
TYPE 'LAST,0' TO END
? HARPO,7300
NAME SALES COMMISSION
HARPO 7300 1095
ENTER NAME,AMOUNT
TYPE 'LAST,0' TO END
? LAST,0
FINISHED

The sales commission program used in Figure 5–9 can be modified to use a counter, as shown in Figure 5–10. Since there are three salespeople, the loop must be executed three times. The counter in this example is X. It is initialized to 0 in line 115. The IF/THEN statement in line 130 tests the number of times the loop has been executed, as represented by the counter X. Line 155 causes X to be incremented each time the loop is executed. The loop instructions will be executed until X equals 3.

LEARNING CHECK

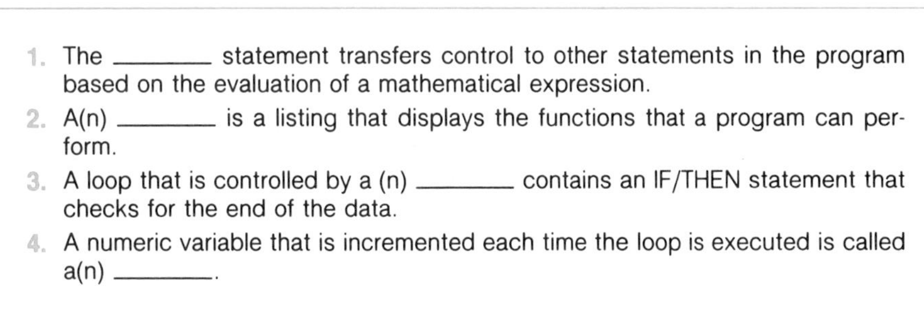

1. The _______ statement transfers control to other statements in the program based on the evaluation of a mathematical expression.
2. A(n) _______ is a listing that displays the functions that a program can perform.
3. A loop that is controlled by a (n) _______ contains an IF/THEN statement that checks for the end of the data.
4. A numeric variable that is incremented each time the loop is executed is called a(n) _______.

Answers

1. ON/GOTO
2. menu
3. trailer value
4. counter

Figure 5–10 SALES COMMISSION PROGRAM WITH COUNTER

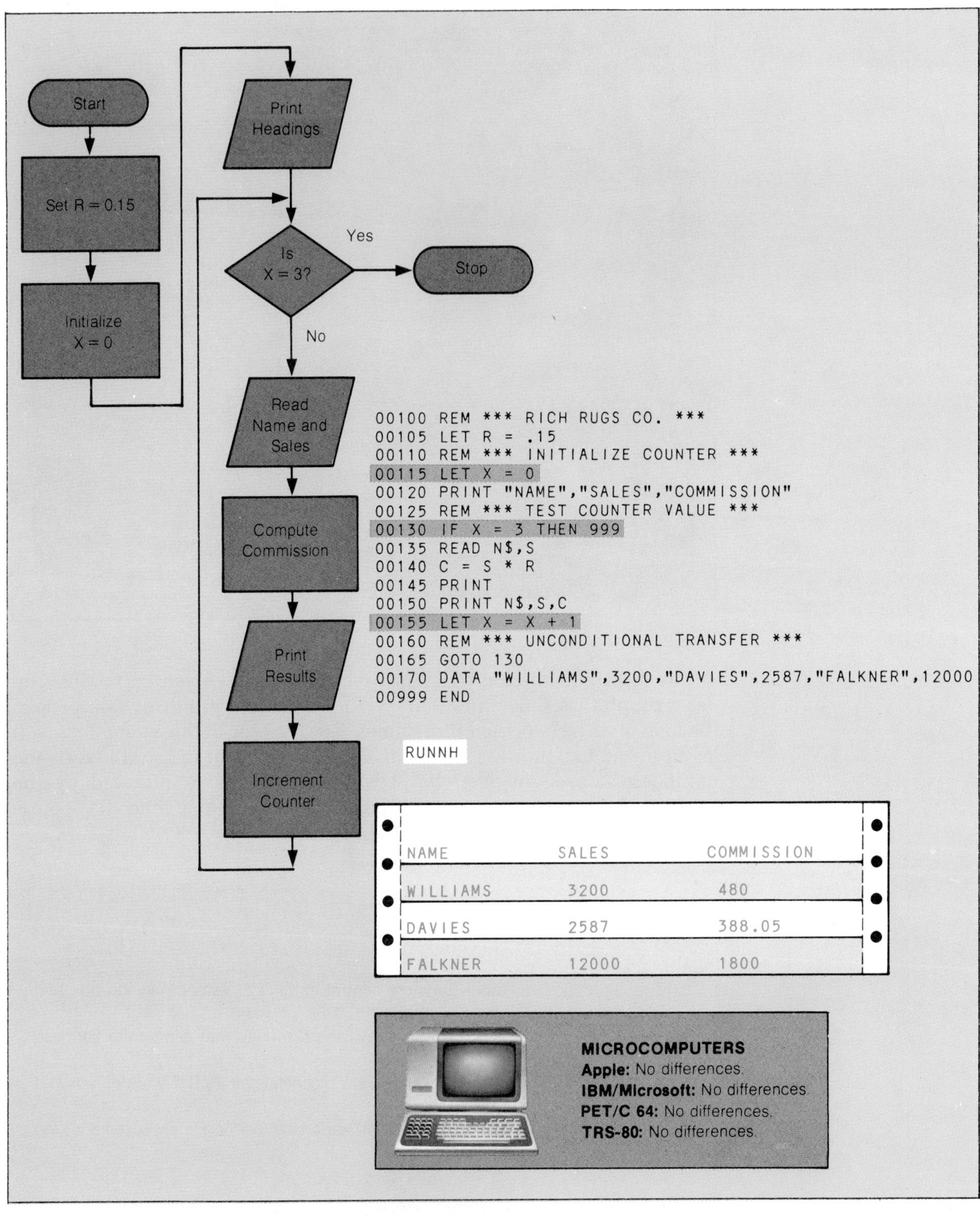

Start
Set R = 0.15
Initialize X = 0
Print Headings
Is X = 3?
Yes
Stop
No
Read Name and Sales
Compute Commission
Print Results
Increment Counter
00100 REM *** RICH RUGS CO. ***
00105 LET R = .15
00110 REM *** INITIALIZE COUNTER ***
00115 LET X = 0
00120 PRINT "NAME","SALES","COMMISSION"
00125 REM *** TEST COUNTER VALUE ***
00130 IF X = 3 THEN 999
00135 READ N$,S
00140 C = S * R
00145 PRINT
00150 PRINT N$,S,C
00155 LET X = X + 1
00160 REM *** UNCONDITIONAL TRANSFER ***
00165 GOTO 130
00170 DATA "WILLIAMS",3200,"DAVIES",2587,"FALKNER",12000
00999 END
RUNNH
NAME SALES COMMISSION
WILLIAMS 3200 480
DAVIES 2587 388.05
FALKNER 12000 1800
MICROCOMPUTERS
Apple: No differences.
IBM/Microsoft: No differences.
PET/C 64: No differences.
TRS-80: No differences.

A Programming Problem

Problem Definition

Ed Hoge, an instructor for Art 101, needs a program that will assign letter grades to students based on their test scores. In addition, he wants to know how many students are in each grade category and how many took the test.

The grading scale is as follows:

Score	Letter Grade
90 or more	A
78 to 89	B
66 to 77	C
54 to 65	D
Less than 54	F

The students and their scores follow:

Student	Score
Nan Barnett	96
Bob Szymanski	93
Jim Strong	89
Bob Tynecki	78
Lynn Probst	90
Bill Brandon	51
Denise Siviy	88
Vic Flynn	66
Karen McKee	98
Anne Tate	77

The Program

The counter variables are initialized to 0 by the READ and DATA statements in lines 115 through 120 of Figure 5–11. The name and grade for each student are read in line 140. Line 155 tests for the trailer value XXX. As long as the student's name does not equal XXX, the loop is reexecuted. The total number of students is accumulated in line 160. The first test to determine the grade is made in line 165. If the number grade is less than 90, it is not an A. Control is transferred to line 185, where the number score is tested again to see if it is less than 78 (less than that required for a B grade). In this fashion, scores less than the lowest number required for a particular grade are passed down to the next lowest level until the correct one is found. Line 245 requires no test; any grade less than 54 is an F. When the trailer value, XXX, is detected, control drops down to line 275, where printing of the totals occurs.

Figure 5–11 LETTER GRADES PROGRAM AND FLOWCHART

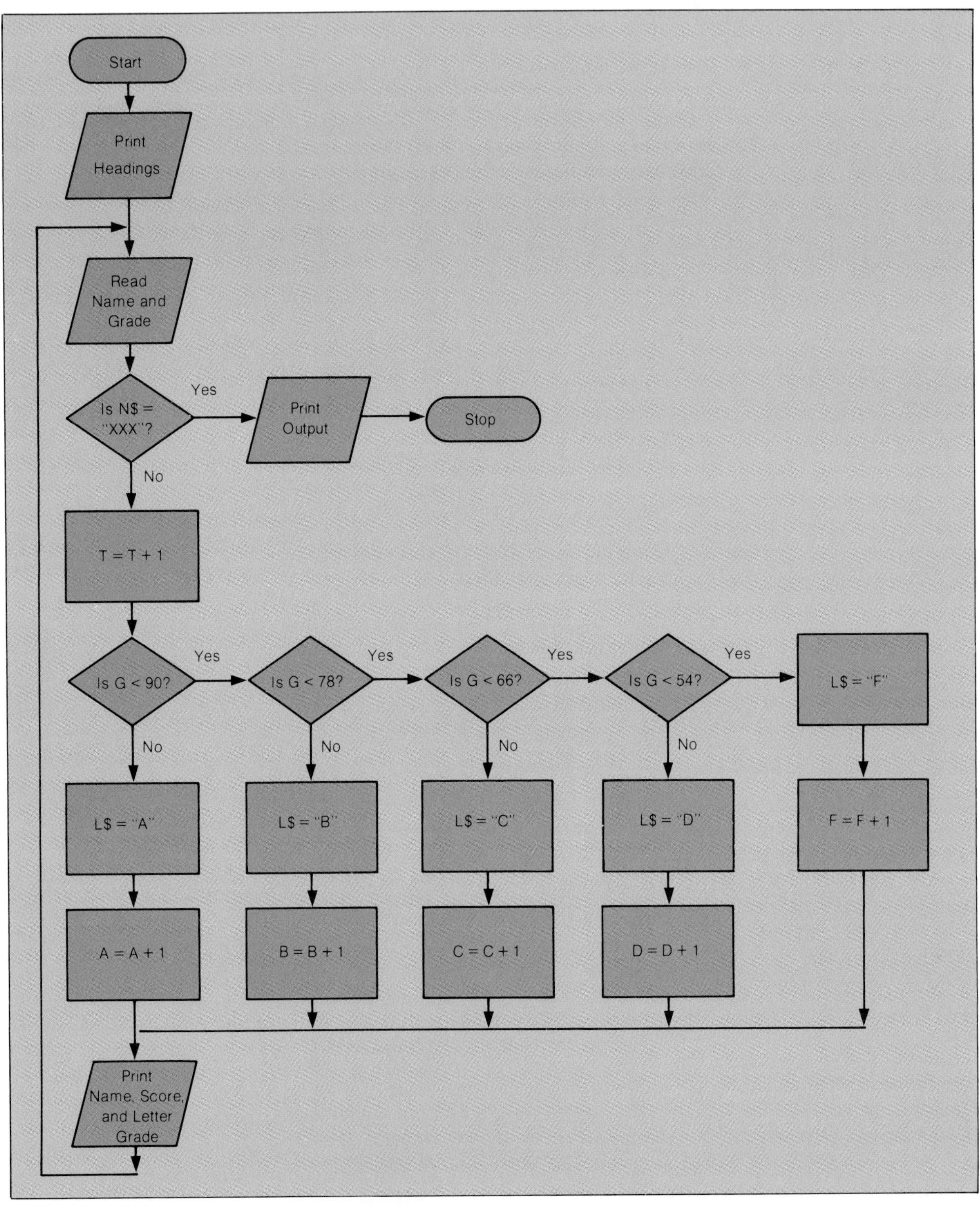

Figure 5–11 LETTER GRADES PROGRAM AND FLOWCHART *(continued)*

```
00100 REM *** ASSIGN LETTER GRADES ***
00105 PRINT
00110 PRINT
00115 DATA 0,0,0,0,0,0
00120 READ A,B,C,D,F,T
00125 PRINT "NAME"," ","SCORE","GRADE"
00130 PRINT
00135 REM *** LOOP BEGINS HERE ***
00140 READ N$,G
00145 REM *** TEST FOR TRAILER VALUE ***
00150 REM *** CONDITIONAL TRANSFER ***
00155 IF N$ = "XXX" THEN 275
00160 LET T = T + 1
00165 IF G < 90 THEN 185
00170 LET L$ = "A"
00175 LET A = A + 1
00180 GOTO 255
00185 IF G < 78 THEN 205
00190 LET L$ = "B"
00195 LET B = B + 1
00200 GOTO 255
00205 IF G < 66 THEN 225
00210 LET L$ = "C"
00215 LET C = C + 1
00220 GOTO 255
00225 IF G < 54 THEN 245
00230 LET L$ = "D"
00235 LET D = D + 1
00240 GOTO 255
00245 LET L$ = "F"
00250 LET F = F + 1
00255 PRINT N$," ",G,L$
00260 REM *** LOOP ENDS HERE ***
00265 REM *** UNCONDITIONAL TRANSFER ***
00270 GOTO 140
00275 PRINT
00280 PRINT "TOTAL # OF A'S = ";A
00285 PRINT "TOTAL # OF B'S = ";B
00290 PRINT "TOTAL # OF C'S = ";C
00295 PRINT "TOTAL # OF D'S = ";D
00300 PRINT "TOTAL # OF F'S = ";F
00305 PRINT
00310 PRINT "TOTAL # OF STUDENTS = ";T
00315 DATA "NAN BARNETT",96,"BOB SZYMANSKI",93,"JIM STRONG",89
00320 DATA "BOB TYNECKI",78,"LYNN PROBST",90,"BILL BRANDON",51
00325 DATA "DENISE SIVIY",88,"VIC FLYNN",66,"KAREN MCKEE",98
00330 DATA "ANNE TATE",77,"XXX",00
00999 END
```

MICROCOMPUTERS
Apple: No differences.
IBM/Microsoft: No differences.
PET/C 64: No differences.
TRS-80: No differences.

(Continued next page)

Figure 5–11 OUTPUT *(continued)*

```
RUNNH

NAME                                  SCORE        GRADE

NAN BARNETT                            96            A
BOB SZYMANSKI                          93            A
JIM STRONG                             89            B
BOB TYNECKI                            78            B
LYNN PROBST                            90            A
BILL BRANDON                           51            F
DENISE SIVIY                           88            B
VIC FLYNN                              66            C
KAREN MCKEE                            98            A
ANNE TATE                              77            C

TOTAL # OF A'S =  4
TOTAL # OF B'S =  3
TOTAL # OF C'S =  2
TOTAL # OF D'S =  0
TOTAL # OF F'S =  1

TOTAL # OF STUDENTS =  10
```

Summary

- The GOTO statement is an unconditional transfer of control that allows the computer to bypass or alter the sequence in which instructions are executed.
- The GOTO statement often is used to set up loops.
- The IF/THEN statement permits control to be transferred only when a specified condition is met. If the condition following IF is true, the clause following the word THEN is given control; if it is false, control passes to the next line.
- The IF/THEN/ELSE statement is an extension of the IF/THEN statement. If the condition following IF is true, the clause following THEN is given control. If the condition is false, control is transferred to the clause following ELSE. IF/THEN/ELSE statements may be nested.
- The ON/GOTO statement instructs the computer to evaluate an expression and, based on its value, to branch to one of several points in a program.
- A menu is a listing that displays the functions a program can perform. The user selects the desired function by entering a code from the keyboard.
- The number of times a loop is executed can be controlled by the use of a trailer value or a counter.

- The trailer value is a dummy value entered at the end of all the data.
- A counter can be set up if the programmer knows ahead of time how many times a loop is to be executed.

Review Questions

1. Why is the GOTO statement an unconditional transfer?
2. Rewrite the following program segment using a GOTO statement:

```
10 READ N$,X,Y
15 LET Z = X + Y
20 PRINT N$,Z
25 READ N$,X,Y
30 LET Z = X + Y
35 PRINT N$,Z
40 READ N$,X,Y
45 LET Z = X + Y
50 PRINT N$,Z
55 DATA "LARRY",10,5,"MOE",25,7,"CURLY",17,41
999 END
```

3. Why is the IF/THEN statement a conditional transfer?
4. Conditions tested in the IF/THEN statement may be either numeric or character string. TRUE FALSE (Circle the correct answer.)
5. If the condition after the IF in an IF/THEN statement is false, control is transferred to ______.
   a. the end of the program
   b. the statement at the line number following the word THEN
   c. the next statement in the program
6. ______ symbols are used in the IF/THEN statement to compare numeric or string variables and constants.
7. Which of these are valid IF/THEN statements?
   a. 10 IF X <> "NO" THEN 30
   b. 60 IF Y = 2 THEN 100
   c. 100 IF A$ = "APPLE" THEN 150
   d. 200 IF X$ = "YES" THEN 250
8. The statement after ELSE in an IF/THEN/ELSE statement is executed when the condition is ______.
   a. true
   b. false
9. What is printed when these statements are executed?

   10 LET X = 4

   20 IF X = 1 THEN PRINT "ONE" ELSE IF X = 3 THEN PRINT "THREE" ELSE PRINT "TWO"

10. The arithmetic expression in an ON/GOTO statement is always evaluated to a(n) ______.

11. If the value of the arithmetic expression in an ON/GOTO statement is evaluated to 3, control is transferred to ______.
    a. the first line number indicated
    b. the next statement in the program
    c. the second line number indicated
    d. the third line number indicated

12. To what line number will control be transferred when this statement is encountered (N = 51)?

```
100 ON N / 17 GOTO 150, 200, 275
```

13. What is a menu?

14. What is a dummy value?

15. A loop controlled by a trailer value contains a(n) ______ statement that checks for the end of the data.

16. What is a counter?

17. What are the three steps involved in setting up a loop control counter?

18. Which of the following symbols represents the IF/THEN test?

a.

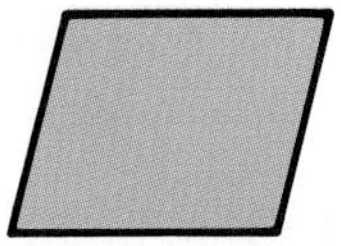

b.

c.

d.

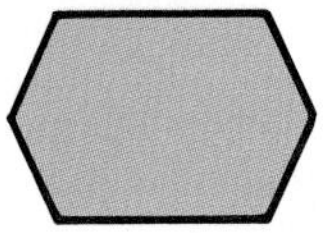

19. In an IF/THEN statement, the THEN clause may be ______.
    a. a line number
    b. a single BASIC statement
    c. multiple BASIC statements
    d. all of the above
    e. a and b only

20. Rewrite the program in Question 2 using the GOTO statement and a trailer value.

Debugging Exercises

Identify the following programs or program segments that contain errors, and debug them.

1.
```
00100 READ X$,A
00105 PRINT X$,A
00110 GOTO 10
00115 DATA "TAMMY",5,"STACY",3
00999 END
```

2.
```
00120 READ A,B
00130 LET X = A + B
00140 IF X THEN 120
00150 PRINT X
```

3.
```
00010 READ C$
00015 IF C = "B" THEN PRINT "BLACK" ELSE PRINT "WHITE"
00020 GOTO 10
00025 DATA "B","B","W","B","W","W"
00999 END
```

4.
```
00010 READ N$,S$
00020 IF S$ <> "M" THEN IF S$ = "D" THEN
         PRINT N$;"DIVORCED" ELSE PRINT "MARRIED
00030 GOTO 10
00040 DATA "CATHY SMITH","D","SONYA APPLE","M"
00050 DATA "JUDY WATERS","D"
00999 END
RUNNH
CATHY SMITH     DIVORCED
SONYA APPLE     MARRIED
JUDY WATERS     DIVORCED
```

5.
```
00010 INPUT "ENTER DRIVER'S NAME";N$
00015 INPUT "ENTER TOTAL POINTS",T
00020 PRINT "ENTER FINISHING POSITION IN RACE"
00025 PRINT "        1 FOR FIRST PLACE"
00030 PRINT "        2 FOR SECOND PLACE"
00035 PRINT "        3 FOR OTHER"
00040 INPUT P
00045 ON P GOTO 50,65,80
00050 LET T = T + 9
00055 PRINT N$,T
00060 GOTO 45
00065 LET T = T + 6
00070 PRINT N$,T
00075 GOTO 45
00080 PRINT N$,T
00085 GOTO 45
00090 DATA "RICHARD PETTY",2,"BOBBY UNSER",1,"A. J. FOYT",5
00999 END
```

6.

```
00010 READ X,Y
00020 LET Z = X / Y
00030 ON Z GOTO 40,60
00040 PRINT "X = Y"
00050 GOTO 10
00060 PRINT "X <> Y"
00070 GOTO 10
00080 DATA 20,10,40,10
00999 END


RUNNH

X <> Y          X <> Y
X <> Y          X = Y  or error message
```

7.

```
00010 PRINT TAB(7);"LEADING MONEY WINNER"
00020 PRINT
00030 PRINT TAB(5);"NAME";TAB(26);"AMOUNT"
00040 PRINT
00050 READ N$,A
00060 IF N$ = "LAST" THEN 999
00070 PRINT TAB(5);N$;TAB(26);A
00080 GOTO 50
00090 DATA "JOHN MCENROE",700,640
00100 DATA "JIMMY CONNER",698,100,
00110 DATA "BJORN BORG",601,830,,"XXX",0
00999 END
```

8.

```
00010 REM *** FINDS THE SUM OF 10 NUMBERS ***
00015 LET X = 1
00020 IF X > 10 THEN 45
00025 PRINT "ENTER NUMBER"
00030 INPUT W
00035 LET S = S + W
00040 GOTO 20
00045 PRINT "SUM = ";S
00999 END
```

9.

```
00010 REM *** CONVERTS MILITARY TIME TO ***
00020 REM *** CIVILIAN TIME ***
00030 INPUT "ENTER MILITARY TIME ";M
00040 IF M >= 13 THEN C = M - 12
00050 IF M >= 13 THEN X$ = "PM" ELSE X$ = "AM"
00060 PRINT "MILITARY TIME";"CIVILIAN TIME"
00070 PRINT "             ","             "
00080 PRINT M,C;X$
00090 END
```

10.
```
00010 REM *** PRINT OUT NAME & COUNTY ***
00015 PRINT 1 = WOOD COUNTY CODE #
00020 PRINT 2 = LUCAS COUNTY CODE #
00025 PRINT 3 = HANCOCK COUNTY CODE #
00030 PRINT 4 = OUT OF STATE
00035 INPUT "ENTER NAME AND COUNTY CODE #";N$,C
00040 ON C GOTO 60,55,50,45
00045 PRINT N$;"LIVES IN WOOD COUNTY" 50 GOTO 999
00055 PRINT N$;"LIVES IN LUCAS COUNTY" 60 GOTO 999
00065 PRINT N$;"LIVES IN HANCOCK COUNTY" 70 GOTO 999
00075 PRINT N$;"LIVES OUT OF STATE"
00999 END
```

Additional Programming Problems

1. Write a program that calculates the gross pay for three employees and outputs employee name and gross pay. Use the GOTO statement and the following data:

Name	Rate	Hours
J. Smith	5.25	40
M. Jones	3.75	35
S. Franks	10.66	40

2. As part of a computer demonstration, you have been asked to write a program that will print out horoscopes. A menu should be used to display the choices. Use the ON/GOTO statement and the following data:

Signs	Horoscope
Aries	YOU WILL BE RICH AND FAMOUS
Taurus	YOU WILL RECEIVE A GREAT JOB OFFER
Gemini	THERE IS HAPPINESS IN YOUR FUTURE

3. You are a graduate assistant for Math 131, and the professor has asked you to calculate the grades. You do not want to do it any more than the professor does, so you have decided to write a program. The program has to find the average of three test scores and assign a letter grade. Here is a list of the five people in the class and their test scores to use for data:

Les Southwick	88	90	84
Sue Fortney	90	96	94
Debbie Knoblock	71	63	69
Dennis Smayer	45	57	59
Anthony Polletti	69	76	81

Use GOTO and IF/THEN statements with a counter to set up the loop. The grading scale is set up like this:

90 to 100	A
80 to 89	B
70 to 79	C
60 to 69	D
59 and below	F

4. The employees of Hard Line, Inc., are given evaluation ratings by three different individuals. These ratings are averaged; based on this average, a report is to be printed recommending the action to be taken by the supervisor. Each of the three evaluations have a maximum value of fifty points. Your job is to compute the average score for each employee and write a report giving the recommended action to be taken for each. The report also should list the total number of employees being evaluated and the total number of employees in each category. The data is as follows:

		Score	
Employee Name	**Evaluation 1**	**Evaluation 2**	**Evaluation 3**
Karen McKee	49	50	48
Bob Szymanski	50	49	50
Ed Pfister	36	21	42
Lisa Lape	15	13	22

Recommended Action

If average score > = 40, recommended for promotion and/or pay raise.

If 40 > average score > = 30, take no action.

If average score < 30, reprimand.

5. B. G. Motors would like a program to quickly calculate the customer costs for a new car. The costs include list price, trade-in consideration, options, tax, and dealer preparation charges. The tax is figured as a percentage of the list price plus the options plus the dealer prep minus the trade-in. Use INPUT statements to enter the values. Design the program to accept any number of option choices. The program is to generate an itemized bill.

6. The bursar's office has requested a program that will calculate and display the general and instructional fees for each student enrolled for the fall term. In addition, a report should be printed out at the end showing total residents and nonresidents, as well as total fees. Use the following data:

Name	Social Security Number	Hours Enrolled	Residency Status
Debarr, Mark M.	265-83-3454	16	Resident
Lindburg, Sally	342-87-8457	17	Nonresident
Schuler, Melissa R.	435-83-8234	15	Resident

General Fees

Resident:	$200
Nonresident:	$500

Instructional Fee

$35 per credit hour

6 Looping with FOR/NEXT and WHILE

Outline

Objectives

After reading this chapter the student should be able to do the following:

- Set up loops using the FOR and NEXT statements.
- Understand the concept of nested FOR and NEXT loops.
- Set up loops using the WHILE and NEXT statements.
- Set up loops using the UNTIL and NEXT statements.

Overview

Chapter 5 discussed two methods of controlling loops—counters and trailer values. The IF/THEN and GOTO statements were used to implement these methods. This chapter presents another method for loop control—FOR and NEXT statements. In addition, it discusses nested loops (loops within loops).

Let us review what happens when a counter is used to control a loop, since the logic of FOR/NEXT loops is very similar. First, the counter variable is set to some initial value. Statements inside the loop are executed once and the counter incremented. The counter variable then is tested to see if the loop has been executed the required number of times. When the variable exceeds the designated terminal value, the looping process ends, and the computer proceeds to the rest of the program. For example, assume we want to write a program that will multiply each of the numbers from 1 to 5 by 5 and then add 2. The program in Figure 6–1 does this using a loop controlled by the counter method. We will see later how the FOR/NEXT loop allows us to accomplish the same steps in a more efficient manner.

The FOR and NEXT Statements

The FOR and NEXT statements allow concise loop definition. The general format of the FOR and NEXT loop is as follows:

line # FOR loop variable = initial expression TO terminal expression STEP step value

.

.

.

line# NEXT loop variable

The FOR statement tells the computer how many times to execute the loop. The loop variable (also called the **index**) is set to an initial value. This value is tested against the terminal value to determine whether or not the loop should be executed. The initial and terminal values may be constants, variables, expressions, or decimals, all of which must be numeric.

To set the initial value and test the counter took two lines (lines 10 and 15) in Figure 6–1. The FOR statement combines these two steps into one statement:

```
00010 FOR N = 1 TO 5 STEP 1
```

Loop Variable (N) · Initial Value (1) · Terminal Value (5) · Step Value (1)

Lines 25 and 30 in Figure 6–1 increment the loop variable (the counter) and send control back to line 15. The functions of these two statements are combined in the NEXT statement. In Figure 6–1, after control is transferred back to line 15, the value of the loop variable is again tested against the terminal value. Once the value is exceeded, control passes to line 999. When FOR and NEXT are used, control goes to the statement immediately following the NEXT statement.

Thus, the loop used in Figure 6–1 can be set up to use FOR and NEXT statements, as shown in Figure 6–2. The FOR statement in line 10 tells the computer to initialize the loop variable, N, to one. Between the FOR and NEXT statements is line 15, the instruction that is to be repeated; it prints out N and the result of N * 5 + 2. Line 20, the NEXT statement, increments the loop variable by the step indicated in the FOR statement. The step value may be a constant, real number, variable, or expression, and it must have a numeric value.

Figure 6–1 LOOPING WITH A COUNTER

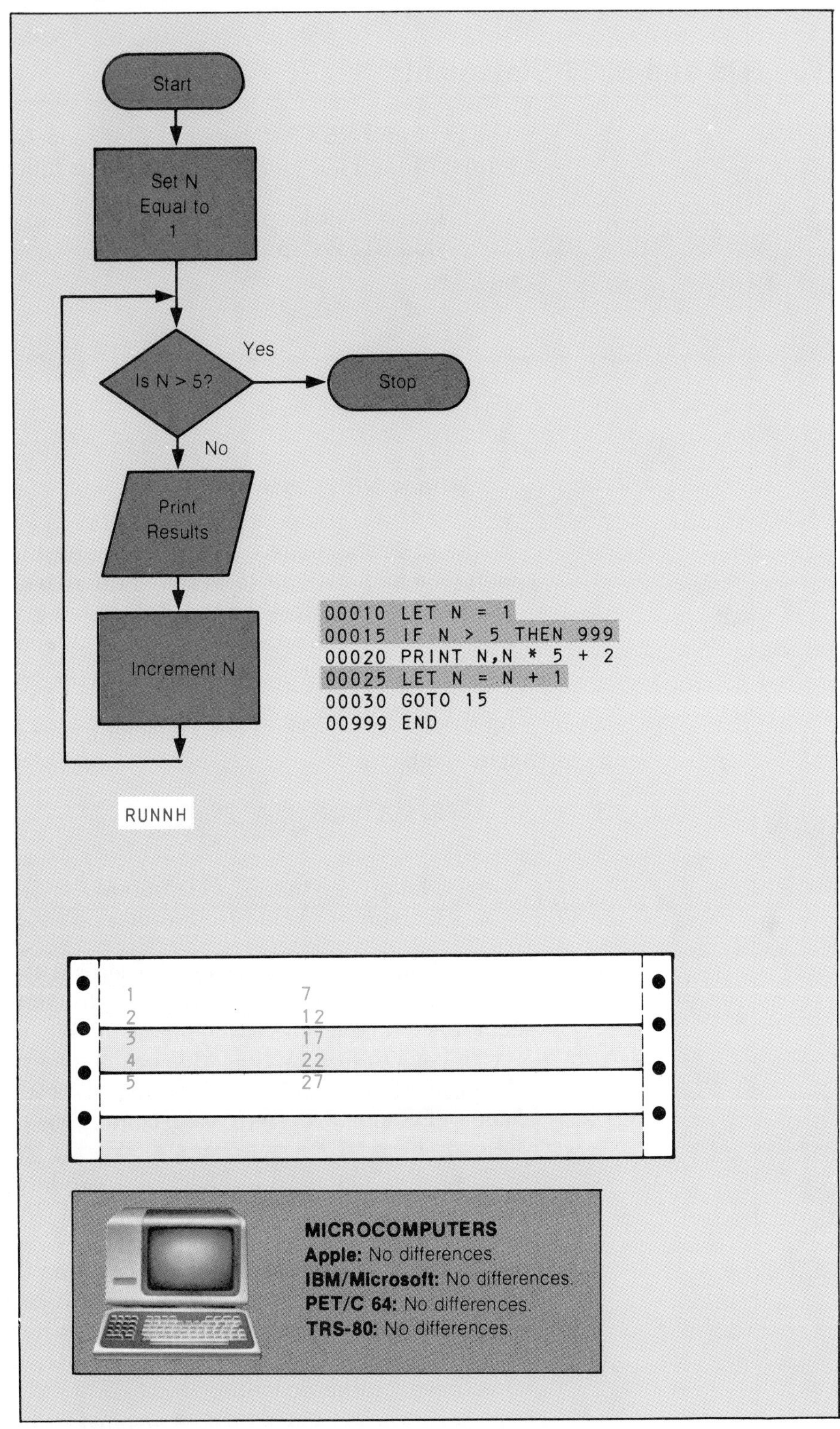
Start
Set N Equal to 1
Is N > 5?
Yes
Stop
No
Print Results
Increment N
00010 LET N = 1
00015 IF N > 5 THEN 999
00020 PRINT N,N * 5 + 2
00025 LET N = N + 1
00030 GOTO 15
00999 END
RUNNH
1 7
2 12
3 17
4 22
5 27
MICROCOMPUTERS
Apple: No differences.
IBM/Microsoft: No differences.
PET/C 64: No differences.
TRS-80: No differences.

Figure 6–2 FOR/NEXT LOOP

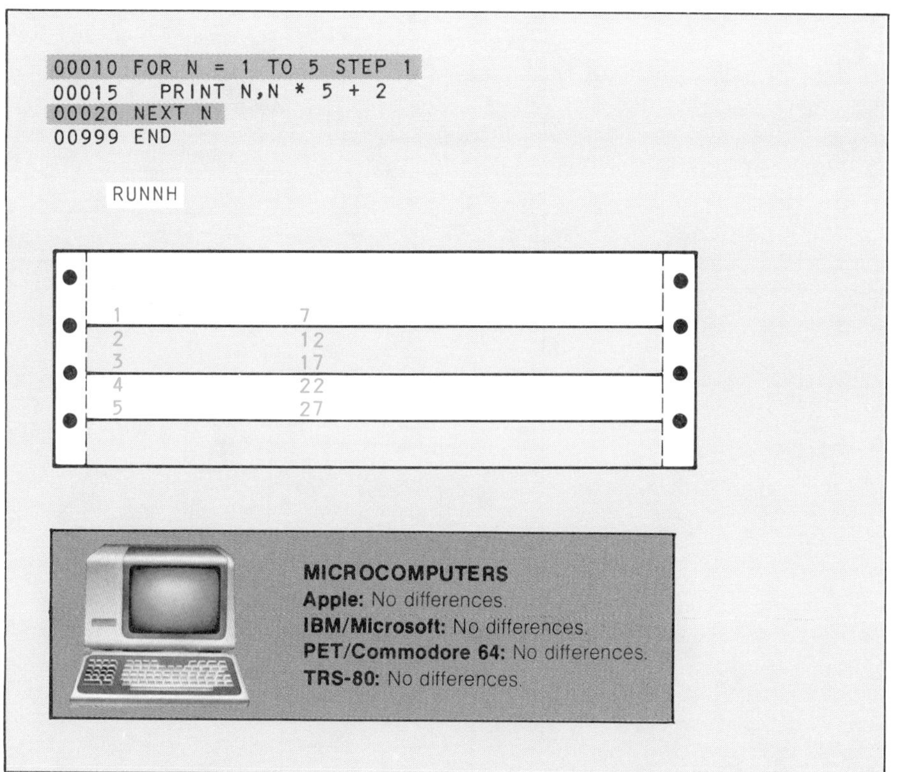
00010 FOR N = 1 TO 5 STEP 1
00015 PRINT N,N * 5 + 2
00020 NEXT N
00999 END
RUNNH
1 7
2 12
3 17
4 22
5 27
MICROCOMPUTERS
Apple: No differences.
IBM/Microsoft: No differences.
PET/Commodore 64: No differences.
TRS-80: No differences.

Flowcharting FOR and NEXT Loops

Figure 6–3a illustrates the standard method of flowcharting the FOR/NEXT loop. We have developed our own shorthand symbol for FOR and NEXT loops, which is shown in Figure 6–3b. This is very convenient for representing a loop, since it shows the initial, terminal, and step values for the loop variable in one symbol.

Processing Steps of FOR and NEXT Loops

Let us review the steps followed by the computer when it encounters a FOR statement:

1. It sets the loop variable to the initial value indicated.
2. It tests to see if the value of the loop variable exceeds the indicated terminal value (this may occur the first time the FOR statement is executed).
3. If the value of the loop variable does not exceed the terminal value, the statements in the loop are executed.

Figure 6–3 FLOWCHARTING FOR/NEXT LOOPS

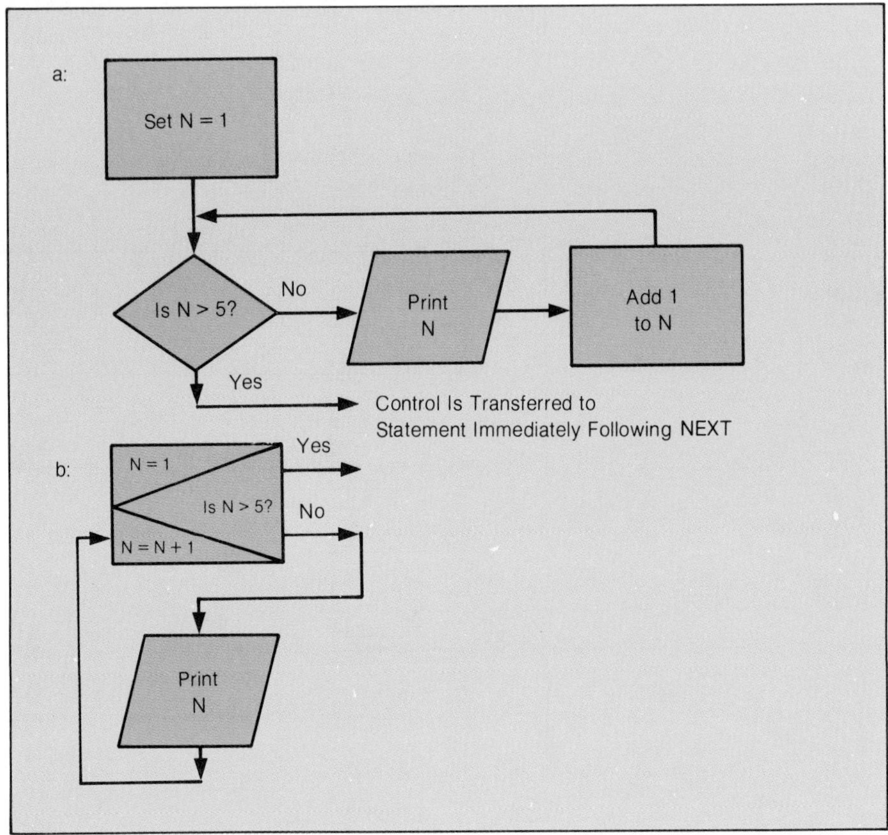

4. If the value of the loop variable exceeds the terminal value, control is transferred to the statement following the NEXT statement.

When the NEXT statement at the end of a loop is encountered, the computer does the following:

1. It adds the step value (given in the FOR statement) to the value of the loop variable. If no step value is indicated in the FOR statement, the value is assumed to be +1. Thus, the following two statements are equivalent:

```
00010 FOR N = 1 TO 5 STEP 1
```

or

```
00010 FOR N = 1 TO 5
```

2. A check is performed to determine if the value of the loop variable exceeds the terminal value.

3. If the loop variable does not exceed the terminal value, control is transferred back to the statement after the FOR statement and the loop is repeated. Otherwise, execution continues with the statement following the NEXT statement.

Rules for Using FOR and NEXT Statements

Some rules to be aware of when you use FOR and NEXT statements follow:

1. The initial value must be less than or equal to the terminal value when using a positive step. Otherwise, the loop will never be executed; for example,

   Valid: `FOR X = 1 TO 10 STEP 2`
   Invalid: `FOR X = 100 TO 50 STEP 5`

2. There are times when it is desirable to use a negative step value, for example, to count backward from 10 by 2s (see Figure 6–4). The loop is terminated when the value of the loop variable, I, "exceeds" the specified terminal value, 2. In this case, though, the value of I "exceeds" in a downward sense—the loop is terminated when I is smaller than the terminal value. The initial value of the loop variable should be greater than the terminal value when using a negative step; for example,

   Valid: `FOR J = 10 TO 1 STEP -2`
   Invalid: `FOR K = 1 TO 10 STEP -2`

3. The step size in a FOR statement should never be 0. This value would cause the computer to loop endlessly. Such an error condition is known as an **infinite loop:**

   Invalid: `FOR X = 20 TO 30 STEP 0`

4. Transfer can be made from one statement to another within a loop. For example, the program in Figure 6–5 reads in four names and the number of hours they worked. It will print out only those people who worked more than 40 hours. Note, however, that a transfer from a statement within the loop to the FOR statement of the loop is illegal. Such a transfer would cause the loop variable to be reset (rather than simply continuing the loop process):

Invalid Transfer

```
00010 FOR I = 900 TO 1000
00020    IF I = 950 THEN 10
00030    PRINT I - 50
00040 NEXT I
```

If you want to continue the looping process but want to bypass some inner instruction, branch (transfer control) to the next statement, as was done in Figure 6–5 (line 20).

Figure 6-4 USING A NEGATIVE STEP VALUE

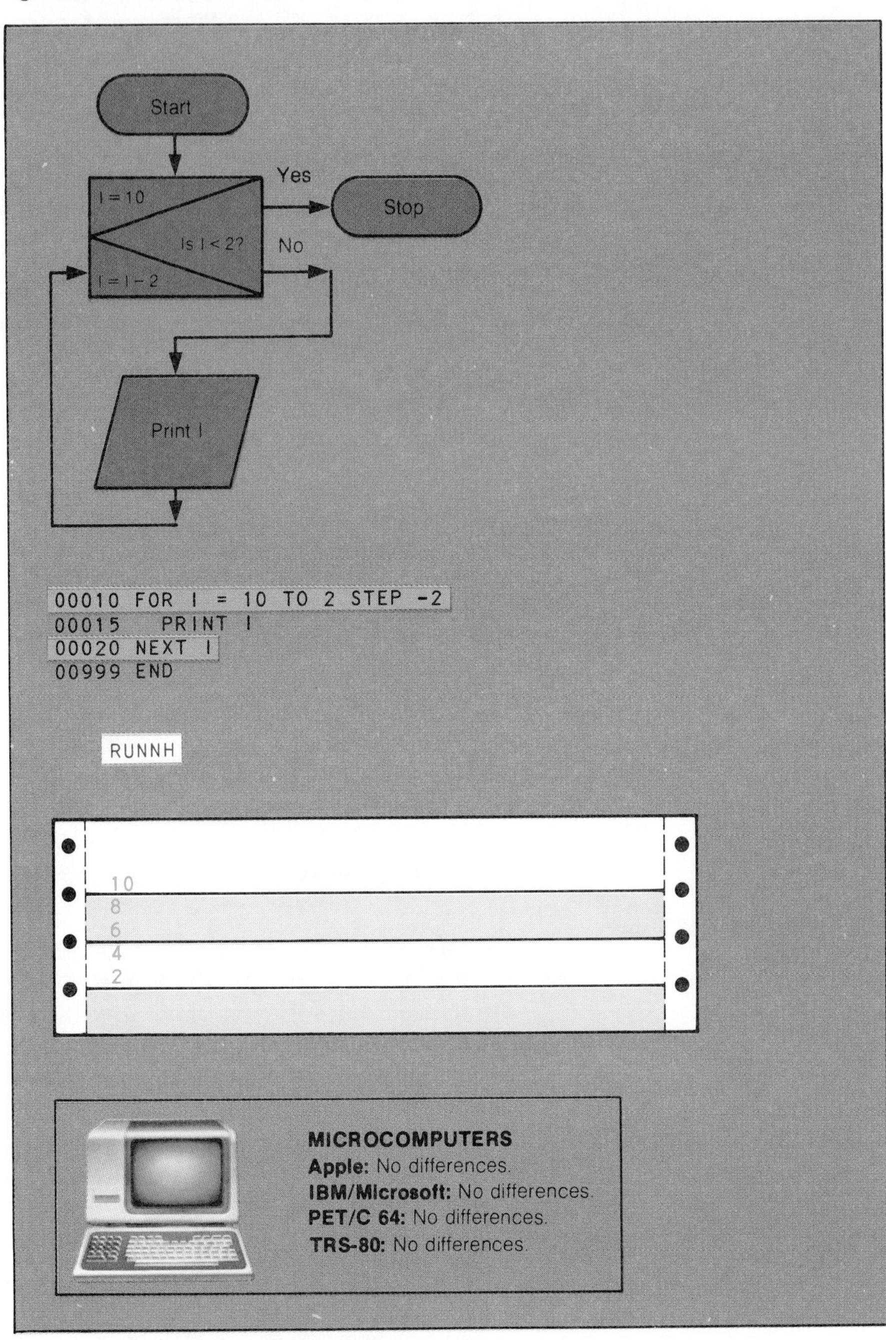
Start
Yes
I = 10
Stop
Is I < 2?
No
I = I - 2
Print I
00010 FOR I = 10 TO 2 STEP -2
00015 PRINT I
00020 NEXT I
00999 END
RUNNH
10
8
6
4
2
MICROCOMPUTERS
Apple: No differences.
IBM/Microsoft: No differences.
PET/C 64: No differences.
TRS-80: No differences.

5. The value of the loop variable should not be modified by program statements within the loop. For example, line 30 here is invalid:

```
00010 FOR J = 1 TO 20
00020    LET S = S + J
00030    LET J = S
00040 NEXT J
```

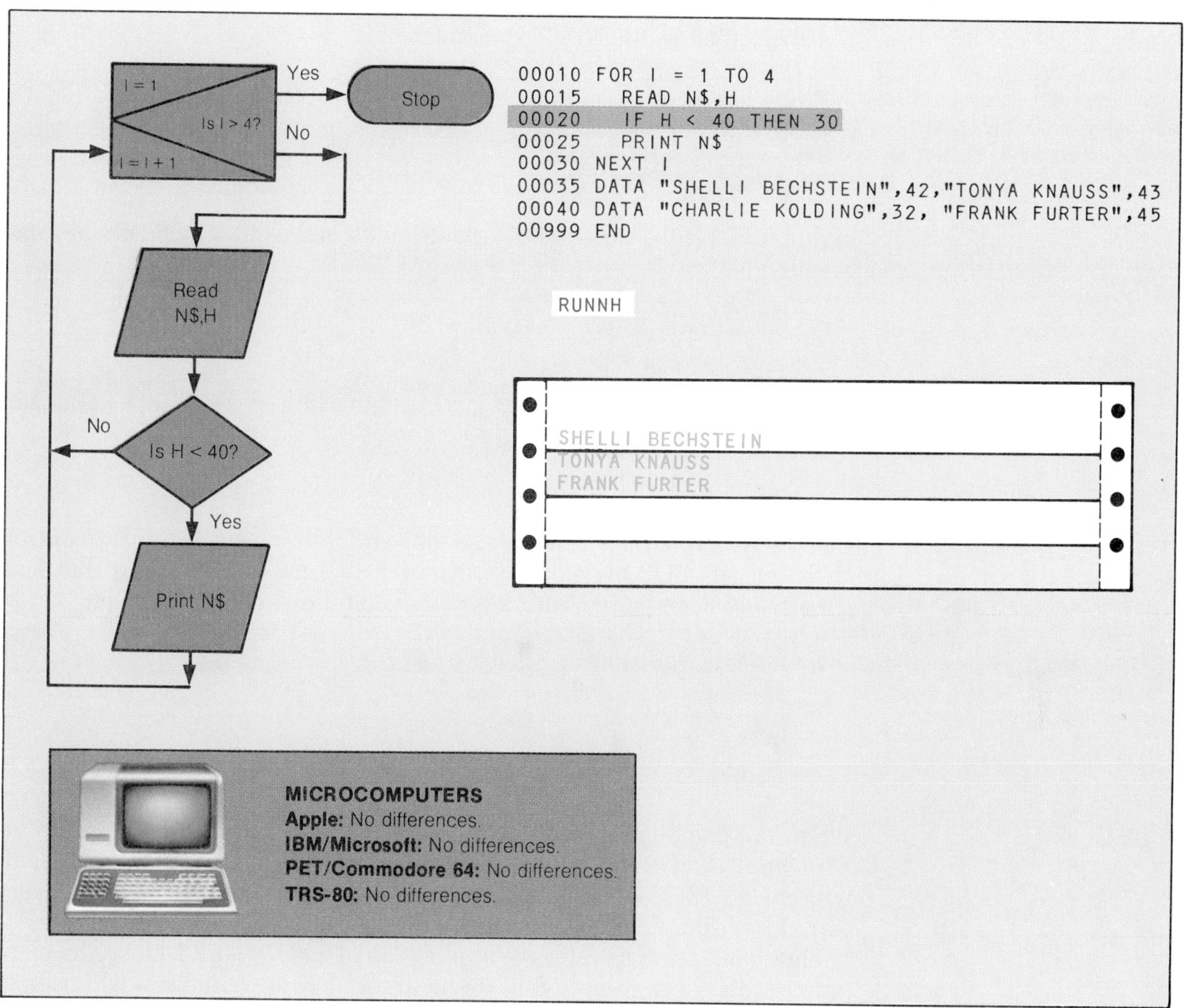

I = 1
Is I > 4?
I = I + 1
Yes
No
Stop
Read N$,H
Is H < 40?
No
Yes
Print N$
00010 FOR I = 1 TO 4
00015 READ N$,H
00020 IF H < 40 THEN 30
00025 PRINT N$
00030 NEXT I
00035 DATA "SHELLI BECHSTEIN",42,"TONYA KNAUSS",43
00040 DATA "CHARLIE KOLDING",32, "FRANK FURTER",45
00999 END
RUNNH
SHELLI BECHSTEIN
TONYA KNAUSS
FRANK FURTER
MICROCOMPUTERS
Apple: No differences.
IBM/Microsoft: No differences.
PET/Commodore 64: No differences.
TRS-80: No differences.

Figure 6–5 TRANSFERRING CONTROL WITHIN A FOR/NEXT LOOP

6. The initial, terminal, and step expressions can be composed of any valid numeric variable, constant, or mathematical formula. The following examples are valid where X = 2, Y = 10, and Z = −2:

```
00010 FOR I = X TO (Y + 20) STEP 1
00020    PRINT I + X
00030 NEXT I
```

```
00010 FOR J = Y TO X STEP Z
00020    LET S = S + J * 3
00030 NEXT J
```

```
00010 FOR K = (X + 1) TO (Y * 2) STEP -Z
00020    PRINT K
00030 NEXT K
```

7. Each FOR statement must be accompanied by an associated NEXT statement. In addition, the loop variable in the FOR statement must be specified in the NEXT statement.

There are some exceptions to Rule 7. Some systems allow nested loops to share a NEXT statement (check your systems manual); for example,

```
00050 NEXT I,J
```

In this case, I is the inner loop variable, and J is the outer loop variable and is equivalent to

```
00050 NEXT I
00060 NEXT J
```

Also, on some systems it is not necessary to follow the NEXT statement with a loop variable. This would be a valid NEXT statement:

```
00050 NEXT
```

When a NEXT statement without a loop variable is used, it returns control to the closest FOR statement (previous to the NEXT statement) that has not already been paired with a NEXT. The following is an example:

```
00010      FOR I = 1 TO 10
00020        FOR J = 1 TO 5
00030          PRINT I,J
00040        NEXT
00050      NEXT
```

When the computer comes to the NEXT statement on line 50, it pairs it with line 10, FOR I = 1 TO 10, because it is the closest FOR statement without a NEXT statement. Line 20, FOR J = 1 TO 5, has already been paired with the first NEXT statement on line 40.

Figure 6–6 demonstrates the application of a FOR/NEXT loop. The purpose of this program is to find the total number of passengers who ride a roller coaster in a half-hour. There are eight runs each half-hour. The FOR/NEXT loop is set to be executed eight times—once for each run of the roller coaster. Each time through the loop, the user enters the number of passengers on the roller coaster, N, and the computer adds that number to the total, T.

Entry and Exit Points

It is good program design to have only one entry point into a loop and one exit point out of a loop. The entry point should be the first statement of the loop. When using the FOR/NEXT loop, the FOR statement is the entry

Figure 6–6 FOR/NEXT LOOP

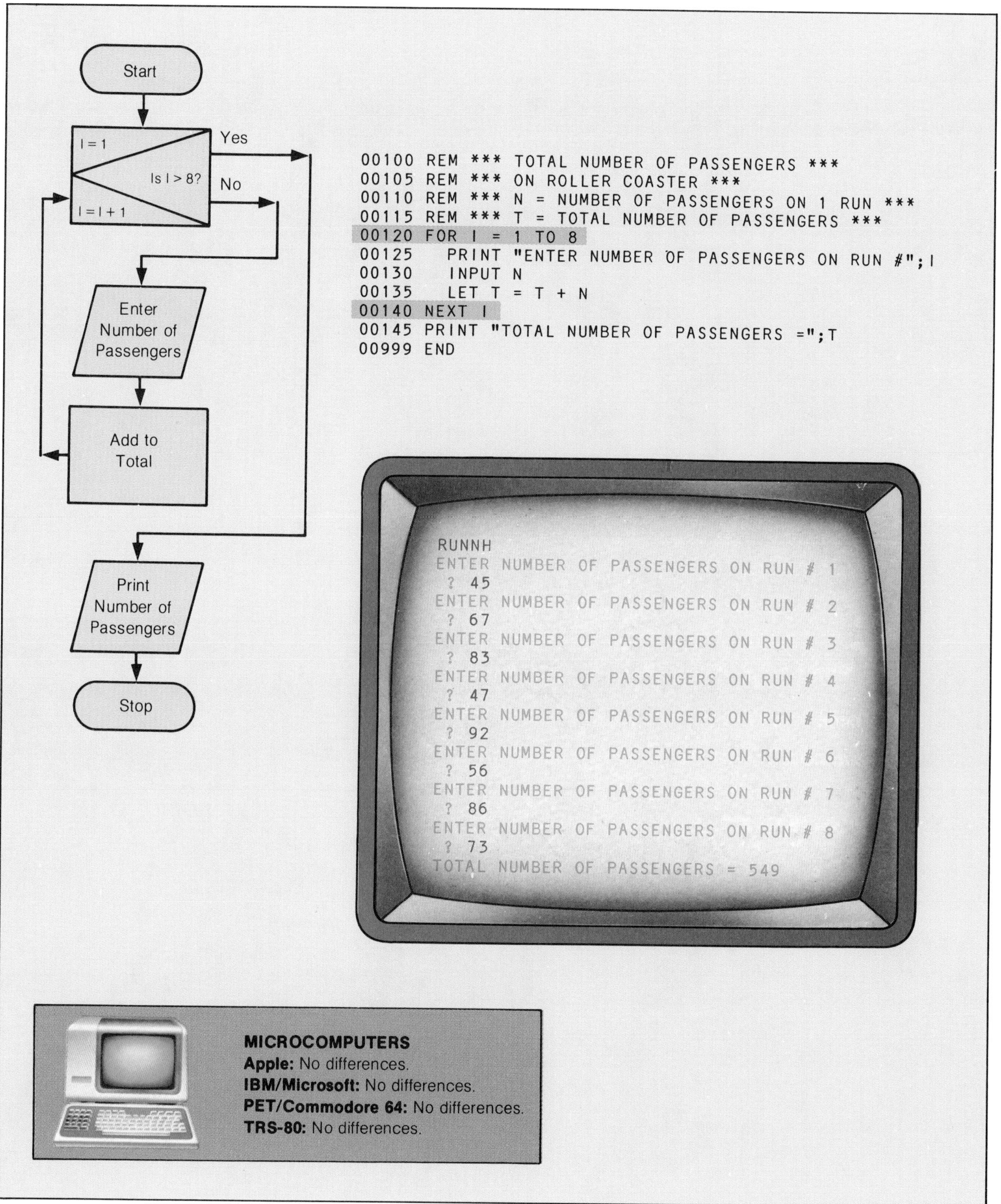

Start
I = 1
Yes
Is I > 8?
No
I = I + 1
Enter Number of Passengers
Add to Total
Print Number of Passengers
Stop
00100 REM *** TOTAL NUMBER OF PASSENGERS ***
00105 REM *** ON ROLLER COASTER ***
00110 REM *** N = NUMBER OF PASSENGERS ON 1 RUN ***
00115 REM *** T = TOTAL NUMBER OF PASSENGERS ***
00120 FOR I = 1 TO 8
00125 PRINT "ENTER NUMBER OF PASSENGERS ON RUN #";I
00130 INPUT N
00135 LET T = T + N
00140 NEXT I
00145 PRINT "TOTAL NUMBER OF PASSENGERS =";T
00999 END
RUNNH
ENTER NUMBER OF PASSENGERS ON RUN # 1
? 45
ENTER NUMBER OF PASSENGERS ON RUN # 2
? 67
ENTER NUMBER OF PASSENGERS ON RUN # 3
? 83
ENTER NUMBER OF PASSENGERS ON RUN # 4
? 47
ENTER NUMBER OF PASSENGERS ON RUN # 5
? 92
ENTER NUMBER OF PASSENGERS ON RUN # 6
? 56
ENTER NUMBER OF PASSENGERS ON RUN # 7
? 86
ENTER NUMBER OF PASSENGERS ON RUN # 8
? 73
TOTAL NUMBER OF PASSENGERS = 549
MICROCOMPUTERS
Apple: No differences.
IBM/Microsoft: No differences.
PET/Commodore 64: No differences.
TRS-80: No differences.

Figure 6–7 MULTIPLE ENTRY POINTS

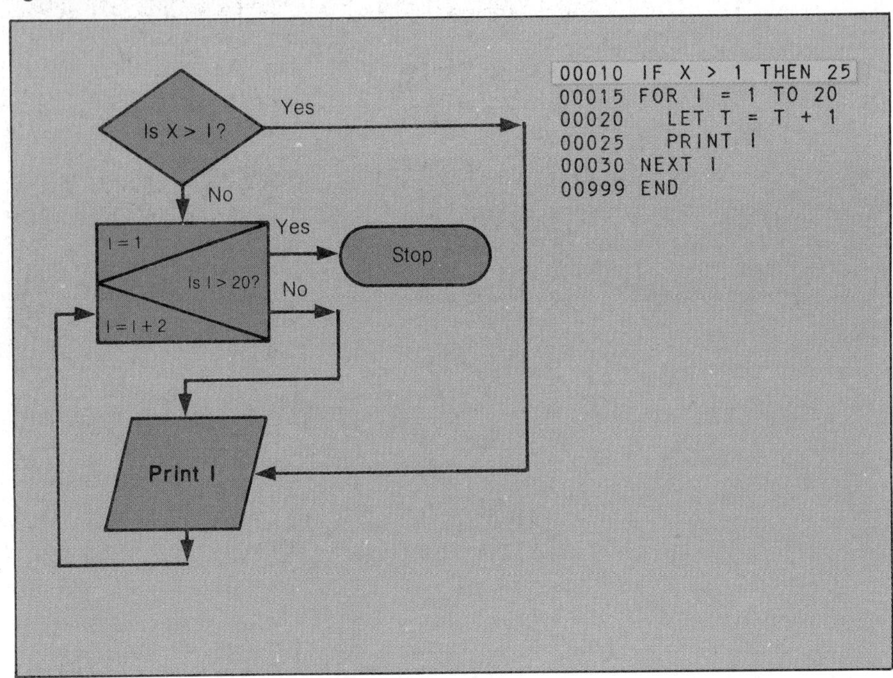

Figure 6–8 MULTIPLE EXIT POINTS

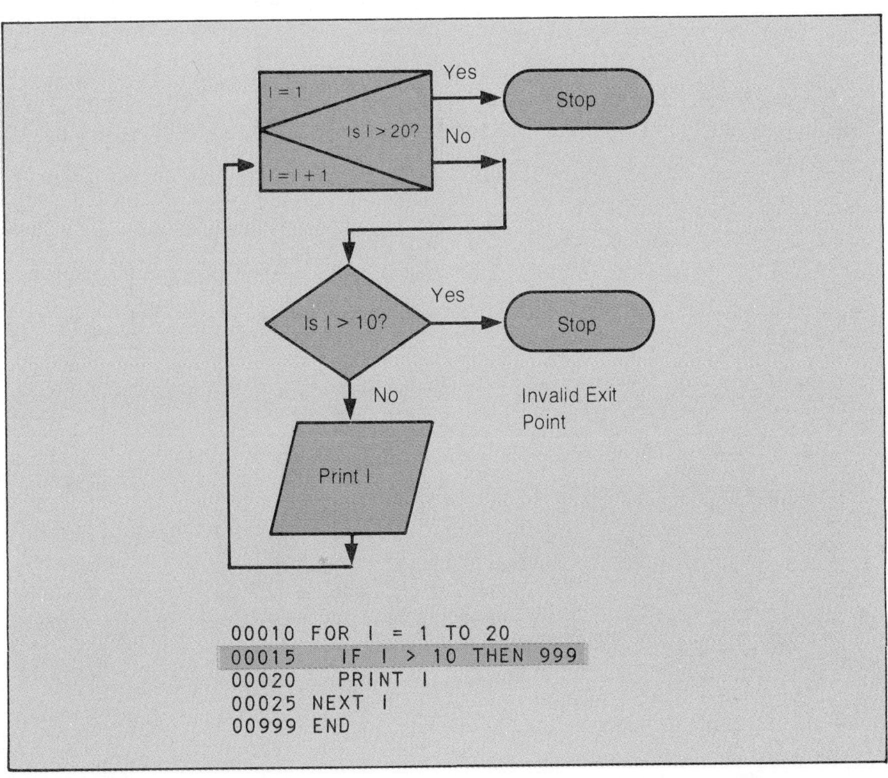

point, and the NEXT statement is the exit point. Figure 6–7 shows an example of poor program design with multiple entry points.

This is invalid according to the single entry point rule, because line 10 sends control to line 25 if X is greater than 1, and line 25 is inside a loop. When this happens, I may not contain a valid value. Also, on some systems, when the computer gets to the NEXT statement it may give you an error, because it has found no corresponding FOR statement.

The exit point should be the last statement of the loop. Figure 6–8 illustrates poor program design using multiple exit points. The program in Figure 6–8 has poor structure because the loop is exited in line 15 if I is greater than 10. The loop will never execute until I equals 20.

LEARNING CHECK

1. In a FOR/NEXT loop, the _______ statement tells the computer how many times to execute the loop.
2. When the terminal value is exceeded in a FOR/NEXT loop, control is transferred to the _______ .
   a. END statement
   b. statement immediately following the NEXT statement
   c. statement preceding the FOR statement
   d. next FOR statement
3. In a FOR statement, if no step value is indicated, the value is assumed to be _______ .
4. Identify the valid FOR/NEXT statements:

   a.
   ```
   FOR X = 8 TO 2 STEP 2
       .
       .
       .
   NEXT X
   ```
   b.
   ```
   FOR I = 1 TO 10
       .
       .
       .
   NEXT I
   ```
   c.
   ```
   FOR J = 10 TO 1 STEP -1
       .
       .
       .
   NEXT I
   ```
   d.
   ```
   FOR M = 1 TO 20 STEP 2
       .
       .
       .
   NEXT M
   ```
5. The step size in a FOR statement may be 0 under certain circumstances. TRUE FALSE (Circle the correct answer.)
6. Transfer can be made from a statement within the loop to the FOR statement of the loop. TRUE FALSE (Circle the correct answer.)

Answers
1. FOR
2. b
3. +1
4. b and d
5. False
6. False

Nested FOR and NEXT Statements

Loops can be nested; that is, all of one loop can be inside another loop or many other loops. An example of a nested loop follows:

```
FOR I = 1 TO 10
   FOR J = 1 TO 10
     .
     .
     .              Valid
   NEXT J
NEXT I
```

The inner loop often is indented to improve readability. In this case, each time the outer loop (I loop) is executed once, the inner loop (J loop) is executed ten times. When the J loop is terminated, control passes to the statement immediately below it, NEXT I. When control is transferred to FOR I (and the value of I does not exceed the terminal value, 10), the FOR J statement is soon encountered again. J is reinitialized, and the J loop is again repeated ten times.

In nested FOR and NEXT statements, be careful not to mix the FOR from one loop with the NEXT from another. In other words, be sure one loop is completely inside another. The following example will not execute:

```
   FOR I = 1 TO 10
FOR J = I TO 10
     .
     .
     .              Invalid
   NEXT I
NEXT J
```

You must also be careful not to give nested loops the same index variable:

```
FOR I = 1 TO 10
   FOR I = 1 TO 5
     .
     .
     .              Invalid
   NEXT I
NEXT I
```

If you do this, each time the inner loop is executed, it changes the value of the outer loop variable. This violates Rule 5.

The following segment illustrates the mechanics of the nested loop. The outer loop will be executed three times, since I varies from 1 to 3. The inner loop will be executed two times each time the outer loop is executed once, so the inner loop will be executed a total of six times (2 × 3):

```
              ┌ FOR I = 1 TO 3
              │  ┌──────────────┐
              │  │ FOR J = 1 TO 2│
Outer Loop ───┤  │ PRINT I,J     ├─── Inner Loop
              │  │ NEXT J        │
              │  └──────────────┘
              └ NEXT I
```

	I	J	
a. First time through outer loop; I = 1	1	1	First time through inner loop; J = 1
	1	2	Second time through inner loop; J = 2
b. Second time through outer loop; I = 2	2	1	Inner loop J = 1
	2	2	Inner loop; J = 2
c. Third time through outer loop; I = 3	3	1	Inner loop; J = 1
	3	2	Inner loop; J = 2

As many loops may be nested within one another as desired, but use caution so that you do not mix the NEXT of one loop with the FOR of another. The brackets must never cross as they do in the invalid example of nested loops. Here is an example of multiple nested loops:

```
Loop 1 [ FOR I = 1 TO 2
           PRINT I
  Loop 2   [ FOR J = 1 TO 3
               PRINT J;
    Loop 3     [ FOR K = 1 TO 3
                   PRINT K
                 NEXT K
             NEXT J
         NEXT I
```

In this example, each nested loop is completely within its outer loop (the brackets never cross each other). Loop 1 is executed two times. Loop 2 is executed six times (2 × 3). Loop 3 is executed eighteen times (2 × 3 × 3).

Figure 6–9 is an application of nested loops that generates three multiplication tables. The inner loop controls the printing of the columns in each row, and the outer loop controls how many rows will be printed.

First, A is initialized to 1. Then execution of the inner loop begins. Line 20 tells the computer (when B = 1) to print "1 × 1 = 1." The comma at the end of that line tells the computer not to start the output of the next PRINT statement on a new line, but rather to continue in the next print zone. Line 25 increments B to 2 and sends control back to line 15. The variable A has not changed. The terminal value of B is not exceeded, so "2 × 1 = 2" is printed in the second print zone. The inner loop executes one more time and prints out "3 × 1 = 3." After the inner loop has executed the third time, one complete row has been printed:

1 × 1 = 1   2 × 1 = 2   3 × 1 = 3

To have printing start on the next line instead of in the next print zone, it is necessary to have the rest of the line printed with blanks. That is accomplished by line 30. Finally, A is incremented when line 35 is encountered. The whole process continues until A exceeds the terminal value, 10.

Figure 6–9 NESTED LOOPS

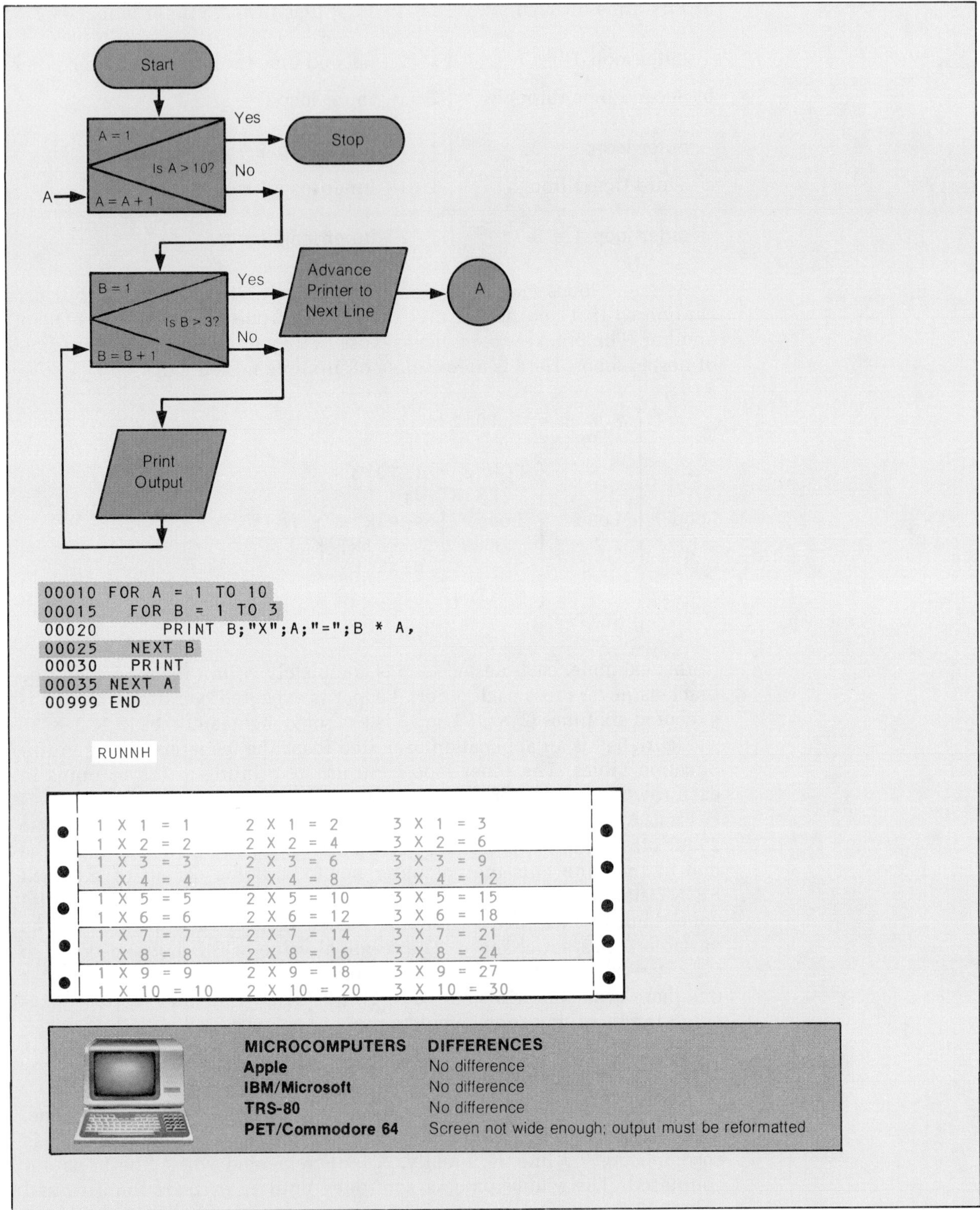


```
00010 FOR A = 1 TO 10
00015    FOR B = 1 TO 3
00020       PRINT B;"X";A;"=";B * A,
00025    NEXT B
00030    PRINT
00035 NEXT A
00999 END
```

```
RUNNH
```

```
1 X 1 = 1        2 X 1 = 2        3 X 1 = 3
1 X 2 = 2        2 X 2 = 4        3 X 2 = 6
1 X 3 = 3        2 X 3 = 6        3 X 3 = 9
1 X 4 = 4        2 X 4 = 8        3 X 4 = 12
1 X 5 = 5        2 X 5 = 10       3 X 5 = 15
1 X 6 = 6        2 X 6 = 12       3 X 6 = 18
1 X 7 = 7        2 X 7 = 14       3 X 7 = 21
1 X 8 = 8        2 X 8 = 16       3 X 8 = 24
1 X 9 = 9        2 X 9 = 18       3 X 9 = 27
1 X 10 = 10      2 X 10 = 20      3 X 10 = 30
```

MICROCOMPUTERS	DIFFERENCES
Apple	No difference
IBM/Microsoft	No difference
TRS-80	No difference
PET/Commodore 64	Screen not wide enough; output must be reformatted

WHILE/NEXT and UNTIL/NEXT Loops

Two additional sets of instructions are used to implement loops: WHILE/NEXT and UNTIL/NEXT. Here is the general format for each of these loops.

WHILE/NEXT Loop:

```
line# WHILE expression
   .
   .
   .
line# NEXT
```

UNTIL/NEXT Loop:

```
line# UNTIL expression
   .
   .
   .
line# NEXT
```

Notice that the NEXT statement in each of these loops is not followed by a variable. Any statements between the WHILE and NEXT or the UNTIL and NEXT statements will be executed each time the loop is repeated. The WHILE loop will be executed as long as the expression in the WHILE statement is true. When the expression is no longer true, control is transferred to the first instruction after the NEXT statement. The UNTIL loop works in just the opposite way. UNTIL loops are executed as long as the expression is false. When the expression in the UNTIL statement is true, control is transferred to the statement immediately after the NEXT statement. The WHILE/NEXT and UNTIL/NEXT loops do not do any counting or incrementing. There must be an instruction within the loop that will alter the WHILE or UNTIL expression so the loop will eventually quit. If there is no instruction within the loop to change the expression's value, the loop will not quit executing and will create an infinite loop. Figure 6–10 illustrates a valid WHILE/NEXT loop.

It is possible to do the same thing as Figure 6–10 does with an UNTIL loop. Figure 6–11 illustrates this.

The following example is invalid. J is never changed, so it never will be greater than 100. The loop will be executed an infinite number of times:

```
00100 WHILE J < 100
00110   PRINT J
00120   LET S = S + J
00130 NEXT
```

WHILE/WEND LOOPS

The BASIC implementation on some microcomputers (for instance, IBM/Microsoft) implements the WHILE loop structure in the following manner.

Figure 6-10 WHILE/NEXT LOOP

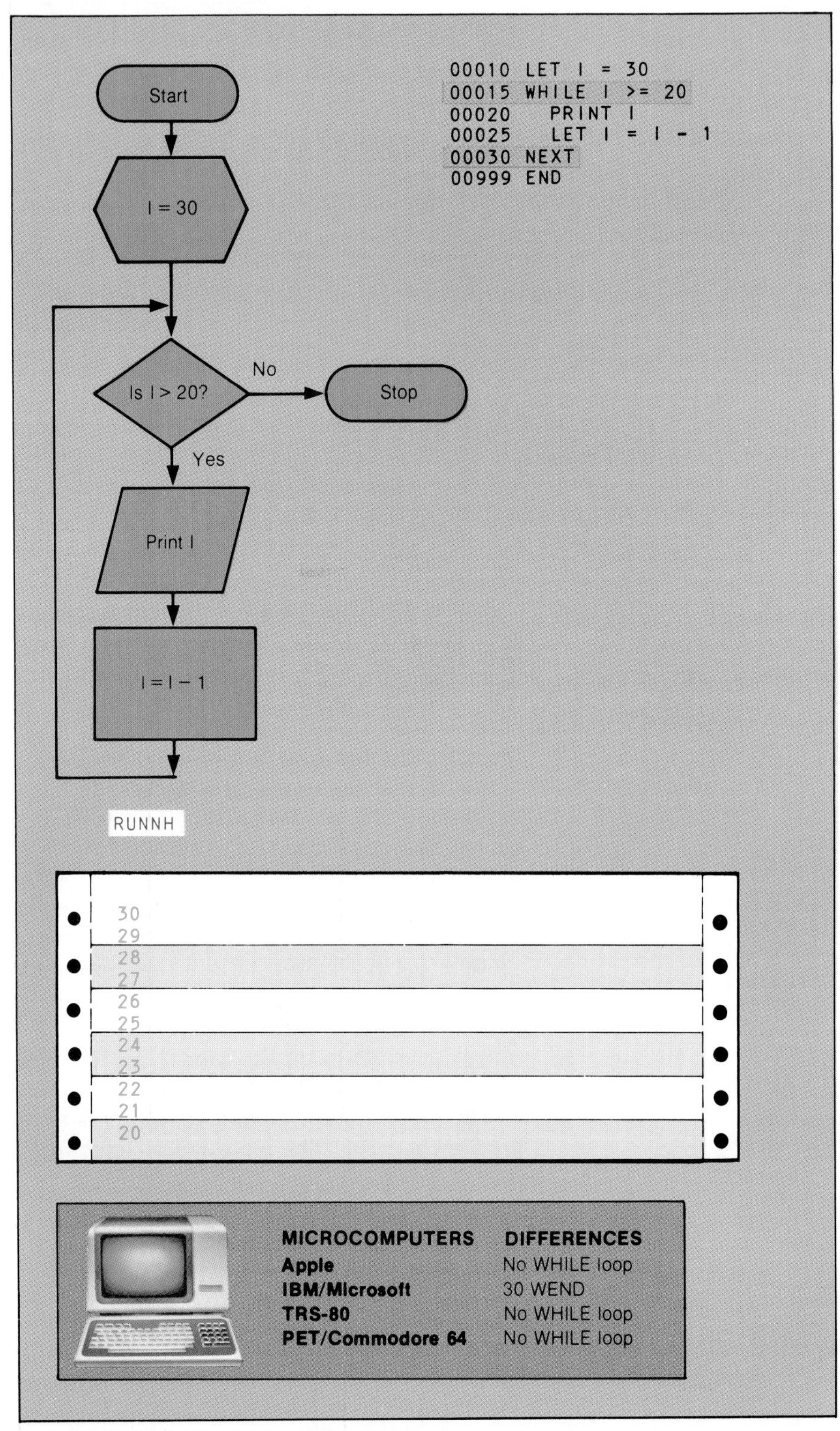

Start
I = 30
Is I > 20?
No
Stop
Yes
Print I
I = I − 1
00010 LET I = 30
00015 WHILE I >= 20
00020 PRINT I
00025 LET I = I - 1
00030 NEXT
00999 END
RUNNH
30
29
28
27
26
25
24
23
22
21
20
MICROCOMPUTERS DIFFERENCES
Apple No WHILE loop
IBM/Microsoft 30 WEND
TRS-80 No WHILE loop
PET/Commodore 64 No WHILE loop

Figure 6–11 UNTIL/NEXT LOOP

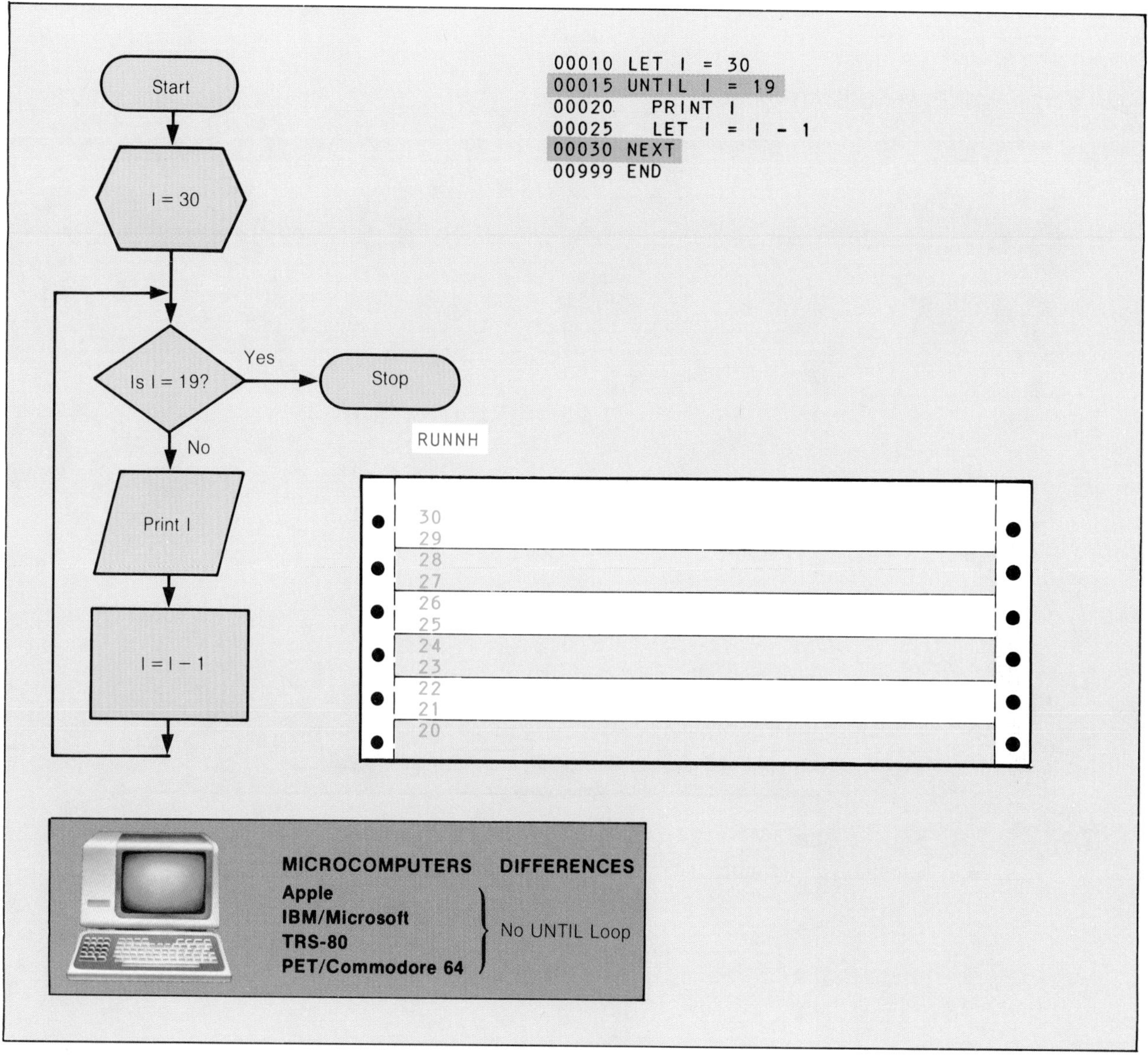
Start
I = 30
Is I = 19?
Yes
Stop
No
Print I
I = I − 1
00010 LET I = 30
00015 UNTIL I = 19
00020 PRINT I
00025 LET I = I - 1
00030 NEXT
00999 END
RUNNH
30
29
28
27
26
25
24
23
22
21
20
MICROCOMPUTERS DIFFERENCES
Apple
IBM/Microsoft
TRS-80
PET/Commodore 64
No UNTIL Loop

The WHILE statement starts and tests the loop, and the WEND statement at the end of the loop sends control back to the WHILE. Here is the general format of the WHILE/WEND loop:

```
line# WHILE expression
      .
      .
      .
line# WEND
```

Figure 6–12 illustrates examples of valid WHILE/WEND statements run on the IBM Personal Computer with Microsoft BASIC.

Figure 6–12 WHILE/WEND STATEMENT

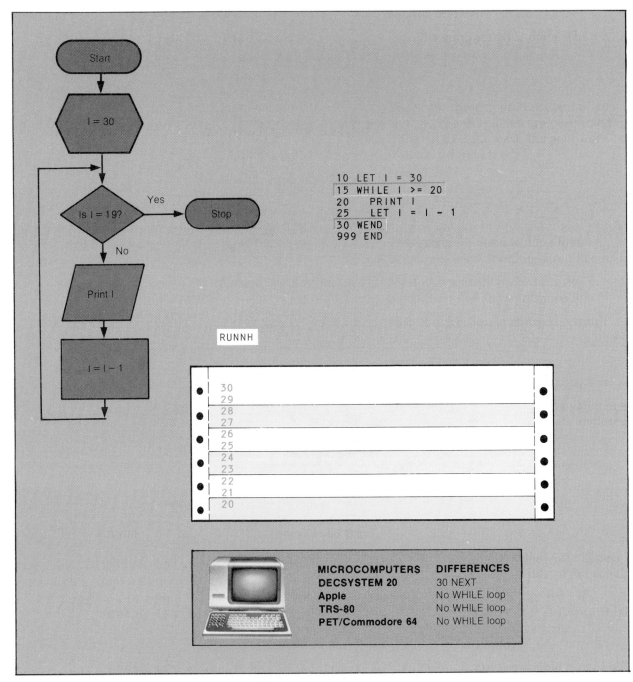

```
10 LET I = 30
15 WHILE I >= 20
20    PRINT I
25    LET I = I - 1
30 WEND
999 END
```

```
RUNNH
```

```
30
29
28
27
26
25
24
23
22
21
20
```

MICROCOMPUTERS	DIFFERENCES
DECSYSTEM 20	30 NEXT
Apple	No WHILE loop
TRS-80	No WHILE loop
PET/Commodore 64	No WHILE loop

LEARNING CHECK

1. When one FOR/NEXT loop is completely inside another FOR/NEXT loop, we have what is referred to as ______ loops.
2. Which of the following are valid nested FOR/NEXT loops?

a.
```
FOR I = 1 TO 10
   FOR J = 2 TO 6
   .
   .
   .
   NEXT I
NEXT J
```
b.
```
FOR I = 10 TO 1 STEP -1
   FOR K = 3 TO 9 STEP 3
   .
   .
   .
   NEXT K
NEXT I
```
c.
```
FOR T = 1 TO 5 STEP 1
   FOR S = 1 TO 3
      FOR R = 1 TO 10
      .
      .
      .
      NEXT R
   NEXT S
NEXT T
```
d.
```
FOR V = 10 TO 1 STEP -2
   FOR X = 1 TO 5
   .
   .
   .
NEXT V
```

3. How many times will loop B be executed?

```
                FOR I = 1 TO 5
                          FOR J = 2 TO 6
Loop A   Loop B              PRINT J
                          NEXT J
                NEXT I
```

4. The following is a valid WHILE loop. TRUE   FALSE (Circle the correct answer.)

```
00010 WHILE X < 10
00020   PRINT X
00030 NEXT
```

5. An UNTIL loop is executed as long as the expression in the UNTIL statement is ______.

Answers

1. nested
2. b and c
3. Twenty-five times
4. False
5. False

Problem Definition

The computer science department needs a program to display a bar graph that shows the number of students enrolled in each of the computer science classes, sections 100 through 109:

100	37
101	28
102	31
103	34
104	26
105	22
106	30
107	21
108	10
109	18

The output should have appropriate headings, and the horizontal bar should be marked off by 10s.

Solution Design

Two loops will be needed—one to give the section number and another to print out an asterisk for each student in that section.

The Program

Figure 6–13 is a good illustration of nested FOR/NEXT loops. Line 125 contains the data—the number of students in sections 100 through 109, respectively. Statements 130 through 160 print out the headings with appropriate spacing. The outer loop (lines 165 through 200) is set to run from 100 to 109, so the variable I represents the section number. Line 170 reads in the number of students; then the inner loop (lines 180 through 190) is set to repeat the PRINT statement (line 185) as many times as there are students. Line 175 printed the section number and tabbed the printer to column 9. Because lines 175 and 185 end with a semicolon, the printer will print the section number and all of the asterisks on one line. After the asterisks have been printed and the inner loop is finished, the printer must be advanced to the next line. This is done in line 195 which prints blanks in the remainder of the line. Because line 195 does not end with a comma or semicolon, the printer moves to the next line.

Many variations can be made to this bar graph display. The asterisk can be replaced by any other character. Also, the limitations placed by the width of the terminal can be overcome by using appropriate scales. For example, each asterisk could represent two students.

Figure 6–13 ENROLLMENT PROGRAM AND FLOWCHART

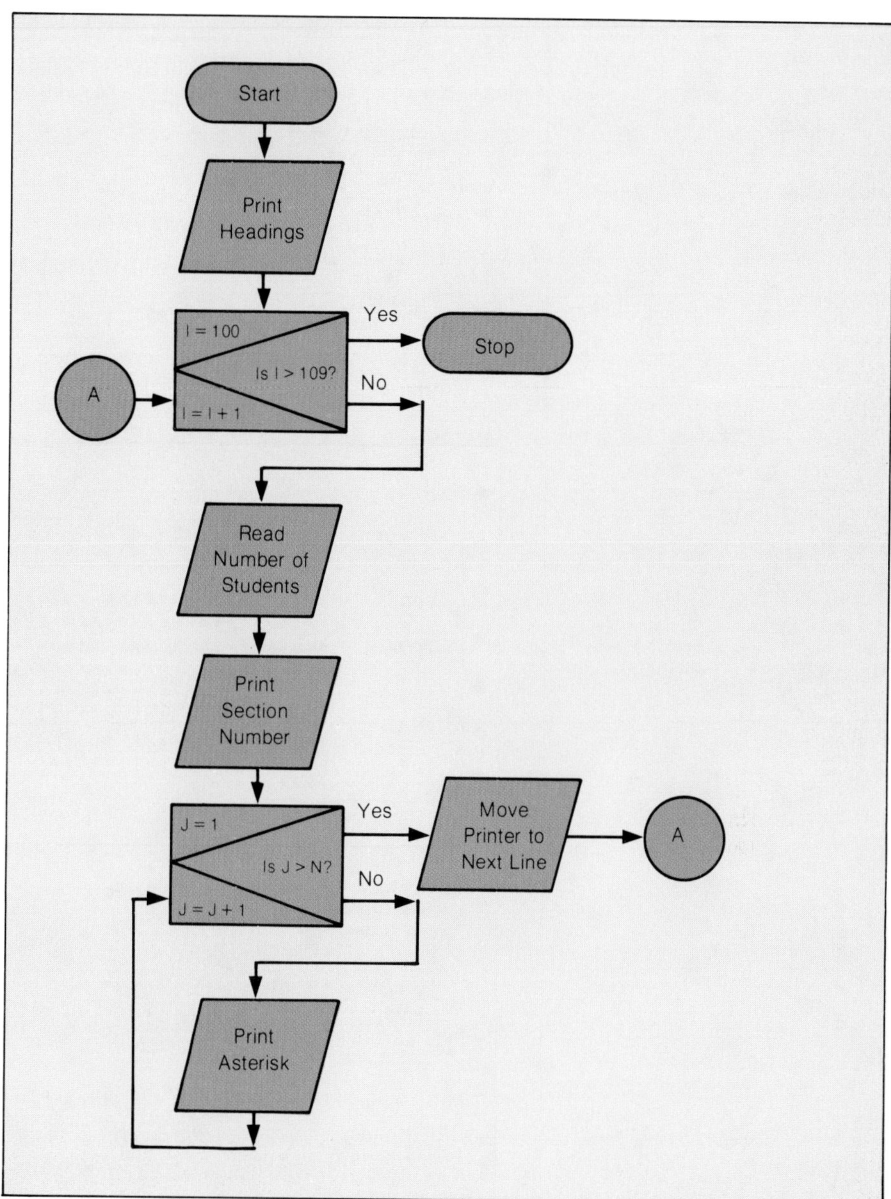

(Figure continued next page)

Figure 6–13 *(continued)*

```
00100 REM *** BAR GRAPH ***
00105 REM *** SHOWS NUMBER OF STUDENTS ENROLLED ***
00110 REM *** IN EACH COMPUTER SCIENCE SECTION ***
00115 REM *** N = NUMBER OF STUDENTS ***
00120 REM
00125 DATA 37,28,31,34,26,22,30,21,10,18
00130 PRINT
00135 PRINT
00140 PRINT TAB(16);"CLASS ENROLLMENT"
00145 PRINT
00150 PRINT "SEC. #";TAB(16);"STUDENTS"
00155 PRINT TAB(8);1;TAB(17);10;TAB(27);20;TAB(37);30
00160 PRINT
00165 FOR I = 100 TO 109
00170   READ N
00175   PRINT I;TAB(9);
00180   FOR J = 1 TO N
00185     PRINT "*";
00190   NEXT J
00195   PRINT
00200 NEXT I
00999 END
```

RUNNH

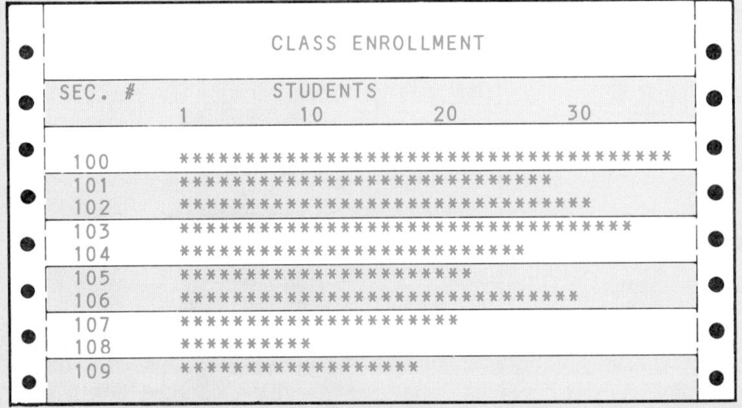

```
               CLASS ENROLLMENT

SEC. #         STUDENTS
       1        10        20        30

100     *************************************
101     ****************************
102     *******************************
103     **********************************
104     **************************
105     **********************
106     ******************************
107     *********************
108     **********
109     ******************
```

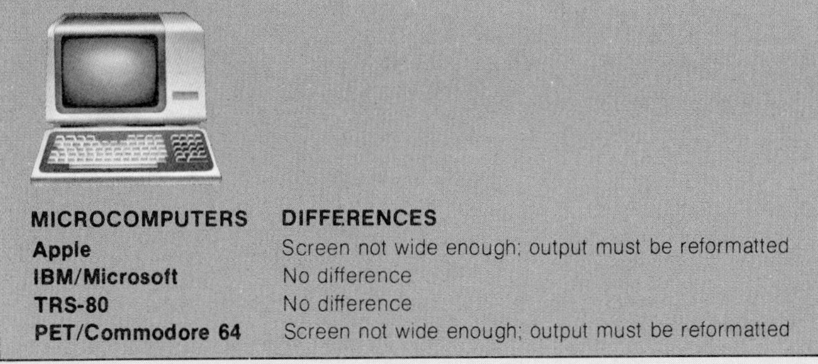

MICROCOMPUTERS	DIFFERENCES
Apple	Screen not wide enough; output must be reformatted
IBM/Microsoft	No difference
TRS-80	No difference
PET/Commodore 64	Screen not wide enough; output must be reformatted

Summary

- BASIC provides for concise loop definition with the FOR and NEXT statements. The FOR statement sets the initial, terminal, and step values and tests to see whether the initial value exceeds the terminal value. The NEXT statement increments the loop variable and sends control back to either the statement following the FOR statement or the statement following the NEXT statement.

- Some rules to remember when using FOR and NEXT loops follow:
  1. The initial value must be less than or equal to the terminal value when using a positive step value.
  2. The step value can be negative. If it is, the initial value must be greater than or equal to the terminal value.
  3. The step value should never be 0, this would cause the computer to loop endlessly.
  4. Transfer can be made from one statement to another within a loop. However, transfer from a statement within a loop to the FOR statement is illegal.
  5. The value of the loop variable should not be modified by program statements within the loop.
  6. The initial, terminal, and step expressions can be composed of any valid numeric variable, constant, or mathematical formula.
  7. Each FOR statement must be accompanied by an associated NEXT statement.
  8. FOR and NEXT loops can be nested.
  9. The NEXT statement of the inner loop must come before the NEXT statement of the outer loop.

- The WHILE statement begins execution of a series of statements in a loop as long as the given condition in the WHILE statement is true.

- The UNTIL statement begins execution of a series of statements in a loop as long as the given condition in the UNTIL statement is false.

Review Questions

1. Is this a valid FOR statement?

```
20 FOR C$ = 1 TO 10 STEP 2
```

2. Is this a valid FOR statement?

```
100 FOR N = 100 TO 1 STEP 25
```

3. What is the output from the following program?

```
30 LET L = 10
40 FOR L = 1 TO 6
50 PRINT L
60 NEXT L
```

4. If the initial value is greater than the terminal value, should the step value be positive or negative?
5. If the step value is negative, will the loop be terminated when the initial value is less than or greater than the terminal value?
6. Is this a valid FOR/NEXT loop?

```
150 FOR J = 5 TO 1 STEP -1
160     PRINT 10 ∧ J
170 NEXT J
```

7. Is this a valid FOR/NEXT loop?

```
200 FOR K = 1 TO 10 STEP 2
210     PRINT K
220 NEXT I
```

8. Can the step value be alphabetic?
9. What is the step value assumed to be if it is not given?
10. Can arithmetic expressions be used as initial and terminal values?
11. What three things does the NEXT statement do?
12. A good program design should have ______.
    a. multiple entry and exit points
    b. single entry and exit points
    c. multiple entry and single exit points
    d. single entry and multiple exit points
13. Is this a valid nested loop?

```
FOR I = 1 TO (X + Y)
  FOR J = 1 TO 5
    PRINT I,J
  NEXT I
NEXT J
```

14. Is this a valid nested loop?

```
FOR I = 10 TO 1 STEP -1
   PRINT I
   FOR J = 2 TO 6 STEP 2
   LET S = I + J
      FOR K = 1 TO 3
         LET S = S + K
         PRINT S
      NEXT J
      PRINT J
   NEXT J
NEXT I
```

15. How many times is the following inner loop executed? How many times is the outer loop executed?

```
FOR I = 1 TO (3 * 4) STEP 2
   FOR J = 1 TO 2 STEP .5
      PRINT I,J
   NEXT J
NEXT I
```

16. How many times is each of the following loops executed?

```
                    FOR I = 100 TO 10 STEP -10
                                 FOR J = 1 TO 5
                                              FOR K = 3 TO 1 STEP -1
Loop 1      Loop 2      Loop 3       PRINT I,J,K
                                              NEXT K
                                 NEXT J
                    NEXT I
```

17. Can control be transferred from one statement to another within a loop? From a statement within a loop to the FOR statement?

18. Is this a valid FOR/NEXT loop?

```
10 FOR I = 1 TO 10
20     READ X
30     IF X > 20 THEN 50
40     LET S = S + W
50 NEXT I
```

19. Which of the following is a valid WHILE loop?

a.
```
WHILE X < 10
    PRINT X
    LET X = X + 1
NEXT
```

b.
```
WHILE Q + 6 < R
    LET S = S + 1
    PRINT S
NEXT
```

20. Explain the differences in constructing an UNTIL/NEXT loop and a WHILE/NEXT loop.

Debugging Exercises

Identify the following programs or program segments that contain errors, and debug them.

1.
```
00010 FOR I = 1 TO 10
00020   READ C
00030   IF C = 1 THEN 10
00040   READ N
00050 NEXT I
```

2.
```
00010 FOR J = 1 TO 20
00020   LET J = J + 1
00030 NEXT J
```

3.
```
00010 FOR J$ = 1 TO (5 * X) STEP 3
00015   PRINT J$
00020 NEXT J$
```

4.
```
00010 FOR X = Y TO Z STEP V
00020   FOR I = 3 TO 12 STEP -2
00030     PRINT I,X
00040   NEXT X
00050 NEXT I
```

5.
```
00020 FOR I = 1 TO 5
00030   FOR J = 1 TO 3
00040     READ X
00050     IF X <> 0 THEN 20
00060     READ H$
00070     PRINT H$
00080   NEXT J
00090 NEXT I
```

6.
```
00010 FOR K = 1 TO 5
00015   FOR J = (3 + X) TO Z
00020     FOR I = 1 TO 2
00025       PRINT K,J,I
00030     NEXT K
00035   NEXT J
00040 NEXT I
```

7.
```
00010 FOR X = T$ TO 5
00020   PRINT X
00030 NEXT X
```

8.
```
00100 UNTIL W = 20
00105   PRINT W
00110 NEXT
```

9.
```
00200 FOR K = 1 TO 100 STEP 10
00210   PRINT K
00220   FOR J = 1 TO 5
00230     READ X
00240     IF X < 10 THEN 250
00250   NEXT J
00260 NEXT K
```

10.
```
00300 FOR P = 10 TO 1 STEP 0
00310   LET S = P + 1
00320 NEXT P
```

Additional Programming Problems

1. The ACME MOVING COMPANY has asked you to write a payroll program that will calculate the weekly net pay for each of its hourly

employees. The employees have the option of participating in a medical insurance plan that deducts $10 per week. The income tax rate is 40 percent. Use a FOR/NEXT loop in your program.

The following is a list of hours worked during the last week, in addition to other data relating to each employee:

Name	Medical Plan	Hours	Wage Rate
Justin Thyme	Yes	40	$ 7.35
Jerry Atrik	No	38	6.25
Kevin Cochran	Yes	40	5.00
Tina Hann	Yes	40	10.25
Scott Main	No	30	4.15
Shelly Vail	Yes	35	3.25

The output should appear as follows:

Name	Net Pay
XXXXXXXXXX	$XXX.XX

2. Write a program to find X^N. The program should calculate X^N by multiplying X times itself N number of times (for example, $X^3 = X * X * X$). The first number of the DATA statement is X, and the second number is N. Use the following DATA statement:

```
DATA 2,7
```

The output should look like this:

```
X RAISED TO THE N = Y.
```

3. Tom and Jerry want to play tic-tac-toe, but they need a tic-tac-toe board. Write a program to print out a tic-tac-toe board. Make the first vertical bar ten spaces from the left margin and the distance between the vertical bars, fifteen spaces. Use the same spacing for the horizontal bars.

4. Vanderwhite Jewelers needs a program to accept five salespersons' sales for each of three months. Output the total sales for each person and the total sales for all three months. Using nested loops, read in the following data:

Dan Lafayette	1,998.30	2,547.00	1,743.55
Mellisa Hayes	2,273.54	1,962.99	2,132.00
David Wolcott	1,872.43	752.52	1,777.63
Dennis Warncke	2,487.66	2,361.69	2,907.59
Beth Daly	1,279.91	1,776.23	1,815.17

Your output should have the following format:

```
SALESPERSON          TOTAL
XXXXXXXXXXX          $XXXXXXXXX
     .                    .
     .                    .
     .                    .
          TOTAL SALES $XXXXXXXXXX
```

5. The wrestling coach at Musclebound High School has a tryout camp each year for the wrestling team. The coach likes to divide the potential team members into three groups based on the following chart:

Weight	**Class**
Less than 150 pounds	Lightweight
150 pounds to 199 pounds	Middleweight
200 pounds or more	Heavyweight

You are to write a program using a WHILE loop that indicates in which class a person belongs. Use the following data:

Name	**Weight**
Jim Lange	165
Don Jackson	200
Bob Bowman	120
Paul Smith	150

6. Given last month's checking account balance, write a program to compute this month's balance. Use the following data:

   Last month's balance: 202.69
   Amount of checks written: 1.28, 58.98, 39.47, 81.67, 0.00

   Use a WHILE loop and the INPUT statement to enter the data. The WHILE loop should execute until 0.00 is entered as a check amount. The Output should follow this format:

   THIS MONTH'S BALANCE IS $XXXX.XX

コサシスセソタチツテト
ヘホマミムメモヤユヨラ
ョッ/ ： *ー ， ． ゛ ゜ x
QRSTUVWXYZ0123456789 アイ
テトナニヌネノハヒフヘホマミムメモヤユヨラリル
x
VWXYZ0123456789 アイウエオカキクケコサシスセソ
ユヨラリルレロワンャュョッ/：*ー，．゛゜x
56789 アイウエオカキクケコサシスセソタチツテトナニヌネノハヒフヘホマミムメモヤユヨラリル
VWXYZ0123456789 アイウエオカキクケコサシスセソ
ユヨラリルレロワンャュョッ/：*ー，．゛゜x
QRSTUVWXYZ0123456789 アイ
テトナニヌネノハヒフヘホマミムメモヤユヨラリル
x
IJKLMNOPQRS
123456789 ア
コサシスセソタチツテト

イウ゜
ナニ
リル
ABCD
ウエオカ
レロワン
ABCDEF
タチツテト
ABCDEFGH
レロワンャュョ
ABCDEF
タチツテト
ABCD
ウエオカ
レロワン
AB
TU
イウ

7 Functions

Outline

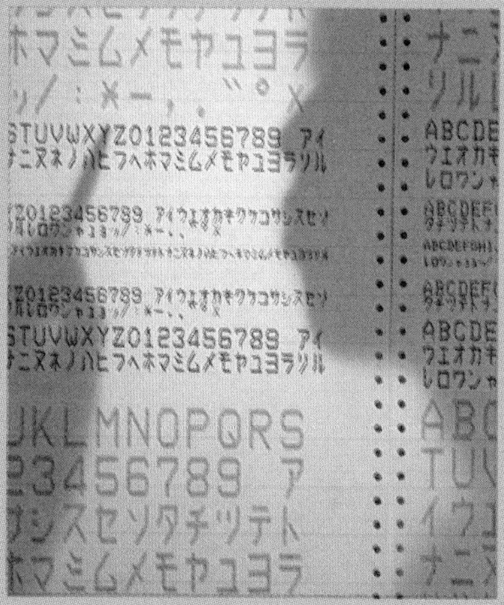

Objectives

After reading this chapter, the student should be able to do the following:

- Understand and use the common ANSI standard library functions.
- Define functions that are not already included in the BASIC language.

Overview

BASIC has numerous built-in functions that perform specific mathematical operations, such as finding the square root of a number or generating random numbers. These functions are useful to the programmer, who is spared the necessity of writing the sequence of statements otherwise needed to perform these operations. At other times, however, it may be useful for the programmer to define a function to meet the particular needs of an application. This chapter discusses these two tools: library functions (also called **built-in,** or **predefined functions**) and user-defined functions.

Library Functions

Table 7–1 lists the ANSI standard library functions found on most systems. The functions have been built into the BASIC language because many applications require these types of mathematical operations. The functions are included in the BASIC language library, where they can be referred to easily—hence, the name **library functions.**

The general format for referencing a library function is as follows:

function name(argument)

In the function references in Table 7–1, the variable X is used as the **argument.** In BASIC, the argument of a function can be a constant, a variable, a mathematical expression, or another function. These functions are used in place of constants, variables, or expressions in BASIC statements such as PRINT, LET, and IF/THEN.

Trigonometric Functions

The first four library functions in Table 7–1—SIN(X), COS(X), TAN(X), and ATN(X)—are trigonometric functions, which are very useful in mathematics, engineering, and scientific applications. They use radian measures of angles, since computers find them easier to understand than degrees. People, however, prefer to use degrees. The following examples show how to convert from one unit to the other:

Table 7–1 Common ANSI Standard Library Functions

Function	Purpose
SIN(X)	Trigonometric sine function, X in radians
COS(X)	Trigonometric cosine function, X in radians
TAN(X)	Trigonometric tangent function, X in radians
ATN(X)	Trigonometric arc tangent function, X in radians
LOG(X)	Natural logarithm function
EXP(X)	e raised to the X power
SQR(X)	Square root of X
INT(X)	Greatest integer less than X
SGN(X)	Sign of X
ABS(X)	Absolute value of X
RND	Random number between 0 and 1

1 radian = 57.29578 degrees. N radians = N * 57.29578 degrees.	To convert 2.5 radians to degrees, multiply 2.5 by 57.29578. The product is about 143 degrees.
1 degree = 0.01745 radians. N degrees = N * 0.01745 radians.	To convert 180 degrees to radians, multiply 180 by 0.01745. The result is 3.14 radians (exactly equal to π).

Exponentiation Functions

The LOG(X), EXP(X), and SQR(X) functions deal with raising a number to a particular power.

EXP (X)

The exponential, or EXP (X), function makes the calculation EXP(X) = e^x. The constant e is equal to 2.718. We will not dwell on e, but it is useful in advanced topics in science, mathematics, and business statistics.

LOG(X)

The **natural logarithm,** or LOG(X), function is the reverse of the EXP(X) function. For example, if X = e^y, then LOG(X) = Y. In other words, Y (the LOG of X) is the power e is raised to in order to find X. If we know X but need Y, we can use the following BASIC statement to find it: 10 Y = LOG(X)

SQR (X)

The square root, or SQR(X), function determines the square root of an argument. In most BASIC implementations, the argument must be a positive number. For example,

X	SQR(X)
4	2
16	4
11.56	3.4

INT(X)

The integer, or INT(X), function is used to compute the greatest integer less than or equal to the value specified as the argument. The integer function does not round a number to the nearest integer. If the argument is a positive value with digits to the right of the decimal point, the digits are truncated (cut off). For example,

X	INT(X)
8	8
5.34	5
16.9	16

Be careful when the argument is a negative number. Remember the number line:

The farther left you go, the less value the number has. For example,

X	INT(X)
−2	−2
−2.5	−3
−6.3	−7

Using INT (X) to Round. Although the INT (X) function does not round by itself, it can be used in an expression that rounds to the nearest integer, tenth, hundredth, or to any degree of accuracy wanted. The program in Figure 7–1 rounds a number to the nearest integer and the nearest tenth. Since the INT (X) function returns the greatest integer less than or equal to the argument, it is necessary to add 0.5 to the argument to round to the nearest integer (see line 110). Line 115 rounds the same number to the nearest tenth. We add 0.05 to A and then multiply that result by 10. The INT (X) function is then applied, and the result is divided by 10.

SGN(X)

The sign or SGN(X), function yields one of three possible values. If $X > 0$, $SGN(X) = +1$; if $X = 0$, $SGN(X) = 0$; and if $X < 0$, $SGN(X) = -1$. For example,

Figure 7–1 ROUNDING PROGRAM

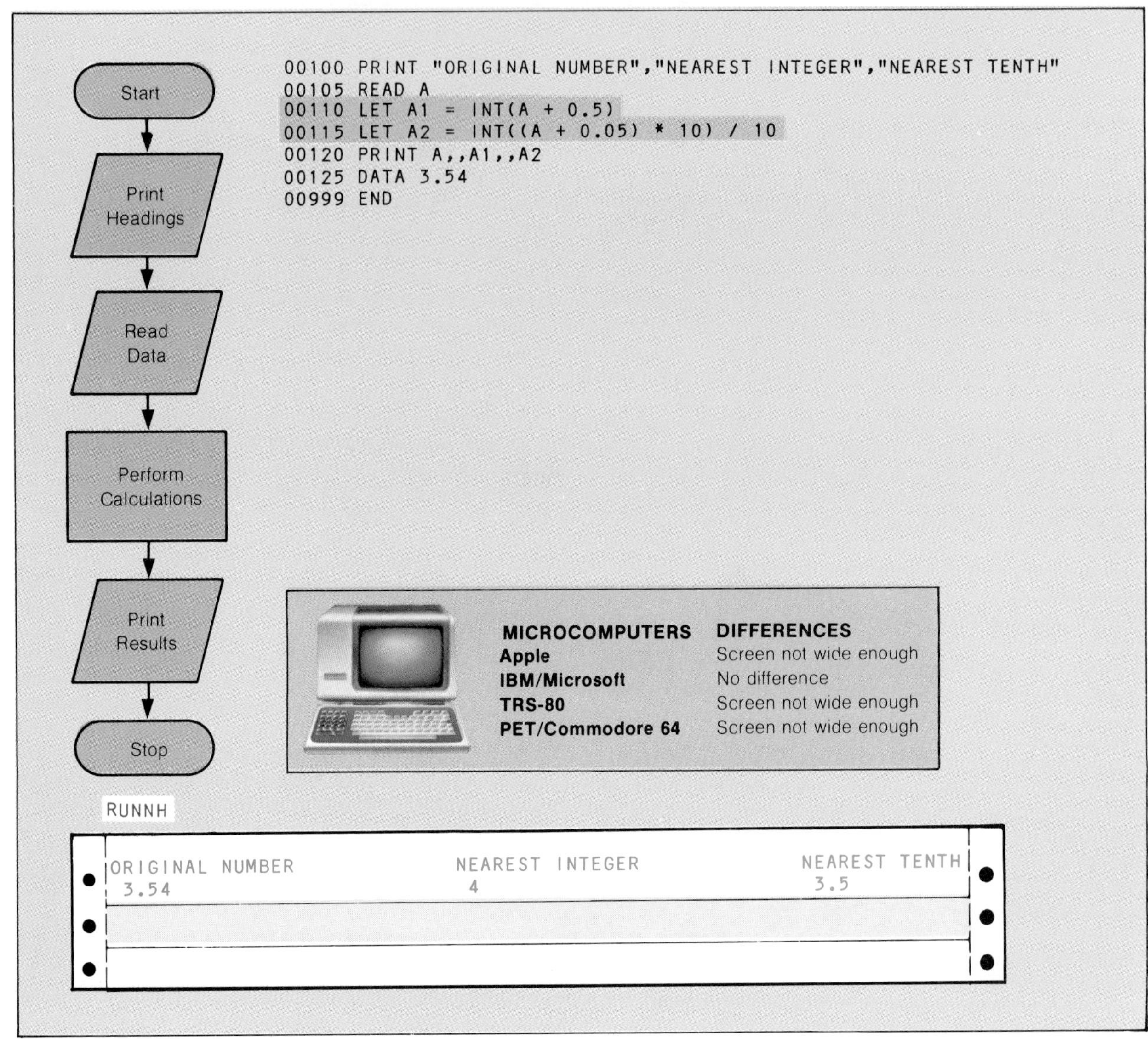

Start
Print Headings
Read Data
Perform Calculations
Print Results
Stop
00100 PRINT "ORIGINAL NUMBER","NEAREST INTEGER","NEAREST TENTH"
00105 READ A
00110 LET A1 = INT(A + 0.5)
00115 LET A2 = INT((A + 0.05) * 10) / 10
00120 PRINT A,,A1,,A2
00125 DATA 3.54
00999 END
MICROCOMPUTERS DIFFERENCES
Apple Screen not wide enough
IBM/Microsoft No difference
TRS-80 Screen not wide enough
PET/Commodore 64 Screen not wide enough
RUNNH
ORIGINAL NUMBER NEAREST INTEGER NEAREST TENTH
3.54 4 3.5

X	SGN(X)
8.34	+1
0	0
−3.5	−1
0.5	+1

This function might be used to quickly identify overdrawn accounts at a bank, as shown in Figure 7–2. After an account number and balance are

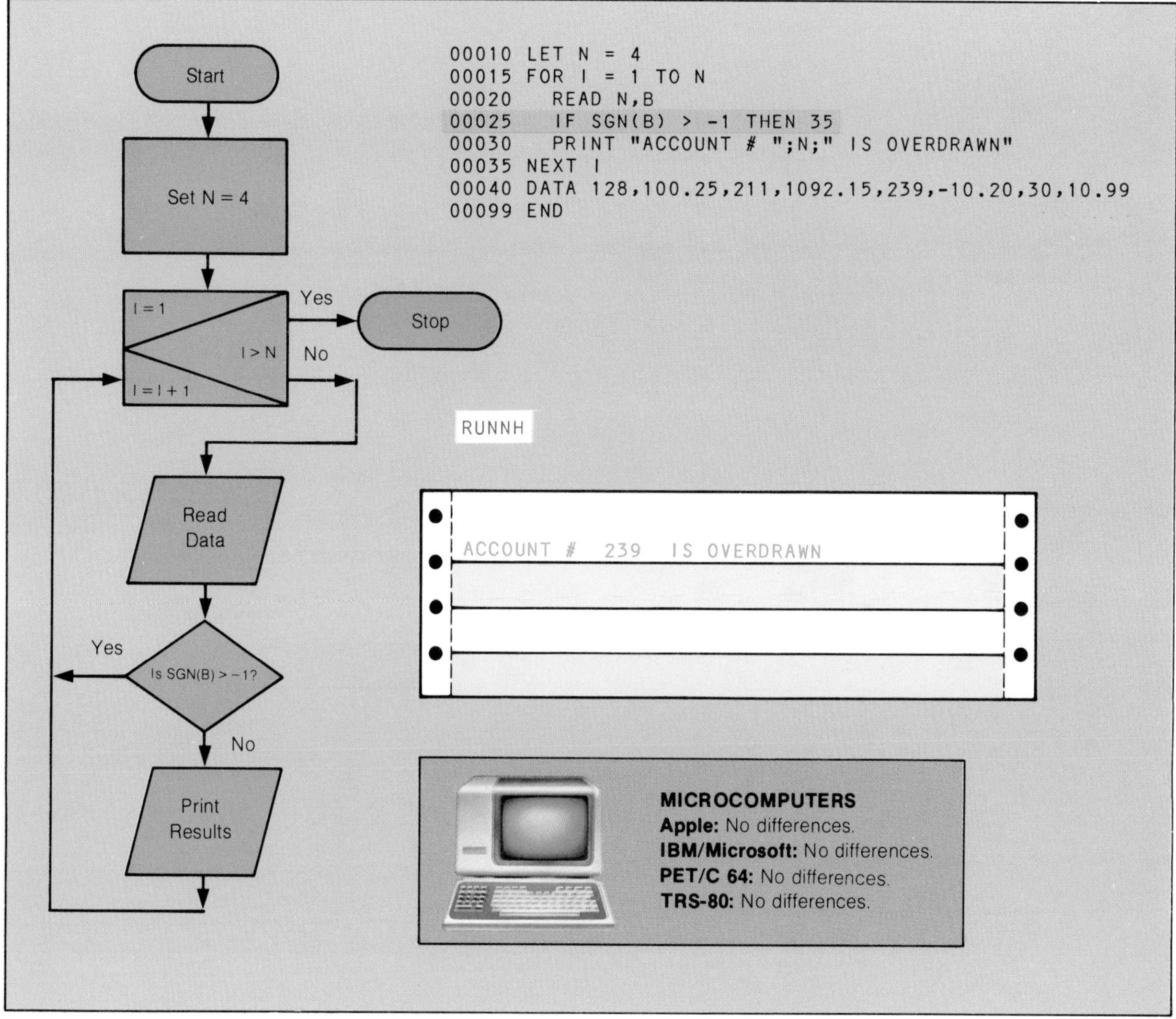
Start
Set N = 4
I = 1
I > N
I = I + 1
Yes
No
Stop
Read Data
Is SGN(B) > −1?
Yes
No
Print Results
00010 LET N = 4
00015 FOR I = 1 TO N
00020 READ N,B
00025 IF SGN(B) > -1 THEN 35
00030 PRINT "ACCOUNT # ";N;" IS OVERDRAWN"
00035 NEXT I
00040 DATA 128,100.25,211,1092.15,239,-10.20,30,10.99
00099 END
RUNNH
ACCOUNT # 239 IS OVERDRAWN
MICROCOMPUTERS
Apple: No differences.
IBM/Microsoft: No differences.
PET/C 64: No differences.
TRS-80: No differences.

Figure 7-2 OVERDRAWN ACCOUNTS PROGRAM

read, the computer checks to see whether the balance is negative (line 25). If the balance is negative, the computer prints the overdrawn message; otherwise, the next account is read.

ABS(X)

The absolute value, or ABS(X), function returns the absolute value of the argument. The absolute value is always positive, even if the argument is a negative value. For example,

Figure 7–3 AUDIT SEARCH PROGRAM

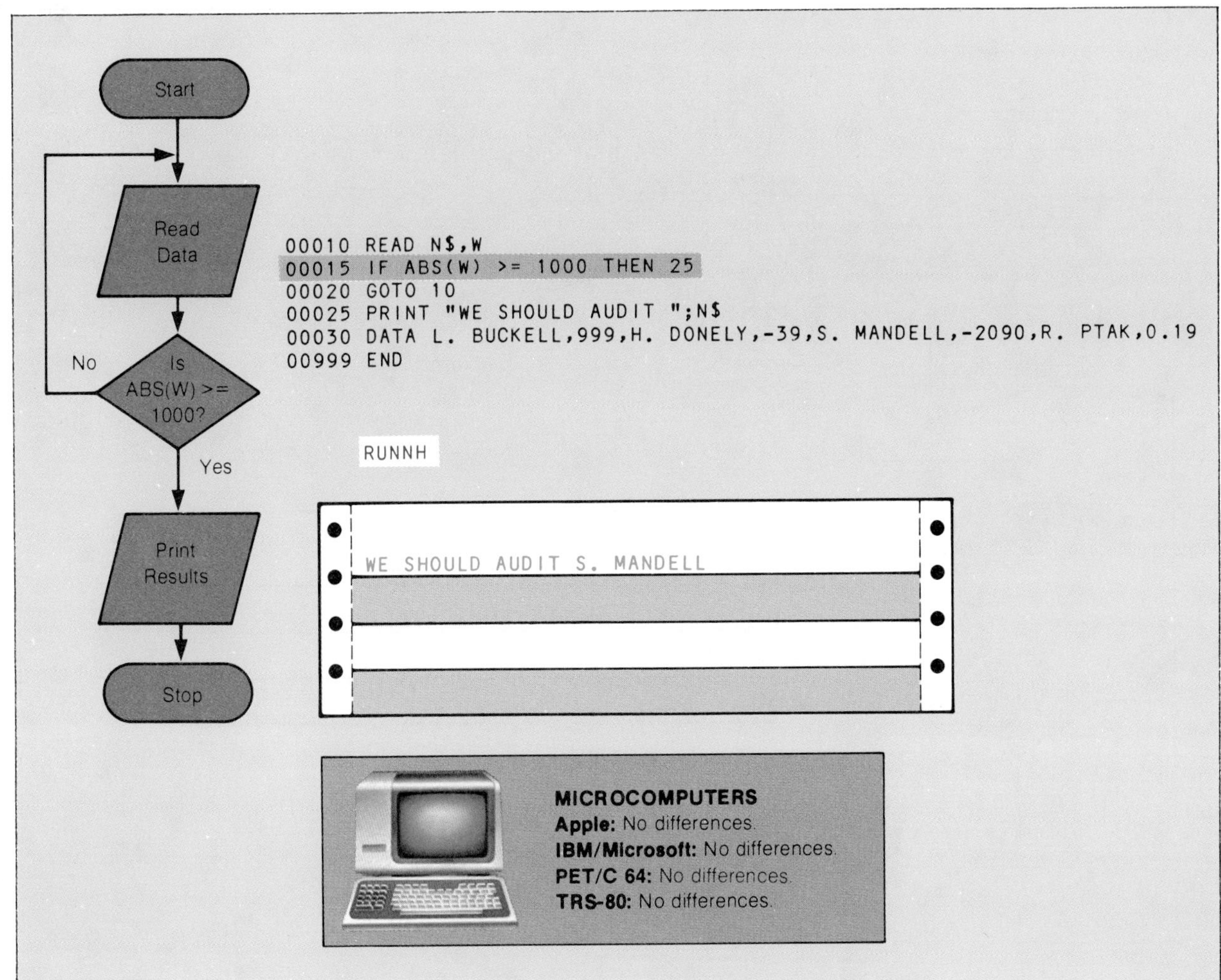
Start
Read Data
No
Is ABS(W) >= 1000?
Yes
Print Results
Stop
00010 READ N$,W
00015 IF ABS(W) >= 1000 THEN 25
00020 GOTO 10
00025 PRINT "WE SHOULD AUDIT ";N$
00030 DATA L. BUCKELL,999,H. DONELY,-39,S. MANDELL,-2090,R. PTAK,0.19
00999 END
RUNNH
WE SHOULD AUDIT S. MANDELL
MICROCOMPUTERS
Apple: No differences.
IBM/Microsoft: No differences.
PET/C 64: No differences.
TRS-80: No differences.

X	ABS(X)
−2	2
0	0
3.54	3.54
−2.68	2.68

We can use this function to identify all values that differ from a given value. For example, the Internal Revenue Service may want to know which individuals owe the government a substantial sum or are owed a substantial sum by the government. Figure 7–3 shows how the absolute value function might be used to help identify these individuals. Line 15 tests for users who either owe at least $1,000 or are being refunded at least $1,000.

RND

The randomize, or RND, function is used to generate a random number between 0 and 1. The term **random** means that any value between 0 and 1 is equally likely to occur. This function is especially important in applications involving statistics, computer simulations, and games. Some systems require that the RND function be used with an argument; other systems do not (see the "Random Numbers" box).

We can use the RND function to generate numbers greater than 1 by using it with other mathematical operations (see Figure 7–4). Suppose we need a random number between 10 and 20 instead of between 0 and 1. Line 15 in Figure 7–4 computes a random number between R1 (the lower limit in a selected range) and R2 (the upper limit in the range).

Line 10 has two numbers read into memory. In line 15, the computer subtracts R2 from R1. The result is multiplied by a random number generated by the RND function. Finally, that product is added to R2. Line 20 finds the integer of R.

Figure 7–4 RANDOM NUMBER PROGRAM

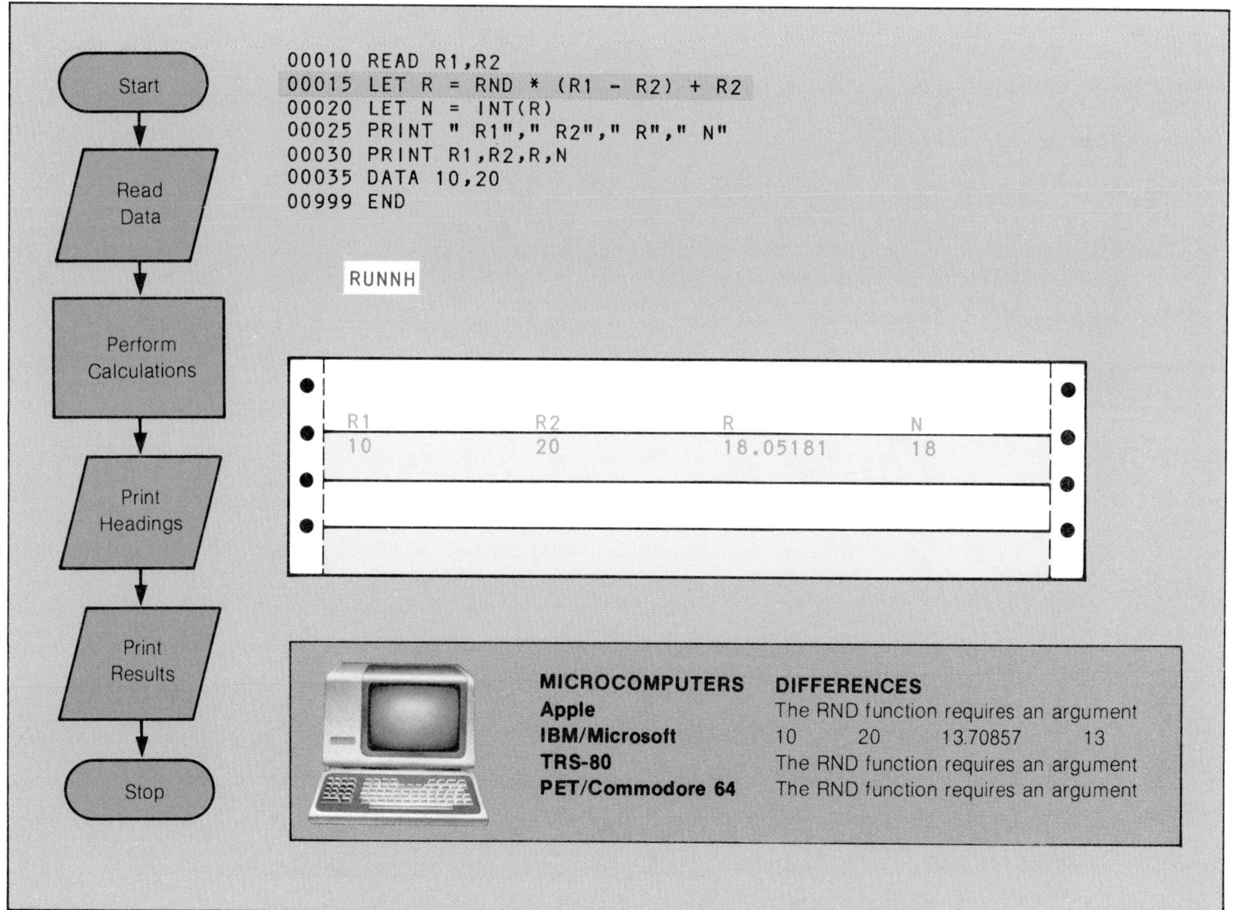

```
00010 READ R1,R2
00015 LET R = RND * (R1 - R2) + R2
00020 LET N = INT(R)
00025 PRINT " R1"," R2"," R"," N"
00030 PRINT R1,R2,R,N
00035 DATA 10,20
00999 END

RUNNH

R1        R2        R           N
10        20        18.05181    18
```


MICROCOMPUTERS	DIFFERENCES
Apple	The RND function requires an argument
IBM/Microsoft	10 20 13.70857 13
TRS-80	The RND function requires an argument
PET/Commodore 64	The RND function requires an argument

Random Numbers

At first it might not seem hard to make up numbers whose values are arrived at only by chance. However, this task is difficult for machines with precise structure and logic (such as computers). The various computer manufacturers use different methods for obtaining random numbers. You can obtain random numbers between 0 and 1 using each of our computers as follows.

DECSYSTEM 20

Two statements are needed with the DECSYSTEM 20 computer. The RND function needs no argument. The function used alone will give the same numbers each time a program is run; therefore, they are not truly random. Once you know that a program works the way you want it to, you should precede the statement containing RND by a RANDOMIZE statement. Now each time the program runs, RND will give a different unpredictable number. An example follows:

```
00025 RANDOMIZE
        .
        .
        .
00070 LET X = RND
```

Apple

Only one statement is needed with the Apple microcomputer. The RND function needs an argument. A positive argument will return a random real number greater than or equal to 0 and less than 1. For example,

```
10 LET X = RND(3)
```

If the argument is 0,

```
10 LET X = RND(0)
```

the most recently generated random number will be returned. A negative argument generates a particular random number that is the same every time RND is used with that argument. If an RND statement with a positive argument follows an RND statement with a negative argument, it will generate a particular, repeatable sequence of random numbers.

LEARNING CHECK

1. ________ are functions that have been built into the BASIC language.
2. In BASIC, the argument of a function can be ________.
   a. a variable
   b. another function
   c. a mathematical expression
   d. all of the above
   e. a and c
3. The functions SIN(X), COS(X), TAN(X), and ATN(X) are called ________.
4. ________ deal with raising a number to a particular power.
5. The ________ function is used to compute the greatest integer less than or equal to the value specified as the argument.
6. The ________ function is used to generate a number between 0 and 1.

Answers

1. Library functions
2. d
3. trigonometric functions
4. Exponentiation functions
5. INT(X)
6. RND

IBM/Microsoft

Two statements are needed to give a truely random result with the IBM/Microsoft microcomputer (works similar to the RND function on the DECSYSTEM 20). The argument for RND is optional. An example follows:

```
15 RANDOMIZE
20 PRINT RND
```

When the program is run, the computer prompts you with: Random number seed (−32768 to 32767)? You must enter a number within this range. Then the processing will continue.

PET/Commodore 64

Two statements are needed to give a truly random result with the PET/Commodore 64 microcomputer. The function RND needs an argument. RND(0) and RND(−N) should precede the use of RND(N). In other words, RND(0) and RND(−N) work much as RANDOMIZE does on the DECSYSTEM 20.
An example follows:

```
40 LET Y = RND(-RND(0))
   .
   .
   .
85 LET X = RND(1)
```

Now X should be a valid random number. Line 40 "seeds" the random number generator.

TRS-80

Two statements are needed with the TRS-80 microcomputer. An argument is needed for RND (you should use 0 to get a number between 0 and 1). An example follows:

```
30 RANDOM
   .
   .
   .
140 LET X = RND(0)
```

User-defined Functions

The definition (DEF) statement can be used by the programmer to define a function not already included in the BASIC language. Once the function has been defined, the programmer can refer to it as a function when necessary. The DEF statement can be placed anywhere before the first reference to it. Its general format is as follows:

line# DEF function name(argument) = expression

The function name consists of the letters FN followed by any one of the twenty-six alphabetic characters. There can be only one argument. However, an argument is not required within the DEF statement. The expression can contain any mathematical operations desired. However a function definition cannot exceed one line.

When the computer encounters line 10 in the following program, it stores in memory the definition for the function FNR. Line 20 initializes B to 5. When the computer encounters line 30, it uses the definition for FNR and substitutes the value of B (5) for X in the expression (X + 20) / 2. The printed result is 12.5:

```
00010 DEF FNR(X) = (X + 20) / 2
00020 LET B = 5
00030 PRINT FNR(B)

RUNNH
12.5
```

Line 100 in Figure 7–5 defines a function to round a number to the nearest hundredth. After the values for name, wage, and hours have been read, the computer is instructed to calculate the salary and round it to the nearest hundredth. This is accomplished by substituting the result of

Figure 7–5 CALCULATING SALARY

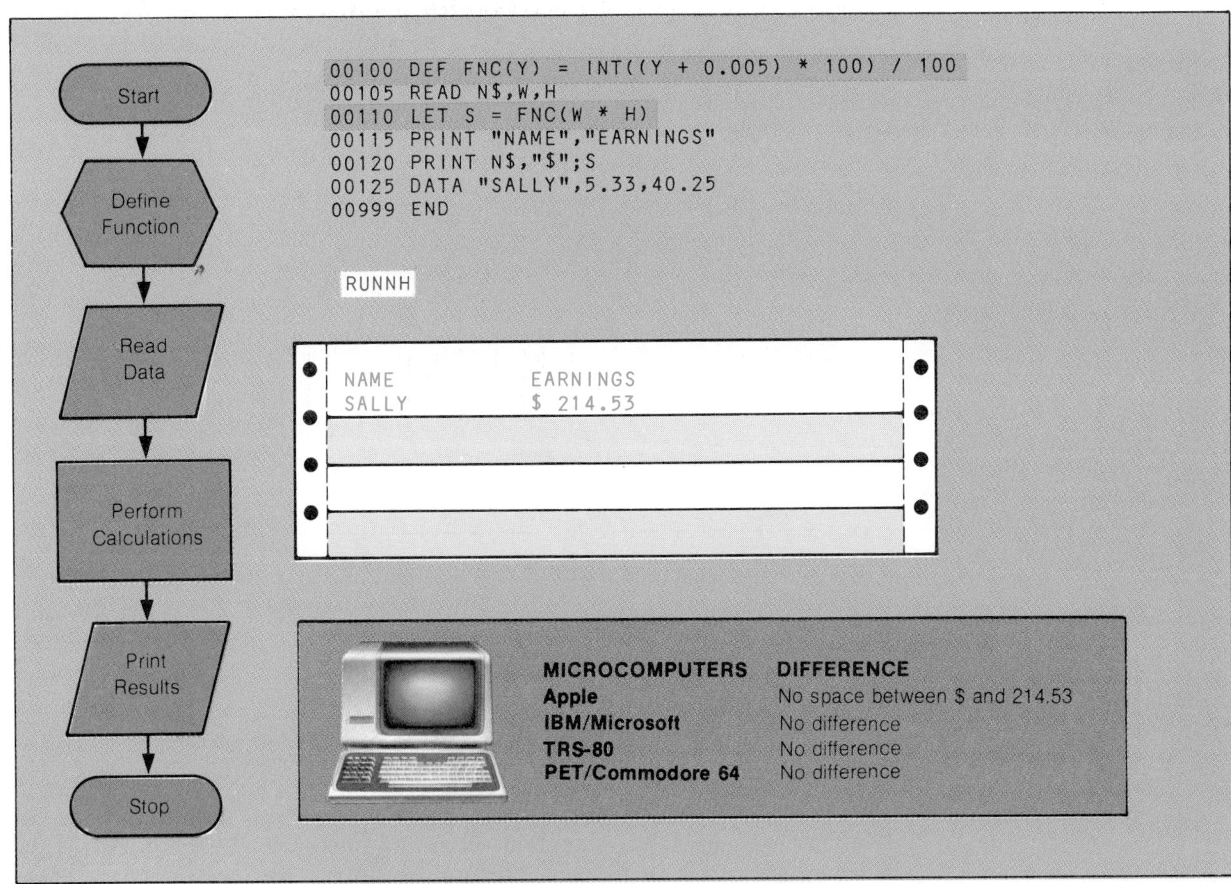

W * HR for Y in the expression defined in line 100. The result is then printed out

---

LEARNING CHECK

1. _______ are functions defined by the programmer that are not already included in the BASIC language library.
2. The DEF statement can be placed _______.
   a. after the reference to the function
   b. anywhere before the first reference to the function
   c. only on the line immediately preceding the reference to the function
   d. none of the above
3. A function definition _______.
   a. cannot exceed one line
   b. may be up to four lines
   c. may be any length

Answers

1. User-defined functions
2. b
3. a

A Programming Problem

The Problem

The ACME Sport Equipment Company manufactures leather basketballs, volleyballs, soccer balls, and softballs. The firm received orders this week for 10,000 baseballs, 5,000 volleyballs, and 250 softballs. The production manager needs to know how much leather will be needed to fill the orders.

Solution Design

If we know the radius of each type of ball ordered, we can figure out the total surface area to be constructed from leather. The formula for computing the surface area of a sphere follows:

$$\text{Surface area} = 4\pi r^2.$$

We can define a function in BASIC to compute this area as follows:

```
FNA(RADIUS) = 4 * 3.1416 * RADIUS ∧ 2
```

The next step is to read the type of ball, its radius, and the number of each to be made. After the surface area is computed, we know how much leather is required to make one ball. By multiplying this value by the number ordered, we know how much leather is needed—in square inches. We must convert this result to square yards by dividing by 1,296 (the number of square inches in a square yard).

Figure 7–6 AREA OF LEATHER SPORT BALLS PROGRAM AND FLOWCHART

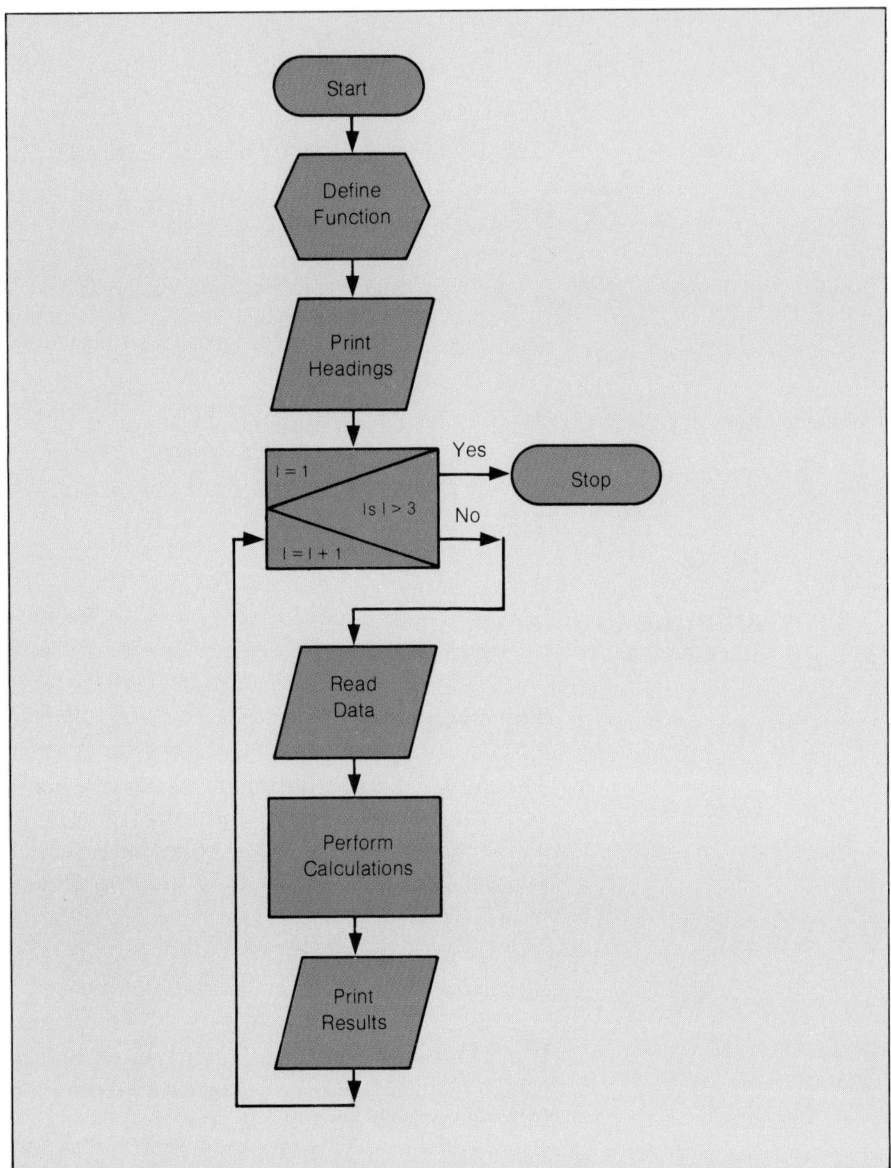

The Program

Line 130 of the program in Figure 7–6 defines a function, FNA, to compute the surface area of a sphere. The next several lines print the headings. Line 165 initiates the FOR and NEXT loop that reads the data, calculates the surface area, converts that result to square yards, and prints the results. In line 175, the programmer refers to FNA to calculate the surface area. Line 205 marks the end of the FOR and NEXT loop.

Figure 7–6 *(continued)*

```
00100 REM *** THE AREA OF LEATHER SPORTS BALLS ***
00105 DATA "BASEBALLS",2,10000,"VOLLEYBALLS",6,5000
00110 DATA "SOFTBALLS",3.5,250
00115 REM *************
00120 REM *** DEFINE FUNCTION TO COMPUTE SURFACE AREA OF BALL ***
00125 REM *************
00130 DEF FNA(X) = 4 * 3.1416 * X ** 2
00135 PRINT
00140 PRINT
00145 PRINT "BALL TYPE","NUMBER","TOTAL AREA"
00150 PRINT ,,"(SQ. YARDS)"
00155 PRINT
00160 REM *** LOOP BEGINS HERE ***
00165 FOR I = 1 TO 3
00170   READ B$,R,N
00175   LET A = FNA(R)
00180   REM *** TOTAL AREA = NUMBER TIMES AREA OF EACH BALL ***
00185   REM *** 1296 CONVERS TO SQUARE YARDS ***
00190   LET T = N * A / 1296
00195   PRINT B$,N,T
00200   PRINT
00205   REM *** LOOP ENDS HERE ***
00210 NEXT I
00999 END
```

```
RUNNH
```

```
BALL TYPE       NUMBER        TOTAL AREA
                              (SQ. YARDS)

BASEBALLS        10000         387.8518

VOLLEYBALLS      5000          1745.333

SOFTBALLS        250           29.69491
```

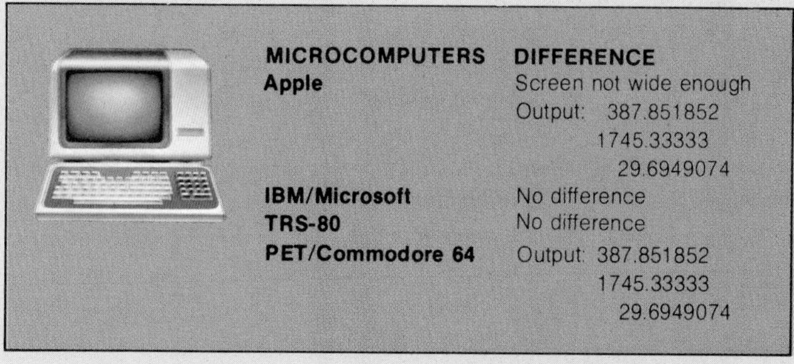

MICROCOMPUTERS	DIFFERENCE
Apple	Screen not wide enough Output: 387.851852 1745.33333 29.6949074
IBM/Microsoft	No difference
TRS-80	No difference
PET/Commodore 64	Output: 387.851852 1745.33333 29.6949074

Summary

- The BASIC language includes several library functions that can make complicated mathematical operations easier to program.
- The trigonometric functions are SIN(X), COS(X), TAN(X), and ATN(X).
- The exponentiation functions are EXP(X), LOG(X), and SQR(X).
- Other mathematical functions are INT(X), SGN(X), ABS(X), and RND.
- It is also possible for the programmer to define functions by using the DEF statement.

Review Questions

1. What are library functions?
2. What are the allowable arguments of a function?
3. Angles, when used as an argument to one of the four trigonometric functions, are measured in ______.
   a. degrees
   b. centimeters
   c. radians
   d. degrees or radians
4. What are the four trigonometric functions?
5. What are the three exponentiation functions?
6. What does the EXP(X) function do?
7. What does the LOG(X) function do?
8. The argument X in SQR(X) can be ______.
   a. any number
   b. any nonnegative number
   c. any positive whole number
   d. any negative number
9. What does the function INT(X) do?
10. What is the result of INT(−3.4)?
11. Write a BASIC statement using the INT(X) function to round a number to the nearest thousandth.
12. What possible values can SGN(X) return?
13. The function ABS(X) always returns ______.
    a. a number greater than or equal to 0
    b. a number less than or equal to 0
    c. a whole number
    d. an even number
14. The RND function generates a random number between what two values?

15. Write a BASIC program using RND to generate a random number between 1 and 25.
16. What BASIC statement is needed to define a user-defined function?
17. What are the rules for naming a user-defined function?
18. How many arguments are allowed for a user-defined function?
19. What limitations, if any, are placed on the length of a function definition?
20. Where is the function definition statement placed within the program?

Debugging Exercises

Identify the following statements and program segments that contain errors, and debug them.

1.
```
00010 READ X
00020 LET Y = COS(X)
00030 PRINT Y
00040 REM *** DATA IS IN DEGREES ***
00050 DATA 60
```

2.
```
00020 READ X
00025 LET Y = SQR(X)
00030 PRINT Y
00035 DATA -169
```

3.
```
00010 READ X
00015 LET Y = LOG(X ^ 2 + 3 * X)
00020 PRINT Y
00025 DATA 3
```

4.
```
00100 INPUT "X = ";X
00110 LET Y = EXP(X,5)
00120 PRINT Y
```

5.
```
00035 READ X
00040 LET Y = INT(ABS(X))
00045 PRINT Y
00050 DATA -7.2
```

6.
```
10 DEF FNA(B,H) = .5 * B1 * H1
20 INPUT "BASE AND HEIGHT OF TRIANGLE: ";B1,H1
30 LET AREA = FNA(B1,H1)
40 PRINT AREA
```

7.
```
00010 READ A
00020 PRINT FNS(A)
00030 DEF FNS(X) = ABS(X) - 256
00040 DATA 5
```

8.
```
00025 REM *** HEADS OR TAILS ***
00030 DEF FND = RND * (1 - 2) + 2
00035 FOR I = 1 TO 5
00040    PRINT INT(FNP + 0.5)
00045 NEXT I
```

9.
```
10 READ A1
15 DEF TAX(A) = A * .06
20 LET T = A1 + TAX(A1)
25 PRINT T
30 DATA 5.99
```

10.
```
10 DEF FNVOL(S) = S ^ 3
20 INPUT "SIDE OF CUBE = ";S1
30 LET V = FNVOL(S1)
40 PRINT V
```

Additional Programming Problems

1. The book company you work for needs a table of square roots and natural logarithms of the numbers from 1 to 100 for its new edition. Write a program to generate such a table. Round each entry to four decimal places.
2. The new Midwestern Trust Bank has timed certificates available with 8 percent interest compounded continuously. Write a program to compute the new balance for the customers listed in the following table. The formula for interest compounded continuously is $A = Pe^{rt}$, where A is the final amount, P is the principal, e is the constant 2.718, r is the interest rate, and t is time in years. Be sure to round to the nearest cent (hundredth) before printing.

Name	Principal	Time (Years)
Joe Brenner	$10,000	3
Barb Spangler	3,000	5
Beverly Brice	7,000	2
Dan Yarnell	5,000	4
Jim Brown	12,000	1

3. The local radio station surveyed ten people in its listening area to determine their opinion on a new program format. The following chart summarizes the results. Negative responses indicate dislike; 0, no opinion; and positive responses, approval. Using the SGN(X) function, determine the percentage with favorable responses, the percentage with no opinion, and the percentage with negative responses. Also determine the average response.

Survey Data +2 +2 −1 0 +2 −2 −1 0 +1 +1

4. Write a program to compute the sine, cosine, and tangent of the angles 30, 45, 60, 90, 120, 135, 150, 180, 210, 225, 240, 270, 300, 315, and 360 degrees, as well as print a table. Use a function to first convert the angles to radians. (*Remember:* 1 degree = 0.01745 radians.)
5. You are computerizing the game of Yahtzee. Write a program to simulate the rolling of the five dice. (*Hint:* Use a function to simulate the rolling of a single die, and call it five times.)
6. The local weather reporter needs a program to print the high, low, and average temperature for the day in degrees Celsius. The reporter takes a varying number of temperature readings in degrees Fahrenheit. (This number is recorded first in the DATA statement.) Write a program to accomplish this task, using a function to perform the conversion from degrees Fahrenheit to degrees Celsius. On this particular day, the temperature readings were 54, 62, 73, 80, 83, 81, 75, and 60. [Remember: The conversion formula is °C = 5/9(°F − 32).]

8 Subroutines and String Functions

Outline

Objectives

After reading this chapter, the student should be able to do the following:

- Understand and use subroutines.
- Understand and use the STOP statement with subroutines and exception handling.
- Understand and use the string functions to manipulate strings.

Overview

Sometimes it is necessary to have the computer execute an identical sequence of instructions at several different points in a program. The programmer need not write the set of instructions over and over again; instead, it can be placed in a subroutine. A **subroutine** is a sequence of statements, typically located at the end of the main program body; it performs a particular function and may be used in several different parts of the main program. By doing this, the instructions need only be written once.

For example, Harry's Haberdashery is having a year-end clearance sale offering a 25 percent discount on all men's clothing. Harry would like a report that lists the sale price for each item, the amount of tax per item (the tax rate is 6 percent), and the total price of the item (including tax). When writing the solution to this problem, we find that the same procedure is needed to round the discounted price and amount of tax to the nearest penny. Instead of writing this rounding procedure two different times, we have written a subroutine that will be executed the required number of times. The program will transfer control to the subroutine and back to the main program through the use of two statements: GOSUB and RETURN. These statements, along with the STOP statement, the ON/GOSUB statement, and the string functions, will be discussed in this chapter.

The GOSUB Statement

The GOSUB statement is used to transfer the flow of control from the main logic of a program to a subroutine. The general format of the GOSUB statement is as follows:

line# GOSUB line#

The line number following GOSUB identifies the first statement of the subroutine.

The GOSUB statement is something like an unconditional GOTO statement. The difference is that the GOSUB command also makes the computer remember where to return after the subroutine has been executed. Here is a typical example of a GOSUB statement:

```
00200 GOSUB 1000
```

Figure 8–1 uses GOSUB statements in lines 195 and 225. Notice the line number of the subroutine. Subroutines often are assigned distinctive line numbers so that they are easier to locate. Although subroutines may be placed anywhere in a program, they are usually at the end, with a line number quite a bit higher than the line numbers in the main program. This leaves sufficient room for statements to be added to the main program.

The RETURN Statement

After processing within a subroutine has been completed, control must be transferred back to the main logic flow of the program. That is accomplished by the RETURN statement. The general format of the RETURN statement is as follows:

line# RETURN

No line number need follow RETURN, because the BASIC interpreter remembers to return to the statement immediately following the most recently executed GOSUB statement. For example,

```
00050 GOSUB 500
00060 PRINT X
.
.
.
00500 REM *** SUBROUTINE ***
.
.
.
00550 RETURN
```

Figure 8–1 CLOTHING DISCOUNT PROGRAM

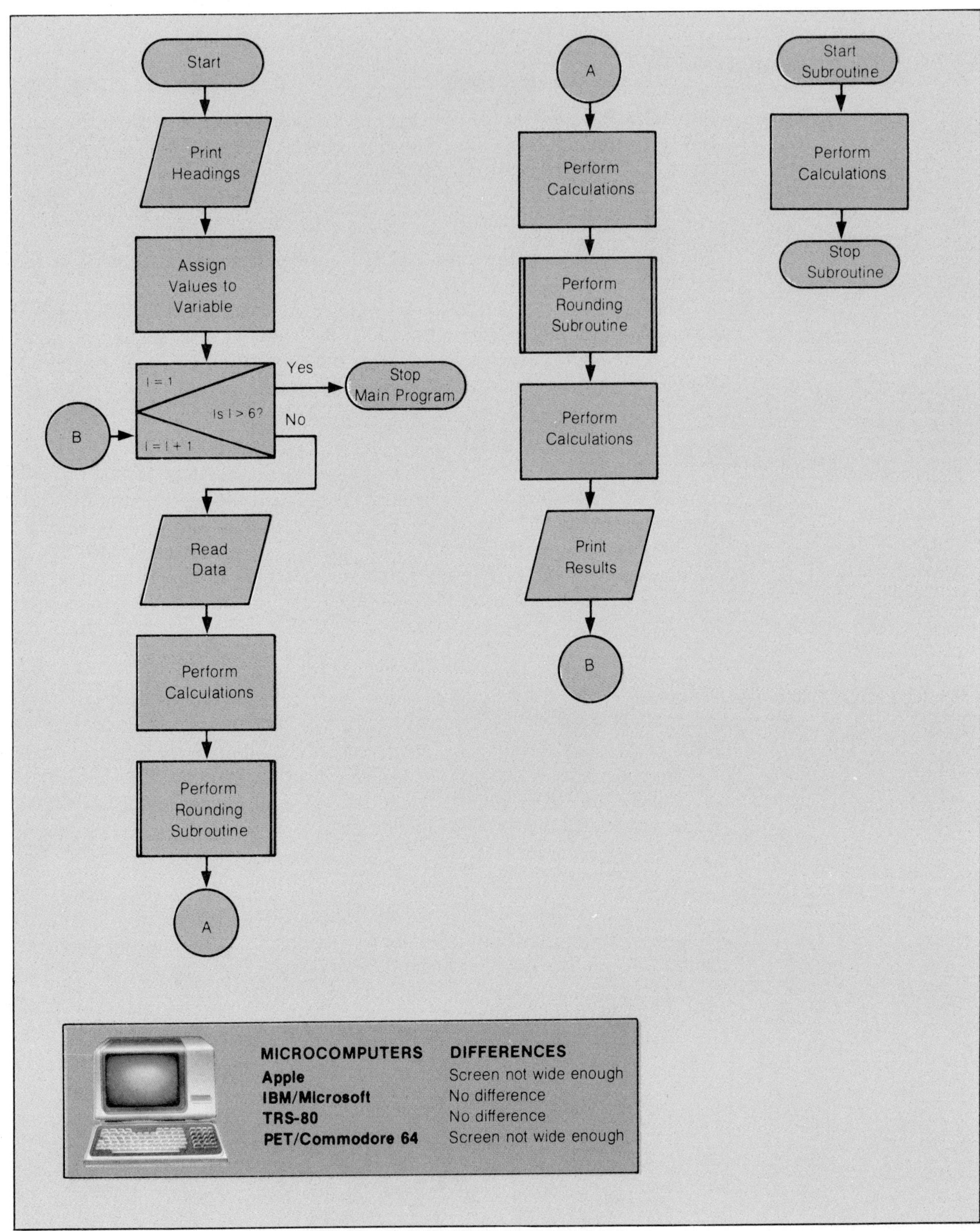

MICROCOMPUTERS	DIFFERENCES
Apple	Screen not wide enough
IBM/Microsoft	No difference
TRS-80	No difference
PET/Commodore 64	Screen not wide enough

Figure 8–1 *(continued)*

```
00100 REM *** THIS PROGRAM GIVES DISCOUNT PRICES ***
00105 REM *** ROUNDED TO THE PENNY ***
00110 DATA "SUITS",189.95,"SHIRTS",14.99,"SLACKS",21.50
00115 DATA "SOCKS",2.19,"UNDERWEAR",6.49,"TIES",9.99
00120 PRINT
00125 PRINT
00130 PRINT
00135 PRINT "ITEM","SALE PRICE","TAX","TOTAL"
00140 REM *** DISCOUNT RATE = 25% ***
00145 LET D = .25
00150 REM *** TAX RATE = 6% ***
00155 LET R = .06
00160 REM *** BEGIN LOOP HERE ***
00165 FOR I = 1 TO 6
00170   READ N$,P1
00175   LET P2 = P1 - D * P1
00180   REM *** NEW PRICE ***
00185   LET X = P2
00190   REM *** ROUND DISCOUNT PRICE ***
00195   GOSUB 1000
00200   LET P2 = X
00210   LET T = P2 * R
00215   LET X = T
00220   REM *** ROUND TAX ***
00225   GOSUB 1000
00230   LET T = X
00235   REM *** TOTAL = NEW PRICE + TAX ***
00240   LET T1 = P2 + T
00245   PRINT
00250   PRINT N$,"$";P2,"$";T,"$";T1
00255   REM *** END OF LOOP ***
00260 NEXT I
00265 PRINT
00270 PRINT
00275 STOP
01000 REM ***************
01005 REM *** SUBROUTINE TO ROUND TO NEAREST CENT ***
01010 REM ***************
01015 LET X = 100 * X + .05
01020 LET X = (INT(X)) / 100
01025 RETURN
09999 END
```

RUNNH

ITEM	SALE PRICE	TAX	TOTAL
SUITS	$ 142.46	$ 8.55	$ 151.01
SHIRTS	$ 11.24	$ 0.67	$ 11.91
SLACKS	$ 16.13	$ 0.97	$ 17.1
SOCKS	$ 1.64	$ 0.1	$ 1.74
UNDERWEAR	$ 4.87	$ 0.29	$ 5.16
TIES	$ 7.49	$ 0.45	$ 7.94

STOP at line 00275 of MAIN PROGRAM

The RETURN statement in line 550 sends control back to the instruction following the GOSUB statement that called the subroutine, so the RETURN statement in line 550 sends the computer back to line 60. The RETURN statement in line 1025 of Figure 8–1 will return control to line 200 if the subroutine was called in line 195. If the subroutine was called in line 225, control will be returned to line 230.

The STOP Statement

The STOP statement halts execution of a program; it is placed wherever a logical end to a program should occur. The general format of the STOP statement follows:

```
line# STOP
```

The STOP statement differs from the END statement in that STOP can appear as often as necessary in a program, whereas the END statement can appear only once and must have the highest line number in the program.

Using STOP with Subroutines

One of the major uses of the STOP statement is with subroutines. For convenience, subroutines generally are placed near the end of a program, but the subroutine may be referred to several times in the program. A STOP statement usually is placed just before the beginning of the first subroutine to prevent unnecessary execution of the subroutine when the computer comes to the logical end of the program. Figure 8–1 illustrates how the STOP statement is used before subroutines (line 275).

Using STOP with Exception Handling

Many programs contain **exception-handling instructions.** These sequences of statements help the computer prevent the input of invalid data, which is referred to as a **garbage in—garbage out error.** The STOP statement can be used to stop execution of a program after such a sequence has been executed.

Figure 8–2 calculates the common logarithm of a number. Since the computer can find the logarithms of positive numbers only, the program includes an exception-handling instruction in line 155. If the user of the program enters a number less than or equal to 0, the computer will branch to line 240, print an error message, and stop processing. Notice that this program also contains a stop statement in line 220; this is the logical end of the main program. In lines 205 through 215, the user is directed to input Y to continue finding the logarithms of numbers. If the user does not wish to continue finding the logarithms of numbers, he or she types N, and program execution ends. The STOP statement prevents subsequent lines from being executed (and thus prevents the error message from being printed unnecessarily).

Figure 8–2 EXCEPTION HANDLING

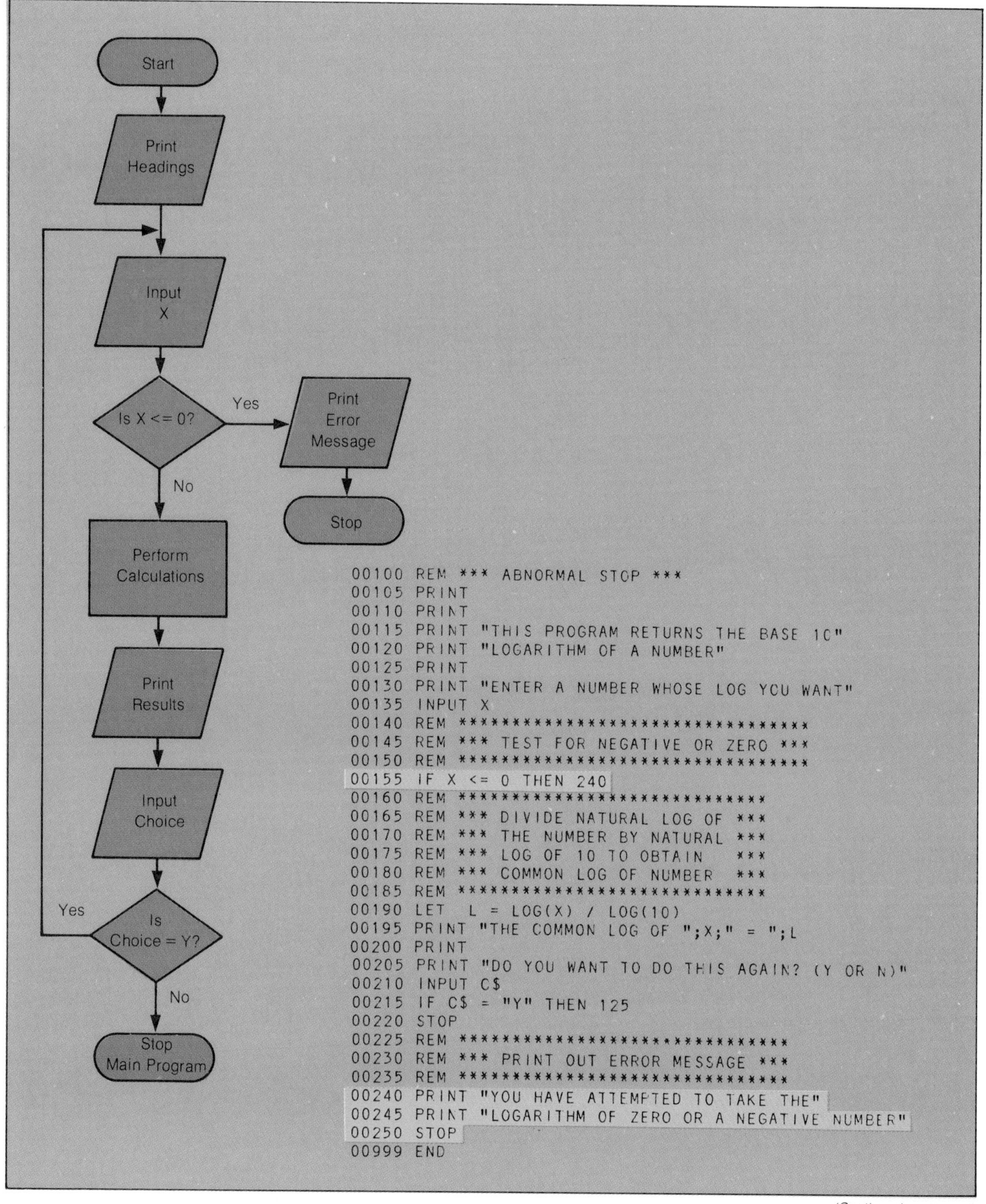


```
00100 REM *** ABNORMAL STOP ***
00105 PRINT
00110 PRINT
00115 PRINT "THIS PROGRAM RETURNS THE BASE 10"
00120 PRINT "LOGARITHM OF A NUMBER"
00125 PRINT
00130 PRINT "ENTER A NUMBER WHOSE LOG YOU WANT"
00135 INPUT X
00140 REM *********************************
00145 REM *** TEST FOR NEGATIVE OR ZERO ***
00150 REM *********************************
00155 IF X <= 0 THEN 240
00160 REM *****************************
00165 REM *** DIVIDE NATURAL LOG OF ***
00170 REM *** THE NUMBER BY NATURAL ***
00175 REM *** LOG OF 10 TO OBTAIN   ***
00180 REM *** COMMON LOG OF NUMBER  ***
00185 REM *****************************
00190 LET  L = LOG(X) / LOG(10)
00195 PRINT "THE COMMON LOG OF ";X;" = ";L
00200 PRINT
00205 PRINT "DO YOU WANT TO DO THIS AGAIN? (Y OR N)"
00210 INPUT C$
00215 IF C$ = "Y" THEN 125
00220 STOP
00225 REM ******************************
00230 REM *** PRINT OUT ERROR MESSAGE ***
00235 REM ******************************
00240 PRINT "YOU HAVE ATTEMPTED TO TAKE THE"
00245 PRINT "LOGARITHM OF ZERO OR A NEGATIVE NUMBER"
00250 STOP
00999 END
```

(Continued next page)

Figure 8–2 *(continued)*

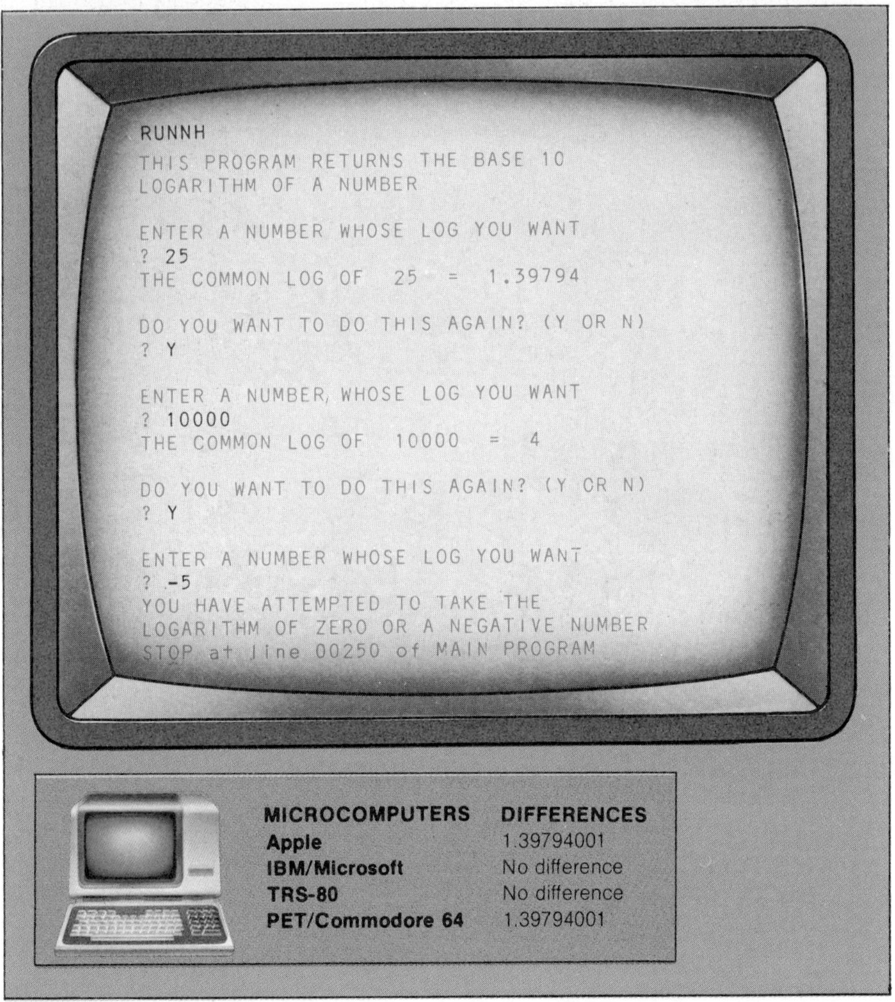

RUNNH
THIS PROGRAM RETURNS THE BASE 10
LOGARITHM OF A NUMBER
ENTER A NUMBER WHOSE LOG YOU WANT
? 25
THE COMMON LOG OF 25 = 1.39794
DO YOU WANT TO DO THIS AGAIN? (Y OR N)
? Y
ENTER A NUMBER WHOSE LOG YOU WANT
? 10000
THE COMMON LOG OF 10000 = 4
DO YOU WANT TO DO THIS AGAIN? (Y OR N)
? Y
ENTER A NUMBER WHOSE LOG YOU WANT
? -5
YOU HAVE ATTEMPTED TO TAKE THE
LOGARITHM OF ZERO OR A NEGATIVE NUMBER
STOP at line 00250 of MAIN PROGRAM
MICROCOMPUTERS DIFFERENCES
Apple 1.39794001
IBM/Microsoft No difference
TRS-80 No difference
PET/Commodore 64 1.39794001

The ON/GOSUB Statement

The ON/GOSUB statement is used to conditionally transfer control to one of several subroutines. Here is the general format for the ON/GOSUB statement:

line# On expression GOSUB line#1, line#2, line#3, . . . line#n

The ON/GOSUB statement operates in the same way as the ON/GOTO statement. The difference is that the line numbers to which control is transferred are not lines in the main program; they are subroutines. The line number to which control is transferred depends on the evaluation of the expression. The arithmetic expression is always evaluated to an integer. If, for instance, the expression evaluates to 2.8 (a real number), the decimal fraction automatically will be truncated so that the expression equals 2. (Some systems round the real number, so this would evaluate to 3. Check your manual.)

The general execution of ON/GOSUB proceeds as follows:

1. If the value of the expression is 1, control is transferred to the subroutine located at line number 1.
2. If the value of the expression is 2, control is transferred to the subroutine located at line number 2.

.

.

.

n. If the value of the expression is n, control is transferred to the subroutine located at line number n.

The following example illustrates the operation of the ON/GOSUB statement:

```
00040 ON X / 10 GOSUB 200,250,300
```

Computer execution is as follows:

If X / 10 = 1, control is passed to the subroutine at line 200.
If X / 10 = 2, control is passed to the subroutine at line 250.
If X / 10 = 3, control is passed to the subroutine at line 300.

The last statement in these subroutines should be RETURN. When the computer executes the RETURN statement, control is transferred back to the line immediately following the last ON/GOSUB or GOSUB statement executed.

If the expression in an ON/GOSUB statement evaluates to a number larger than the number of statements indicated, or if the number evaluated is less than 1 or greater than the maximum allowed, either the program will terminate with an error message or the ON/GOSUB statement will be bypassed. The "ON/GOSUB" box illustrates how various BASIC systems respond to these conditions.

ON/GOSUB Errors

Computer	Action Taken If Number Evaluated Is Greater Than Number of Line Numbers	Action Taken If Number Evaluated Is Less Than 1 or Greater Than Maximum Allowed
DECSYSTEM 20	"?58 ON statement out of range"	"?58 ON statement out of range"
Apple	BASIC continues with the next executable line	"?Illegal quantity error in 20"
IBM/Microsoft	BASIC continues with the next executable line	"Illegal function call" error
TRS-80	BASIC continues with the next executable line	"FC error in 20"
PET/Commodore 64	BASIC continues with the next executable line	"Illegal quantity error in 20"

LEARNING CHECK

1. The ________ statement is used to unconditionally transfer the flow from the main line of the program to a subroutine.
2. After processing within a subroutine, control is transferred back to the main logic flow of the program by the ________ statement.
3. The STOP statement may ________.
   a. be placed wherever a logical end to the program should occur
   b. only appear once in the program and have the highest line number
   c. be placed just before subroutines to prevent unnecessary execution of subroutines
   d. all of the above
   e. a and c
4. The ________ statement is used to conditionally transfer control to one of several subroutines.
5. What is the line number of the subroutine to which control will be transferred when Z = 2?

```
00100 ON Z GOSUB 200,300,400
```

Answers

1. GOSUB
2. RETURN
3. e
4. ON/GOSUB
5. 300

String Functions

Up to this point, we have manipulated numbers but have done little with strings except print them out or compare them in IF and THEN tests. Many business applications require more sophisticated manipulations of strings.

A string is simply a series of alphanumeric characters such as #OJQ$P or HORNBLOWER, H. Usually, BASIC requires that quotation marks be placed around strings.

BASIC string functions allow programmers to modify, **concatenate** (join together), compare, and analyze the composition of strings. These functions are useful for sorting lists of names, finding out subject matter in text, printing mailing lists, and so forth. For example, we can help the computer understand that John J. Simmons is the same as Simmons, John J. The most common string functions are listed in Table 8–1.

The Concatenation Function

It is possible to join strings together using the concatenation function. In business this is often desirable when working with names or addresses. The program in Figure 8–3 demonstrates what happens:

Table 8–1 STRING FUNCTIONS

Basic String Function	Operation	Example
string 1$ + string 2$	Concatenates; joins two strings together	KUNG + FU is KUNGFU
LEN(string)	Finds the length of a string	If H$ is HELLO HOWARD, then LEN(H$) is 12
LEFT$(string,expression)	Returns the number of leftmost characters of a string specified by the expression	LEFT$("ABCDE",2) is AB
RIGHT$(string,expression)	Returns the rightmost characters of a string, starting with the character specified by the expression	RIGHT$("ABCDE",2) is BCDE
MID$(string,expression 1,expression 2)	Starting with the character at expression 1, returns the number of characters specified by expression 2	MID$("ABCDE",3,2) is CD
ASCII(string)	Returns the ASCII code for the first character in the string	If A$ contains DOG, then ASCII(A$) is 68
CHR$(expression)	Returns the string representation of the ASCII code of the expression	If CHR$(F$) > Z, then 20
VAL(expression)	Returns the numeric equivalent of the string expression	X = VAL(H$)
STR$(expression)	Converts a number to its string equivalent	STR$(123) is 123

The LEN Function

The LEN function returns the number of characters in the string. An example of now the LEN function might be used is given in Figure 8–4. In this example, if the value in H$ is less than fourteen characters long, it can be printed within the predefined print zones. Otherwise, we might wish to use the TAB function to print out the next value.

The LEFT$ and RIGHT$ Functions

The LEFT$ function returns the number of characters specified in the argument starting from the beginning of the string. The RIGHT$ function returns a substring, which starts with the character specified by the expression. The LEFT$ and RIGHT$ functions are illustrated in Figure 8–5. In this example, the computer stores a character string in B$. Line 20 tells the computer to print the first six characters of B$. Line 30 tells the computer to start printing with the eighth character. The microcomputers handle the RIGHT$ function differently than the DECSYSTEM 20. On the microcomputers, the instruction

Figure 8-3 CONCATENATION

```
00005 PRINT
00010 PRINT "1 - DUE TO LACK OF INTEREST"
00015 PRINT "2 - ON ACCOUNT OF RAIN"
00020 PRINT "3 - DUE TO LACK OF PLAYERS"
00025 LET A$ = "GAME CALLED "
00030 PRINT
00035 INPUT "ENTER # OF REASON FOR CALLING GAME";X
00040 PRINT
00045 ON X GOTO 50,60,70
00050 PRINT A$ + "DUE TO LACK OF INTEREST"
00055 GOTO 999
00060 PRINT A$ + "ON ACCOUNT OF RAIN"
00065 GOTO 999
00070 PRINT A$ + "DUE TO LACK OF PLAYERS"
00999 END
```

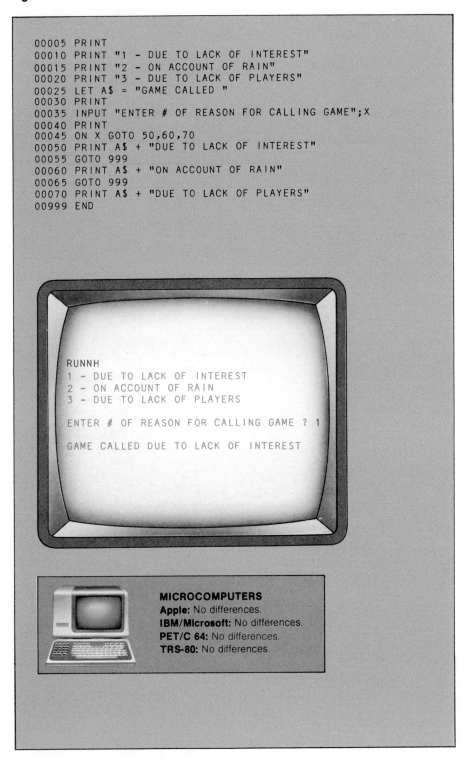

```
RUNNH
1 - DUE TO LACK OF INTEREST
2 - ON ACCOUNT OF RAIN
3 - DUE TO LACK OF PLAYERS

ENTER # OF REASON FOR CALLING GAME ? 1

GAME CALLED DUE TO LACK OF INTEREST
```

MICROCOMPUTERS
Apple: No differences.
IBM/Microsoft: No differences.
PET/C 64: No differences.
TRS-80: No differences.

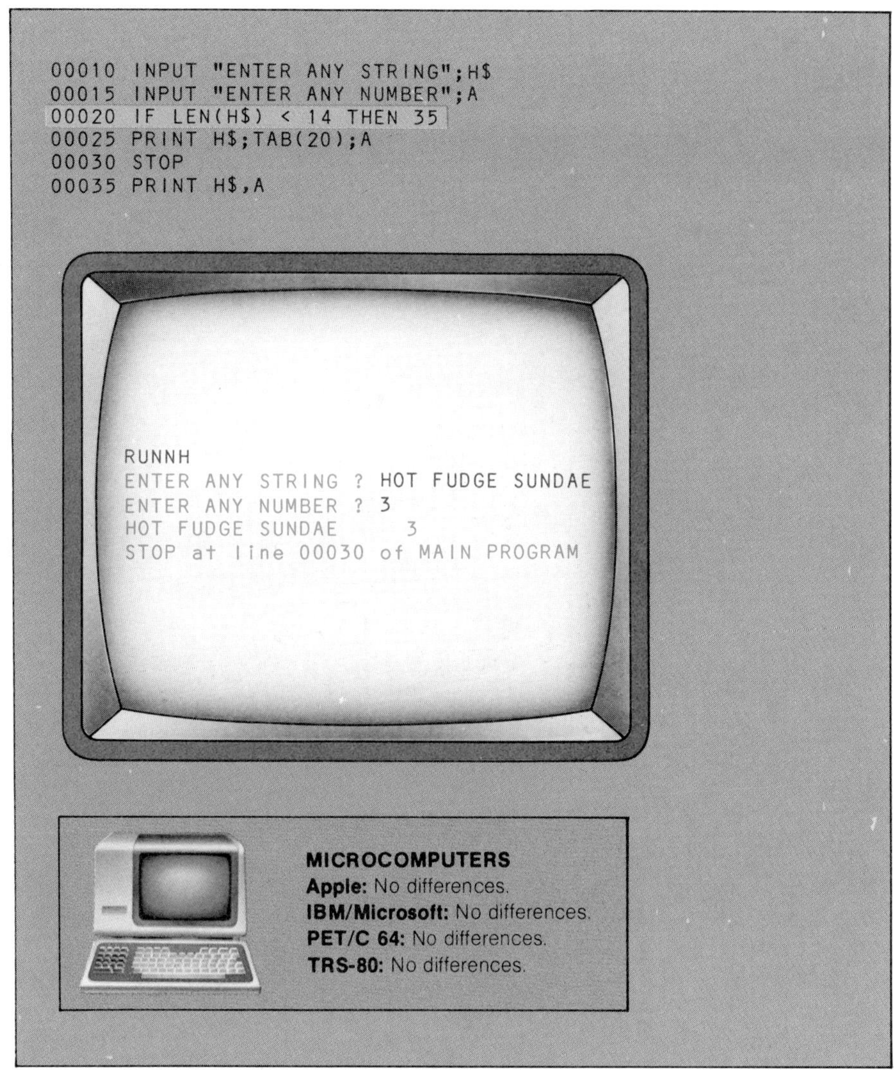
00010 INPUT "ENTER ANY STRING";H$
00015 INPUT "ENTER ANY NUMBER";A
00020 IF LEN(H$) < 14 THEN 35
00025 PRINT H$;TAB(20);A
00030 STOP
00035 PRINT H$,A
RUNNH
ENTER ANY STRING ? HOT FUDGE SUNDAE
ENTER ANY NUMBER ? 3
HOT FUDGE SUNDAE 3
STOP at line 00030 of MAIN PROGRAM
MICROCOMPUTERS
Apple: No differences.
IBM/Microsoft: No differences.
PET/C 64: No differences.
TRS-80: No differences.

Figure 8-4 THE LEN FUNCTION

```
30 PRINT RIGHT$(B$,8)
```

instructs the computer to print the last eight characters of the string. The output would look like this:

```
HAVE A
IFIC DAY
```

The LEFT$ function is often useful when comparing character strings. Suppose a program asks the user to answer a yes or no question but does not specify whether the question should be answered by typing the entire

Figure 8–5 THE LEFT$ AND RIGHT$ FUNCTION

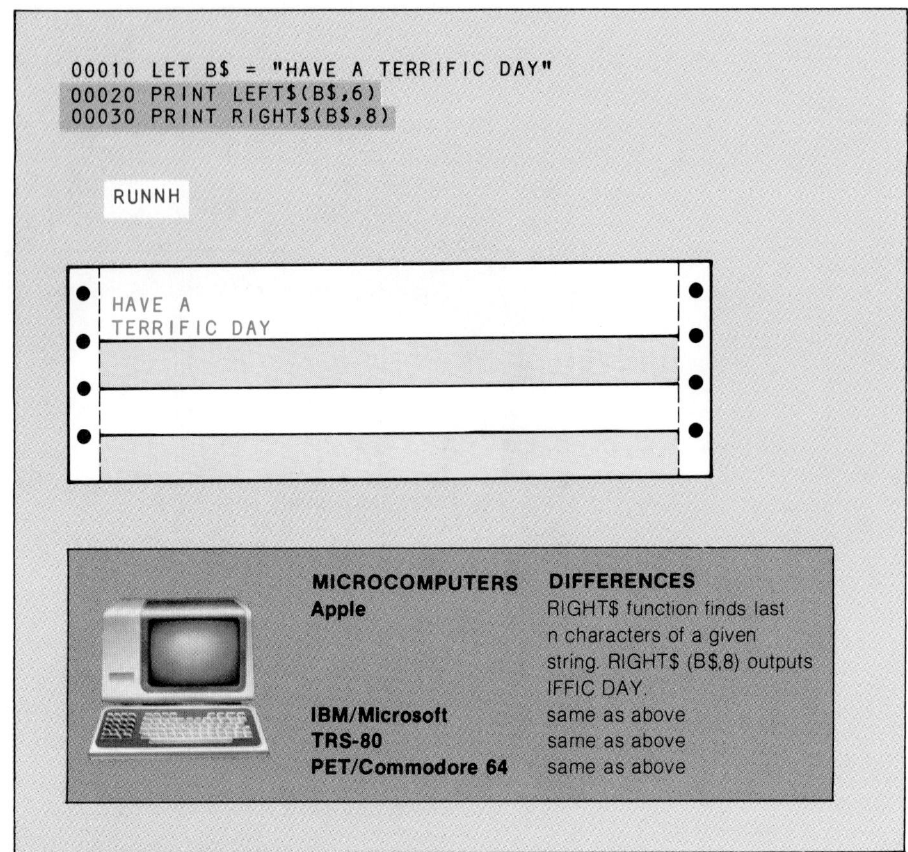
00010 LET B$ = "HAVE A TERRIFIC DAY"
00020 PRINT LEFT$(B$,6)
00030 PRINT RIGHT$(B$,8)
RUNNH
HAVE A
TERRIFIC DAY
MICROCOMPUTERS
DIFFERENCES
Apple
RIGHT$ function finds last n characters of a given string. RIGHT$ (B$,8) outputs IFFIC DAY.
IBM/Microsoft
same as above
TRS-80
same as above
PET/Commodore 64
same as above

word YES or NO or just the first letter Y or N. We can use the LEFT$ function to compare just the first character of the user's response, allowing the user to type either YES/NO or Y/N. The program in Figure 8–6 illustrated this.

The MID$ Function

The MID$ function is more complicated. Here is the general format:

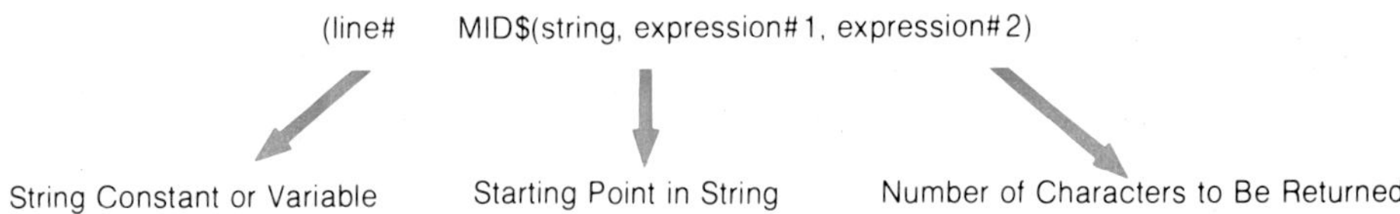
(line#
MID$(string, expression#1, expression#2)
String Constant or Variable
Starting Point in String
Number of Characters to Be Returned

Sometimes expression 2 is omitted; in that case, the characters—from the starting point to the end of the string—are returned. This function is use-

Figure 8–6 COMPARING CHARACTER STRINGS

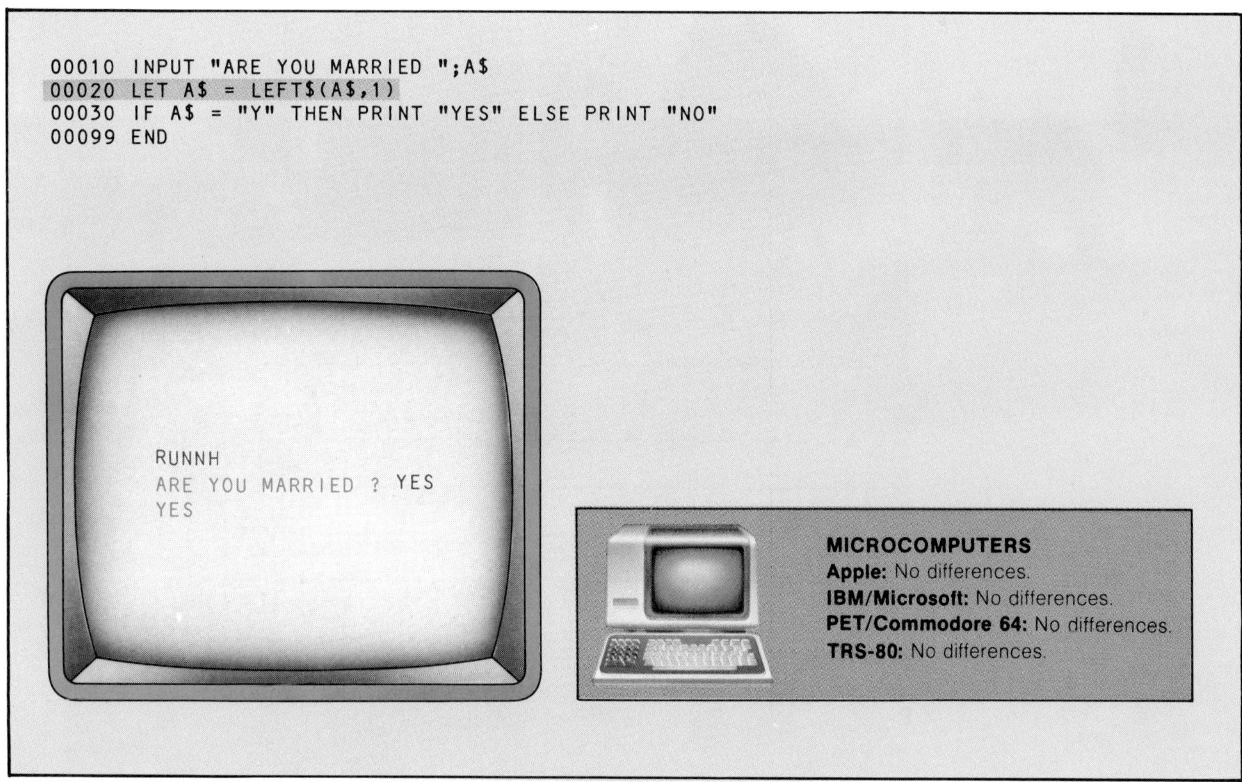
00010 INPUT "ARE YOU MARRIED ";A$
00020 LET A$ = LEFT$(A$,1)
00030 IF A$ = "Y" THEN PRINT "YES" ELSE PRINT "NO"
00099 END
RUNNH
ARE YOU MARRIED ? YES
YES
MICROCOMPUTERS
Apple: No differences.
IBM/Microsoft: No differences.
PET/Commodore 64: No differences.
TRS-80: No differences.

ful when you want to look at some middle characters of a string. For instance, assume you have a file of telephone numbers, and you want to print out only those with an exchange of 352. Here are the telephone numbers:

491–354–1070
491–353–0011
491–352–3520
491–352–1910
491–352–7350
491–353–9822

The program in Figure 8–7 will compare the exchange to "352" and print the telephone numbers that qualify:

The ASCII and CHR$ Functions

The ASCII function—optional on some systems—returns the decimal ASCII value of the first character specified in the string argument. The

Figure 8–7 THE MID$ FUNCTION

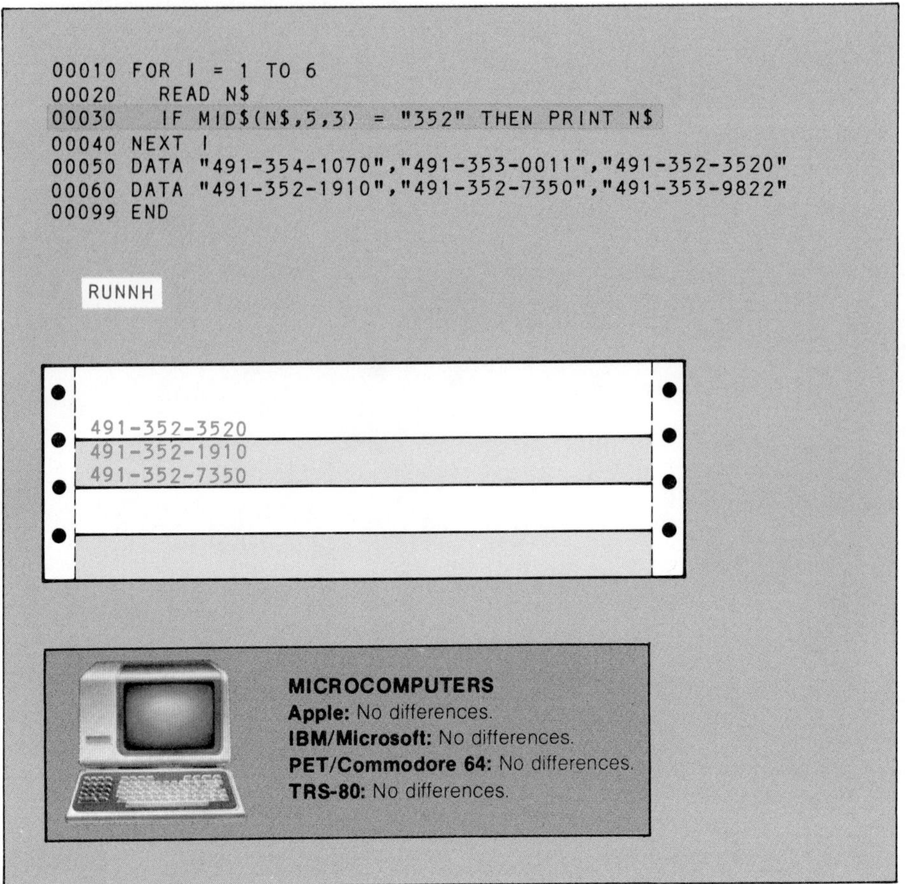
00010 FOR I = 1 TO 6
00020 READ N$
00030 IF MID$(N$,5,3) = "352" THEN PRINT N$
00040 NEXT I
00050 DATA "491-354-1070","491-353-0011","491-352-3520"
00060 DATA "491-352-1910","491-352-7350","491-353-9822"
00099 END
RUNNH
491-352-3520
491-352-1910
491-352-7350
MICROCOMPUTERS
Apple: No differences.
IBM/Microsoft: No differences.
PET/Commodore 64: No differences.
TRS-80: No differences.

argument must be a variable name. Figure 8–8 lists characters and their corresponding ASCII value. An example is shown in Figure 8–9.

The CHR$ function works just the opposite of the ASCII function. This function returns the character that corresponds to the decimal ASCII value. The program in Figure 8–10 illustrater the use of the CHR$ function.

The ASCII and CHR$ functions are helpful in allowing programs to respond to both lowercase and uppercase input. By using these functions, we can write a program that will allow the user to answer a yes or no question with either y or Y and n or N. Looking at Figure 8–3, you can see that lowercase letters range from 97 to 122, and uppercase letters range from 65 to 90. An IF/THEN statement can be used to compare the ASCII value to 96. If the value is greater than 96, a lowercase letter has been typed; if the value is less than 96, the letter is uppercase. Once you know what type of letter you have, it can be converted to either uppercase or lowercase for comparison. An uppercase letter can be changed to lower-

Figure 8–8 ASCII CODES

```
   32      ! 33      " 34      # 35
$ 36       % 37      & 38      ' 39
( 40       ) 41      * 42      + 43
, 44       - 45      . 46      / 47
0 48       1 49      2 50      3 51
4 52       5 53      6 54      7 55
8 56       9 57      : 58      ; 59
< 60       = 61      > 62      ? 63
@ 64       A 65      B 66      C 67
D 68       E 69      F 70      G 71
H 72       I 73      J 74      K 75
L 76       M 77      N 78      O 79
P 80       Q 81      R 82      S 83
T 84       U 85      V 86      W 87
X 88       Y 89      Z 90      [ 91
\ 92       ] 93      ^ 94      _ 95
` 96       a 97      b 98      c 99
d 100      e 101     f 102     g 103
h 104      i 105     j 106     k 107
l 108      m 109     n 110     o 111
p 112      q 113     r 114     s 115
t 116      u 117     v 118     w 119
x 120      y 121     z 122     { 123
| 124
```

Figure 8–9 THE ASCII FUNCTION

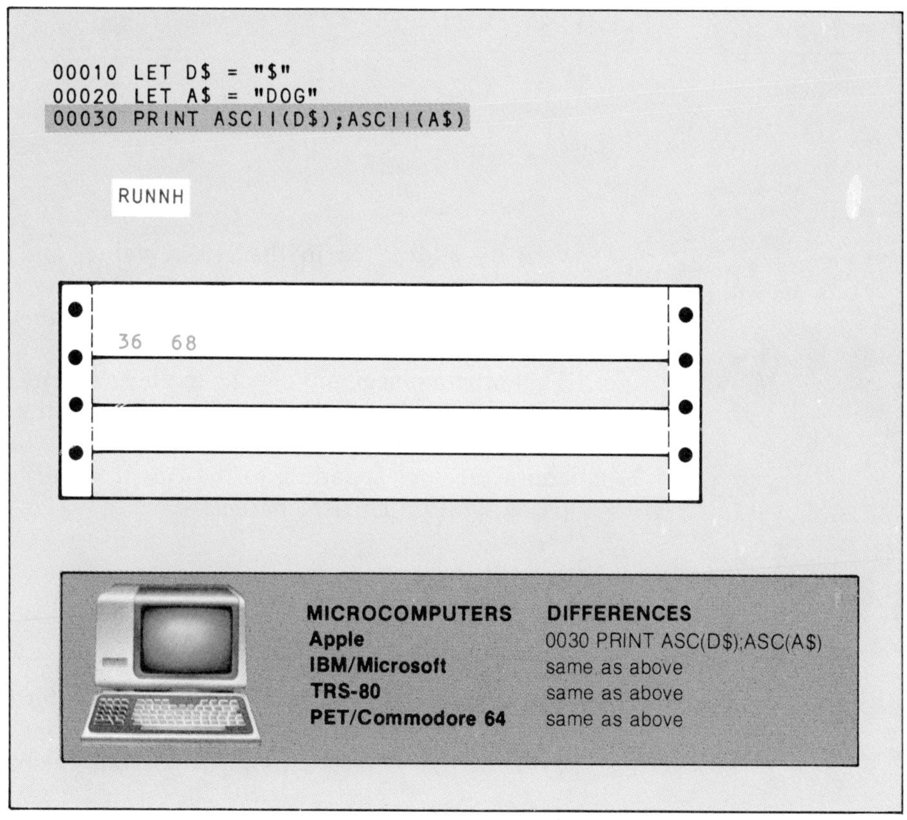

```
00010 LET D$ = "$"
00020 LET A$ = "DOG"
00030 PRINT ASCII(D$);ASCII(A$)
```

RUNNH

```
36  68
```

MICROCOMPUTERS	DIFFERENCES
Apple	0030 PRINT ASC(D$);ASC(A$)
IBM/Microsoft	same as above
TRS-80	same as above
PET/Commodore 64	same as above

Figure 8–10 THE CHR$ FUNCTION

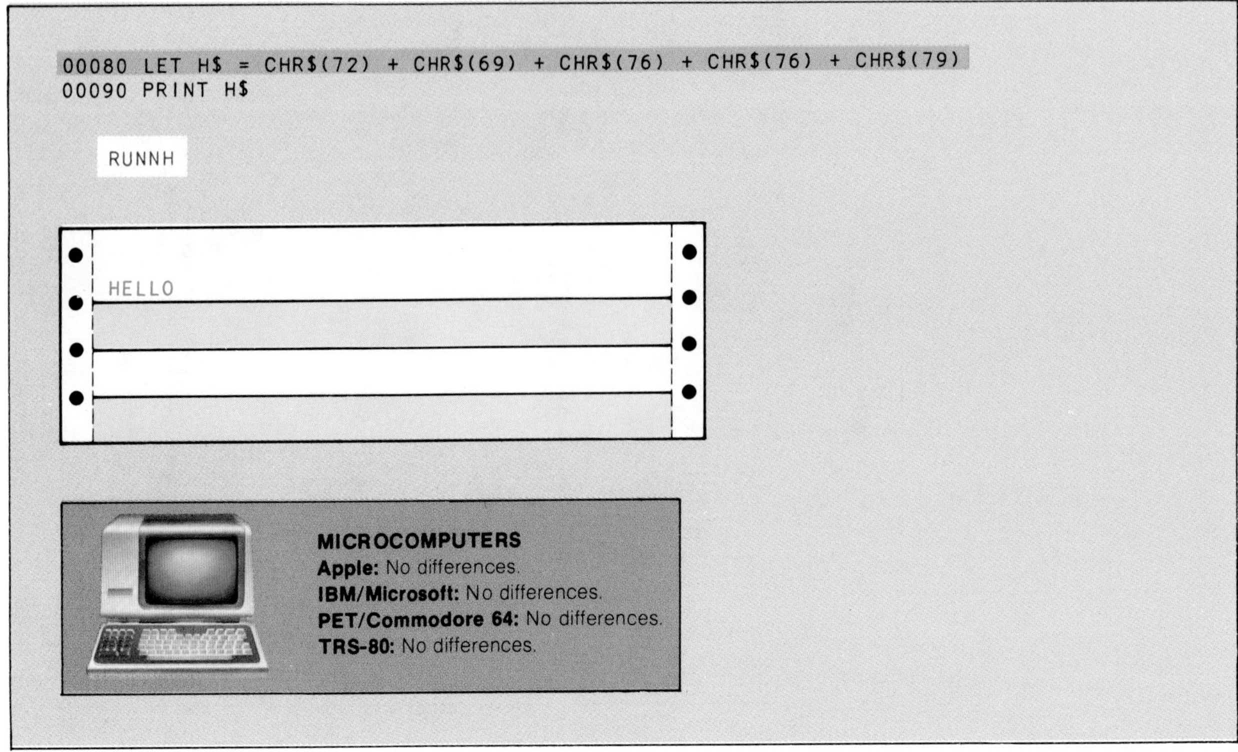

case by adding 32 to the ASCII value, and a lowercase letter can be changed to uppercase by subtracting 32.

00080 LET H$ = CHR$(72) + CHR$(69) + CHR$(76) + CHR$(76) + CHR$(79)
00090 PRINT H$
RUNNH
HELLO
MICROCOMPUTERS
Apple: No differences.
IBM/Microsoft: No differences.
PET/Commodore 64: No differences.
TRS-80: No differences.

The program segment in Figure 8–11 illustrates this use of the ASCII and CHR$ functions:

This program segment checks the user's reply to see if it is lowercase. If it is lowercase, 32 is subtracted from the ASCII value to give the ASCII value for the uppercase of the same letter. After subtracting, CHR$ assigns the character corresponding to the ASCII value to A$. A$ then can be compared with uppercase characters.

The VAL Function

The VAL function turns a numeric string (for example, 5280) into a number that can be used in arithmetic calculations. Figure 8–12 illustrates this. By using the VAL function, it is possible to change the number in charac-

Figure 8–11 CONVERTING LOWERCASE LETTERS TO UPPERCASE LETTERS

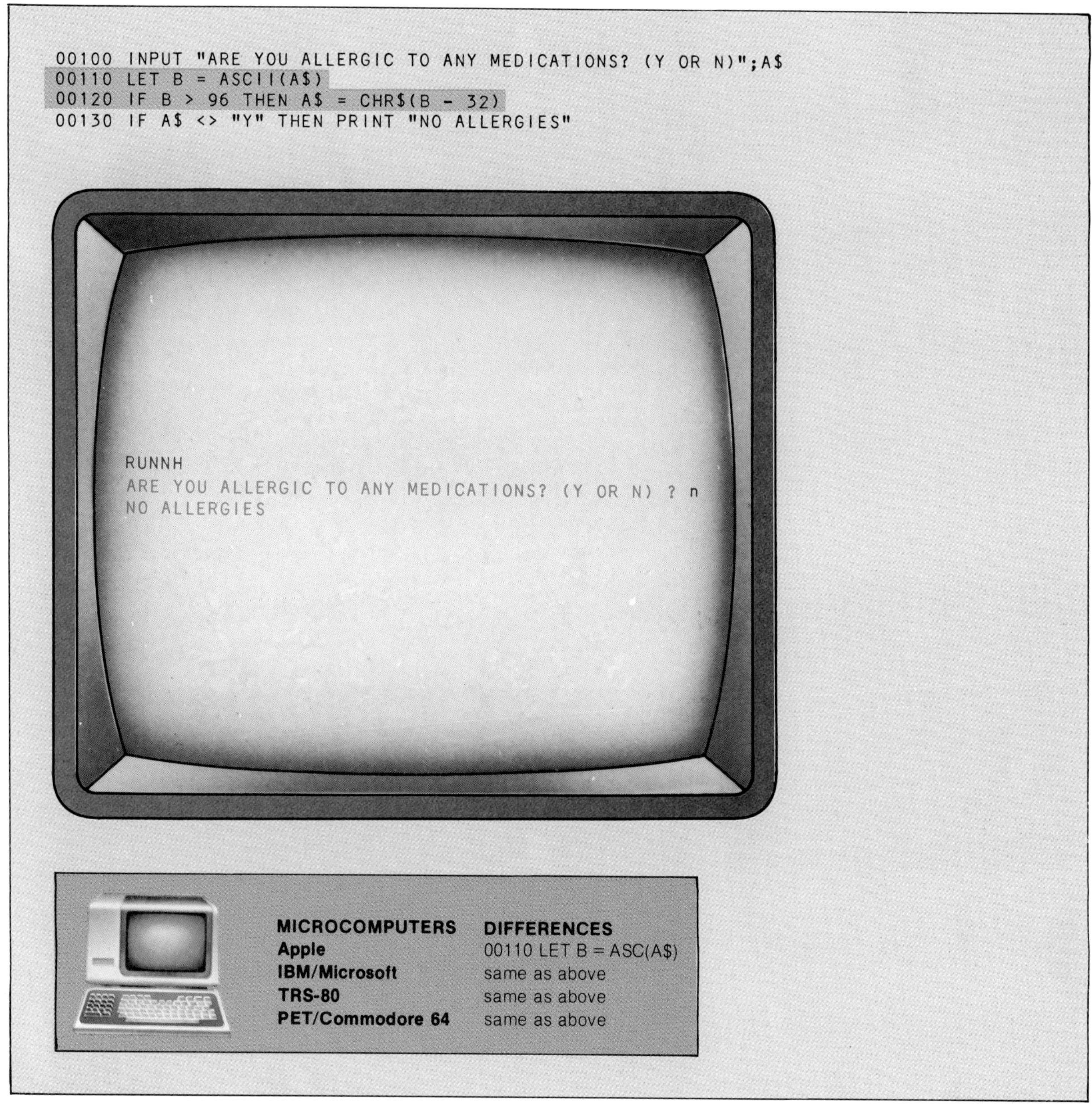

ter string format to a real number so that the number can be used in mathematical computations. If the character string contains any nonnumeric characters, the VAL function will replace these with zeros.

00100 INPUT "ARE YOU ALLERGIC TO ANY MEDICATIONS? (Y OR N)";A$
00110 LET B = ASCII(A$)
00120 IF B > 96 THEN A$ = CHR$(B - 32)
00130 IF A$ <> "Y" THEN PRINT "NO ALLERGIES"
RUNNH
ARE YOU ALLERGIC TO ANY MEDICATIONS? (Y OR N) ? n
NO ALLERGIES
MICROCOMPUTERS
DIFFERENCES
Apple
00110 LET B = ASC(A$)
IBM/Microsoft
same as above
TRS-80
same as above
PET/Commodore 64
same as above

Figure 8–12 THE VAL FUNCTION

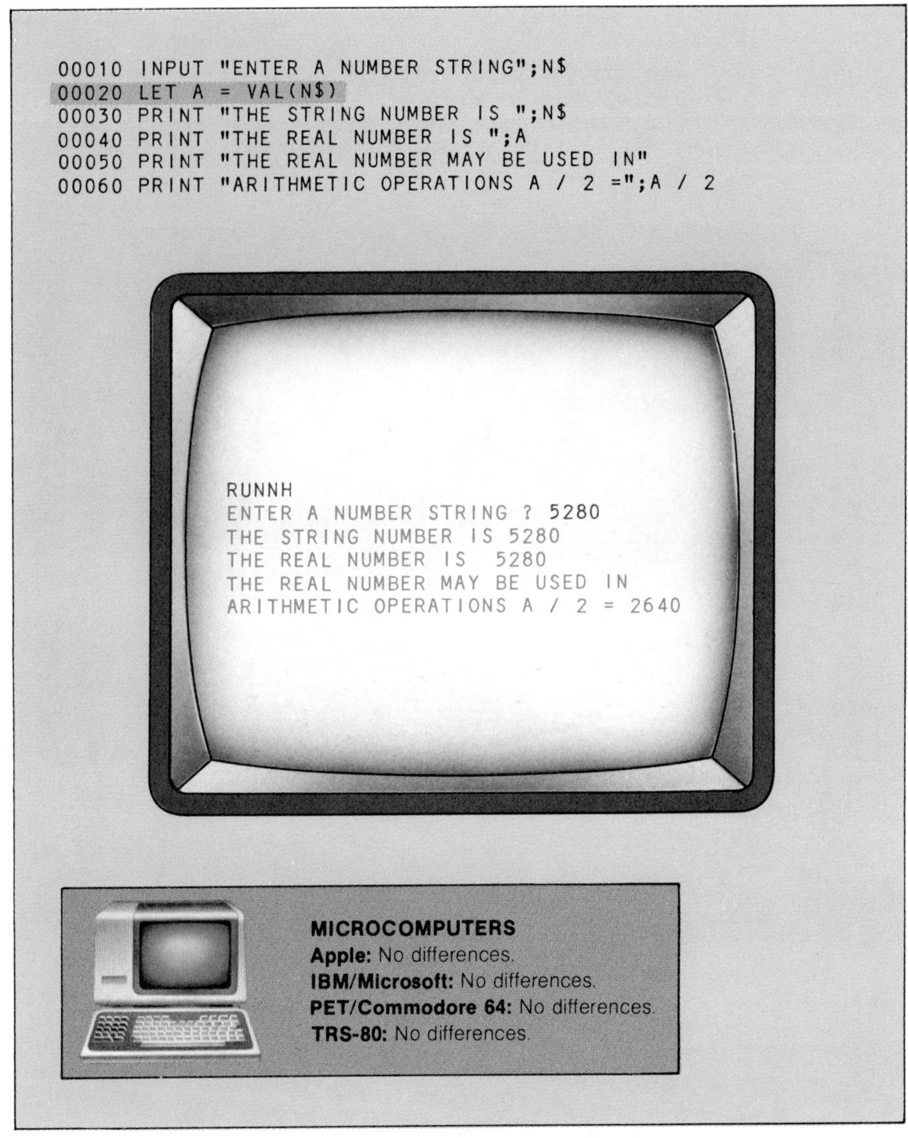

00010 INPUT "ENTER A NUMBER STRING";N$
00020 LET A = VAL(N$)
00030 PRINT "THE STRING NUMBER IS ";N$
00040 PRINT "THE REAL NUMBER IS ";A
00050 PRINT "THE REAL NUMBER MAY BE USED IN"
00060 PRINT "ARITHMETIC OPERATIONS A / 2 =";A / 2
RUNNH
ENTER A NUMBER STRING ? 5280
THE STRING NUMBER IS 5280
THE REAL NUMBER IS 5280
THE REAL NUMBER MAY BE USED IN
ARITHMETIC OPERATIONS A / 2 = 2640
MICROCOMPUTERS
Apple: No differences.
IBM/Microsoft: No differences.
PET/Commodore 64: No differences.
TRS-80: No differences.

The STR$ Function

The STR$ function is just the opposite of the VAL function; it converts a real number to a string. Figure 8–13 illustrates the STR$ functions. Remember that once a number has been converted to a character string, it no longer can be used in mathematical computations.

Figure 8–13 THE STR$ FUNCTION

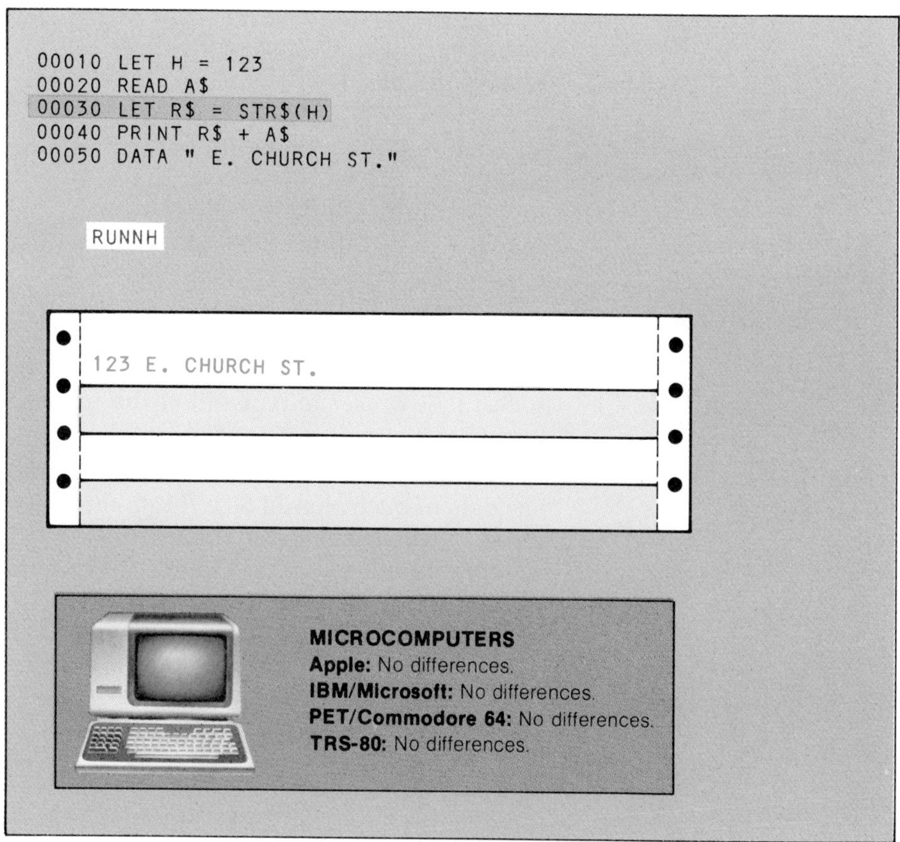

00010 LET H = 123
00020 READ A$
00030 LET R$ = STR$(H)
00040 PRINT R$ + A$
00050 DATA " E. CHURCH ST."
RUNNH
123 E. CHURCH ST.
MICROCOMPUTERS
Apple: No differences.
IBM/Microsoft: No differences.
PET/Commodore 64: No differences.
TRS-80: No differences.

LEARNING CHECK

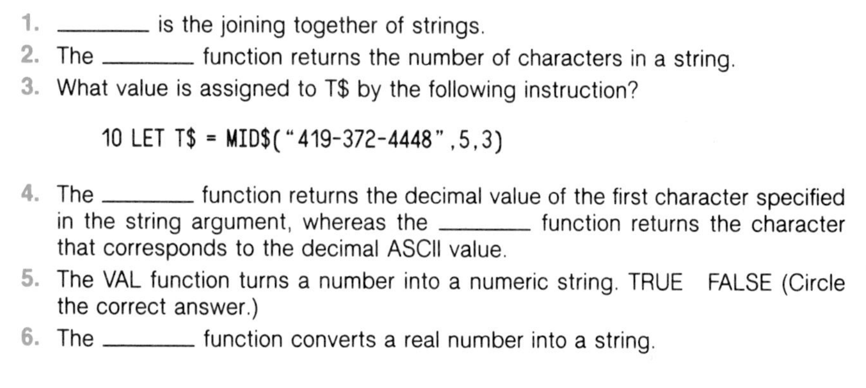

1. ________ is the joining together of strings.
2. The ________ function returns the number of characters in a string.
3. What value is assigned to T$ by the following instruction?

```
10 LET T$ = MID$("419-372-4448",5,3)
```

4. The ________ function returns the decimal value of the first character specified in the string argument, whereas the ________ function returns the character that corresponds to the decimal ASCII value.
5. The VAL function turns a number into a numeric string. TRUE FALSE (Circle the correct answer.)
6. The ________ function converts a real number into a string.

Answers

1. Concatenation
2. LEN
3. 372
4. ASCII; CHR$
5. False
6. STR$

A Programming Problem

The Problem

We want to write a program that will ask the user for the following information:

1. Name to be input in this format: first, blank, last.
2. Month of birth (for example, 02).
3. Day of birth (for example, 04).
4. Year of birth (for example, 1963).
5. Sex (allow user to type either the full word or the first letter).
6. Current date in the format mm/dd/yy (for example, 08/16/83).

The date of birth should be put into the same format as the current date so that they can be compared. Using the ON/GOSUB statement, we will print the appropriate message: either "HAPPY nth BIRTHDAY first name" or "first name, YOUR BIRTHDAY ISN'T UNTIL mm/dd."

The output will have the following format:

LAST, FIRST   SEX = m or f
BORN mm/dd/yy
blank line
appropriate birthday message

Solution Design

1. Collect information.
2. Switch name so that the last name comes first.
3. Put birthday in mm/dd/yy format.
4. Compare birth date to current date.
5. Assign 1 to X if birthday.
6. Assign 2 to X if not birthday.
7. Use ON/GOSUB to transfer control.
8. Print appropriate message.

The Program

In the program in Figure 8–14, lines 150 through 175 ask the user for data. Line 190 initializes I to 0. Line 195 increments I. Line 195 picks off the leftmost I characters and places them in L$. Line 205 picks off the rightmost character of L$. Line 215 tests whether T$ is a blank by using the CHR$ function (the ASCII code for a blank or space is 32). If a blank is

Figure 8–14 NAME AND BIRTHDAY PROGRAM AND FLOWCHART

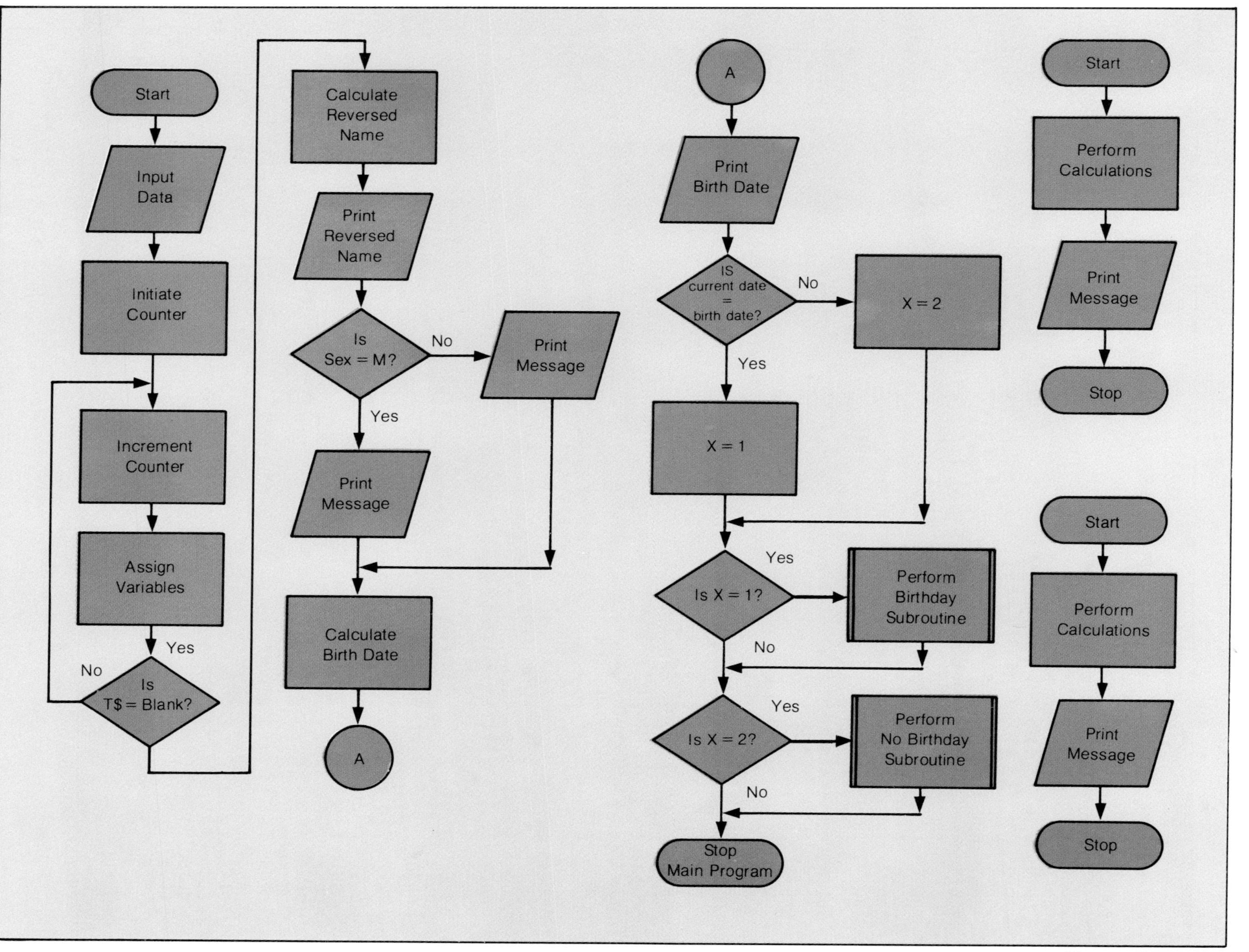

(Figure continued next page)

Figure 8–14 *(continued)*

```
00100 REM *** N$ = NAME (FIRST NAME FIRST) ***
00105 REM *** M$ = MONTH OF BIRTH ***
00110 REM *** D$ = DAY OF BIRTH ***
00115 REM *** Y$ = YEAR OF BIRTH ***
00120 REM *** S$ = SEX ***
00125 REM *** C$ = CURRENT DATE ***
00130 REM *** B$ = BIRTH DATE ***
00135 REM *** R$ = REVERSED NAME ***
00140 REM
00145 REM
00150 INPUT "ENTER YOUR NAME, FIRST THEN LAST ";N$
00155 INPUT "ENTER MONTH OF BIRTH (e.g. 02 FOR FEB.) ";M$
00160 INPUT "ENTER DAY OF BIRTH (e.g. 04) ";D$
00165 INPUT "ENTER YEAR OF BIRTH (e.g. 1963) ";Y$
00170 INPUT "ENTER SEX MALE OR FEMALE ";S$
00175 INPUT "ENTER TODAY'S DATE (e.g. 08/16/83) ";C$
00180 REM *** SWITCH NAME SO LAST NAME COMES FIRST ***
00185 REM *** SEARCH LOOP UPTO LENGTH OF NAME ***
00190 LET I = 0
00195 LET I = I + 1
00200 LET L$ = LEFT$(N$,I)
00205 LET T$ = RIGHT$(L$,I)
00210 REM *** TEST FOR BLANK ***
00215 IF T$ = CHR$(32) THEN 230
00220 REM *** IF NOT BLANK THEN CONTINUE  LOOP ***
00230 LET R$ = RIGHT$(N$,I +1) + ", " + L$
00235 PRINT
00240 PRINT
00245 PRINT R$;"     ";
00250 REM *** COMPARE SEX ***
00255 IF LEFT$(S$,1) = "M" THEN PRINT "SEX = M" ELSE PRINT "SEX = F"
00260 REM *** PUT TOGETHER DATE OF BIRTH ***
00265 LET Y$ = RIGHT$(Y$,3)
00270 LET B$ = M$ + "/" + D$ + "/" + Y$
00275 PRINT "BORN ";B$
00280 IF LEFT$(B$,5) = LEFT$(C$,5) THEN X = 1 ELSE X = 2
00285 ON X GOSUB 295,340
00290 STOP
00295 REM *** SUBROUTINE TO PRINT BIRTHDAY MESSAGE ***
00300 LET C = VAL(RIGHT$(C$,7))
00305 LET B = VAL(RIGHT$(B$,7))
00310 LET A = C - B
00315 PRINT
00320 PRINT "HAPPY";A;"BIRTHDAY ";L$
00325 PRINT
00330 PRINT
00335 RETURN
00340 REM *** SUBROUTINE FOR NO BIRTHDAY ***
00345 LET X$ = LEFT$(B$,5)
00350 PRINT
00355 PRINT L$;", YOUR BIRTHDAY ISN'T UNTIL ";X$
00360 PRINT
00365 PRINT
00370 RETURN
00999 END
```

Figure 8–14 *(continued)*

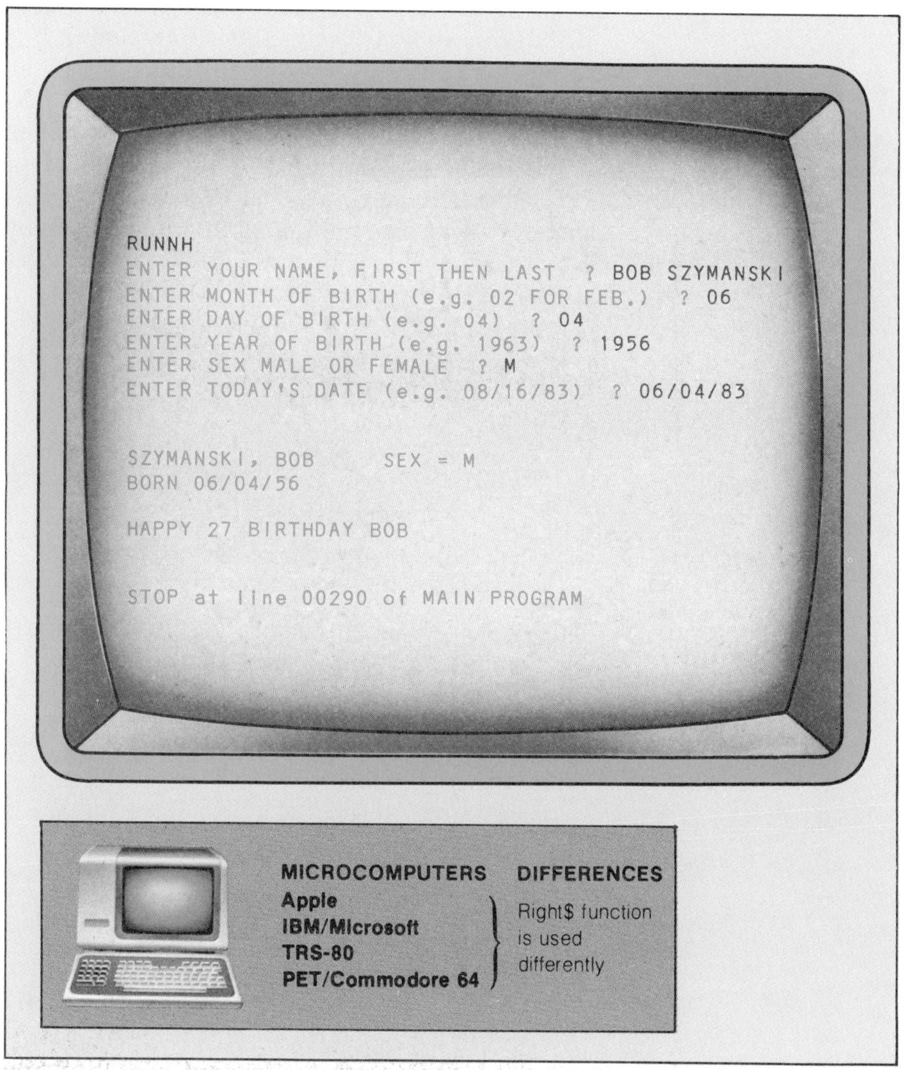
RUNNH
ENTER YOUR NAME, FIRST THEN LAST ? BOB SZYMANSKI
ENTER MONTH OF BIRTH (e.g. 02 FOR FEB.) ? 06
ENTER DAY OF BIRTH (e.g. 04) ? 04
ENTER YEAR OF BIRTH (e.g. 1963) ? 1956
ENTER SEX MALE OR FEMALE ? M
ENTER TODAY'S DATE (e.g. 08/16/83) ? 06/04/83
SZYMANSKI, BOB SEX = M
BORN 06/04/56
HAPPY 27 BIRTHDAY BOB
STOP at line 00290 of MAIN PROGRAM
MICROCOMPUTERS
Apple
IBM/Microsoft
TRS-80
PET/Commodore 64
DIFFERENCES
Right$ function is used differently

found, line 215 sends the computer to line 230, which assigns the reversed name to R$. The name is printed out in reverse by line 245. Notice that the PRINT statement is ended with a semicolon so that the next PRINT statement will be continued on the same line. Line 255 compares the first character of the reply for M or F and prints out the sex. Line 265 assigns the last two numbers of the year of birth to Y$. Line 270 then puts the birth date into the same format as the current date. After the birth date is printed out in line 275, line 280 compares the dates (only month and day). If they are the same, line 440—an ON/GOSUB statement—transfers control to line 295. If they are not equal, control is transferred to the subroutine at line 340. Line 290 contains the STOP statement to keep the subroutines from being executed unnecessarily. The subroutine starting at line 295 prints the happy birthday message, Lines 300 and 305 convert the years to integers so that they can be subtracted in line 310 to find the individual's age. Lines 315 through 330 print the output, and control is then transferred back to the main program by the RETURN statement in line 335. The second subroutine, which is executed when the individual does not have a birthday, starts in line 340. The month and day of birth are assigned to X$ in line 345, and lines 350 through 365 print the output. After control is returned to the main program (this is done by line 370 in the second subroutine), the first statement to be executed is the STOP in line 290. Execution of this statement results in the message STOP at line 290 of the main program.

Summary

- Two statements define a subroutine: GOSUB and RETURN.
- The GOSUB statement is used to transfer the flow of control from the main logic of a program to a subroutine.
- The RETURN statement transfers control from a subroutine back to the line in the main program immediately following the last GOSUB or ON/GOSUB statement that was executed.
- The STOP statement halts execution of a program.
- The ON/GOSUB statement is used to conditionally transfer control from the main program to one of several subroutines.
- BASIC string functions permit modification, concatenation, comparison, and analysis of the composition of strings.

Review Questions

1. What is the purpose of using subroutines?
2. What does the GOSUB statement do?
3. Identify which of the following are valid GOSUB statements:

a.
```
170 GOSUB
 .
 .
 .
900 REM SUBROUTINE
```

b.
```
210 GOSUB 600
 .
 .
 .
600 REM SUBROUTINE
```

c. 125 GOSUB 950

```
125 GOSUB 950
.
.
.
800 REM SUBROUTINE
.
.
.
950 REM SUBROUTINE
```

d. 340 GOSUB 1000

```
340 GOSUB 1000
.
.
.
800 REM SUBROUTINE
```

4. What is the purpose of the RETURN statement?
5. Where is the RETURN statement placed in a program?
6. What is the difference between the STOP and END statements?
7. How is the STOP statement used with subroutines?
8. What is the purpose of using the STOP statement with exception handling?
9. What is the difference between the GOSUB statement and the ON/GOSUB statement?
10. If X equals 3, what is the line number of the subroutine to which control will be transferred when the following line is executed?

```
240 ON X GOSUB 300,350,400,450
```

11. Is line 100 a valid ON/GOSUB statement? Why or why not?

```
 90 LET Z = 4
100 on Z GOSUB 200,250,300
.
.
.
200 REM SUBROUTINE
.
.
.
250 REM SUBROUTINE
.
.
.
300 REM SUBROUTINE
.
.
.
400 END
```

12. Write a BASIC statement that will join A$ and B$ to produce C$. If A$ = "EDWARD" and B$ = " ERLANGER", what will C$ be equal to after this statement is executed?

13. After the following statement is executed, what does R equal?

    20 LET R = LEN("123 SANDRIDGE RD")

14. Using the LEFT$ function, change the value of A$ from "COMPUTER" to "COMPUTATION".
15. Give the output from the following statement:

    10 PRINT RIGHT$("MICHAEL JACKSON",9)

16. Give the output from the following statement:

    20 PRINT MID$("MICHAEL JACKSON",9,4)

17. Using Figure 8–3, what will this instruction print out?

    10 PRINT ASCII(APPLE)

18. What will this instruction print?

    20 PRINT CHR$(75) + CHR$(97) + CHR$(114) + CHR$(101) + CHR$(110)

19. What is the purpose of the VAL function?
20. What will the output from this instruction be?

    30 PRINT STR$(342) + STR$(58)

Debugging Exercises

Identify the programs or program segments that contain errors, and debug them. If output is given, correct the program or segment so that it will give the desired output.

1.
```
00010 GOSUB 150
00015 STOP
00100 REM *** SUBROUTINE ***
00105 PRINT "HELP"
00110 RETURN
00999 END
```

2.
```
00010 GOSUB 300
00020 PRINT Z
  .
  .
  .
00290 STOP
00300 REM *** SUBROUTINE ***
00310 PRINT Z * 2
00999 END
```

3.
```
00010 LET X = 4
00020 ON X GOSUB 100,200,300
  .
  .
  .
00100 REM *** SUBROUTINE ***
  .
  .
  .
00200 REM *** SUBROUTINE ***
  .
  .
  .
00300 REM *** SUBROUTINE ***
  .
  .
  .
00999 END
```

4.
```
00010 LET A$ = "TOM"
00015 LET B$ = "TERRIFIC"
00020 LET C$ = A$ + B$
00025 PRINT C$


RUNNH
T. TERRIFIC
```

5.
```
00010 LET X$ = "
00015 LET A$ = LEFT$(X$,LEN(X$) / 2)
00020 LET B$ = RIGHT$(X$,LEN(X$) / 2 + 1)
00025 PRINT A$
00030 PRINT B$
```

6.
```
10 REM *** LIST PEOPLE WITH MIDDLE INITIAL A ***
20 FOR I = 1 TO 5
30   READ N$
40   FOR J = 1 TO 5
50     LET L$ = LEFT$(N$,I)
60     LET R$ = RIGHT$(L$,1)
70     IF R$ = "   " THEN 90
80   NEXT J
90   IF MID$(N$,I + 1,1) = "A" THEN PRINT N$
100 NEXT I
110 DATA "KAREN ANNE MCKEE","JOHN DANIEL MANN"
120 DATA "ERIC ALEXANDER RED"
130 DATA "ALICE KAY OTTEN","BOB ALAN SZYMANSKI"
140 END


RUNNH
KAREN ANNE MCKEE
ERIC ALEXANDER RED
BOB ALAN SZYMANSKI
```

7.
```
00005 FOR I = 1 TO 3
00010   READ A$
00015   LET A = STR$(A$)
00020   LET A = A / 2
00025   PRINT A
00030 NEXT I
00035 DATA 596,634,310

RUNNH
 298    317    155
```

8.
```
00010 PRINT "HELLO"

RUNNH
"HELLO"
```

9.
```
00010 INPUT "ARE YOU 21 OR OLDER?";A$
00015 IF A$ <> "YES" THEN GOTO 999
00020 INPUT "ENTER AGE";N$
00025 LET N = N * 2
00030 PRINT "YOU ARE ELIGIBLE FOR $";N
00999 END

RUNNH
ARE YOU 21 OR OLDER?? Y
ENTER AGE? 32
YOU ARE ELIGIBLE FOR $ 64
```

10.
```
00010 PRINT ASCII(A),ASCII(B),ASCII(C)

RUNNH
 64             65             66
```

Additional Programming Problems

1. Write a program to compute the gross pay of hourly employees. If the employee works more than forty hours, this program should call a subroutine that will calculate the overtime pay:

   (Hours worked − 40) × 1.5 × Wage rate) = Overtime pay.

   Use this data:

Name	Hours	Wage
Tim Novak	45	$10.90
Edwin Peter	39	8.65
Dave Lee	47	9.30
Joe Szchmit	33	5.15

The output should have this format:

NAME	HOURS	GROSS PAY
XXXXX	XX	$XXX.XX
.	.	.
.	.	.
.	.	.

2. Write a program to print any word entered by a user in one of these three formats:

FIVE	FIVE	F
FIV	IVE	I
FI	VE	V
F	V	E

Subroutines should be called by an ON/GOUSB statement to print the word in the format specified by the user.

3. Write a program that reads a list of words and prints only those words that begin with whatever prefix is entered by the user. Use the following data: PREPARE, PREFIX, INTEREST, INCOME, UNDER, UNFORTUNATE, PROFFER, PROGRAM, PROFESSIONAL

4. The gas company has its customer names on file in the format of last name, first name, and middle initial. It needs a program that will reverse the names so that they are printed on the customer's bill in the format of first name, middle initial, and last name. Here is a list of customers:

Customer Name
Hough, Charlie J.
Niekro, Joe G.
Stilwell, Hazel Z.
Miller, Risa A.
Wilhelm, Hoyt H.
Rudolph, Wilma P.

5. Write a program to print a chart of the capital letters from A to Z and their corresponding ASCII value in the following format:

CHAR	VALUE	CHAR	VALUE
A	65	B	66
C	67	D	68
.	.	.	.
.	.	.	.
.	.	.	.
Y	89	Z	90

No data are needed. Use a FOR/NEXT loop that starts with the ASCII value of A and goes to the ASCII value of Z.

6. The residents of Morton Avenue want to add 100 to their street addresses. They need a program to change their current addresses and list their new addresses. Read these addresses into a string variable, and add 100 to each house number:

   35 Morton Avenue
   41 Morton Avenue
   67 Morton Avenue

   OUTPUT:

   135 Morton Avenue
   141 Morton Avenue
   167 Morton Avenue

9 Arrays

Outline

Objectives

After reading this chapter, the student should be able to do the following:

- Understand the function of subscripts.
- Understand and use the DIM statement.
- Program and manipulate one- and two-dimensional arrays.
- Sort data items using both the bubble and Shell sorts.

Overview

So far, our programs have used simple variables such as A, N$, and D2 to represent single values. Now let us say we want to write a program that reads the daily television viewing hours for five people, calculates the average, and prints the difference between each person's viewing time and the average in the following format:

```
NAME            VIEWING HRS.  DIFFERENCE FROM AVERAGE

M. STOOTS        5                 1

B. KOOL          3                -1

K. DAVIS         6                 2

H. WARD          4                 0

V. JONS          2                -2


AVERAGE DAILY VIEWING HRS. =  4
```

Up to this point, we have been calculating averages by reading one value at a time into a single variable when using the READ/DATA statements and accumulating the values as they are read. In this procedure, however, each time a new value is read, the previous value stored in the variable is destroyed; thus, in the previous example, we would not be able to compare each person's viewing time with the calculated average viewing time. To make the comparison, each person's viewing time would need to be stored in a separate memory location. One way of accomplishing this is by using a distinct variable name for each value. This approach will work (provided you know the number of values you will be working with beforehand) but can become cumbersome when dealing with a large number of values.

There is an easier way: BASIC permits us to deal with groups of related values as **arrays.** Figure 9–1 shows the coding necessary to produce the previously listed output.

Figure 9–1 ARRAY EXAMPLE

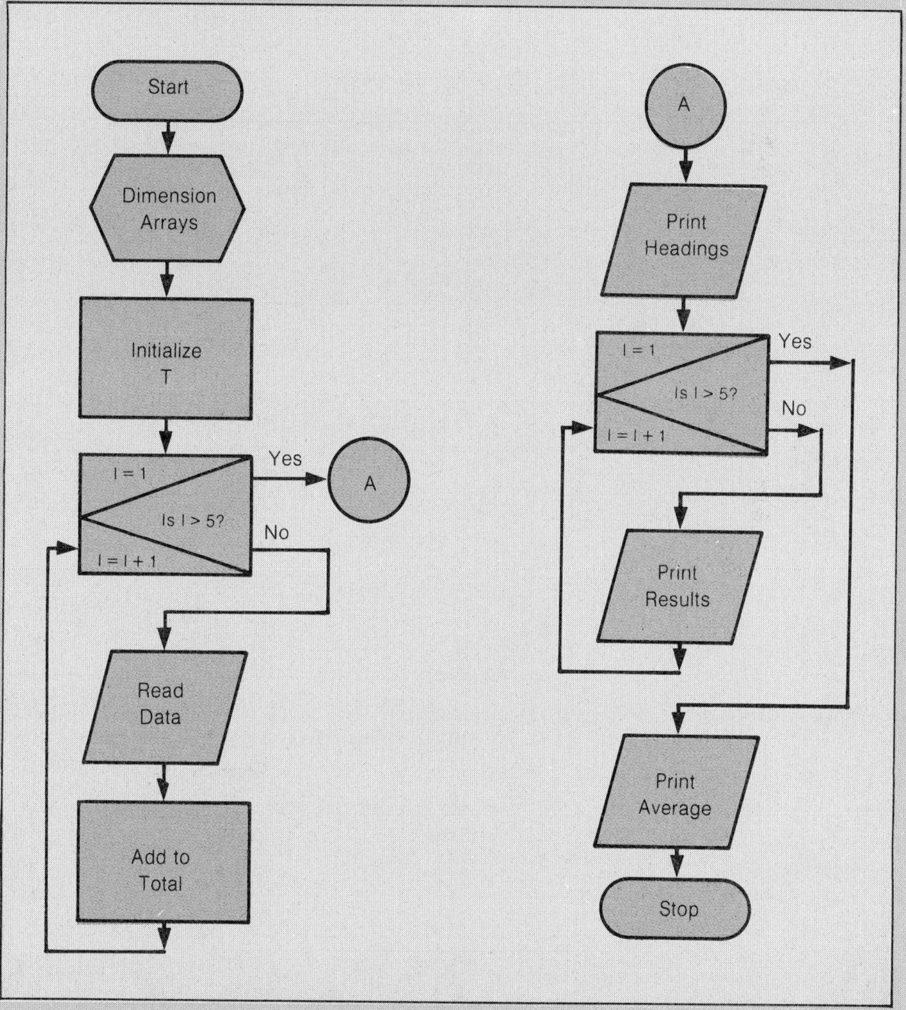

(Figure continued on next page)

Figure 9–1 *(continued)*

```
00010 REM *** T.V. VIEWING HRS. SURVEY ***
00015 DIM N$(5)
00020 DIM H(5)
00025 LET T = 0
00030 FOR I = 1 TO 5
00035   READ N$(I)
00040   READ H(I)
00045   LET T = T + H(I)
00050 NEXT I
00055 LET A = T / 5
00060 PRINT "NAME","VIEWING HRS.","DIFFERENCE FROM AVERAGE"
00065 FOR I = 1 TO 5
00070   PRINT
00075   PRINT N$(I),H(I),H(I) - A
00080 NEXT I
00085 PRINT
00090 PRINT
00095 PRINT "AVERAGE DAILY VIEWING HRS. = ";A
000100 DATA "M. STOOTS",5,"B. KOOL",3,"K. DAVIS",6,"H. WARD",4,"V. JONS",2
00999 END
```

MICROCOMPUTERS	DIFFERENCES
Apple	Screen not wide enough
IBM/Microsoft	No difference
TRS-80	No difference
PET/Commodore 64	Screen not wide enough

Array names are distinguished from simple variable names through the use of subscripts. The DIM statement tells the computer how much storage is necessary to hold an array. Arrays may be one-dimensional (sometimes called **lists**), two-dimensional (often called **tables,** or **matrices**), or of higher dimensions. A method for sorting arrays also is discussed in this chapter.

Subscripts

An array is a group of storage locations in memory in which data elements can be stored. The entire array is given one name; the programmer indicates individual elements in the array by referring to their positions. The general concept is simple. Let us say there are three students in a computer science class. We would like to store the names of the students in an array called C$. It might look like this:

Array C$

C$(1)	JONNY
C$(2)	RACHEL
C$(3)	SUE

We can gain access to an individual name within the array by telling the computer which position in the list it occupies. This is done through the use of **subscripts.** For example, Jonny is in the first position in the array—that is, C$(1). Rachel is in the second location, C$(2). Sue is in C$(3). The subscripts are enclosed in parentheses.

In BASIC, the same rules that apply to naming simple variables apply to naming arrays. Remember that only numbers can be stored in numeric variable array names, and only character strings can be stored in string variable arrays. It is good programming practice not to use the same name for both a simple variable and an array in a program.

The subscript (index) enclosed in parentheses can be any legal expression; for example, A(K), J(2), and X(B + C) are valid references to array elements.

When an array element is indicated by an expression, the computer carries out the following steps:

1. It evaluates the expression inside the parentheses.
2. It translates the result to the nearest integer.
3. It accesses the indicated element in the array.

For example, if the computer encounters A(K), it looks at the current value of K. This value indicates the position of the desired element in array A.

Array A
10
15
16
17
32

Assume that I = 2, N = 3, and K = 5. Then

A(I) refers to A(2)—the second element in array A, or 15.

A(N) refers to A(3)—the third element in array A, or 16.

A(I + N) refers to A(5)—the fifth element in array A, or 32.

A(K) refers to A(5)—the fifth element in array A, or 32.

References to specific elements of arrays are called **subscripted variables.** In contrast, simple variables are **unsubscripted variables.** An unsubscripted variable—say, P3—is used to refer to a single storage location named P3; the subscripted variable P(3), in contrast, represents the third item in an array called P.

The DIM Statement

When a programmer uses an array, the BASIC compiler does not automatically know how many elements the array will contain. Unless told otherwise, it makes provisions for a limited number. Usually the compiler is designed to assume that an array will have no more than ten elements (eleven elements in some systems: 0 through 10). Consequently, it reserves space for ten elements in the array. The programmer cannot write a statement that refers to an array element for which space has not been reserved.

The programmer can specify the number of elements for which space must be reserved by means of a DIM (dimension) statement. A DIM statement is not required for arrays of ten or less elements (or whatever number of elements the system assumes); however, many programmers will specify DIM statements for small arrays to help document the array usage.

The general format of the DIM statement follows:

line# DIM variable 1(limit 1),variable 2(limit 2), . . .

The variables are the names of arrays. Each limit is an integer constant that represents the maximum number of storage locations required for a particular array.

Assume that space is needed to store twenty-five elements in an array named X. The following statement reserves storage for twenty-five elements:

```
00010 DIM X(25)
```

There is no problem if fewer than twenty-five values are actually read into array X, but it cannot contain more. Array subscripts can vary in the program from 0 to the limit declared in the DIM statement, but no subscript can exceed that limit.

More than one array can be declared in a DIM statement; for example,

```
00020 DIM A(30),B(20),J(100)
```

declares A, B, and J as arrays. Array A may contain up to 30 elements; B, up to 20 elements, and J, up to 100 elements. (If an index of 0 is used, up to 31, 21, and 101 elements can be stored, respectively.)

DIM statements must appear in a program before the first references to arrays they describe. A good programming practice is to place them at the beginning of the program. The following standard preparation symbol is often used to flowchart the DIM statement:

One-Dimensional Arrays

This section has been discussing lists of related values stored under a single variable name—one-dimensional arrays. Let us look at some applications involving the use of one-dimensional arrays.

Reading Data into an Array

Using FOR and NEXT statements can be an efficient method of reading data into an array. The following program segment reads and stores a list of ten numbers in an array named J:

```
00010 FOR S = 1 TO 10
00020    READ J(S)
00030 NEXT S
00040 DATA 10,20,30,40,50
00050 DATA 60,70,80,90,100
```

The first time through this program loop, the loop variable S equals 1. When statement 20 is executed, the computer reads a number from the data lists and stores it in J(1)—the first storage location in array J. The second time through the loop, S equals 2. The next number is read into J(2)—the second location in the array. The loop processing continues until all ten numbers have been read and stored.

Printing Data in an Array

Now assume we are to print the first eight numbers in array J in a single column. The following statements do just that:

```
00060 FOR N = 1 TO 8
00070    PRINT J(N)
00080 NEXT N
```

```
RUNNH
 10
 20
 30
 40
 50
 60
 70
 80
```

As the loop variable N varies from 1 to 8, the index changes, and the computer prints elements 1 through 8 of array J.

Computations with Arrays

The program in Figure 9–2 generates a sales report that outlines the current prices of several items, the quantities sold, and the sales revenues that resulted. In addition, the program prints out the total amount of all sales.

This problem solution can be broken into the following steps:

1. Read the data into arrays.
2. Calculate the sales revenue for each item by multiplying price and quantity.
3. Calculate the total revenue by adding the sales revenues.

Three arrays are used in Figure 9–2. Two one-dimensional arrays are read as input: a price list, stored in array P, contains a list of the prices of six items; a quantity list, stored in array Q, contains a list of the quantities sold of the items. In the main part of the program a third array, T, is generated. It is a list of the gross sales of the items.

The program begins with a segment that establishes the price array, P. In lines 30 through 40, the variable J is set equal to 1, and a number is read from the data list and assigned to P(1). As the looping continues, P(2) is given a value, then P(3), and so on. When the looping is finished, array P contains the prices of the items. That is, P(1) is 0.75, P(2) is 2.98, and so on.

The next segment of the program fills array Q with values in the same manner. The values read into Q are the quantities of the six items sold. Thus, after execution of the loop (lines 45 through 55) has been completed, Q(1) is 11, Q(2) is 95, and so on.

Once the array elements have been stored, it is possible to manipulate them to obtain the desired information. For example, the main part of the program calculates the gross sales for each of the six items and stores the results in the array T. These computations are accomplished by multiplication of the elements in the price array P by the corresponding elements in the quantity array Q. All these arrays are then printed.

We also are to determine the total amount of all sales. We know that the array T contains the sales for each item. Therefore, we need to add all the elements in array T. This is accomplished in lines 80 through 95.

If we wanted the total sales of only the first two items, we could simply alter the number of times the FOR/NEXT loop is executed:

```
00080 LET T1 = 0
00085 FOR K = 1 TO 2
00090    LET T1 = T1 + T(K)
00095 NEXT K
```

Figure 9–2 SALES TOTALS PROGRAM

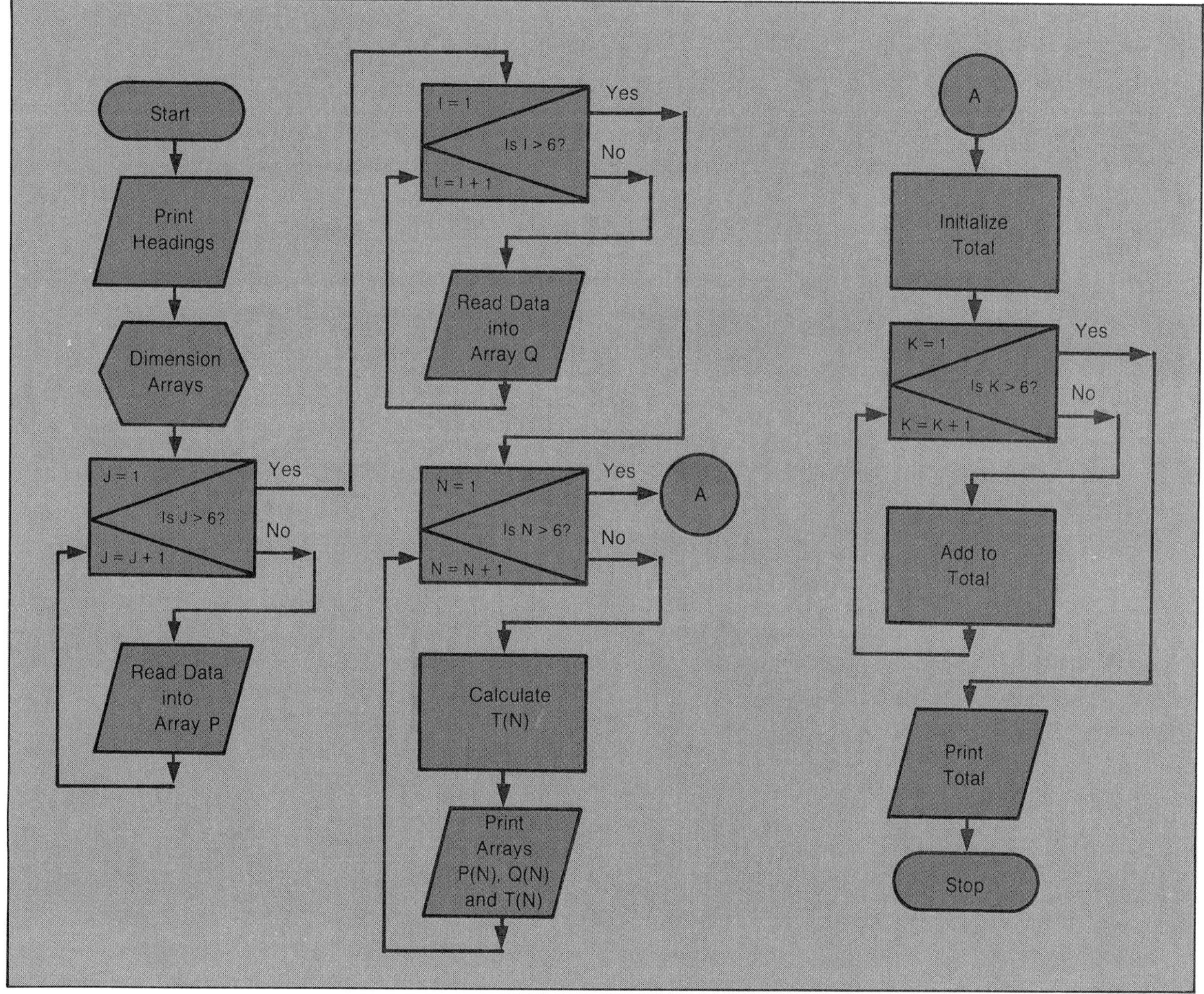

(Figure continued next page)

Figure 9–2 *(continued)*

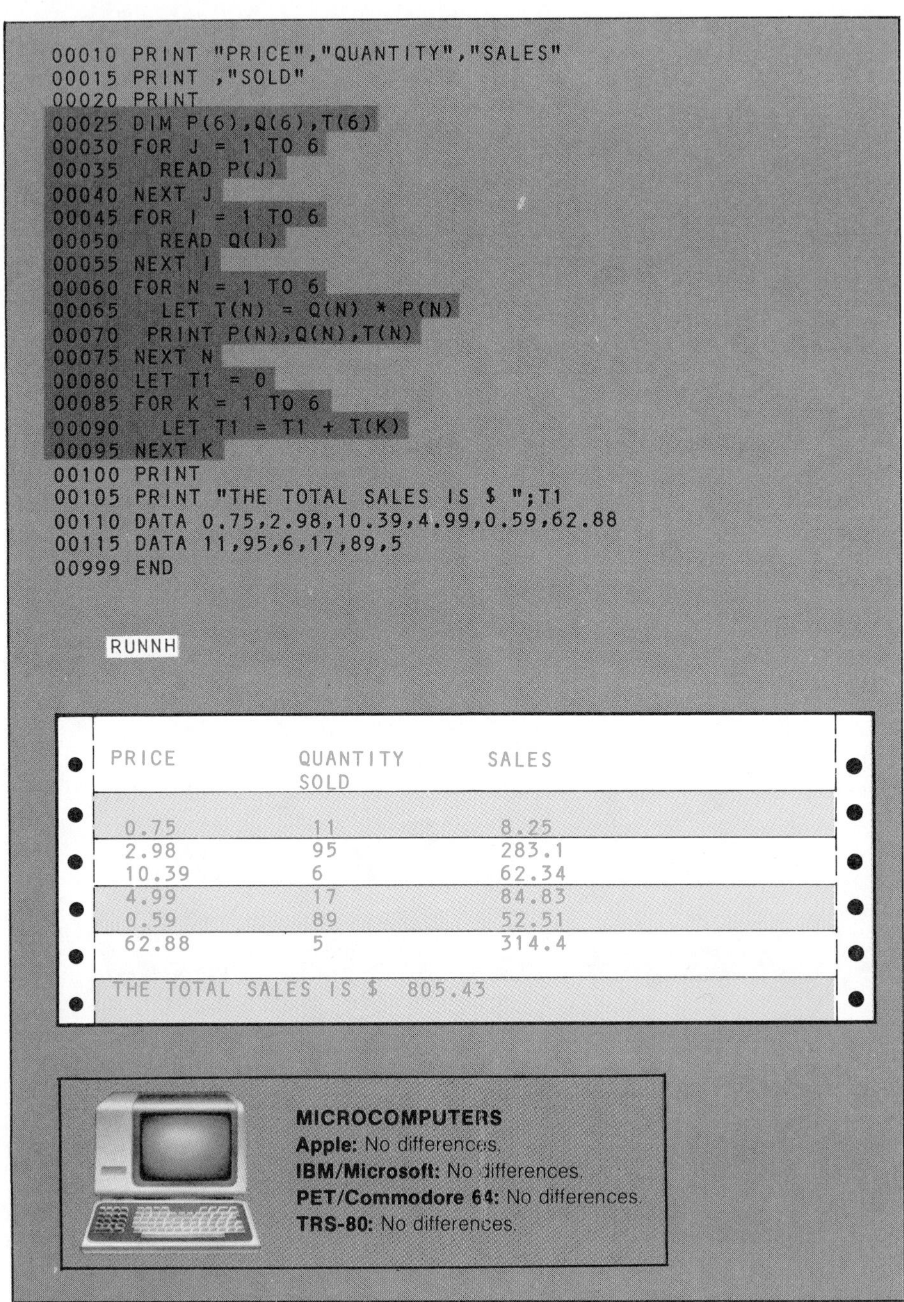

```
00010 PRINT "PRICE","QUANTITY","SALES"
00015 PRINT ,"SOLD"
00020 PRINT
00025 DIM P(6),Q(6),T(6)
00030 FOR J = 1 TO 6
00035   READ P(J)
00040 NEXT J
00045 FOR I = 1 TO 6
00050   READ Q(I)
00055 NEXT I
00060 FOR N = 1 TO 6
00065   LET T(N) = Q(N) * P(N)
00070  PRINT P(N),Q(N),T(N)
00075 NEXT N
00080 LET T1 = 0
00085 FOR K = 1 TO 6
00090   LET T1 = T1 + T(K)
00095 NEXT K
00100 PRINT
00105 PRINT "THE TOTAL SALES IS $ ";T1
00110 DATA 0.75,2.98,10.39,4.99,0.59,62.88
00115 DATA 11,95,6,17,89,5
00999 END

RUNNH
```

PRICE	QUANTITY SOLD	SALES
0.75	11	8.25
2.98	95	283.1
10.39	6	62.34
4.99	17	84.83
0.59	89	52.51
62.88	5	314.4

THE TOTAL SALES IS $ 805.43

MICROCOMPUTERS
Apple: No differences.
IBM/Microsoft: No differences.
PET/Commodore 64: No differences.
TRS-80: No differences.

Two-Dimensional Arrays

An array does not have to be a single list of data; it can be a table or matrix. For example, assume that Andy's Hamburger Chain operates nine restaurants—three in each of three different cities. Andy has received the following table of data concerning the number of hamburgers sold by each of the nine restaurants:

	Restaurant		
City	Main	Branch	Drive-through
Toledo	100	50	35
Detroit	95	60	50
Columbus	110	80	100

The rows in the table refer to the cities, and the columns refer to the restaurants. Thus, the number of hamburgers sold in Andy's main restaurant in Columbus can be found in the third row, first column.

This arrangement of data—a table consisting of rows and columns—is called a **two-dimensional array.** In this case, the two-dimensional array of data comprises three rows and three columns—a total of nine elements (3 × 3).

Two-dimensional arrays are named in the same way as other variables. A name used for a two-dimensional array cannot be used for a one-dimensional array in the same program (and vice versa). An individual element in a table is indicated by a pair of subscripts in parentheses. The first subscript indicates the row; the second, the column. The row and column subscripts are separated by a comma.

If we name the array H for Andy's Hamburger Chain, the number of hamburgers sold at the individual restaurants can be indicated by H(r,c), where r stands for the row in which a value is found, an c stands for the column in which it is found:

Array H

H(1,1) 100	H(1,2) 50	H(1,3) 35
H(2,1) 95	H(2,2) 60	H(2,3) 50
H(3,1) 110	H(3,2) 80	H(3,3) 100

Thus, H(2,3) represents the number of hamburgers sold at the drive-through in Detroit, found in row 2, column 3. H(1,1) indicates the number of hamburgers sold at the Toledo main restaurant.

Notice that it is necessary to store the cities' names in a separate array, because we cannot mix character string values with numeric values in the same array:

Array C$

C$(1) Toledo
C$(2) Detroit
C$(3) Columbus

As with one-dimensional arrays, individual subscripts in two-dimensional arrays may be indicated with any legal expression:

X(3,5)
X(I,5)
X(I,J)
X(2,I + J)

The 4 × 8 array X contains the following thirty-two elements:

Array X

10	15	20	25	30	35	40	45
50	55	60	65	70	75	80	85
90	95	100	105	110	115	120	125
130	135	140	145	150	155	160	165

Assume that I = 4 and J = 2. Then

X(J,I) refers to X(2,4)—the element in the second row, fourth column of array X, which is 65.

X(4,I) refers to X(4,4)—the element in the fourth row, fourth column of array X, which is 145.

X(3,J + 4) refers to X(3,6)—the element in the third row, sixth column of array X, which is 115.

X(I,5) refers to X(4,5)—the element in the fourth row, fifth column of array X, which is 150.

As with one-dimensional arrays, the space needed to store a two-dimensional array must be stated if the array size exceeds a certain limit. Unless told otherwise, most BASIC compilers reserve enough space for an array with up to ten rows and up to ten columns. Therefore, for an array to exceed either the row limit or the column limit, the programmer must specify its size in a DIM statement. For example,

```
00010 DIM X(20,5)
```

reserves space for array X, which has twenty rows and five columns.

Reading and Printing Data in Two-Dimensional Arrays

Reading data into and printing data from two-dimensional arrays can be accomplished with nested FOR/NEXT statements. Thus, in Figure 9–3, we read Andy's hamburger sales data into a two-dimensional array called H. The reading of the table follows a row-by-row sequence from left to right across each column. The loops in lines 20 through 55 perform this reading process:

```
00020 FOR I = 1 TO 3
00025    FOR J = 1 TO 3
00030       READ H(I,J)
00035    NEXT J
00040 NEXT I
00045 DATA 100,50,35
00050 DATA 95,60,50
00055 DATA 110,80,100
```

When the program is executed, each data value is represented by the variable H followed by a unique pair of subscripts telling its location by row, I, and column, J. As the data values are read, they fill the table row by row (that is, after row 1 has been filled, row 2 is filled, and then row 3). The outer FOR/NEXT loop controls the rows (using the variable I); the inner loop controls the columns (using the variable J). Thus, every time the outer loop is executed once, the inner loop is executed three times. While I is equal to 1, J is equal to 1, 2, and 3. The first three numbers from the data list are read into H(1,1), H(1,2), and H(1,3). Then I is incremented to 2. The inner loop again is executed three times, and the next three numbers from the data list are read into the second row, H(2,1), H(2,2), and H(2,3). I is finally incremented to 3, and the third row of the table is filled.

To print the entire table, a PRINT statement in a nested loop can be used. This is illustrated in lines 80 through 115. Let us examine the PRINT statements in this segment:

```
00080 FOR I = 1 TO 3
00085    READ C$
00090    PRINT C$,
00095    FOR J = 1 TO 3
00100      PRINT H(I,J),
00105   NEXT J
00110   PRINT
00115 NEXT I
```

The comma in line 100 signals the computer to print the three values in predefined print zones on the same line. After the inner loop has been executed, the blank PRINT in line 110 sets the carriage return so that the next row is printed on the next line.

Adding Rows of Items

After data has been read and stored as an array, it is possible to manipulate the array elements. For example, Andy may want to find out how many hamburgers were sold in Detroit or how many hamburgers were sold at drive-throughs.

Since the data for each city are contained in a row of the array, we need to total the elements in one row of the array (the second row) to find out

Figure 9–3 HAMBURGER SALES PROGRAM

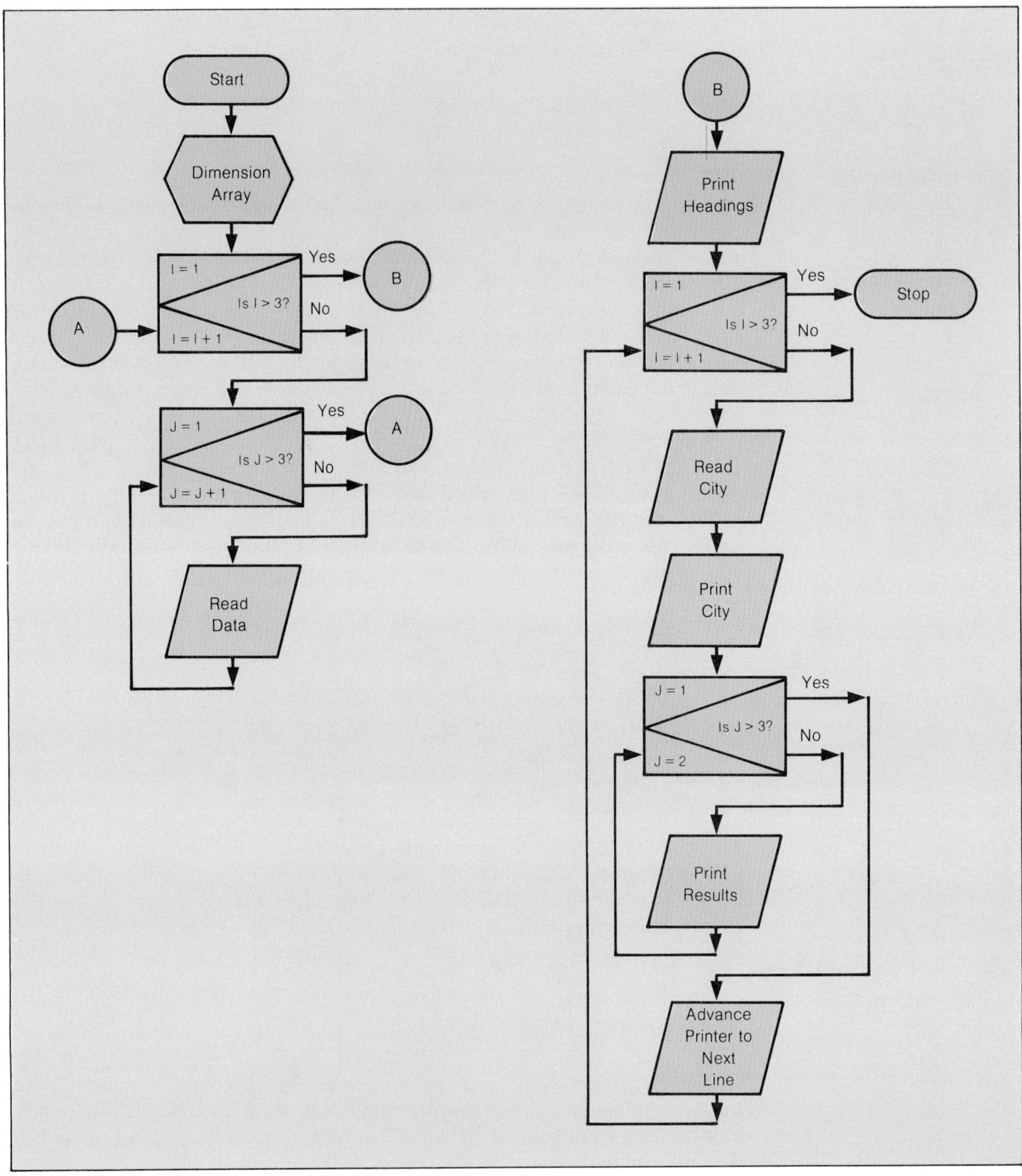

Figure 9–3 *(continued)*

```
00010 REM *** ANDY'S HAMBURGER CHAIN SALES INFORMATION ***
00015 DIM H(3,3)
00020 FOR I = 1 TO 3
00025   FOR J = 1 TO 3
00030     READ H(I,J)
00035   NEXT J
00040 NEXT I
00045 DATA 100,50,35
00050 DATA 95,60,50
00055 DATA 110,80,100
00060 DATA "TOLEDO","DETROIT","COLUMBUS"
00065 PRINT
00070 PRINT "CITY","MAIN","BRANCH","DRIVE-THROUGH"
00075 PRINT
00080 FOR I = 1 TO 3
00085   READ C$
00090   PRINT C$,
00095   FOR J = 1 TO 3
00100     PRINT H(I,J),
00105   NEXT J
00110   PRINT
00115 NEXT I
00999 END
```

```
RUNNH
```

CITY	MAIN	BRANCH	DRIVE-THROUGH
TOLEDO	100	50	35
DETROIT	95	60	50
COLUMBUS	110	80	100

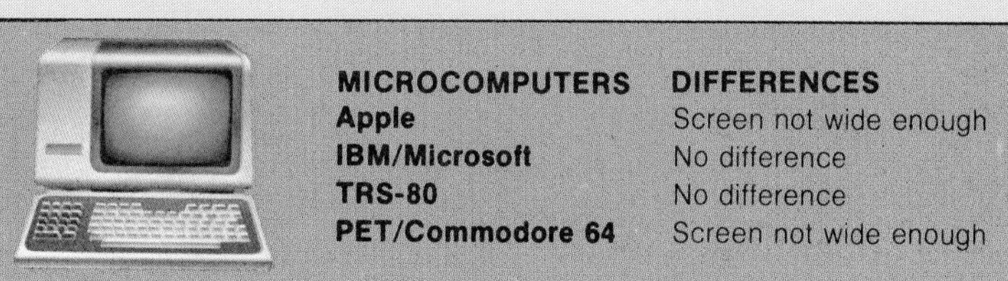

MICROCOMPUTERS	DIFFERENCES
Apple	Screen not wide enough
IBM/Microsoft	No difference
TRS-80	No difference
PET/Commodore 64	Screen not wide enough

how many hamburgers were sold in Detroit. This can be done with the following statements:

```
00120 LET T = 0
00125 FOR J = 1 TO 3
00130    LET T = T + H(2,J)
00135 NEXT J
```

Notice that H(2,J) restricts the computations to the elements in row 2, while the column, J, varies from 1 to 3.

Adding Columns of Items

To find the number of hamburgers sold at drive-throughs, we want to total the elements in the third column of the array:

```
00150 LET D = 0
00155 FOR I = 1 TO 3
00160    LET D = D + H(I,3)
00165 NEXT I
```

In these statements, H(I,3) restricts the computations to the elements in the third column, while the row, I, varies from 1 to 3.

Totaling a Two-Dimensional Array

Now suppose we need to know how many Andy's hamburgers were sold altogether. This means we must add all the elements in the array:

```
00175 LET A = 0
00180 FOR I = 1 TO 3
00185    FOR J = 1 TO 3
00190       LET A = A + H(I,J)
00195    NEXT J
00200 NEXT I
```

A is the variable that will be used to accumulate the total. It is initialized outside the loop. To add all the elements in array H, we are going to use a nested loop. The outer loop will control the rows and the inner loop, the columns. Line 190 does the actual accumulation. The first time through the loop, both I and J equal 1; thus, H(1,1) is added to 0. J is then incremented, and H(1,2) is added to A to make 150. Then H(1,3), or 35, is added. At this point, I is incremented to 2 so that we can begin adding the second-row values and so on until all the elements in H have been totaled. Figure 9–4 shows the complete program for Andy's Hamburger Chain and the resulting output.

Figure 9–4 Complete Hamburger Sales Program

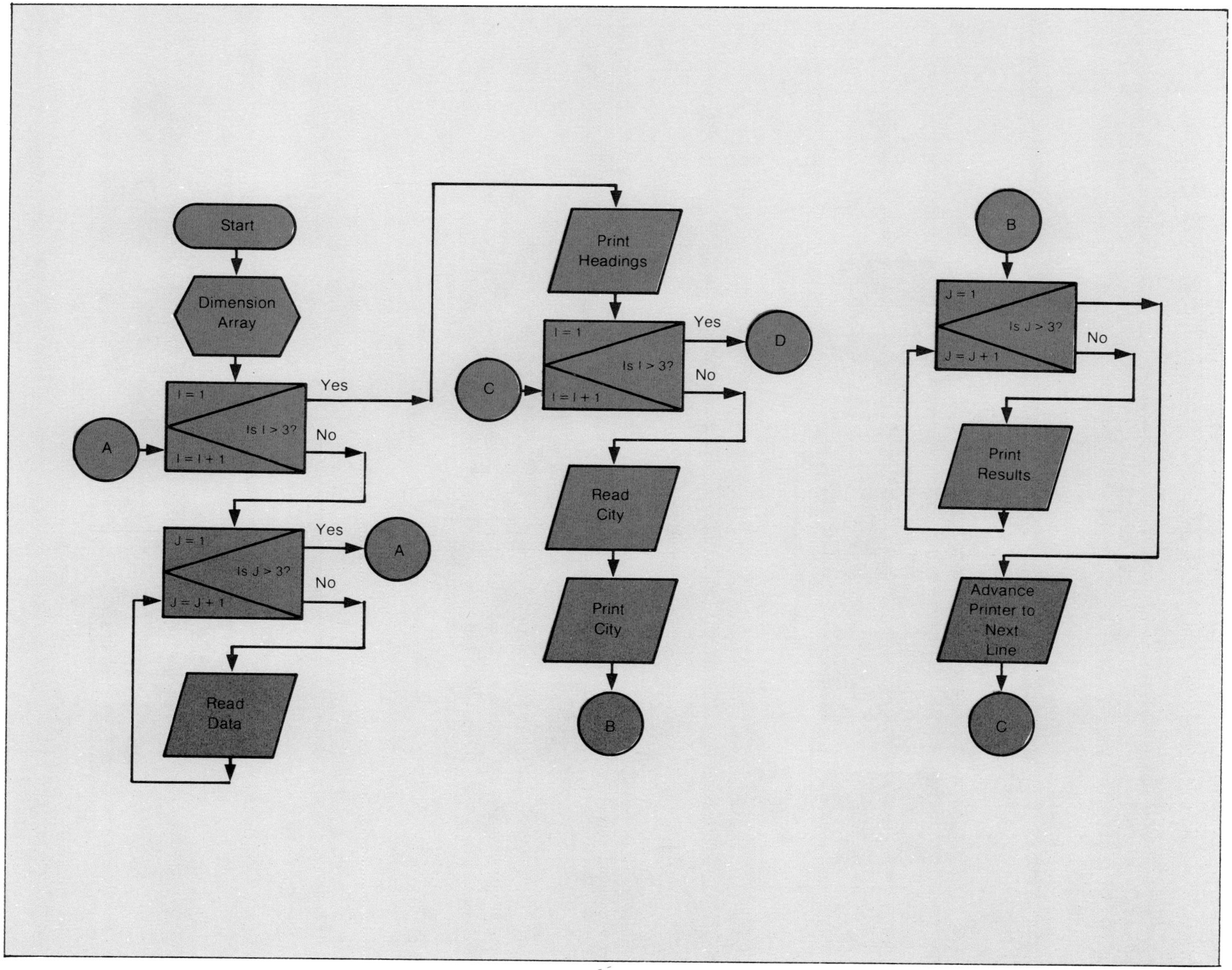

(Figure continued next page)

Figure 9–4 *(continued)*

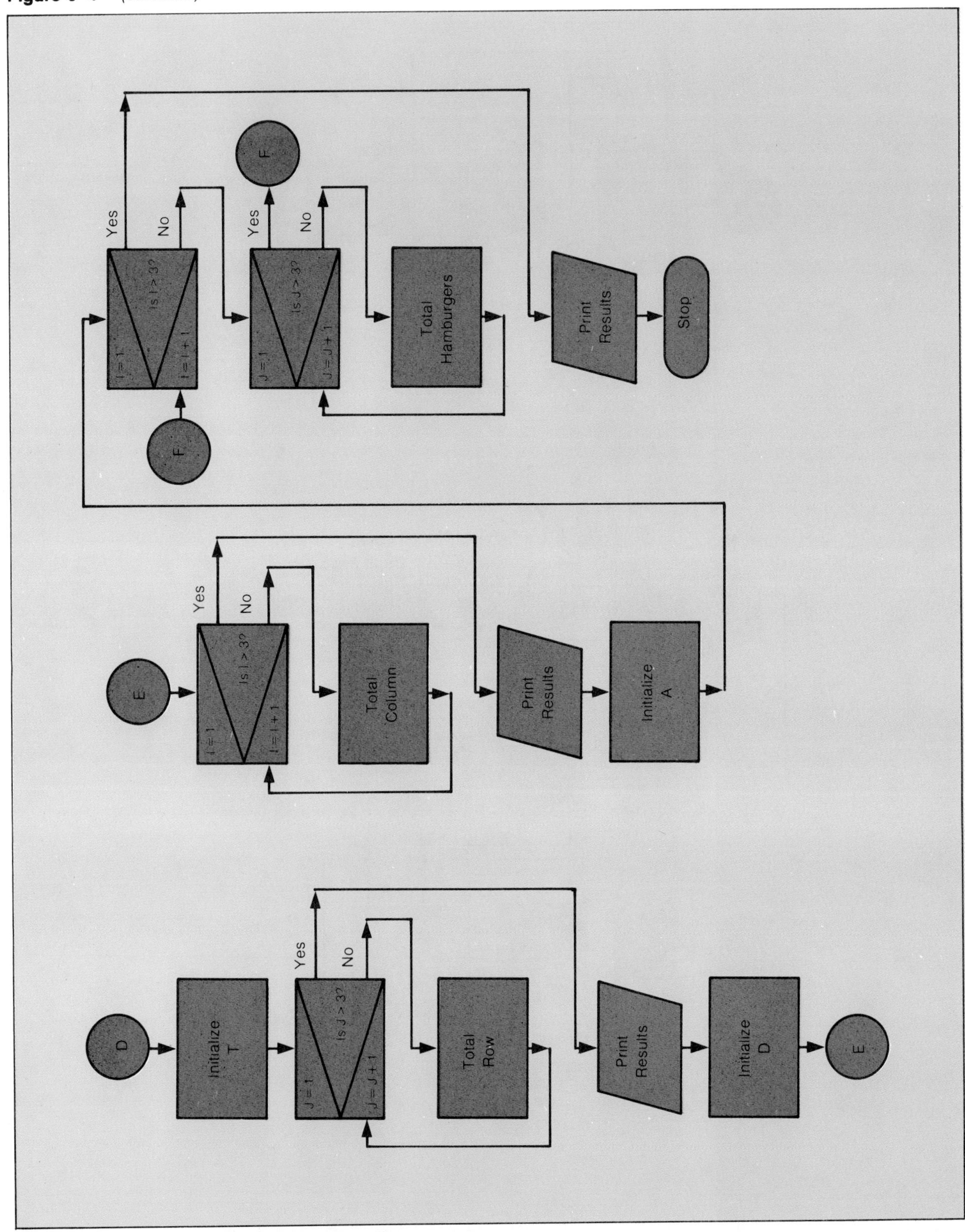

Figure 9–4
(continued)

```
00010 REM *** ANDY'S HAMBURGER CHAIN SALES INFORMATION ***
00015 DIM H(3,3)
00020 FOR I = 1 TO 3
00025   FOR J = 1 TO 3
00030     READ H(I,J)
00035   NEXT J
00040 NEXT I
00045 DATA 100,50,35
00050 DATA 95,60,50
00055 DATA 110,80,100
00060 DATA "TOLEDO","DETROIT","COLUMBUS"
00065 PRINT
00070 PRINT "CITY","MAIN","BRANCH","DRIVE-THROUGH"
00075 PRINT
00080 FOR I = 1 TO 3
00085   READ C$
00090   PRINT C$,
00095   FOR J = 1 TO 3
00100    PRINT H(I,J),
00105  NEXT J
00110  PRINT
00115 NEXT I
00120 LET T = 0
00125 FOR J = 1 TO 3
00130   LET T = T + H(2,J)
00135 NEXT J
00140 PRINT
00145 PRINT T;"HAMBURGERS WERE SOLD IN DETROIT"
00150 LET D = 0
00155 FOR I = 1 TO 3
00160   LET D = D + H(I,3)
00165 NEXT I
00170 PRINT D;"HAMBURGERS WERE SOLD AT DRIVE THROUGHS"
00175 LET A = 0
00180 FOR I = 1 TO 3
00185   FOR J = 1 TO 3
00190     LET A = A + H(I,J)
00195   NEXT J
00200 NEXT I
00205 PRINT A;"HAMBURGERS WERE SOLD ALTOGETHER"
00999 END
```

```
RUNNH
```

```
CITY          MAIN          BRANCH          DRIVE-THROUGH

TOLEDO         100           50              35
DETROIT        95            60              50
COLUMBUS       110           80              100

 205 HAMBURGERS WERE SOLD IN DETROIT
 185 HAMBURGERS WERE SOLD AT DRIVE THROUGHS
 680 HAMBURGERS WERE SOLD ALTOGETHER
```

MICROCOMPUTERS	DIFFERENCES
Apple	Screen not wide enough
IBM/Microsoft	No difference
TRS-80	No difference
PET/Commodore 64	Screen not wide enough

LEARNING CHECK

1. ________ tell the computer the position of an element in an array.
2. The subscript enclosed in parentheses can be any legal expression. TRUE FALSE (Circle the correct answer.)
3. The ________ statement reserves storage space for the elements in an array.
4. A(n) ________ is a list of related values stored under a single variable name.
5. A(n) ________ is a table with rows and columns of elements.
6. Two-dimensional arrays may be read in or printed out using ________ FOR/NEXT loops.
7. The first subscript of a two-dimensional array refers to the ________ of the element, and the second subscript refers to the ________.

Answers

1. Subscripts
2. True
3. DIM
4. one-dimensional array
5. two-dimensional array
6. nested
7. row; column

Advantages of Arrays

Although it may not be obvious at this point, arrays are useful in many applications. By using arrays, we can avoid having to make up names for numerous items. Also, once data are stored in an array, the data items (elements) can be referred to over and over again without being reread. Arrays also are used extensively in file processing (discussed in Chapter 10).

Arrays also can be manipulated in a number of ways besides the basic computational examples previously given. For instance, some of the more common manipulation techniques include array merges and array searches.

Array Merge

Two arrays can be merged into one (see Figure 9–5). For example, if we had two arrays—A and B, each with five elements—and we wanted to merge them into an array C that contained the data A_1, B_1, A_2, B_2, . . . , A_5, B_5 (arranged in that order), we could use any of the following codes:

```
00010 LET X = 1
00020 FOR I = 1 TO 5
00030    LET C(X) = A(I)
00040    LET X = X + 1
00050    LET C(X) = B(I)
00060    LET X = X + 1
00070 NEXT I
```

Figure 9–5 MERGING TWO ARRAYS

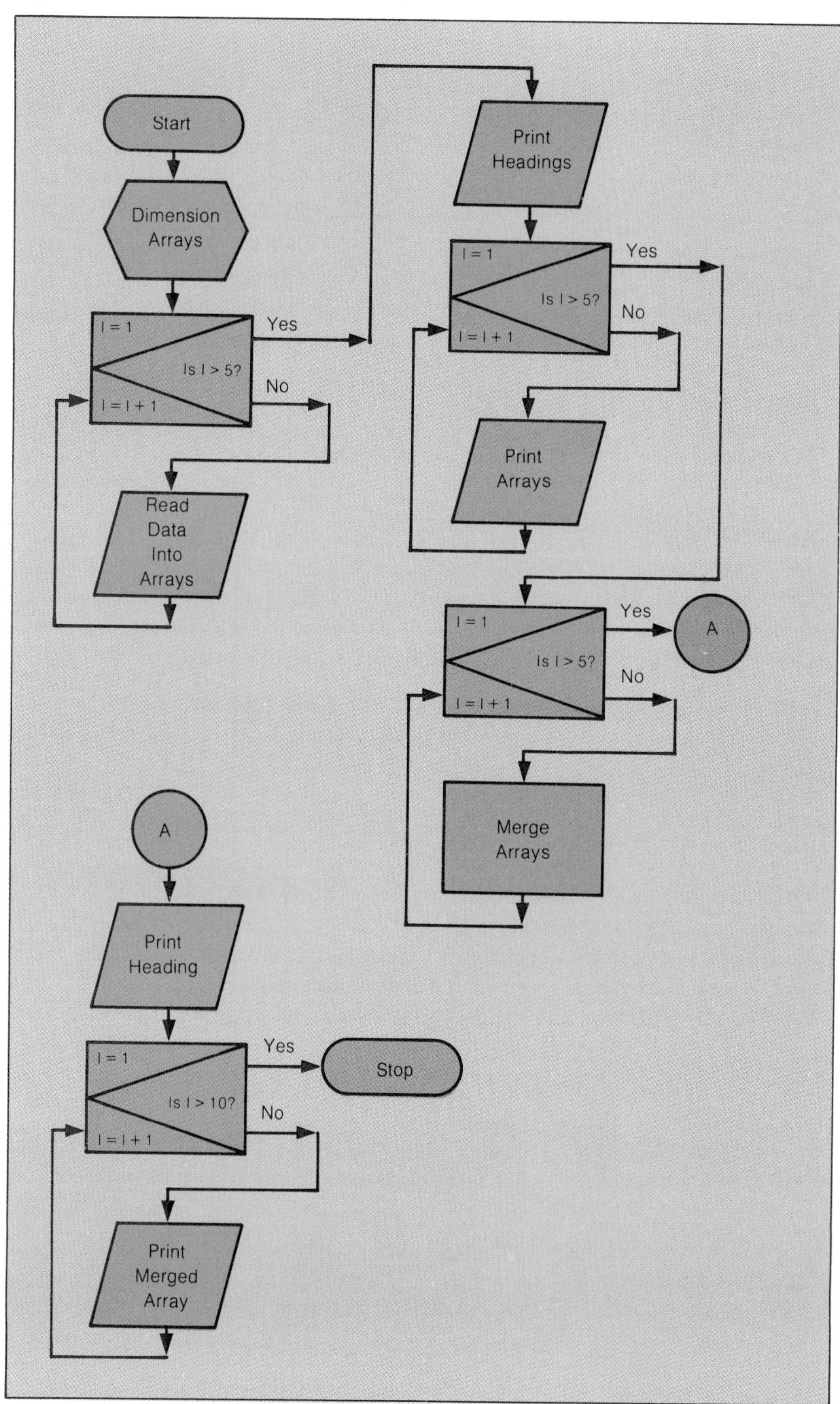

(Figure continued next page)

Figure 9–5 *(continued)*

```
00010 DIM A(5),B(5),C(10)
00015 FOR I = 1 TO 5
00020   READ A(I)
00025   READ B(I)
00030 NEXT I
00035 PRINT "ARRAY A","ARRAY B"
00040 FOR I = 1 TO 5
00045   PRINT A(I),
00050   PRINT B(I)
00055 NEXT I
00060 FOR I = 1 TO 5
00065   LET C(2 * I - 1) = A(I)
00070   LET C(2 * I) = B(I)
00075 NEXT I
00080 PRINT
00085 PRINT
00090 PRINT "ARRAY C"
00095 FOR I = 1 TO 10
00100   PRINT C(I)
00105 NEXT I
00110 DATA 1,2,3,4,5,6,7,8,9,10
00999 END

RUNNH
```

```
ARRAY A        ARRAY B
 1              2
 3              4
 5              6
 7              8
 9              10

ARRAY C
 1
 2
 3
 4
 5
 6
 7
 8
 9
 10
```

MICROCOMPUTERS
Apple: No differences.
IBM/Microsoft: No differences.
PET/Commodore 64: No differences.
TRS-80: No differences.

or

```
00010 LET X = 1
00020 FOR I = 1 TO 10 STEP 2
00030    LET C(I) = A(X)
00040    LET C(I + 1) = B(X)
00050    LET X = X + 1
00060 NEXT I
```

or

```
00010 FOR I = 1 TO 5
00020    LET C(2 * I - 1) = A(I)
00030    LET C(2 * I) = B(I)
00040 NEXT I
```

Figure 9–5 illustrates a merging of two arrays.

Array Search

An array search consists of searching an array until a desired value or values are found. For example, you may want to know the number of scores higher then 89 in a particular array, or you may be searching for a single value.

In the first case, assume that the array A contains thirty-five grades, and you want to know the number of scores higher than 89. The following segment could be used to search the array A and obtain the results:

```
00100 LET X = 0
00110 FOR I = 1 TO 35
00120    IF A(I) <= 89 THEN 140
00130    LET X = X + 1
00140 NEXT I
```

The variable X is used to count the number of scores higher than 89. Line 120 checks to see if the score is less than or equal to 89. If it is, the computer skips down to line 140 without incrementing the counter. If the score is greater than 89, line 130 is executed, and the counter is incremented. Later in the program, the value of X could be printed out, giving the total number of grades greater than 89 in array A.

In the latter case, suppose you wanted to find out information for the August 19 concert at the local concert hall. The computer might prompt you to enter the date of the concert in which you are interested. It then would search a list of concert dates until it matched the two dates. Finally, the computer would extract the corresponding values from the other arrays and display them on the CRT screen. Note that if more than one array holds corresponding (related) data, the data must be contained in the same relative position in each array. (See Figure 9–6.)

Figure 9–6 CONCERT INFORMATION EXAMPLE

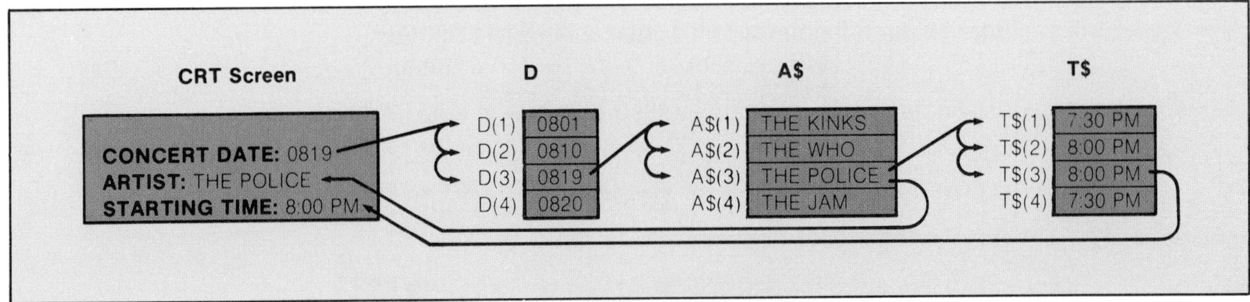

The two types of searches just discussed were sequential array searches. In this type of search, the first element of the array is examined, then the second, then the third, and so on, one after another until the end of the array is reached. This type of search is adequate until we start dealing with larger arrays (one hundred or more elements). After that point, sequential searches may become noticeably slow. If, however, the elements in the array can be arranged in an ascending or descending sequence, a more efficient technique for searching the array is the binary search.

In a binary search, portions of the array that do not contain the value being searched for are eliminated. (Remember, the data must be in ascending or descending order.) For example, in our concert information example, we could list the concert dates in an array in ascending order (the numbers are coded to reflect the month and the date in the following manner: MM/DD), such as in Figure 9–7.

To conduct a binary search on array D, the following steps are taken. First, the data item to be found in the array is entered from the keyboard—0819 in this case. The data item entered (0819) then is compared to the middle item in the array (0822), which in this case is the sixth element.

Figure 9–7 BINARY SEARCH

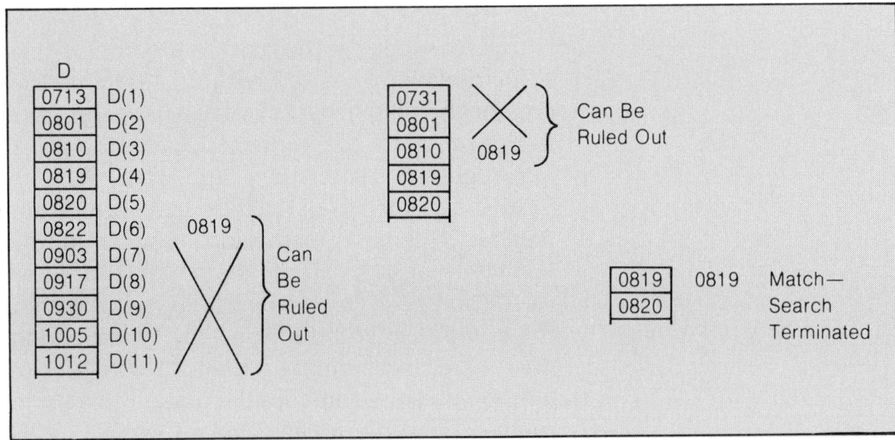

The date we are searching for is less than the date at D(6). Therefore, since the list is in ascending order, the computer knows that the elements D(6) through D(11) need not be searched. With only one comparison, we have already eliminated half the array.

The next step is to compare the desired data with the middle value of the remaining elements, D(1) through D(5), in array D. This would be D(3), or 0810. Our date is larger than 0810; therefore, D(1) through D(3) can be ruled out for further searching. This leaves us with D(4) and D(5) left to search. Since there is no single middle element between 4 and 5, the lower-numbered element is chosen for the comparison. When D(4) is matched to 0819, it is found that they are equal, and the search is terminated. The logic to perform a binary search must calculate which element within the array is to be compared on each pass through the search. The search will continue until an equal element is found or until all possible elements have been compared and found to be not equal. Figure 9–8 gives the coding and flowchart for the binary search segment.

Using a binary search is much more efficient than a sequential search when dealing with very large arrays. For example, if we had an array with one thousand elements, the maximum number of comparisons a binary search would need to make to find an equal element is 10, as compared with possibly 999 comparisons in a sequential search if the element we were searching for was the last one in the array.

Sorting

Many applications require that data items be sorted, or ordered, in some way. For example, names must be alphabetized, Social Security numbers arranged from lowest to highest, basketball players ranked from high scorer to low scorer, and the like.

Suppose that an array, BA, contains five prices that we would like ordered from lowest to highest:

Array BA (Unsorted)
2.03
4.95
1.13
3.89
2.56

It is a simple matter for us to mentally reorder this list as follows:

Array BA (Sorted)
1.13
2.03
2.56
4.95
3.89

Figure 9–8 BINARY SEARCH PROGRAM SEGMENT

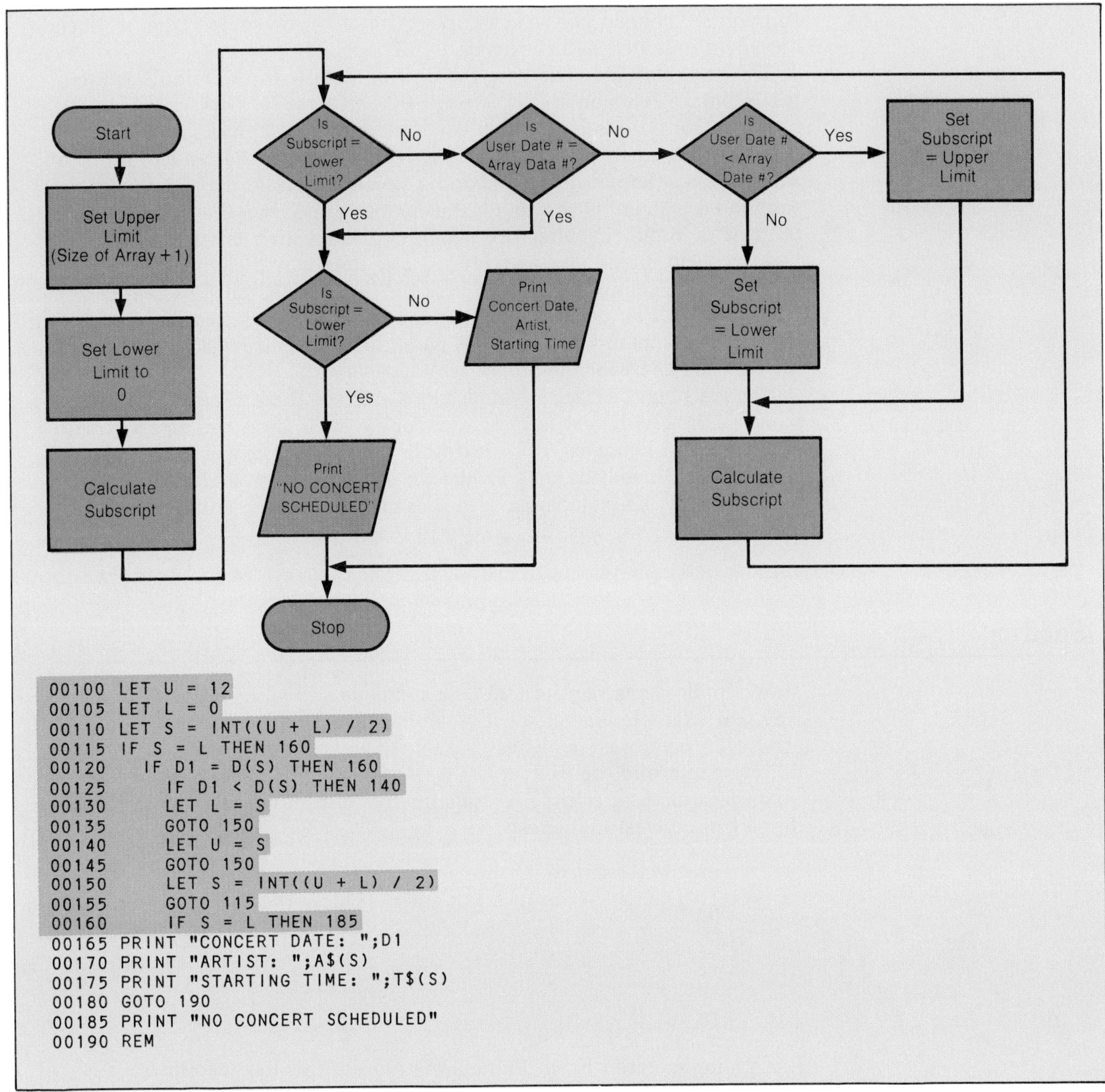


```
00100 LET U = 12
00105 LET L = 0
00110 LET S = INT((U + L) / 2)
00115 IF S = L THEN 160
00120   IF D1 = D(S) THEN 160
00125     IF D1 < D(S) THEN 140
00130     LET L = S
00135     GOTO 150
00140     LET U = S
00145     GOTO 150
00150     LET S = INT((U + L) / 2)
00155     GOTO 115
00160     IF S = L THEN 185
00165 PRINT "CONCERT DATE: ";D1
00170 PRINT "ARTIST: ";A$(S)
00175 PRINT "STARTING TIME: ";T$(S)
00180 GOTO 190
00185 PRINT "NO CONCERT SCHEDULED"
00190 REM
```

What if there were seven hundred prices instead of five? Then it would not be so easy for us to order the price list. However, the computer is perfectly suited for such tasks. One method of sorting with the computer is illustrated in Figure 9–9.

The Bubble Sort

The **bubble sort** works by comparing two adjacent values in an array and then interchanging them according to the desired order—either ascending or descending order.

The program in Figure 9–9 sorts fifteen student names into alphabetical order. To the computer, the letter A is less than the letter B, B is less than C, and so on. Lines 135 through 145 simply read the student names into an array called S$ and prints them. Lines 160 through 205 perform the bubble sort. Let us examine them carefully to see what happens.

Line 165 refers to the variable F, short for **flag.** It is initialized to 0. Its value is checked later by the computer to determine if the entire array has been sorted.

Notice the terminal value of the FOR/NEXT loop that sorts the array. The terminal value is one less than the number of items to be sorted. This is because two items at a time are compared. J varies from 1 to 14, which means that the computer eventually will compare item 14 with item 14 + 1. If the terminal value were 15 (the number of names), the computer would try to compare item 15 with item 16, which does not exist in our array.

The IF/THEN statement in line 175 tells the computer whether to interchange two compared values. For example, when J = 1, the computer compares JANELLE with SUE. Since J comes before S in the alphabet, there is no need to switch these two items:

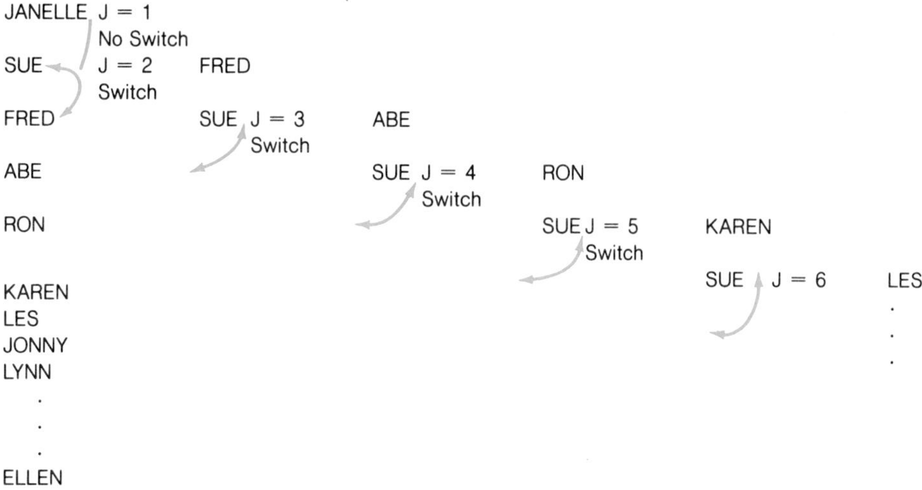

Then J is incremented to 2, and SUE is compared with FRED. These two names must be interchanged. This is performed by lines 180 through 190. Note that we have created a holding area, H$, so that the switch can be made. We move SUE to the holding area, H$, and then move FRED to SUE's previous position. Now SUE is placed in the position previously occupied by FRED. Whenever the computer interchanges two values, F is set to 1 in line 195. This loop continues until every item in the array has

Figure 9–9 SORTING PROGRAM

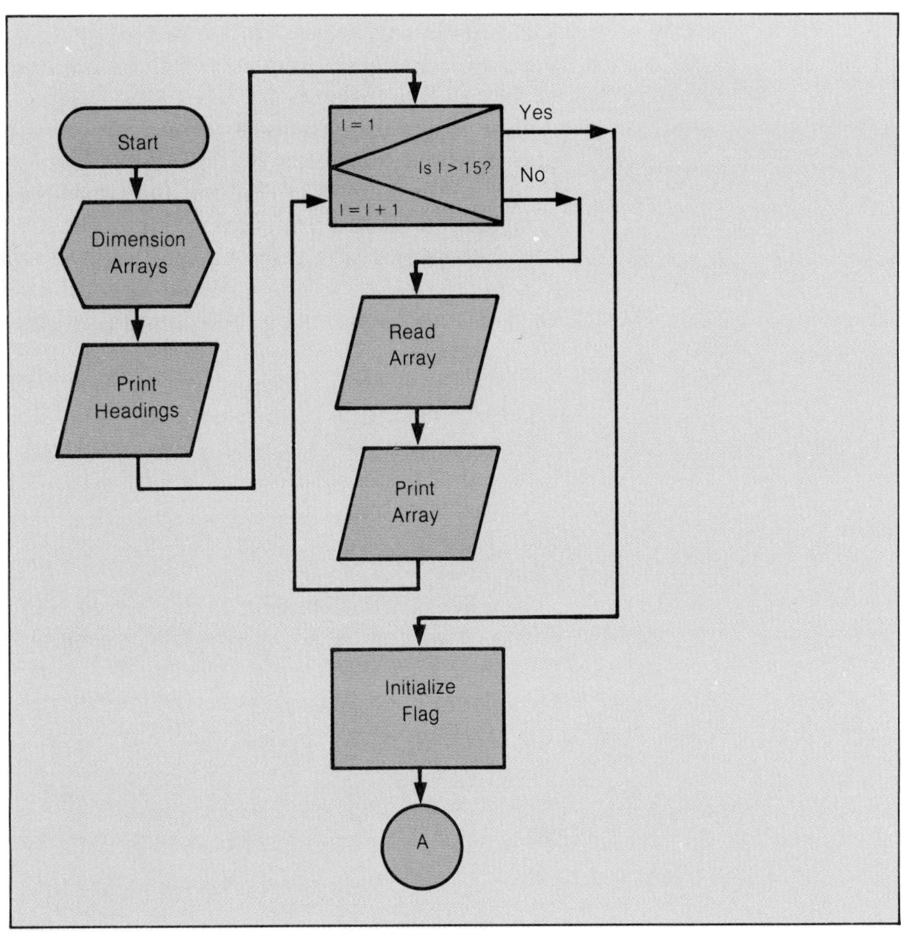

been examined. After once through this entire loop, the array S$ looks like this:

JANELLE
FRED
ABE
RON
KAREN
LES
JONNY
LYNN
RACHEL
KEN
BENJI
SONJA
KRIS
ELLEN
SUE

Figure 9–9 *(continued)*

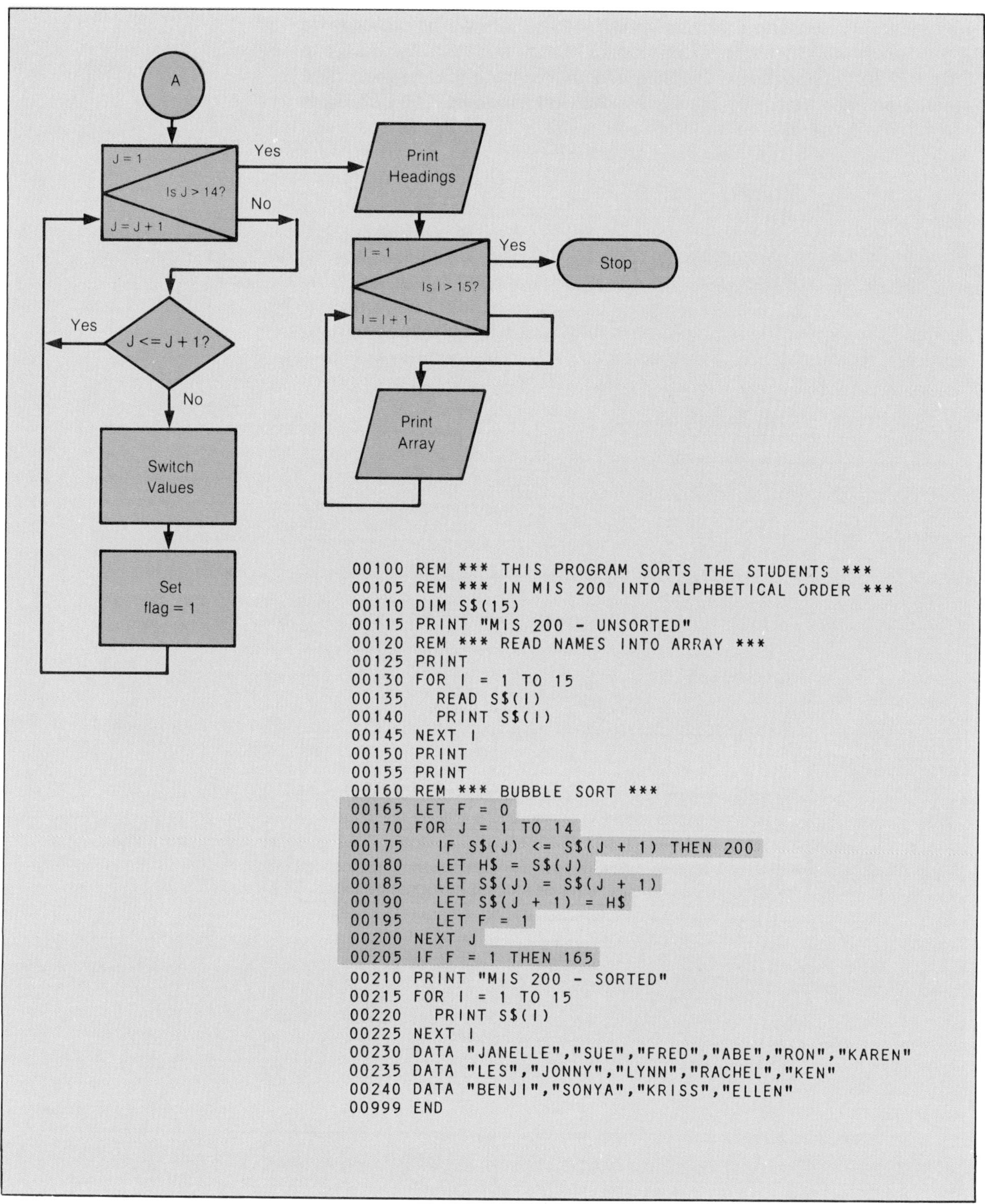


```
00100 REM *** THIS PROGRAM SORTS THE STUDENTS ***
00105 REM *** IN MIS 200 INTO ALPHBETICAL ORDER ***
00110 DIM S$(15)
00115 PRINT "MIS 200 - UNSORTED"
00120 REM *** READ NAMES INTO ARRAY ***
00125 PRINT
00130 FOR I = 1 TO 15
00135   READ S$(I)
00140   PRINT S$(I)
00145 NEXT I
00150 PRINT
00155 PRINT
00160 REM *** BUBBLE SORT ***
00165 LET F = 0
00170 FOR J = 1 TO 14
00175   IF S$(J) <= S$(J + 1) THEN 200
00180   LET H$ = S$(J)
00185   LET S$(J) = S$(J + 1)
00190   LET S$(J + 1) = H$
00195   LET F = 1
00200 NEXT J
00205 IF F = 1 THEN 165
00210 PRINT "MIS 200 - SORTED"
00215 FOR I = 1 TO 15
00220   PRINT S$(I)
00225 NEXT I
00230 DATA "JANELLE","SUE","FRED","ABE","RON","KAREN"
00235 DATA "LES","JONNY","LYNN","RACHEL","KEN"
00240 DATA "BENJI","SONYA","KRISS","ELLEN"
00999 END
```

(Figure continued next page)

Figure 9–9 *(continued)*

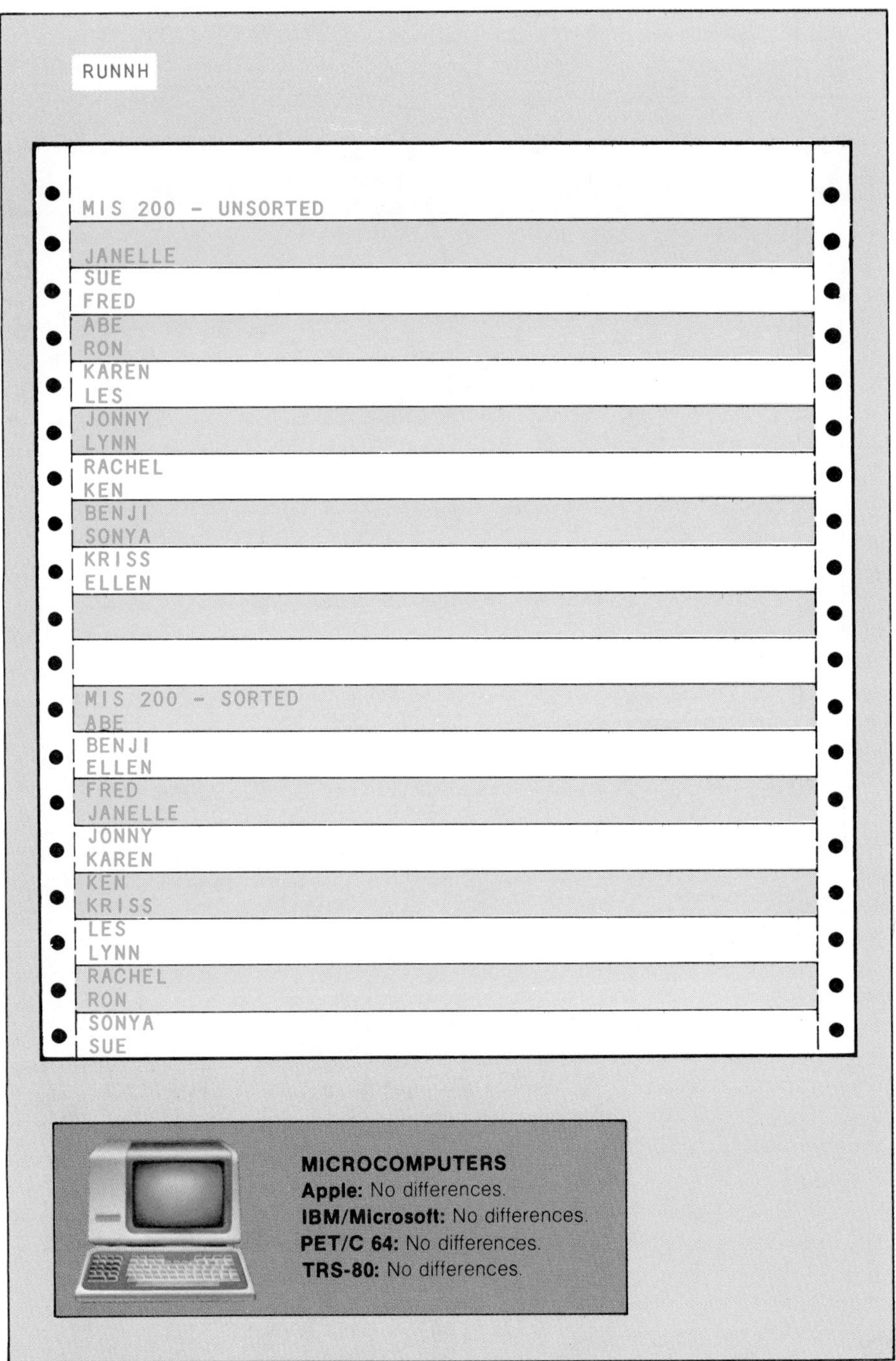
RUNNH
MIS 200 - UNSORTED
JANELLE
SUE
FRED
ABE
RON
KAREN
LES
JONNY
LYNN
RACHEL
KEN
BENJI
SONYA
KRISS
ELLEN
MIS 200 - SORTED
ABE
BENJI
ELLEN
FRED
JANELLE
JONNY
KAREN
KEN
KRISS
LES
LYNN
RACHEL
RON
SONYA
SUE
MICROCOMPUTERS
Apple: No differences.
IBM/Microsoft: No differences.
PET/C 64: No differences.
TRS-80: No differences.

Although several switches have been made, the list is not sorted completely. That is why we need line 205. As long as F equals 1, the computer knows that switches have been made, and the sorting process must continue.

When the computer loops through the entire array without setting F equal to 1—that is, when no switches are made—the computer finds F equal to 0 and knows that the list is ordered.

Numbers, of course, can be sorted by this same method. Two-dimensional arrays can be sorted with nested loops.

The Shell Sort

The bubble sort just discussed is very simple to understand and code. However, it is not very efficient, because the bubble sort can only exchange adjacent elements of the list being sorted. If an element is far from its proper position in the list, many exchanges will be necessary to bring it to its proper position. The **Shell sort,** named after its inventor, Donald Shell, avoids this difficulty. Figure 9–10 illustrates how one version of the Shell sort works.

After defining the list to be sorted, a gap is chosen that is equal to one-half the size of the list. In the example in Figure 9–10, the gap is equal to 4. The elements of the list to be sorted are separated by the chosen gap and

Figure 9–10 THE SHELL SORT

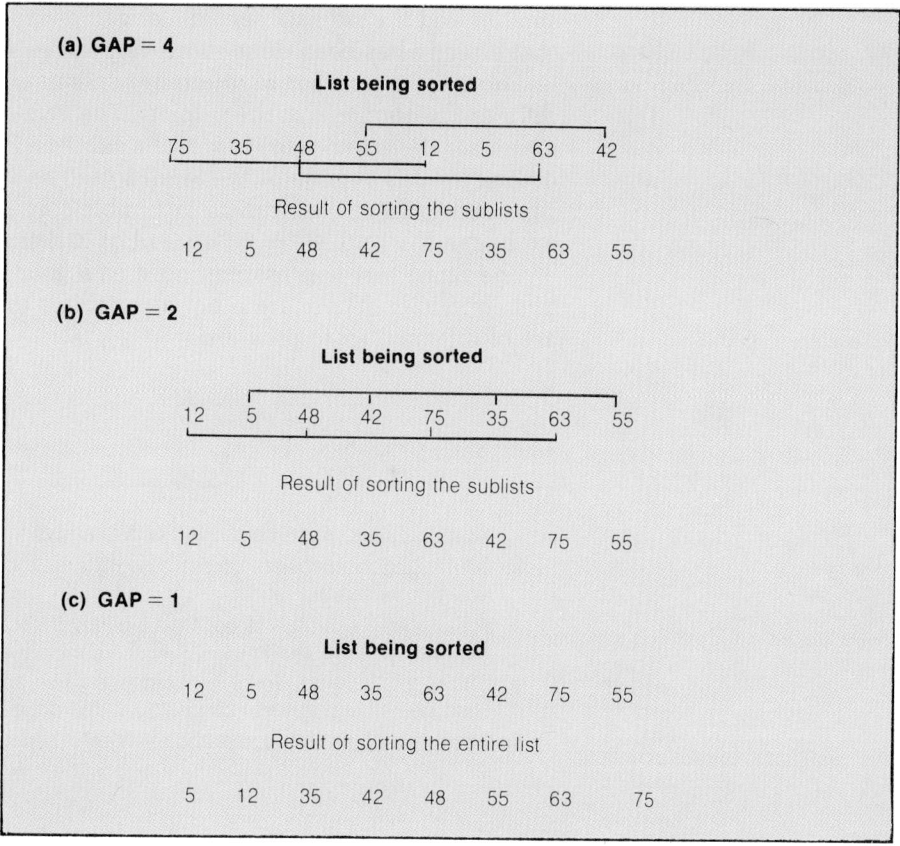

grouped into sublists. Our example has four sublists, each consisting of two elements (see Figure 9–10a). The first and the fifth elements of the list make up one sublist to be sorted; the second and sixth elements, another sublist; the third and seventh elements, another sublist, and the fourth and eighth elements, the final sublist.

The sublists are sorted independently of each other, and the results are shown in Figure 9–10a. Two points should be made at this time. First, because the sublists are short, the sorting proceeds rapidly; second, because the gap between the elements in each sublist is large, out-of-place elements make considerable movement toward their final positions.

Next, the gap is divided in half, and the previously described process is repeated with a gap of two. This will give us two sublists, one consisting of all the elements in odd-numbered positions and one consisting of all the elements in even-numbered positions of the list being sorted. Each sublist is sorted independently; the results of sorting are shown in Figure 9–10b.

The final step involves dividing the gap in half again, giving us a gap of one. This leaves us with only one sublist, which gives us the final result shown in Figure 9–10c.

At first glance, the Shell sort may appear less efficient than the bubble sort. In fact, the entire sequence of sorts called for by the Shell sort takes much less time than a single bubble sort applied to the same list. This is because the earlier sorts of the Shell sort proceed rapidly, since the sublists are short. As we proceed through the Shell sort, the gap becomes smaller and the sublists become longer; because of the preliminary sorting that already has been done, however, the sublists are easier to sort.

There are a number of different versions of the Shell sort, each using a different method to sort the sublists. The version of the Shell sort presented here uses the bubble sort to sort the sublists. Figure 9–11 shows the BASIC coding for this version of the Shell sort. The variable G is the value of the gap used to form the sublists. A bubble sort is used, but we compare and exchange X(I) and X(I + G) instead of X(I) and X(I + 1).

The Shell sort is presented here as a good compromise between speed and simplicity. There are other algorithims that sort faster; however, they are often complex to program.

LEARNING CHECK

1. A(n) ________ is the combining of two arrays into one.
2. A(n) ________ consists of searching the elements of an array until a desired value or values are found.
3. A sequential search is faster than a binary search when searching arrays of one hundred or more elements. TRUE FALSE (Circle the correct answer.)
4. The ________ sort works by comparing two adjacent values in an array and then interchanging them according to the desired order.
5. The ________ sort compares elements separated by a chosen gap and grouped into sublists and interchanges them according to the desired order.

Answers

1. array merge
2. array search
3. False
4. bubble
5. Shell

Figure 9–11 SHELL SORT

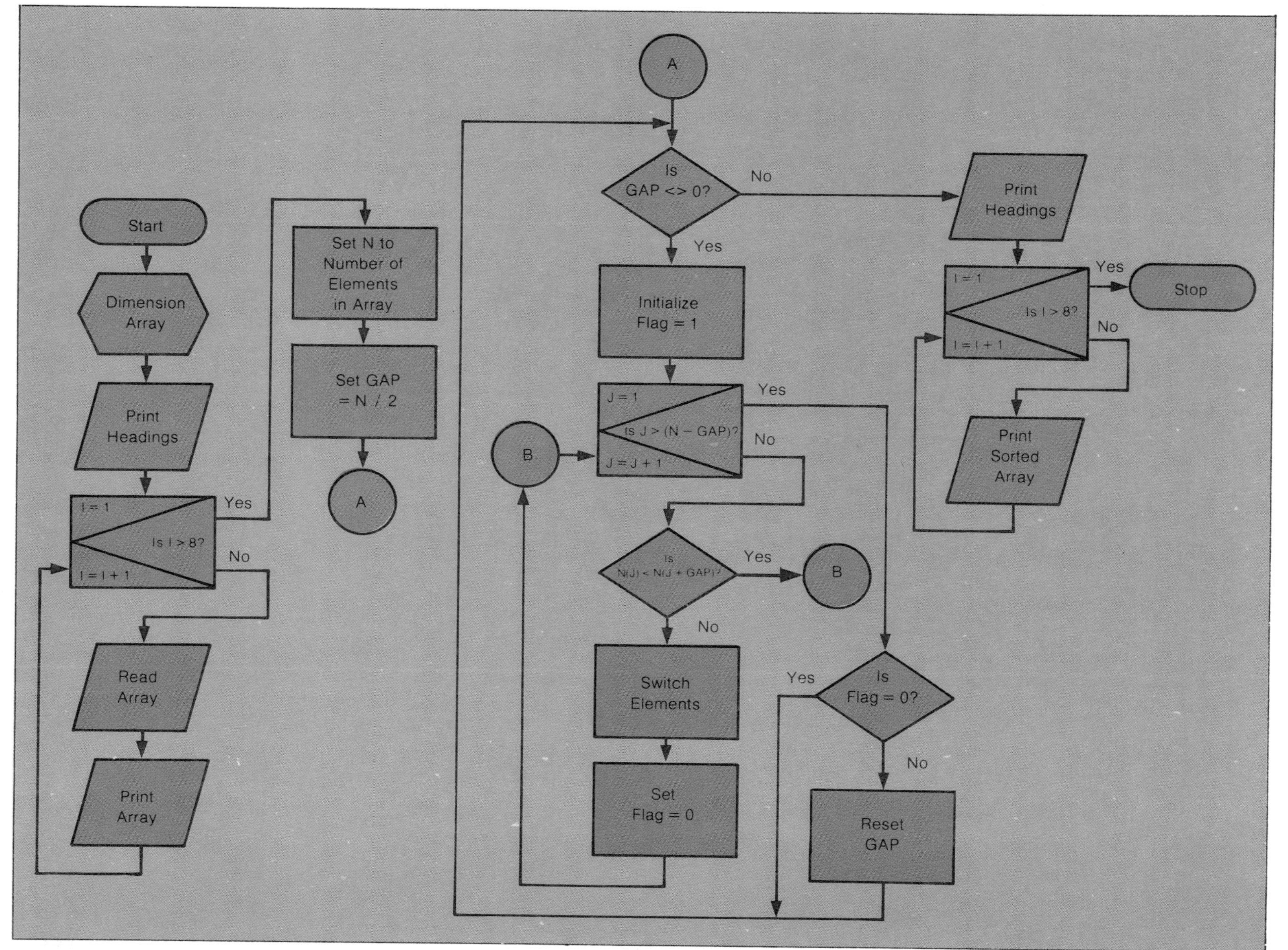

Figure 9–11
(continued)

```
00100 REM *** THIS PROGRAM SORTS NUMBERS INTO ***
00105 REM *** NUMERICAL ORDER ***
00110 DIM N(10)
00115 PRINT "UNSORTED NUMBERS"
00120 REM *** READ NUMBERS INTO ARRAY ***
00125 FOR I = 1 TO 8
00130   READ N(I)
00135   PRINT N(I)
00140 NEXT I
00145 PRINT
00150 PRINT
00155 REM *** SHELL SORT ***
00160 LET N = 8
00165 LET G = INT(N / 2)
00170 WHILE G <> 0
00175   LET F = 1
00180   FOR J = 1 TO (N - G)
00185     IF N(J) <= N(J + G) THEN 210
00190     LET H = N(J)
00195     LET N(J) = N(J + G)
00200     LET N(J + G) = H
00205     LET F = 0
00210 NEXT J
00215   IF F = 0 THEN 175
00220   LET G = INT(G / 2)
00225 NEXT
00230 PRINT "SORTED NUMBERS"
00235 FOR I = 1 TO 8
00240   PRINT N(I)
00245 NEXT I
00250 DATA 75,35,48,55,12,5,63,42
00999 END
```

```
UNSORTED NUMBERS
 75
 35
 48
 55
 12
 5
 63
 42


SORTED NUMBERS
 5
 12
 35
 42
 48
 55
 63
 75
```

MICROCOMPUTERS	DIFFERENCES
Apple	No WHILE loop
IBM/Microsoft	Line 287 should be WEND
TRS-80	No WHILE loop
PET/Commodore 64	No WHILE loop

A Programming Problem

The Problem

The Norm Crosby Swamp Classic Golf Tournament needs to determine quickly the tournament winner after the final round of scores is in. Five golfers have a chance to win. Their names and scores for the first three rounds follow:

Tom Watson	69	69	70
Lee Trevino	65	70	72
Fuzzy Zoeller	66	71	70
Bruce Lietzke	67	72	68
Jack Nicklaus	71	66	70

Solution Design

Since the early round scores are known, they can be introduced to the program along with the golfers' names in READ and DATA statements. The final round scores should be entered by an INPUT statement. Next, the total scores must be calculated and then sorted from lowest to highest. A crucial point is that as the scores are rearranged in the sorting section, the corresponding golfer's name must be carried with each score (although the name is not sorted). Finally, the results must be printed.

The Program

Figure 9–12 shows this problem's solution. Line 105 sets aside room for the variables (although this DIM statement is not strictly necessary, since the arrays have fewer than ten elements per index). Lines 150 through 175, a nested FOR/NEXT loop, read the data. Lines 195 through 210 enter the final round scores. Line 230 through 250 accumulate the total scores in a nested FOR/NEXT loop. The scores are sorted from lowest to highest in lines 270 through 305. The variable H in line 285 is the temporary storage area for scores during sorting. The variable H$ in line 290 performs the same duty for the golfers' names. Every time the computer switches a total, T(J), it also must switch the corresponding golfer's name. The computer performs the switches in lines 295 through 310. Lines 345 through 380 print the results.

Figure 9–12 SORTING GOLF SCORES PROGRAM AND FLOWCHART

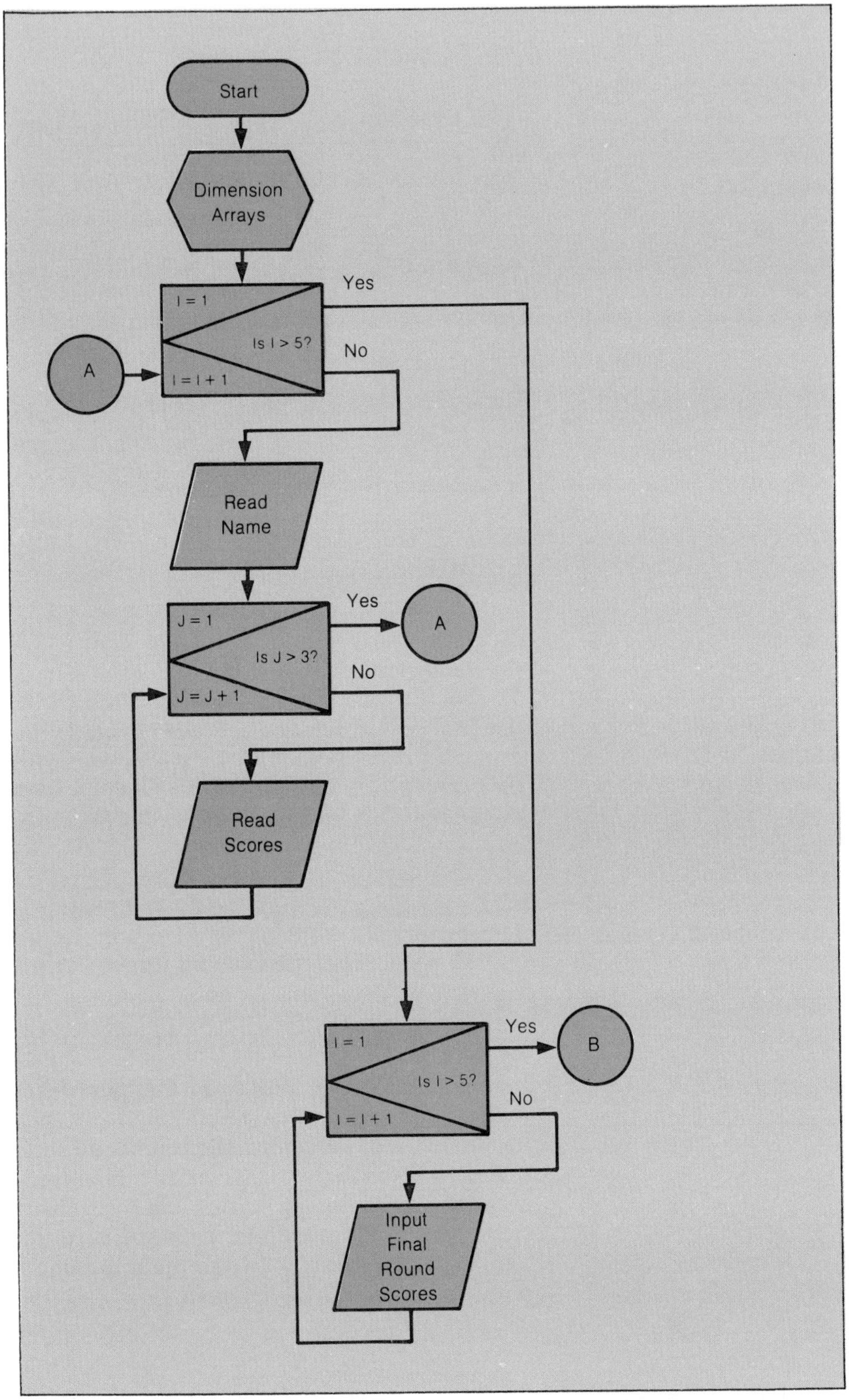

Figure 9–12 *(continued)*

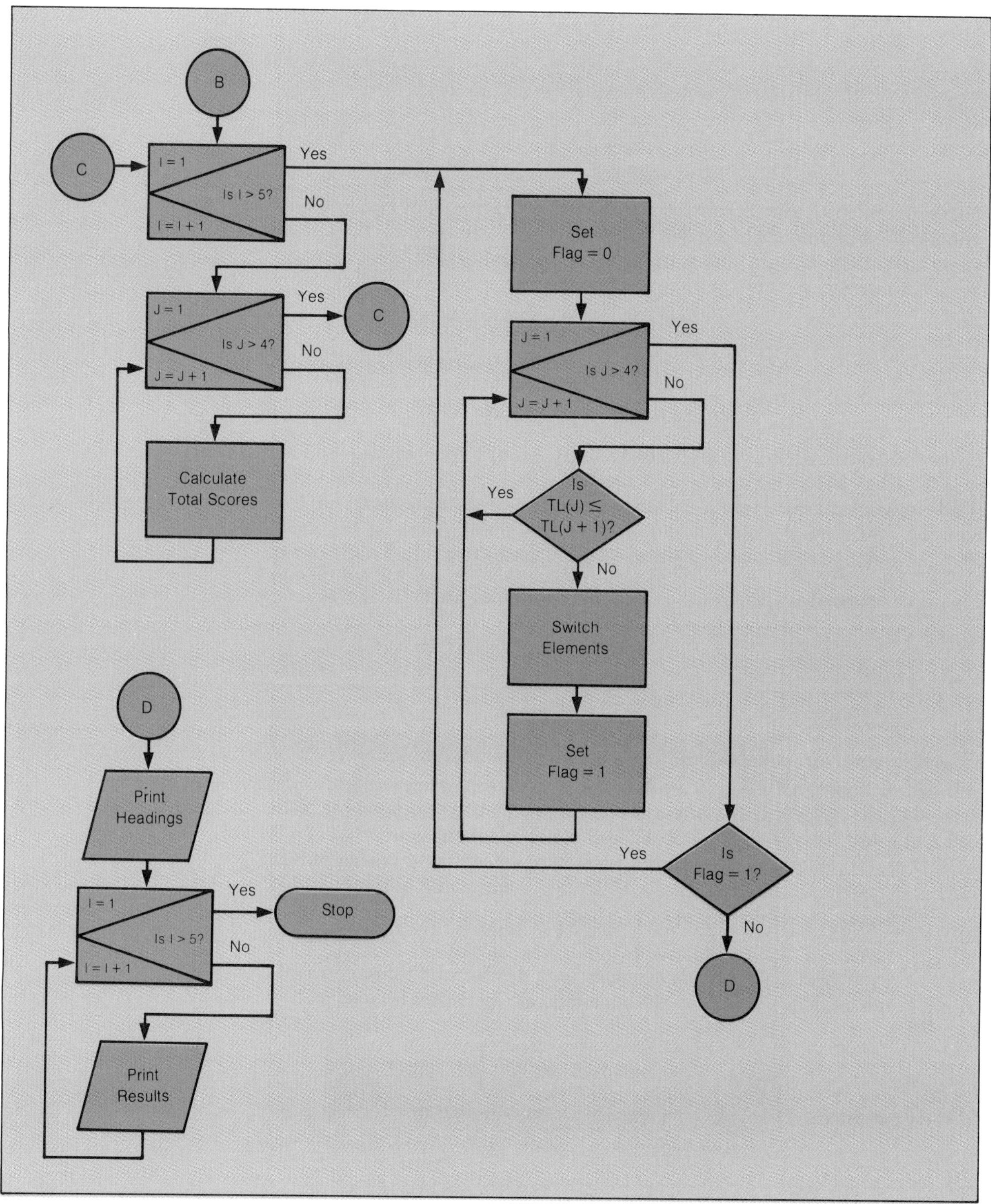

Figure 9-12—*Continued*

Figure 9–12 *(continued)*

```
00100 REM *** GOLF SCORES ***
00105 DIM N$(5),S(5,4),T(5)
00110 PRINT
00115 PRINT
00120 DATA "TOM WATSON",69,69,70,"LEE TREVINO",65,70,72
00125 DATA "FUZZY ZOELLER",66,71,70,"BRUCE LIETZKE",67,72,68
00130 DATA "JACK NICKLAUS",71,66,70
00135 REM **********
00140 REM READ IN DATA FOR FIRST 3 ROUNDS ***
00145 REM **********
00150 FOR I = 1 TO 5
00155   READ N$(I)
00160   FOR J = 1 TO 3
00165     READ S(I,J)
00170   NEXT J
00175 NEXT I
00180 REM **********
00185 REM *** INPUT FINAL ROUND SCORES ***
00190 REM **********
00195 FOR I = 1 TO 5
00200   PRINT "ENTER FINAL ROUND SCORES ";N$(I)
00205   INPUT S(I,4)
00210 NEXT I
00215 REM **********
00220 REM *** CALCULATE TOTAL SCORES ***
00225 REM **********
00230 FOR I = 1 TO 5
00235   FOR J = 1 TO 4
00240     T(I) = T(I) + S(I,J)
00245   NEXT J
00250 NEXT I
00255 REM **********
00260 REM *** SORT SCORES ***
00265 REM **********
00270 LET F = 0
00275 FOR J = 1 TO 4
00280   IF T(J) <= T(J + 1) THEN 320
00285   LET H = T(J)
00290   LET H$ = N$(J)
00295   LET T(J) = T(J + 1)
00300   LET N$(J) = N$(J + 1)
00305   LET T(J + 1) = H
00310   LET N$(J + 1) = H$
00315   LET F = 1
00320 NEXT J
00325 IF F = 1 THEN 270
00330 REM ***********
00335 REM *** PRINT OUT PLACES ***
00340 REM ***********
00345 PRINT
00350 PRINT
00355 PRINT "PLACE";TAB(10);"GOLFER";TAB(30);"SCORE"
00360 PRINT
00365 FOR I = 1 TO 5
00370   PRINT I;TAB(10);N$(I);TAB(30);T(I)
00375   PRINT
00380 NEXT I
00999 END
```

Figure 9–12 *(continued)*

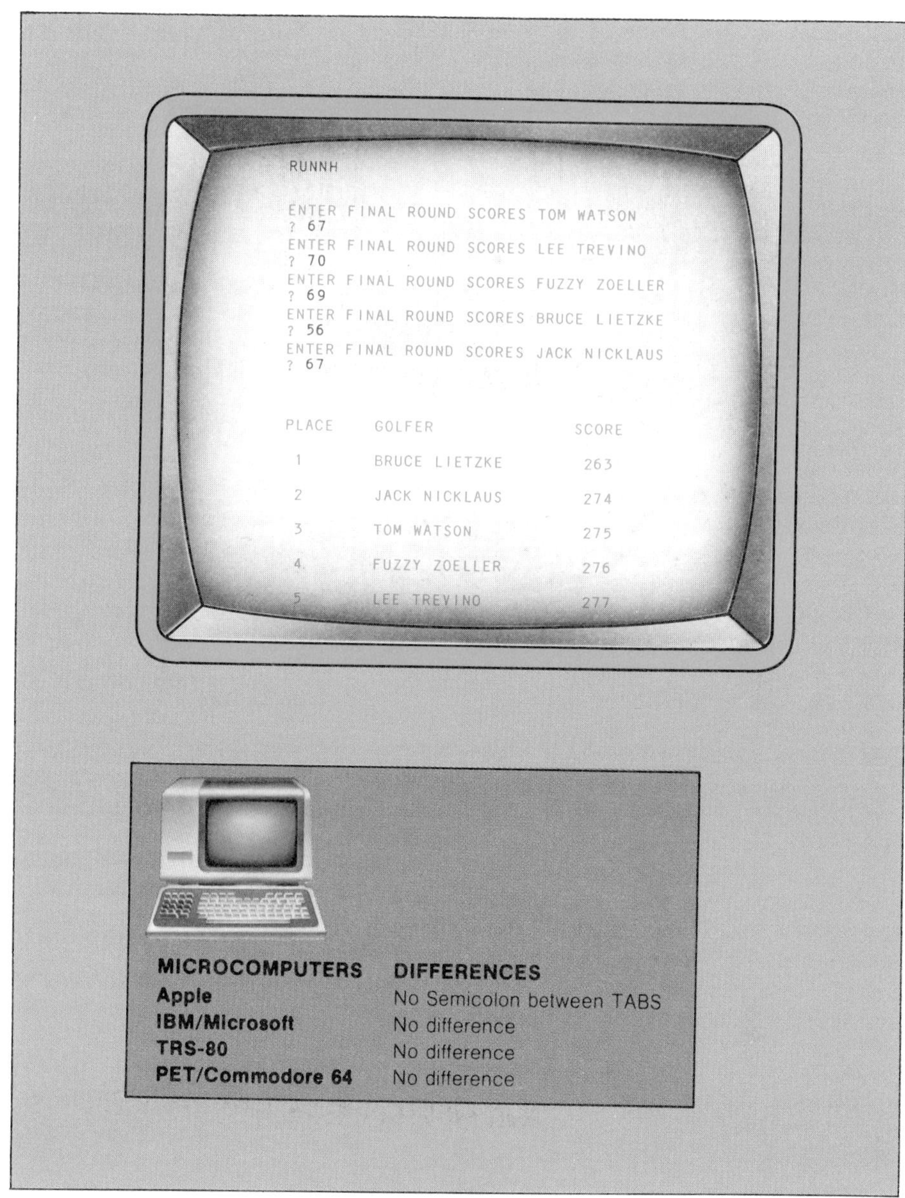

RUNNH
ENTER FINAL ROUND SCORES TOM WATSON
? 67
ENTER FINAL ROUND SCORES LEE TREVINO
? 70
ENTER FINAL ROUND SCORES FUZZY ZOELLER
? 69
ENTER FINAL ROUND SCORES BRUCE LIETZKE
? 56
ENTER FINAL ROUND SCORES JACK NICKLAUS
? 67
PLACE GOLFER SCORE
1 BRUCE LIETZKE 263
2 JACK NICKLAUS 274
3 TOM WATSON 275
4 FUZZY ZOELLER 276
5 LEE TREVINO 277
MICROCOMPUTERS DIFFERENCES
Apple No Semicolon between TABS
IBM/Microsoft No difference
TRS-80 No difference
PET/Commodore 64 No difference

Summary

- Arrays are lists or tables of related values stored under a single variable name.
- Access to individual elements in an array can be gained through the use of subscripts.
- The DIM statement sets up storage space for arrays.
- Array manipulation is carried out through the use of FOR/NEXT loops.
- Two-dimensional arrays also are called tables or matrices.
- Two subscript numbers identify individual items in a matrix. The first number indicates the row; the second indicates the column.
- The bubble sort and the Shell sort are two methods of ordering values contained in an array.

Review Questions

1. What is an array?
2. We can make reference to individual elements in an array by referring to their position. This is done through the use of ______.
3. When an array element is indicated by an expression, what three steps are carried out by the computer?
4. Variables that are references to specific elements in an array are called ______ variables, whereas simple variables are called ______ variables.
5. What is the purpose of the DIM statement?
6. DIM statements must appear where in a program?
7. Array subscripts can vary in value from 0 to ______.
8. Which of the following flowchart symbols often is used for the DIM statement?

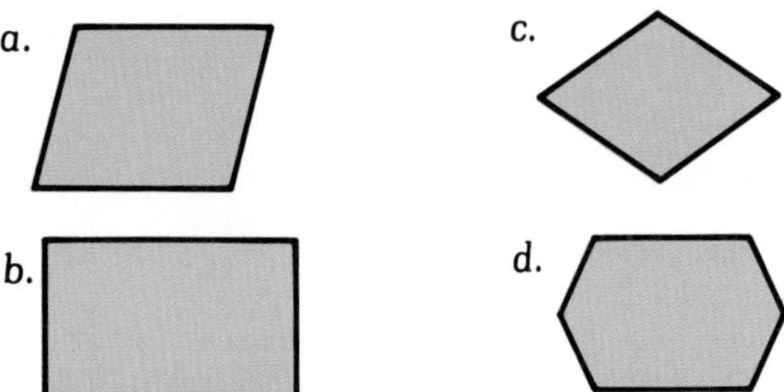

9. A list of related values stored under a single variable name is a (n) ______.
10. The ______ statements are an efficient method of reading data into and printing data out of a one-dimensional array.

11. Write a set of instructions that will find the sum of the four elements in array A.
12. A table consisting of rows and columns is called a(n) ______.
13. What would the DIM statement for array B, with four rows and six columns, look like? For how many elements would this DIM statement reserve space?
14. Reading data into and printing data from two-dimensional arrays can be accomplished using ______ statements.
15. Give two advantages of arrays.
16. What is an array merge? Write a sequence of instructions to merge two arrays of seven elements each.
17. When searching large arrays (one hundred or more elements), is a sequential or binary search faster? Why?
18. When searching an array using a binary search, the elements must be arranged in ______.
19. Describe how a bubble sort works.
20. Why is the bubble sort less efficient than the Shell sort?

Debugging Exercises

1.
```
00010 DIM A(10),B(5)
00020 LET B = A(1) + A(2)
00030 PRINT B
```

2.
```
00010 DIM L(15)
00015 FOR I = 1 TO 16
00020    PRINT L(I)
00025 NEXT I
```

3.
```
00050 DIM R(25)
00060 FOR J = 1 TO 25
00070    READ R(I)
00080 NEXT J
```

4.
```
00090 *** TOTAL ELEMENTS OF ARRAY G ***
00095 DIM G(12)
00100 LET T = 0
00105 FOR N = 1 TO 12
00110    LET T = T + G(1)
00115 NEXT N
```

5.
```
00100 DIM X(3,2)
00110 FOR I = 1 TO 2
00120    FOR J = 1 TO 3
00130       READ X(I,J)
00140    NEXT J
00150 NEXT I
```

6.
```
00090 DIM X(5,4)
00100 REM *** ADD COLUMN 4 OF A TWO-DIMENSIONAL ARRAY ***
00110 FOR I = 1 TO 4
00120   READ Y(5,I)
00130 NEXT
```

7.
```
00200 REM *** MERGE ARRAY A AND B ***
00205 DIM A(10),B(10)
00210 LET X = 1
00215 FOR I = 1 TO 10
00220   LET C(I) = A(X)
00225   LET C(I + 1) = B(X)
00230 NEXT I
```

8.
```
00070 REM *** TOTAL NUMBER OF MALES IN CLASS ***
00080 DIM C(30)
00090 FOR I = 1 TO 30
00100   IF C(I) = "M" THEN 120
00110 LET T = T + 1
00120 NEXT I
```

9.
```
00100 DIM T$(100)
00110 REM *** BINARY SEARCH FOR TELEPHONE NUMBER ***
00120 LET N$ = "352-3270"
00130 LET U = 100
00140 LET L = 0
00150 LET M = INT((U + L) / 2)
00160 IF M = L THEN 220
00170   IF N$ = T$(M) THEN 220
00180   LET L = M
00190   GOTO 150
00200   LET U = M
00210   GOTO 150
00220   IF M = L THEN 250
00230 PRINT "FOUND"
00240 GOTO 999
00250 PRINT "NOT FOUND"
00999 END
```

10.
```
00110 DIM G(27)
00115 REM *** BUBLE SORT GRADES IN DESCENDING ORDER ***
00120 LET F = 0
00125 FOR I = 1 TO 26
00130   IF G(I) < G(I + 1) THEN 155
00135   LET H = G(I + 1)
00140   LET G(I + 1) = G(I)
00145   LET G(I) = H
00150   LET F = 1
00155 NEXT I
00160 IF F = 0 THEN 120
```

Additional Programming Problems

1. A furniture store is having a year-end clearance sale. It needs a program that will contain all its prices in one array and the corresponding rate of discount in a second array. A third array should be built to hold the sale price of each item (sale price = price − rate × price). Use the following data:

   Print out the original prices and their corresponding sale price.

Price	Rate of Discount
$178.89	0.25
59.95	0.20
402.25	0.30
295.00	0.25
589.98	0.30
42.99	0.20

2. Write a program to fill in a two-dimensional array that is a 6 by 4 multiplication table, and print it out as follows:

X	1	2	3	4
1	1	2	3	4
2	2	4	6	8
3	3	6	9	12
4	4	8	12	16
5	5	10	15	20
6	6	12	18	24

3. Bowling Green State University set up two sections of advanced Latin, both scheduled to meet at 8:00 a.m. Many of the students found this class too early to attend, so they dropped out. There are now ten students left in each class, so the university has decided to combine the two classes. Now it needs a program to merge the two lists of remaining students. Use the following data:

Class A	Class B
Wahl	Yoon
Pattera	Smoyer
Pontello	Rittenhouse
Main	Christoph
Panham	Navarre
Beerman	Mayers
Yodzis	O'Conner
York	Thomas
Saylor	Kaase
Kim	Savage

   Print out the merged list.

4. Junior Johnson likes to play on computers, and now he wants a program that will keep track of all his baseball cards. He is tired of looking through all his cards whenever he wants to know something about a certain player. He would like to be able to enter the player's name and have the computer print out the team the person is on, the number of games he has played, the number of at bats, the number of RBIs, and the player's batting average.

The output should look like this:

```
NAME: Last name, first initial
CLUB: Club name
GAMES: XX
AT BATS: XXX
RBI'S: XX
AVERAGE: 0.XXX
```

Use this data:

Player	Club	Games	At Bats	RBIs	Average
Ramos	Expos	26	41	3	0.195
Hisle	Brewers	27	87	11	0.230
Driessen	Reds	82	233	33	0.236
Bonnel	Blue Jays	66	227	28	0.220
Murcer	Yankees	50	117	24	0.260
Ayala	Orioles	44	86	13	0.279

The players, clubs, games, at bats, RBIs, and averages all should be in separate arrays. The data items for each player should be in the same position in their arrays as the position of the corresponding player. Test the program by entering any of the player's names and checking the output with the data list.

5. The Casket Company needs a program to list its employees' names and I.D. numbers in ascending order by I.D. number. Use a bubble sort to sort the following data. (Remember that when you change the position of an I.D. in the array, the position of the name also must be changed so that they correspond.)

I.D. Number	Name
467217	Alston, M.
624719	Cioffari, R.
784609	Chilson, D.
290013	Sergent, D.
502977	Layman, F.
207827	Kock, D.
389662	Wymer, E.
443279	Toalston, A.
302621	Kehmer, C.
196325	McKee, K.

6. Write a program to provide the weather reporter with a list of major cities and their high temperatures for the day. The program should arrange the cities in alphabetical order using a Shell sort. The weather reporter then should be able to request a city and have its high temperature printed out. Use a binary search to find the requested city. Here are the data:

City	Temperature
Miami	92
New York	80
Chicago	86
Denver	78
Los Angeles	83
Houston	95
Boston	73
Fresno	85

10 File Processing

Outline

Objectives

After reading this chapter the student should be able to do the following:

- Understand and discuss the structure of a file.
- Understand and use sequential files.
- Understand and use random relative files.

Overview

Business applications often involve large amounts of data. It is not uncommon for programs dealing with inventory, payroll, or customer balances to process hundreds, thousands, or millions of data items. Since the main memory of the computer is limited, users need some means of storing programs and data so that they do not have to retype them into the computer every time it is necessary to run the programs. Some microcomputers are so small that they cannot store internally all the data needed. In addition, it is useful to establish a single data file that several programs can use in different ways at different times. For example, personnel data can be used in applications such as handling payroll, processing medical claims, and printing mailing lists. For all these reasons, data often is stored on external storage media (secondary storage devices)—usually magnetic disks and tapes. Groups of data stored on disks or tapes are known as files.

Unfortunately, there is no standardized method for performing operations on files stored on secondary storage devices. Many BASIC implementations include unique file manipulation commands. Fortunately, the principles on which the commands are based are similar. We look first at the fundamentals of file processing and later differentiate among implementations on the computers we have been discussing.

What Is a File?

A file is a way of organizing data. Think of a typical office, which probably has a number of file drawers. Usually each file drawer contains related information about one general topic. For example, one drawer might contain all the information about the firm's clients and be called the **client file.** Within this drawer might be a separate information sheet for each client giving the name, address, and so on. Each of these information sheets are referred to as a record. The individual data items, such as the client's name recorded on the information sheet, are called **fields.** A group of one or more related fields is known as a **record,** and a group of one or more related records is known as a **file** (see figure 10–1).

The computer has allowed us to store and manipulate files much more efficiently than its predecessor, the file cabinet. The computer uses two main types of file access methods: sequential and random access.

Sequential Data Files

Magnetic tape is one type of sequential media (see Figure 10–2). In a sequential file, the data items are recorded one after another and must also be read one after another in the same order in which the recording took place. For example, to recall the fifth item stored in a sequential file, you must start at the beginning of the file and read the first four items successfully to get to the fifth one.

Figure 10–1 FILE ORGANIZATION

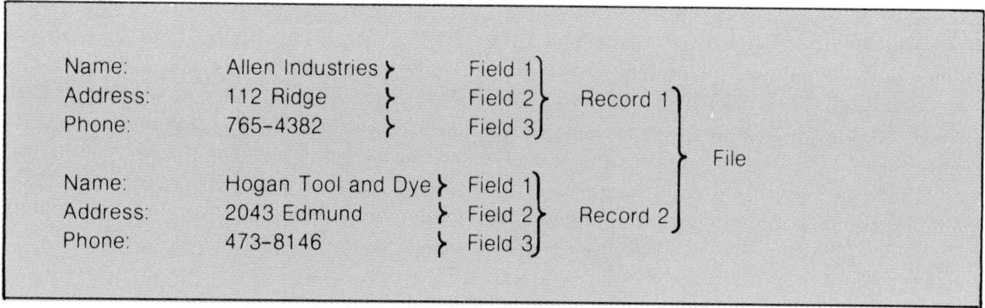

Figure 10–2 MAGNETIC TAPE

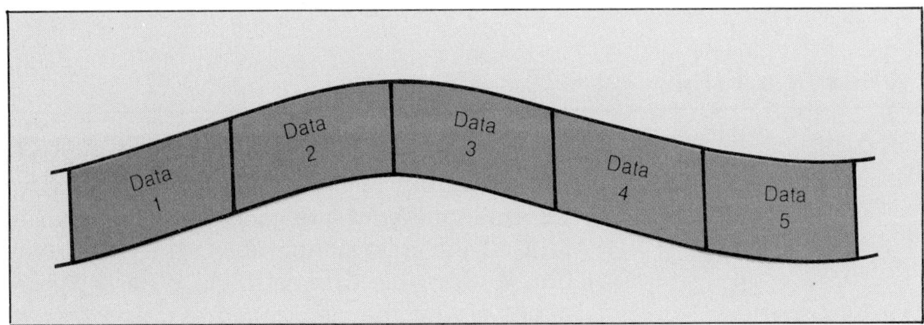

Data also can be stored sequentially on disk (see Figure 10–3). A disk is divided into concentric circles called **tracks.** The data items are recorded one after another on the tracks of the disk. Figure 10–3 shows how a disk containing our client file might be organized. The number 13 is the ASCII code for the carriage return, which is used to separate fields.

In a sequential file, each field takes only the amount of space required by its length. To record data in a sequential file, the following three steps are needed:

1. *Opening a sequential data file for writing to the file.* When opening a file, the programmer must tell the computer the name of the file to which it is to output the data. Using this name, the computer sets up a location on a disk or tape in which the data are to be placed.

Figure 10–3 DISK

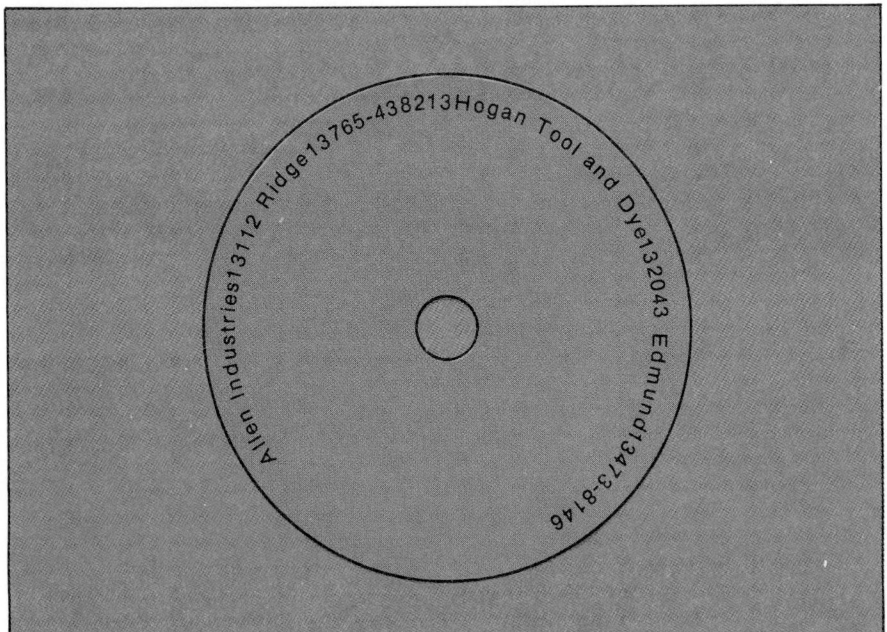

2. *Writing data to a sequential data file.* After opening a data file, data may be written onto the disk. A special statement is used to write data onto a disk, with the processing being similar to printing output on the screen or printer, except the data are being written onto the disk instead.
3. *Closing a sequential data file.* The last step in creating a sequential data file is to close it. After all the data have been written on the disk, the file must be closed to prevent loss of its contents. Closing also indicates to the computer that the use of the file is finished for the present time.

Reading from a sequential file also requires three steps:

1. *Opening a sequential data file for reading from the file.* The opening of a sequential file for reading may be either identical to the opening format for writing to a file or slightly modified. For example, to open a data file to write to a disk may require that a word or character be included to indicate this, such as WRITE or W. To read from the data file, these might need to be changed to READ or R.
2. *Reading data from a sequential data file.* After the file has been opened, the data can be read from the disk and placed in variables—numeric data in numeric variables and string data in string variables. Remember that in a sequential file, data are always read in the same order in which they were written.
3. *Closing a sequential data file.* Closing the file after reading the disk is identical to closing it after writing to the disk.

No matter what type of computer you are using, these general steps apply in using sequential data files. An example follows of sequential data file use on the DECSYSTEM 20 (also referred to as **terminal format files**). Following this, we will show the same example for each of our computers, the Apple, IBM/Microsoft TRS-80, and the PET/Commodore 64. Refer to the appropriate section for your computer. The discussion on implementing files will be limited to files on disk. Consult your manual for any differences in commands for tape.

Decsystem 20

Creating or Accessing a Sequential Data (Terminal Format) File

The general format of the command that creates or accesses a data file for the DECSYSTEM 20 is as follows:

line# OPEN "filename" AS FILE #number

If a file already exists with the filename specified, the computer will give us access to it. Otherwise, a new file will be created. The number can be used to refer to the file. The following is an example:

```
00010 OPEN "ALBUMS" AS FILE #2
```

Writing Data to a File

After the file has been created, we can write data to it:

line# PRINT #number,expression

The number is the one used in the OPEN statement. The expression is the data to be written onto the disk. For example,

```
00020 PRINT #2,"THE JAM -- SETTING SONS"
```

Pressing RETURN at the end of the line tells the computer that this is the end of the data item.

Closing a File

The general format of the CLOSE command is as follows:

line# CLOSE #number

The program in Figure 10–4 creates a file called ALBUMS as file #2 and writes some data to it.

Line 10 creates a file called ALBUMS. The file number at the end of the line is used later to refer to the file. Line 15 sets up a FOR/NEXT loop to read some data items (in line 40) and write them to the file. Line 25 prints the values in A$ to file #2, ALBUMS. Line 35 closes the file.

Reading Data from a File

To use the data stored on a file, we read it. The general format of the INPUT command is as follows:

Figure 10–4 CREATING AND WRITING DATA TO A FILE.

```
00010 OPEN "ALBUMS" AS FILE #2
00015 FOR I = 1 TO 4
00020   READ A$
00025   PRINT #2,A$
00030 NEXT I
00035 CLOSE #2
00040 DATA "THE JAM -- SETTING SONS","TOM WAITS -- SMALL CHANGE"
00045 DATA "DIRE STRAITS -- MAKING MOVIES","THE KINKS -- LOW BUDGET"
00999 END
```

Figure 10–5 READING DATA FROM A FILE.

```
00010 OPEN "ALBUMS" AS FILE #2
00015 FOR I = 1 TO 4
00020    INPUT #2,A$(I)
00025    PRINT A$(I)
00030 NEXT I
00035 CLOSE #2
```

line# INPUT #file number,variable list

The following is an example:

```
00020 INPUT #2,A$
```

The program in Figure 10–5 reads data stored in the file called ALBUMS.

Line 10 gives access to ALBUMS as file #2. Line 15 sets up a FOR/NEXT loop that reads the items from the file one by one into an array, A$, and prints them out for us to see. Line 25 prints the data on the screen. Line 35 closes the file.

Apple

Creating or Accessing a Sequential Data File

The Apple system calls data files **text files.** To tell the system to use the disk, we need to cue the computer by pressing the control (CTRL) key and the D key simultaneously. Since this has to be done several times in a file manipulation program, we may want to initialize a variable, D$, to CTRL-D by doing the following:

```
10 LET D$ = CHR$(4)
```

Check Chapter 8 to refresh your memory about what CHR$ does.

The general format of the command for creating or opening a text file is the following:

line# PRINT D$; "OPEN filename"

D$ is the CTRL-D command. The file name must begin with a letter and be less than thirty characters long. An example follows:

```
10 LET D$ = CHR$(4)
15 PRINT D$;"OPEN ALBUMS"
```

A file called ALBUMS now is listed in our **catalog.** A catalog is a program that supplies a complete alphabetical list of a users files. It is designated as a text (data) file by the letter T in the catalog listing. The OPEN command is used in this manner whenever we want to gain access to data in a file.

Writing Data to a File

After the file has been created, we can alert the computer that we want to put some data into the file by using this command:

line# PRINT D$; "WRITE filename"

This line is followed by the command that actually does the writing to the disk:

line# PRINT expression

This PRINT command writes the expression to the disk. Since a sequential file is simply a long list of data, the computer needs to know where one data item ends and the next one begins. Pressing the RETURN button at the end of the PRINT line tells the computer this.

Closing a File

The general format of the CLOSE command is as follows:

line# PRINT D$; "CLOSE filename"

The program in Figure 10–6 opens a file named ALBUMS, writes some data out to it, and finally closes it.

Line 10 initializes D$ to the disk command. Line 15 creates the file. Line 20 tells the computer that we are going to write some data to the disk.

In this example, the data items are different lengths: THE JAM—SETTING SONS is twenty-one characters long, TOM WAITS—SMALL CHANGE is twenty-three characters long, and so forth. The items are sep-

Figure 10–6 CREATING AND WRITING DATA TO A FILE

```
10 LET D$ = CHR$(4)
15 PRINT D$;"OPEN ALBUMS"
20 PRINT D$;"WRITE ALBUMS"
25 PRINT "THE JAM -- SETTING SONS"
30 PRINT "TOM WAITS -- SMALL CHANGE"
35 PRINT "DIRE STRAITS -- MAKING MOVIES"
40 PRINT "THE KINKS --LOW BUDGET"
45 PRINT D$;"CLOSE ALBUMS"
99 END
```

arated from one another by the fact that they are on different lines. Therefore, the file is a list of items, each of which ends with the ASCII character 13, the carriage return:

> ALBUM: THE JAM—SETTING SONS13TOM WAITS—SMALL CHANGE13DIRE STRAITS . . .

Reading Data from a File

Once a file has been established, it can be read whenever the user wants to use the data. The following command alerts the computer that reading from a file on disk is to occur:

> line# PRINT D$; "READ filename"

To read the data items, we use an INPUT statement, as shown in Figure 10–7. After the file is opened, line 70 signals the computer that we are going to read data from it. The FOR/NEXT loop then reads the data into an array, W$. The file is closed by line 90.

IBM/Microsoft

Creating or Accessing a Sequential Data File

The general format for creating or accessing a sequential data file for the IBM/Microsoft microcomputer follows:

> line# OPEN "filename" FOR OUTPUT AS #number
> line# OPEN "filename" FOR INPUT AS #number

The filename in quotes must be less than or equal to eight characters. OUTPUT specifies sequential output mode; it allows data to be written to the specified file on disk. INPUT specifies sequential input mode; it allows

Figure 10–7 READING DATA FROM A FILE

```
60 LET D$ = CHR$(4)
65 PRINT D$;"OPEN ALBUMS"
70 PRINT D$;"WRITE ALBUMS"
75 FOR I = 1 TO 4
80    INPUT W$(I)
85 NEXT I
90 PRINT D$;"CLOSE ALBUMS"
99 END
```

data to be read from the specified file on disk. The number after the pound (#) sign will be used later as a shorthand reference to the file in the program. An example statement creating a file called ALBUMS follows:

```
10 OPEN "ALBUMS" FOR OUTPUT AS #1
```

Writing Data to a File

Once a file has been created, we can write some data to it by using a variation of the PRINT statement. Notice, however, that the following PRINT statement looks different from that used to display the results of processing:

line# PRINT#number,expression

The #number distinguishes this statement from a regular PRINT command. The number should be the same one that was specified in the OPEN statement. The expression can be any valid variable, string, numeric constant, and so on. Since a sequential file is simply a long list of items, the computer knows where one data item ends and the next one begins by the pressing of the carriage return at the end of the PRINT line.

Closing a File

The general format of the CLOSE command follows:

line# CLOSE #number

Again, the number should be the same one that was used to open the file.

The program in Figure 10–8 opens a file named ALBUMS, writes some data to it, and closes the file.

Line 10 creates the file as #1. That same number is used throughout the program in the file statements as a shorthand reference to ALBUMS. Lines 15 through 30 simply write four data items to the file. Line 35 closes the file.

Figure 10–8 CREATING AND WRITING DATA TO A FILE

```
10 OPEN "ALBUMS" FOR OUTPUT AS #1
15 PRINT#1,"THE JAM -- SETTING SONS"
20 PRINT#1,"TOM WAITS -- SMALL CHANGE"
25 PRINT#1,"DIRE STRAITS -- MAKING MOVIES"
30 PRINT#1,"THE KINKS -- LOW BUDGET"
35 CLOSE #1
999 END
```

Figure 10–9 READING DATA FROM A FILE

```
10 OPEN "ALBUMS" FOR OUTPUT AS #2
15 FOR I = 1 TO 4
20    INPUT#2,B$(I)
25    PRINT B$(I)
30 NEXT I
35 CLOSE #2
999 END
```

Reading Data from a File

Once a file has been created, it can be read to access the data using the following:

line# INPUT #number, expression

The #number distinguishes this as a file statement. The following is an example:

```
20 INPUT#1,B$
```

The program in Figure 10–9 reads data stored in a file called ALBUMS:

Line 10 accesses ALBUMS as file #2. Line 15 sets up a FOR/NEXT loop that reads the items from the file one by one into an array, B$. The items are displayed by line 25. Line 35 closes the file.

TRS-80

Creating or Accessing a Sequential Data File

After you have turned the TRS-80 on, the computer will ask,

```
HOW MANY FILES?
```

Since we are going to deal with fewer than three files, we can simply press the ENTER button in response.

The following command permits access to a file:

line# OPEN "mode," buffer number, "filename"

The "mode" will be either I for sequential input (reading data from an existing file) or 0 for sequential output (writing data on the disk). After the "mode" is specified, we designate the number of the buffer where data temporarily will be held. The filename can be from one to eight characters long; the first character must be alphabetic (do not embed any blanks). An example follows:

```
10 OPEN "O",1"ALBUMS"
```

This line creates a file called ALBUMS. After the file is opened, we can use buffer 1 to write data to the file ("mode" = 0). We will see how this works later.

Writing Data to a File

After a file has been created (opened), data can be written to it. The general format of the PRINT command follows:

line# PRINT #buffer number, expression

For example,

```
15 PRINT #1,"THE JAM -- SETTING SONS"
```

prints the character string THE JAM—SETTING SONS as the first item in the file called ALBUMS. The #1 is the buffer number used in the OPEN statement for ALBUMS above.

Now we can write a simple program that creates a file and writes some data to it, as shown in Figure 10–10.

Line 10 opens the file called ALBUMS. We use buffer #1 to write data to the file. Pressing ENTER at the end of each line separates one item from another on the disk file. Line 35 closes the file.

Closing a File

The following command closes a file:

line# CLOSE #buffer number

Make sure that the buffer number is the one specified in the OPEN statement for the file. (See lines 10 and 35.)

Figure 10–10 CREATING AND WRITING DATA TO A FILE

```
10 OPEN "O",1,"ALBUMS"
15 PRINT #1,"THE JAM -- SETTING SONS"
20 PRINT #1,"TOM WAITS -- SMALL CHANGE"
25 PRINT #1,"DIRE STRAITS -- MAKING MOVIES"
30 PRINT #1,"THE KINKS -- LOW BUDGET"
35 CLOSE #1
999 END
```

Figure 10–11 READING DATA FROM A FILE

```
10 OPEN "I",1,"ALBUMS"
15 FOR I = 1 TO 4
20    INPUT #1,B$(I)
25 NEXT I
30 FOR J = 1 TO 4
35    PRINT B$(J)
40 NEXT J
45 CLOSE #1
999 END
```

Reading Data from a File

To read data from a file, we first must gain access to it by using the OPEN statement. However, the mode is now I, for sequential input. The following statement should be used to gain access on an already existing file:

line# OPEN"I",buffer number,"filename"

The command that reads data from the file follows:

line# INPUT #buffer number,variable

The program segment in Figure 10–11 reads data that have been stored in ALBUMS.

Line 10 gives access to an already existing file called ALBUMS. A FOR/NEXT loop then is established to read the data into an array, B$. Data is read from the file by line 20. Note that the buffer number is the same as was designated in the OPEN statement. Lines 30 through 40 simply print out the file. Line 45 closes the file.

PET/Commodore 64

Creating or Accessing a Sequential Data File

The general format of the command for creating or accessing a data file for the PET/Commodore 64 microcomputer follows:

line# OPEN file#,device#,channel#,"0:name,type,direction"

The file# is used to refer to the file. The device# is 8, which tells the computer to open the file on disk. The channel# is a data channel, numbers 2 through 14. For convenience, it is suggested that you use the same number for both the channel# and file# to keep them straight. The name is the file name. For our purposes here, the type is SEQ (sequential), which can be abbreviated by using just the first letter, S. The direction must be READ or WRITE, or at least the first letter of each. An example follows:

```
10 OPEN 2,8,2,"0:ALBUMS,S,W"
```

If the file ALBUMS already exists and we need only read what is on it, the W should be changed to R. The following example gives us access to an existing file called ALBUMS:

```
10 OPEN 2,8,2,"0:ALBUMS,S,R"
```

Writing Data to a File

After a filename has been created, we can write data to the file by using a PRINT command. The general format follows:

line# PRINT#file number, expression

The file number is the one specified in the OPEN statement. The expression is the data to be written onto the disk. For example,

```
15 PRINT#2,"THE JAM -- SETTING SONS"
```

writes THE JAM–SETTING SONS to file #2. Pressing RETURN at the end of the line signals the computer that this is the end of the data item.

Closing a File

The general format of the CLOSE statement follows:

line# CLOSE#file number

Let us put these commands together in Figure 10–12 to create a file called ALBUMS, write some data to it, and close it.

Reading Data from a File

Once a file has been established, it can be read so that manipulations can be performed on the data. First, the file should be reopened:

Figure 10–12 CREATING AND WRITING DATA TO A FILE

```
10 OPEN 2,8,2,"0:ALBUMS,S,W"
15 PRINT#2,"THE JAM -- SETTING SONS"
20 PRINT#2,"TOM WAITS -- SMALL CHANGE"
25 PRINT#2,"DIRE STRAITS -- MAKING MOVIES"
30 PRINT#2,"THE KINKS -- LOW BUDGET"
35 CLOSE#2
```

Figure 10–13 READING DATA FROM A FILE

```
10 OPEN 2,8,2,"0:ALBUMS,S,R"
15 FOR I = 1 TO 4
20    INPUT#2,A$(I)
25    PRINT A$(I)
30 NEXT I
35 CLOSE#2
```

line# OPEN file#, device#,channel#, "O:name, type, direction"

Then we use the following command to read the data items:

line# INPUT#file number, expression

The file number, of course, must be the same as the file number in the OPEN statement. The expression is the variable that specifies where the data will be stored in internal memory.

The program in Figure 10–13 reads data from the file called ALBUMS: Line 10 opens file #2. Since the file already has been established, R is specified as the direction (that is, to read from the file). A FOR/NEXT loop is initiated in line 15. Line 20 reads data from file #2 into an array, A$. Line 25 is a PRINT statement. No file number is specified; it simply prints the data items on the screen of the PET/Commodore 64. Finally, the file is closed in line 35.

LEARNING CHECK

1. A(n) ________ is a group of one or more related records.
2. ________ and ________ are two main types of file access methods.
3. Records in sequential files are written to and read from the disk one after the other starting with the first record. TRUE FALSE (Circle the correct answer.)
4. The three steps needed to read data from a file are ________.
   a. open file for writing, read data from file, close file.
   b. open file for reading, read data from file, close file.
   c. open file for reading, write data to file, close file.

Answers
1. file
2. Sequential; random access
3. True
4. b

Random Data Files

Random data files are files that allow you to write to or read from a file in random order. Figure 10–14 illustrates how a random file is organized on disk. For the purposes of this book, all records must be the same length in a random file. (Check your manual for other options.) This enables the computer to find them without reading all the preceding records. Since the fields that make up each record may not be the same length, blank characters are placed after them. Because of this, random files tend to take up more disk space than sequential files, but this disadvantage is outweighed by the associated advantages, such as speed of access.

Our discussions of random files for each computer will deal with relative files. A record file with relative organization contains records that are stored in numbered locations. The number associated with a position represents its location relative to the beginning of the file. For example, record 1 would occupy the first record position; record 2, the second record position; and so forth. Thus, with a relative file we can access a record either sequentially or randomly by record number.

Like sequential files, random files have to be opened before use and closed after use. When reading or writing with a random file, the number of the record to be read or written to must be specified. Record numbers start with 1 and continue to as high as necessary to store all the records. The methods used to perform these steps vary from computer to computer.

The following examples are programs that provide random access to relative files. These programs demonstrate how to create a file, write data to a file, read data from a file, and close a file.

Figure 10–14 RANDOM DATA FILES

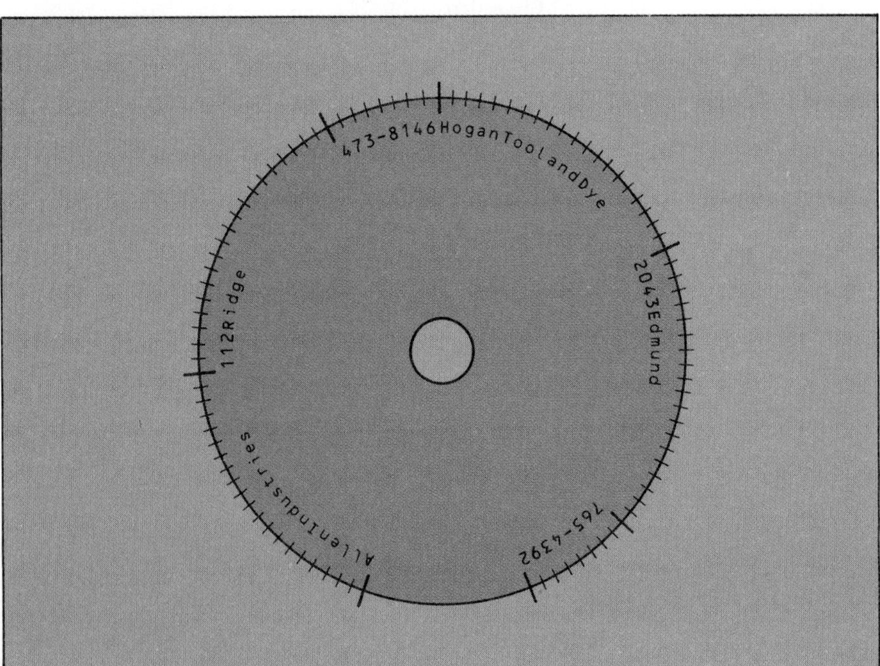

DECSYSTEM 20

To access records in a file for the DECSYSTEM 20, you must establish a buffer for input and output. The MAP statement establishes and names the buffer and describes the characteristics of the records in a particular file. The MAP statement specifies that certain variables are contained in the buffer. Its general format follows:

line# MAP (name) elements(s)

where (name) is the name given to the buffer (parentheses are optional), and element(s) is a list of elements separated by commas that defines the characteristics of the record. Each element represents a field in the record. The length of a string variable must be specified by the syntax:

string variable = n

where string variable is any string variable, and n is the number of characters in the string (n must be a constant). For example,

```
00010 MAP BUFF1 A$ = 15,N$ = 15
```

Creating or Accessing a Random Relative File

A random relative file can be created or accessed through the use of the OPEN statement. The syntax of the OPEN statement includes many keywords that describe attributes of the file. These keywords generally are followed by a name, numeric expression, or line number and are separated by commas. Many of these keywords do not concern us in a book of this level. As such, the following general format of the OPEN statement is abbreviated to include only the relevant keywords. Consult your manual for a more complete discussion.

$$\text{Line\# OPEN “filename” FOR} \left\{ \begin{array}{c} \text{INPUT} \\ \text{OUTPUT} \end{array} \right\} \text{AS FILE \# expression,}$$

$$\left\{ \begin{array}{c} \text{SEQUENTIAL} \\ \text{RELATIVE} \end{array} \right\} \text{FIXED} \left\{ \begin{array}{l} \text{,MAP map name} \\ \text{,RECORD SIZE num exp} \end{array} \right\}$$

The “filename” is a string expression that identifies the files. The FOR OUTPUT clause creates a new file with the “filename” you specify. The FOR INPUT clause requires that the specified file already exist. The clause “AS FILE # expression” associates the file with a file number. This file number will be used as a shorthand reference to the file later in the program. The SEQUENTIAL and the RELATIVE clauses arrange records sequentially by order of input and by numbered position in the file, respectively. FIXED specifies that the records are of a fixed length. The clause “MAP map name” references a MAP statement. The map buffer you reference defines the buffer used to store the file's data temporarily. The “MAP map name” clause also can be used to define the record size. If no "MAP map name" clause is specified, the maximum length of records (in characters) in the file must be specified using the "RECORD SIZE num exp" clause.

An example of an OPEN statement to create a file called ALBUMS and write data to the file follows:

```
00015 OPEN "ALBUMS" FOR OUTPUT AS FILE #1,RELATIVE FIXED,MAP BUFF1
```

To access the file ALBUMS after it has been created and read data from it, the following statement is used:

```
00015 OPEN "ALBUMS" FOR INPUT AS FILE #1,RELATIVE FIXED,MAP BUFF1
```

Writing Data to a File

The PUT statement writes a new record from the buffer to the file. The general format of the PUT statement as we will use it follows:

PUT file exp,RECORD num exp

For example,

```
PUT #1,RECORD 3
```

This statement writes the data in the buffer to record position 3 in file #1. If the "RECORD num exp" portion of the statement is left off, the data will be written to the next record in the sequence from where the pointer presently is. That is, if the last record written was record 5, the data will be written to record 6.

Closing a File

The general format of the CLOSE command follows:

line# CLOSE #file number(s)

For example,

```
00090 CLOSE #1
```

The program in Figure 10–15 creates a file called ALBUMS and writes some data to it.

Line 10 creates the buffer. Line 15 creates the file called ALBUMS. The WHILE loop in line 20 checks to see if the user wants to write another record. The number of the record to be written to is input in line 25. Lines 30 and 35 input the data into the buffer. Line 40 writes the data in the buffer into the file in the record position specified in the variable R. The file is closed in line 55.

Figure 10–15 CREATING AND WRITING DATA TO A FILE

```
00010 MAP BUFF1 A$ = 15,N$ = 15
00015 OPEN "ALBUMS" FOR OUTPUT AS FILE #1,RELATIVE FIXED,MAP BUFF1
00020 WHILE X$ <> "N"
00025    INPUT "WRITE WHAT RECORD #";R
00030    INPUT "ARTIST NAME";A$
00035    INPUT "ALBUM TITLE";N$
00040    PUT #1,RECORD R
00045    INPUT "WRITE ANOTHER RECORD?(Y OR N)";X$
00050 NEXT
00055 CLOSE #1
00999 END
```

```
RUNNH
WRITE WHAT RECORD # ? 1
ARTIST NAME ? THE JAM
ALBUM TITLE ? SETTING SONS
WRITE ANOTHER RECORD?(Y OR N) ? Y
WRITE WHAT RECORD # ? 3
ARTIST NAME ? DIRE STRAITS
ALBUM TITLE ? MAKING MOVIES
WRITE ANOTHER RECORD?(Y OR N) ? Y
WRITE WHAT RECORD # ? 2
ARTIST NAME ? TOM WAITS
ALBUM TITLE ? SMALL CHANGE
WRITE ANOTHER RECORD?(Y OR N) ? Y
WRITE WHAT RECORD # ? 4
ARTIST NAME ? THE KINKS
ALBUM TITLE ? LOW BUDGET
WRITE ANOTHER RECORD?(Y OR N) ? N
```

Reading Data from a File

The GET statement reads a record from the file into a buffer. The general format of the GET statement as we will use it follows:

GET file exp,RECORD num exp

For example,

```
GET #1,RECORD 3
```

This statement reads the data in record 3 from File#1 into the buffer. As with the PUT statement, if the ",RECORD num exp" portion of the GET statement is left off, the data will be read from the next record in the sequence from where the pointer presently is.

Figure 10–16 READING DATA FROM A FILE

```
00010 MAP BUFF1 A$ = 15,N$ = 15
00015 OPEN "ALBUMS" FOR INPUT AS FILE #1,RELATIVE FIXED,MAP BUFF1
00020 WHILE X$ <> "N"
00025   INPUT "READ WHAT RECORD #";R
00030   GET #1,RECORD R
00035   PRINT A$,N$
00040   INPUT "READ ANOTHER RECORD?(Y OR N)";X$
00045 NEXT
00050 CLOSE #1
00999 END
```

```
RUNNH
READ WHAT RECORD # ? 3
DIRE STRAITS                 MAKING MOVIES
READ ANOTHER RECORD?(Y OR N) ? Y
READ WHAT RECORD # ? 1
THE JAM                      SETTING SONS
READ ANOTHER RECORD?(Y OR N) ? Y
READ WHAT RECORD # ? 4
THE KINKS                    LOW BUDGET
READ ANOTHER RECORD?(Y OR N) ? Y
READ WHAT RECORD # ? 2
TOM WAITS                    SMALL CHANGE
READ ANOTHER RECORD?(Y OR N) ? N
```

The program in Figure 10–16 reads data stored in a file called ALBUMS. Line 10 creates the buffer. The existing file ALBUMS is accessed by the OPEN statement in line 15. The WHILE statement in line 20 checks to see if the user wants to read another record. The record number the user wishes to read is entered in line 25. Line 30 reads the data from a given record into the file buffer. The PRINT statement in line 35 prints the contents of the buffer to the screen. Line 50 closes the file.

Apple

Creating or Accessing a Random Relative File

The general format of the command for creating or opening a random relative file for the Apple microcomputer follows:

line# PRINT D$;"OPEN filename,L record length"

See the earlier discussion on PRINT D$ for the Apple Microcomputer. The filename must begin with a letter and be less than thirty characters long. The record length is the total number of characters in each record. An example follows:

```
15 PRINT D$;"OPEN ALBUMS,L 30"
```

Writing Data to a File.

The general format of the command that tells the computer we want to write data into the file is as follows:

line# PRINT D$;"WRITE filename,R";record number

For example,

```
40 PRINT D$"WRITE ALBUMS,R";3
```

tells the computer that we want to write data into record position 3 of the file. This line is followed by the line that actually does the writing to the disk:

line# PRINT expression

For example,

```
45 PRINT A$,N$
```

This command actually prints the data to record position 3 in the file.

Closing a File

The general format of the CLOSE command follows:

line# PRINT D$;"CLOSE filename"

The program in Figure 10–17 opens a file named ALBUMS, writes data to the specified records, and finally closes it.

Line 10 initializes D$ to the disk command. Line 15 creates the file ALBUMS, and each record contains thirty characters. Line 20 checks to see if the user wants to write another record. Line 25 allows the user to enter the record number to which he or she wishes to write. The data are input into a file buffer in lines 30 and 35. The computer prepares to write to the file in line 40, and lines 45 and 50 actually write the data to the file. Line 55 tells the computer to stop writing to the disk. The file is closed in line 70.

Figure 10-17 CREATING AND WRITING DATA TO A FILE

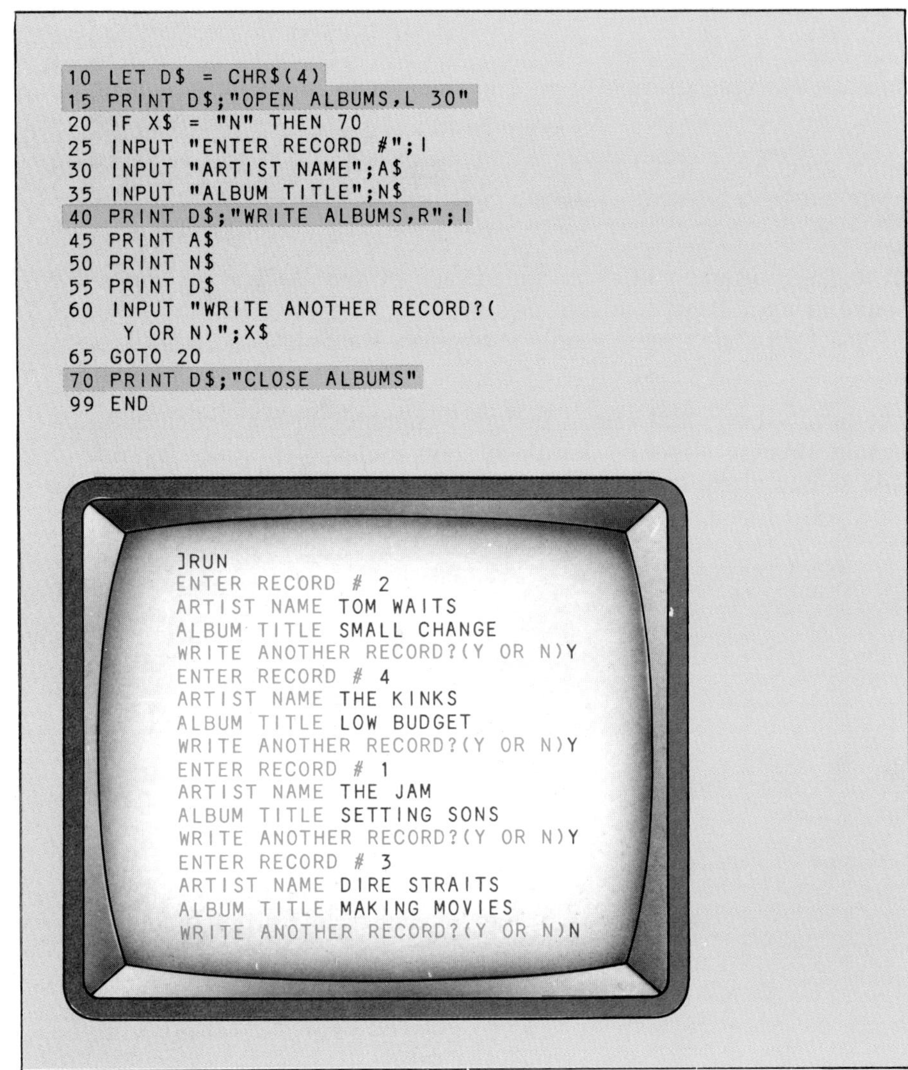

```
10 LET D$ = CHR$(4)
15 PRINT D$;"OPEN ALBUMS,L 30"
20 IF X$ = "N" THEN 70
25 INPUT "ENTER RECORD #";I
30 INPUT "ARTIST NAME";A$
35 INPUT "ALBUM TITLE";N$
40 PRINT D$;"WRITE ALBUMS,R";I
45 PRINT A$
50 PRINT N$
55 PRINT D$
60 INPUT "WRITE ANOTHER RECORD?(
    Y OR N)";X$
65 GOTO 20
70 PRINT D$;"CLOSE ALBUMS"
99 END
```

```
]RUN
ENTER RECORD # 2
ARTIST NAME TOM WAITS
ALBUM TITLE SMALL CHANGE
WRITE ANOTHER RECORD?(Y OR N)Y
ENTER RECORD # 4
ARTIST NAME THE KINKS
ALBUM TITLE LOW BUDGET
WRITE ANOTHER RECORD?(Y OR N)Y
ENTER RECORD # 1
ARTIST NAME THE JAM
ALBUM TITLE SETTING SONS
WRITE ANOTHER RECORD?(Y OR N)Y
ENTER RECORD # 3
ARTIST NAME DIRE STRAITS
ALBUM TITLE MAKING MOVIES
WRITE ANOTHER RECORD?(Y OR N)N
```

Reading Data from a File

To read data from a file, you must first alert the computer with the following command:

line# PRINT D$;"READ filename"; record number

For example,

```
30 PRINT D$;"READ ALBUMS,R";2
```

This command readies the computer to read data from record position 2 of the file.

To actually read the data, the INPUT command is used as follows:

line# INPUT expression(s)

For example,

```
40 INPUT A$,N$
```

The program in Figure 10–18 reads records from the file ALBUMS. Line 30, 35, and 40 perform the READ functions. See the discussion of the previous program for a description of the other statements. Line 30 readies the com-

Figure 10–18 READING DATA FROM A FILE

```
10 LET D$ = CHR$(4)
15 PRINT D$;"OPEN ALBUMS,L 30"
20 IF X$ = "N" THEN 60
25 INPUT "ENTER RECORD #";I
30 PRINT D$;"READ ALBUMS,R";I
35 INPUT A$,N$
40 PRINT A$,N$
45 PRINT D$
50 INPUT "READ ANOTHER RECORD?(Y
     OR N)";X$
55 GOTO 20
60 PRINT D$;"CLOSE ALBUMS"
999 END
```

```
]RUN
ENTER RECORD #2
TOM WAITS           SMALL CHANGE
READ ANOTHER RECORD?(Y OR N)Y
ENTER RECORD #4
THE KINKS           LOW BUDGET
READ ANOTHER RECORD?(Y OR N)Y
ENTER RECORD #1
THE JAM             SETTING SONS
READ ANOTHER RECORD?(Y OR N)Y
ENTER RECORD #3
DIRE STRAITS        MAKING MOVIES
READ ANOTHER RECORD?(Y OR N)N
```

puter to read data from a specific record position in the file. Line 35 transfers the contents of the record to a file buffer, and line 40 prints the record to the screen.

IBM/Microsoft

Creating or Acessing a Random Relative File

The general format for creating or accessing a random relative file for the IBM/Microsoft microcomputer follows:

line# OPEN "filename" AS #number LEN = number

For example,

```
10 OPEN "ALBUMS" AS #1 LEN = 30
```

The filename in quotes must be less than or equal to eight characters. The number after the pound sign (#) will be used later as a shorthand reference to the file in the program. The LEN = 30 clause defines the length of a record to be thirty characters long.

Writing Data to a File

When using random relative files, FIELD statements must be used to allocate space in the random buffer for the variables that will be written to the random file. The general format of the FIELD statement follows:

line# FIELD #filename, width AS string variable,width AS string variable, . . .

For example,

```
15 FIELD #1,15 AS B$,15 AS B1$
```

The LSET or RSET commands are needed to move the data into the random buffer. LSET left-justifies the string in the field, and RSET right-justifies the string, with spaces used to pad the extra positions. For example, if the string HELLO is to be printed in a field with ten positions, the RSET command will fill the field like this:

_ _ _ _ _ H E L L O

This is called right-justifying. If the LSET command were used, the field will be filled like this:

H E L L O _ _ _ _ _

This is called left-justifying.

Numeric values must be converted to strings when placed into the buffer. This is accomplished by the functions MKI$ to make an integer value into a string, MKS$ for a single precision value, and MKD$ for a double precision value. For example, to convert the following single precision value to a string:

```
10 LET  A = 101.96
```

use

```
10 LSET A$ = MKS$(A)
```

Numeric values must be converted back to numbers using the "convert" functions: CVI for integers, CVS for single precision values, and CVD for double precision values. For example,

```
100 PRINT CVS(A)
```

converts the string A back to a single precision value.

In the following program, the line

```
80 LSET B$ = A$
```

places the data in A$ into the file buffer and left-justifies it.

The PUT statement is used to write data from the buffer to the disk. The general format of the PUT statement follows:

line# PUT #filename,number

where filename is the number under which the file was opened, and number is the record number for the record to be written. For example,

```
50 PUT #1,3
```

writes the data in the file buffer to record position 3 in the random file.

Closing a File

The general format of the CLOSE command follows:

line# CLOSE #number

For example,

```
65 CLOSE #1
```

The number should be the same one used to open the file.

The program in Figure 10–19 opens a random file named ALBUMS, writes some data to it, and closes the file. Line 10 opens the file ALBUMS and specifies a record length of thirty bytes. The field lengths are defined by the FIELD command in line 15. Line 20 checks to see if another record is to be entered. The record number to be written is entered in line 25. The

Figure 10–19 CREATING AND WRITING DATA TO A FILE

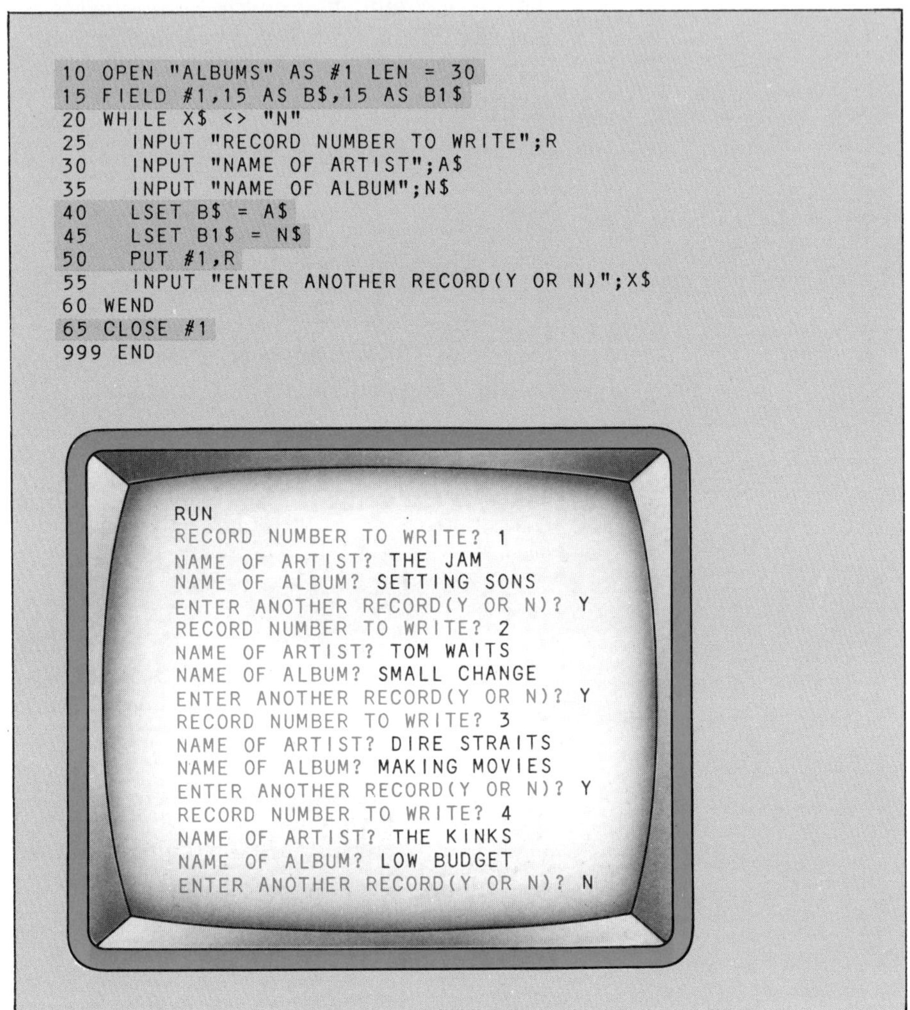

```
10 OPEN "ALBUMS" AS #1 LEN = 30
15 FIELD #1,15 AS B$,15 AS B1$
20 WHILE X$ <> "N"
25    INPUT "RECORD NUMBER TO WRITE";R
30    INPUT "NAME OF ARTIST";A$
35    INPUT "NAME OF ALBUM";N$
40    LSET B$ = A$
45    LSET B1$ = N$
50    PUT #1,R
55    INPUT "ENTER ANOTHER RECORD(Y OR N)";X$
60 WEND
65 CLOSE #1
999 END
```

```
RUN
RECORD NUMBER TO WRITE? 1
NAME OF ARTIST? THE JAM
NAME OF ALBUM? SETTING SONS
ENTER ANOTHER RECORD(Y OR N)? Y
RECORD NUMBER TO WRITE? 2
NAME OF ARTIST? TOM WAITS
NAME OF ALBUM? SMALL CHANGE
ENTER ANOTHER RECORD(Y OR N)? Y
RECORD NUMBER TO WRITE? 3
NAME OF ARTIST? DIRE STRAITS
NAME OF ALBUM? MAKING MOVIES
ENTER ANOTHER RECORD(Y OR N)? Y
RECORD NUMBER TO WRITE? 4
NAME OF ARTIST? THE KINKS
NAME OF ALBUM? LOW BUDGET
ENTER ANOTHER RECORD(Y OR N)? N
```

data are entered in line 30 and 35 and are placed into the file buffer in lines 40 and 45. Line 50 writes the data in the buffer to the disk. The file is closed in line 65.

Reading Data from a File

The GET command is used to move a record from a file into the random buffer. The general format of the GET statement follows:

Get #filename,number

where filename is the number under which the file was opened, and number is the number of the record to be read in the range of 1 to 32767. For example,

```
30 GET #1,2
```

would place the contents of record 2 into the file buffer.

The program in Figure 10–20 reads data stored in a file called ALBUMS. Line 10 opens the file. The field lengths are defined in line 15. The WHILE

Figure 10–20 READING DATA FROM A FILE

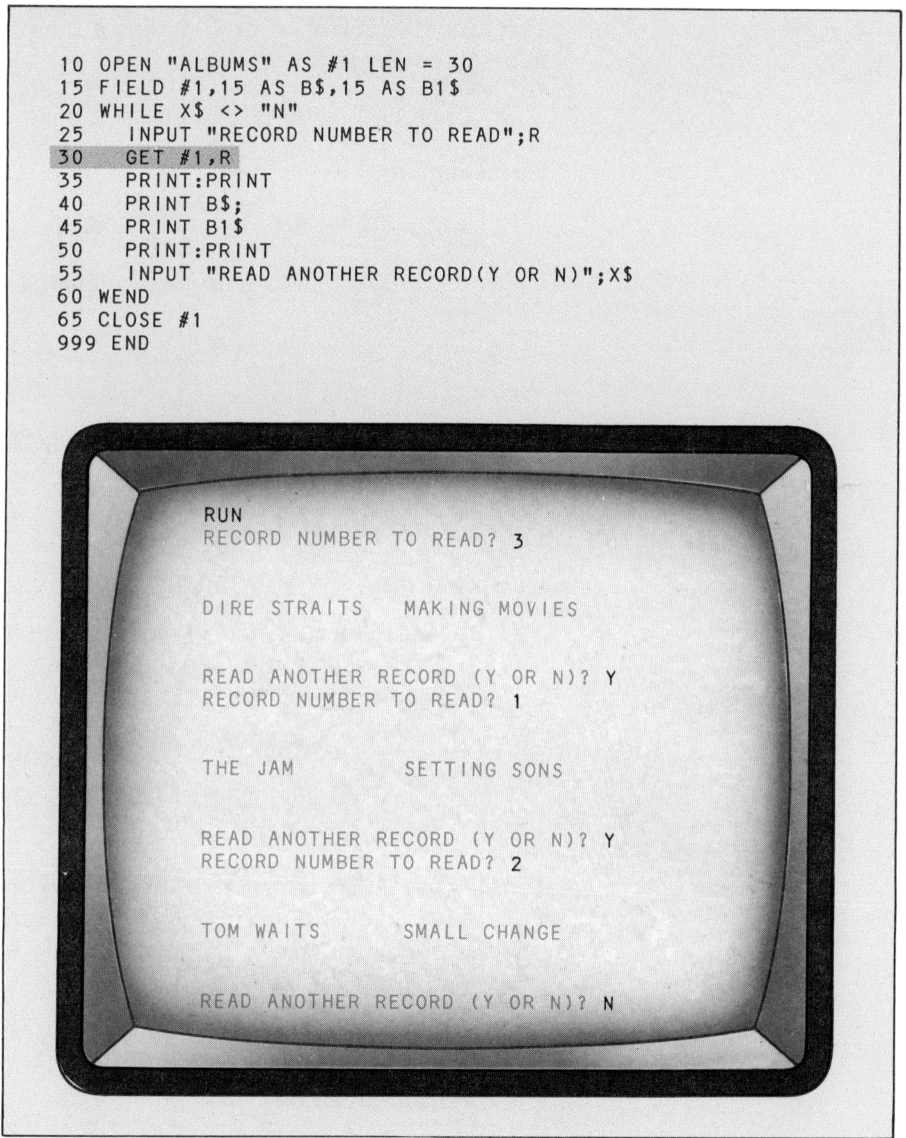

```
10 OPEN "ALBUMS" AS #1 LEN = 30
15 FIELD #1,15 AS B$,15 AS B1$
20 WHILE X$ <> "N"
25    INPUT "RECORD NUMBER TO READ";R
30    GET #1,R
35    PRINT:PRINT
40    PRINT B$;
45    PRINT B1$
50    PRINT:PRINT
55    INPUT "READ ANOTHER RECORD(Y OR N)";X$
60 WEND
65 CLOSE #1
999 END
```

RUN
RECORD NUMBER TO READ? 3
DIRE STRAITS   MAKING MOVIES
READ ANOTHER RECORD (Y OR N)? Y
RECORD NUMBER TO READ? 1
THE JAM   SETTING SONS
READ ANOTHER RECORD (Y OR N)? Y
RECORD NUMBER TO READ? 2
TOM WAITS   SMALL CHANGE
READ ANOTHER RECORD (Y OR N)? N

statement in line 20 checks to see if another record is to be read. The record number to be read is entered in line 25. Line 30 places the record into the file buffer. Lines 40 and 45 print the contents of the file buffer to the screen. Line 65 closes the file.

TRS-80

Creating or Accessing a Random Relative File

The format for creating or accessing a random relative file for the TRS-80 microcomputer follows:

line# OPEN "R",file number,"filename",record length

For example,

```
10 OPEN "R",1,"ALBUMS",30
```

opens the file ALBUMS with record lengths of thirty bytes.

Writing Data to a File

See the previous discussion of the IBM/Microsoft microcomputer. The procedure for writing data to a file is the same.

Closing a File

The procedure for closing a file for the TRS-80 is the same as for the IBM/ Microsoft microcomputer. See the previous discussion.

The program in Figure 10–21 opens a file, writes some data to it, and closes the file.

Reading Data from a File

See the previous discussion of the IBM/Microsoft microcomputer; the procedure for reading data from a file is the same.

The program in Figure 10–22 opens the file ALBUMS, reads some records, and closes the file.

PET/Commodore 64

Relative files are not implemented on the PET/Commodore 64.

Figure 10–21 CREATING AND WRITING DATA TO A FILE

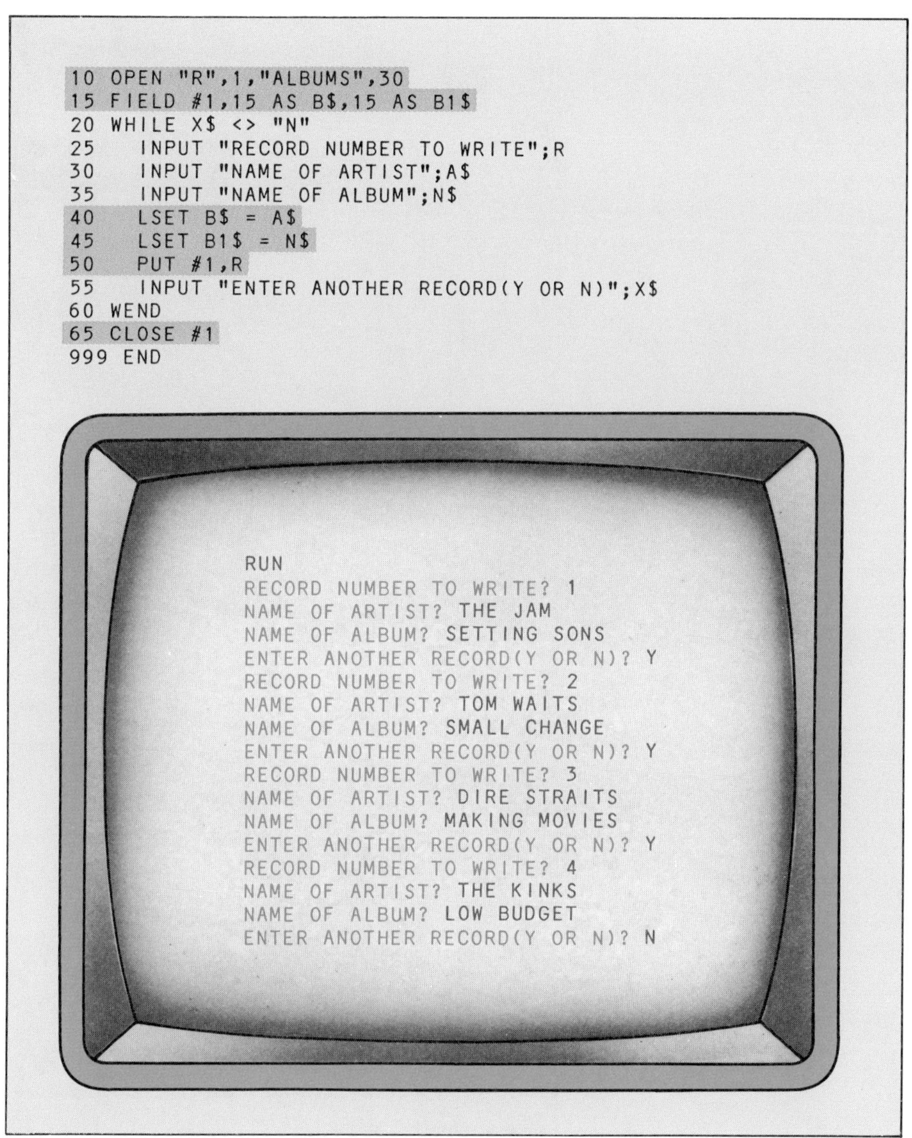
10 OPEN "R",1,"ALBUMS",30
15 FIELD #1,15 AS B$,15 AS B1$
20 WHILE X$ <> "N"
25 INPUT "RECORD NUMBER TO WRITE";R
30 INPUT "NAME OF ARTIST";A$
35 INPUT "NAME OF ALBUM";N$
40 LSET B$ = A$
45 LSET B1$ = N$
50 PUT #1,R
55 INPUT "ENTER ANOTHER RECORD(Y OR N)";X$
60 WEND
65 CLOSE #1
999 END
RUN
RECORD NUMBER TO WRITE? 1
NAME OF ARTIST? THE JAM
NAME OF ALBUM? SETTING SONS
ENTER ANOTHER RECORD(Y OR N)? Y
RECORD NUMBER TO WRITE? 2
NAME OF ARTIST? TOM WAITS
NAME OF ALBUM? SMALL CHANGE
ENTER ANOTHER RECORD(Y OR N)? Y
RECORD NUMBER TO WRITE? 3
NAME OF ARTIST? DIRE STRAITS
NAME OF ALBUM? MAKING MOVIES
ENTER ANOTHER RECORD(Y OR N)? Y
RECORD NUMBER TO WRITE? 4
NAME OF ARTIST? THE KINKS
NAME OF ALBUM? LOW BUDGET
ENTER ANOTHER RECORD(Y OR N)? N

Random versus Sequential Files

The following is a short summary of the differences between random and sequential files:

- Records in sequential files are written to the disk one after the other, starting with record 1.

Figure 10-22 READING DATA FROM A FILE

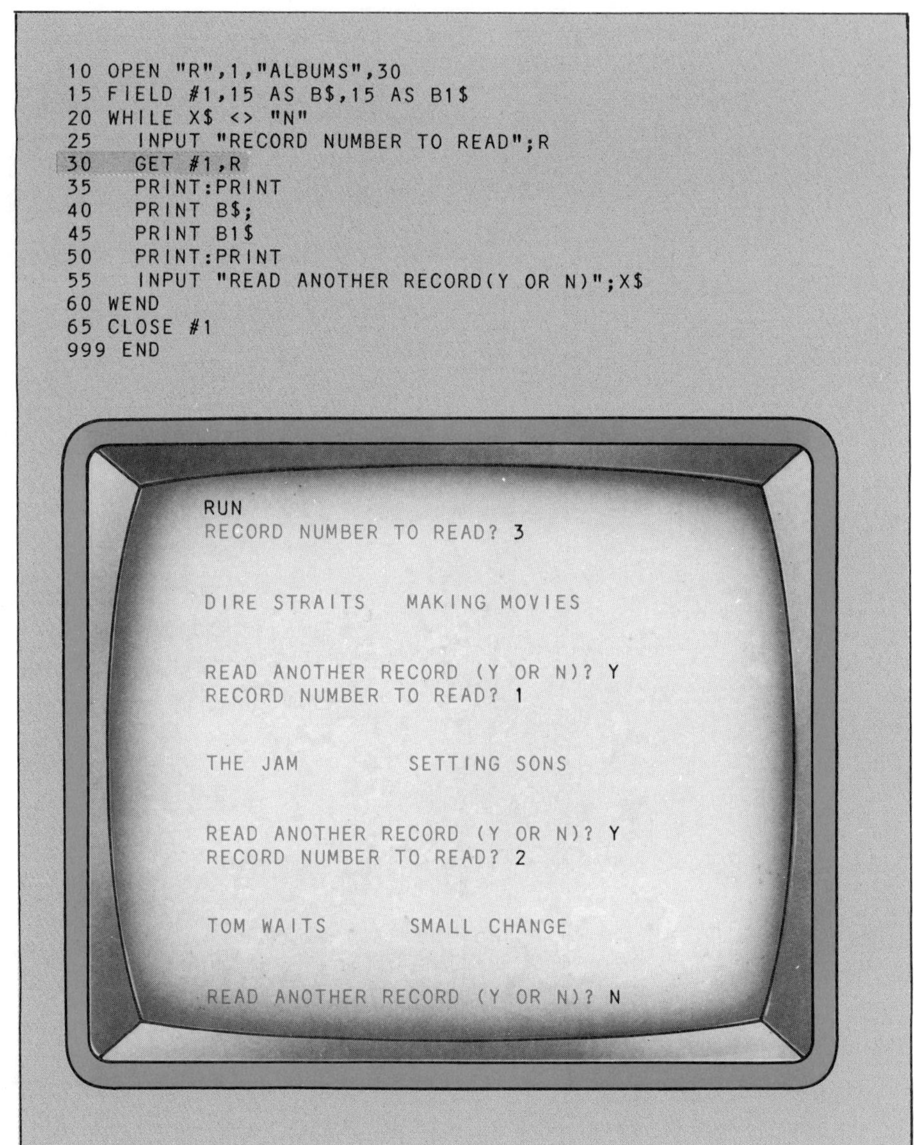

```
10 OPEN "R",1,"ALBUMS",30
15 FIELD #1,15 AS B$,15 AS B1$
20 WHILE X$ <> "N"
25   INPUT "RECORD NUMBER TO READ";R
30   GET #1,R
35   PRINT:PRINT
40   PRINT B$;
45   PRINT B1$
50   PRINT:PRINT
55   INPUT "READ ANOTHER RECORD(Y OR N)";X$
60 WEND
65 CLOSE #1
999 END
```

```
RUN
RECORD NUMBER TO READ? 3


DIRE STRAITS   MAKING MOVIES


READ ANOTHER RECORD (Y OR N)? Y
RECORD NUMBER TO READ? 1


THE JAM        SETTING SONS


READ ANOTHER RECORD (Y OR N)? Y
RECORD NUMBER TO READ? 2


TOM WAITS      SMALL CHANGE


READ ANOTHER RECORD (Y OR N)? N
```

- Records in sequential files are read from the disk one after the other, starting with record 1.
- Records in random files may be written in any order desired.
- Records in random files may be read in any order desired.
- Records in sequential files can be of varying lengths.
- Records in random files must all be the same length.

Another method of randomly accessing data in a file is through the use of indexed files. Indexed files initiate random access by means of a key, or a field within a record that uniquely identifies the contents of a particular record. For a more detailed discussion of indexed files, see your systems manual.

LEARNING CHECK

1. _______ files allow you to write to or read from a file in random order.
2. All records in a random file must be the same length. TRUE FALSE (Circle the correct answer.)
3. Records in a relative file may be accessed sequentially or randomly by _______.
4. Records in a random file may be written in any order desired. TRUE FALSE (Circle the correct answer.)

Answers

1. Random data
2. True
3. record number
4. True

A Programming Problem

The Problem

Because of the smaller enrollment in karate class during the summer, the continuing education department of Whatsamatter U. has decided to merge the intermediate and advanced classes into one. The class instructor wants a list of all students in alphabetical order.

Solution Design

The fifteen students in the intermediate class are described on a file called INT.FILE. The ten students in the advanced class are described on a file called ADV.FILE. The data in these files can be read into an array. Then the names can be alphabetized and written to a new file called SUMMER.-FILE.

The Program

Figure 10–23 gives the program listing. Line 105 sets dimensions for the array that will hold the twenty-five names. Line 110 creates the new file

Figure 10–23 FILE PROCESSING PROGRAM AND FLOWCHART

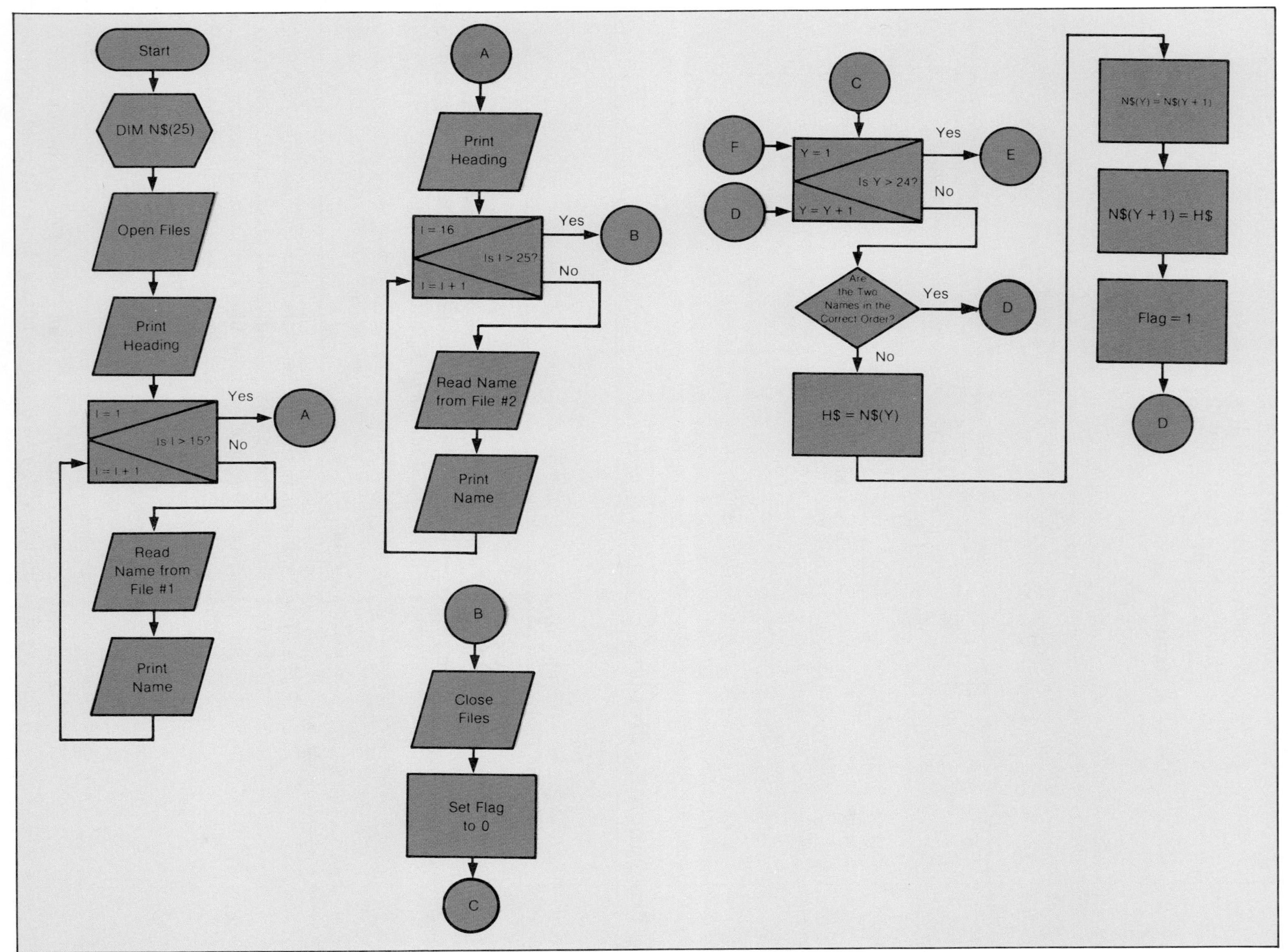

Figure 10–23 *(continued)*

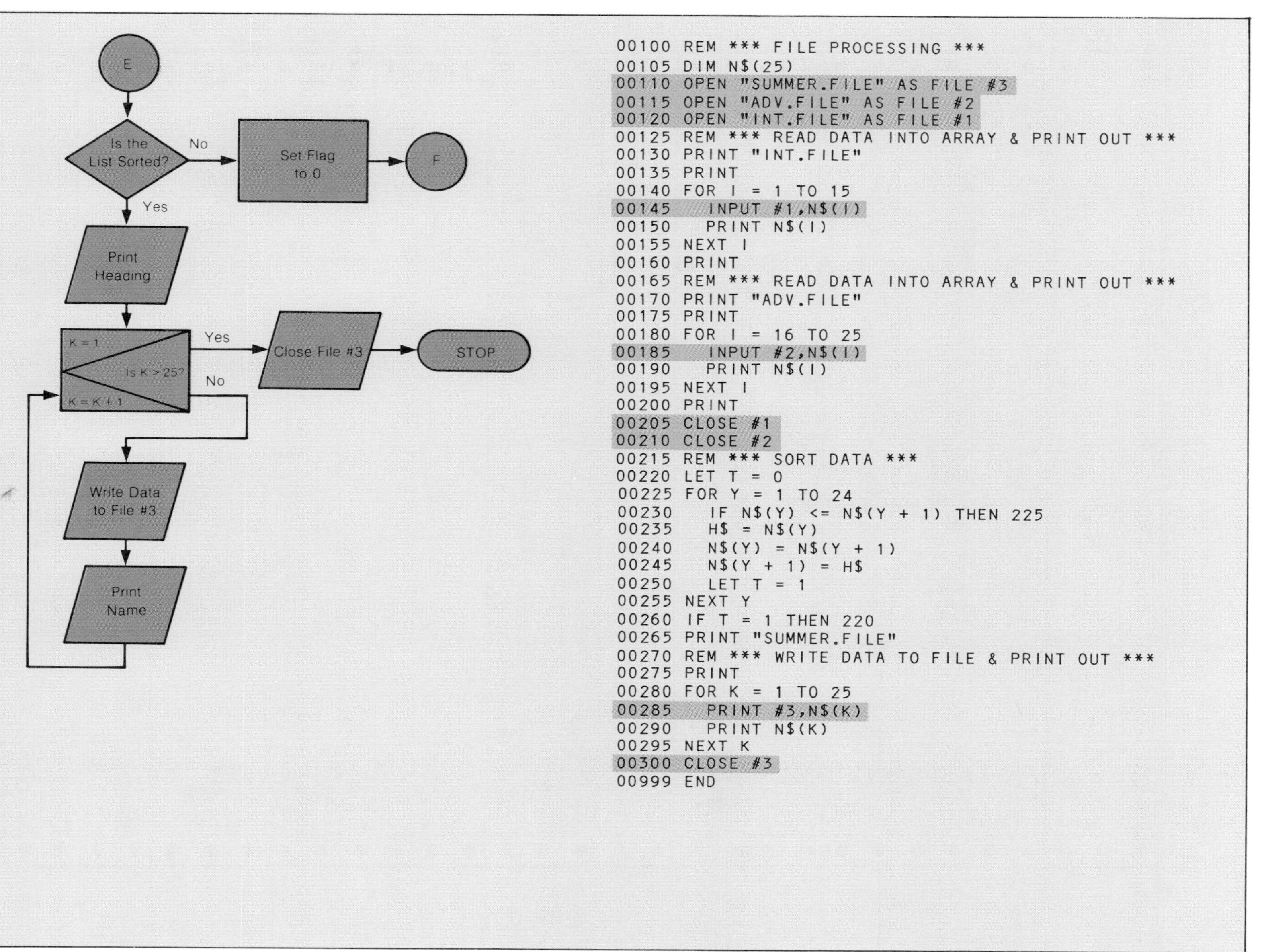


```
00100 REM *** FILE PROCESSING ***
00105 DIM N$(25)
00110 OPEN "SUMMER.FILE" AS FILE #3
00115 OPEN "ADV.FILE" AS FILE #2
00120 OPEN "INT.FILE" AS FILE #1
00125 REM *** READ DATA INTO ARRAY & PRINT OUT ***
00130 PRINT "INT.FILE"
00135 PRINT
00140 FOR I = 1 TO 15
00145   INPUT #1,N$(I)
00150   PRINT N$(I)
00155 NEXT I
00160 PRINT
00165 REM *** READ DATA INTO ARRAY & PRINT OUT ***
00170 PRINT "ADV.FILE"
00175 PRINT
00180 FOR I = 16 TO 25
00185   INPUT #2,N$(I)
00190   PRINT N$(I)
00195 NEXT I
00200 PRINT
00205 CLOSE #1
00210 CLOSE #2
00215 REM *** SORT DATA ***
00220 LET T = 0
00225 FOR Y = 1 TO 24
00230   IF N$(Y) <= N$(Y + 1) THEN 225
00235   H$ = N$(Y)
00240   N$(Y) = N$(Y + 1)
00245   N$(Y + 1) = H$
00250   LET T = 1
00255 NEXT Y
00260 IF T = 1 THEN 220
00265 PRINT "SUMMER.FILE"
00270 REM *** WRITE DATA TO FILE & PRINT OUT ***
00275 PRINT
00280 FOR K = 1 TO 25
00285   PRINT #3,N$(K)
00290   PRINT N$(K)
00295 NEXT K
00300 CLOSE #3
00999 END
```

Figure 10–23 *(continued)*

```
INT.FILE

RIDGE
BABHA
AMOS
RYMER
GORBY
WELLS
WEIR
EVANS
TAHNY
PIKE
DUGAN
LEWIS
CARBER
FRARY
DYERY


ADV.FILE

MCNUTT
LEE
MAAS
GORSH
BROWN
MEADOWS
TRAVERS
HAAS
MOHR
WILLS


SUMMER.FILE

AMOS
BABHA
BROWN
CARBER
DUGAN
DYERY
EVANS
FRARY
GORBY
GORSH
HAAS
MCNUTT
MEADOWS
MOHR
PIKE
RIDGE
RYMER
TAHNY
TRAVERS
WEIR
WELLS
WILLS
```

that will hold the combined student data. The next two lines open the two existing files. Lines 140 through 155 put data from INT.FILE into the first fifteen positions of the array N$. Line 150 simply prints them out for us to see. The next loop, in lines 180 through 195 does the same thing for ADV.-FILE. Note the initial and terminal values of the FOR statement in line 180. This lets us put the data from ADV.FILE into positions 16 through 25 of the N$ array.

Now we have a combined student list, but it is not alphabetized. We close files 1 and 2 with lines 205 through 210. Lines 220 through 260 alphabetize the student array. Since we probably will need these names in the future, they are stored on disk by line 285. Line 290 prints out the list for the instructor.

Summary

- Data is organized in the following manner. A single data item is called a field. Related fields are organized into a record. A file is composed of a group of related records.
- There are two main types of files: sequential and random access.
- There is no standardized method for performing operations on files stored on secondary storage devices.

Review Questions

1. A file contains ______.
2. What is a record?
3. Each individual data item in a record is called a ______.
4. Name the two types of file access methods that are discussed.
5. In a ______, the data items are recorded one after another and also must be read one after another in the same order in which they were recorded.
6. How much space does each field of a sequential file require?
7. Give the three steps needed to record data in a sequential file.
8. What must the programmer tell the computer when opening a file?
9. Data may be written to the disk only after the file has been ______.
10. Closing a sequential file does what two things?
11. List the three steps required for reading from a sequential file.
12. Data may be read from a sequential data file in any order. TRUE FALSE (Circle the correct answer.)

13. Give the general format of the command used to write data to a sequential file on your computer.
14. Random files allow you to write or read from a file in random order. TRUE FALSE (Circle the correct answer.)
15. The records in a relative random file must be the same length. TRUE FALSE (Circle the correct answer.)
16. To find a record, the computer must read all preceding records in a random access file. TRUE FALSE (Circle the correct answer.)
17. Random files have to be ______ before use and ______ after use.
18. A record with relative organization contains records that are stored in ______ locations.
19. Relative files may be accessed ______.
    a. sequentially
    b. randomly by record number
    c. a and b
    d. none of the above
20. What is a key, and what is it used for?

Debugging Exercises

Identify the programs or program segments that contain errors, and debug them.

1.
```
00010 OPEN BOOKS AS FILE #1
```

2.
```
00010 OPEN "DATA" AS FILE #3
00015 FOR I = 1 TO 10
00020   READ X
00025   PRINT #3,X
00030 NEXT I
00035 CLOSE #3
```

3.
```
00100 OPEN "PAYMENTS" AS FILE #1
00110 FOR I = 1 TO 100
00120   READ P$
00130   PRINT #2,P$
00140 NEXT I
00150 CLOSE #2
```

4.
```
00010 OPEN "SUPPLIES AS FILE #6
00020 FOR I = 1 TO 100
00030   INPUT #6,S$(I),N(I)
00040   PRINT S$(I),N(I)
00050 NEXT I
00060 CLOSE
```

5.
```
00010 OPEN "ORDERS" AS #1
00015 FOR I = 1 TO 100
00020   READ Y
00025   PRINT 1,Y
00030 NEXT I
00035 CLOSE #1
```

6.
```
00035 OPEN "TICKETS" AS FILE 5
00040 FOR I = 1 TO 10
00045   INPUT "ENTER NAME AND # OF TICKETS REQUESTED";X$
00050   PRINT 5,X5
00055 NEXT I
00060 CLOSE 5
```

7.
```
00010 OPEN INVENTORY AS FILE #1
00015 WHILE X$ <> "N"
00020   INPUT "ENTER PART"P$
00025   PRINT P$
00030   INPUT "WRITE ANOTHER RECORD (Y OR N)?";X$
00035 NEXT
00040 CLOSE #1
00099 END
```

8. Does the following program segment correctly set up a buffer area and open the file ADDRESS? Correct it, if necessary.

```
10 MAP BUF#1 N$ = 20,A$ = 30
20 OPEN "ADDRESS" FOR INPUT AS FILE #1,
        RELATIVE FIXED
```

9.
```
10 MAP BUFF1 N$ = 20
20 OPEN "FILMS" FOR OUTPUT AS FILE #1,
        RELATIVE FIXED,MAPBUFF1
30 INPUT "NAME OF FILM";N$
40 PUT #2,RECORD 3
50 CLOSE #2
```

10. Does the following program correctly create a file called CLIENTS? Correct it, if necessary.

```
10 MAP BUFF1 N$ = 20,A$ = 30
20 OPEN "CLIENTS" FOR INPUT AS FILE #1,
        RELATIVE FIXED,MAP BUFF1
30 WHILE D$ <> "N"
40   INPUT "WRITE WHAT RECORD #";R
50   INPUT "CLIENT NAME;N$
60   INPUT "CLIENT ADDRESS;A$
70   GET #1,RECORD R
80   PRINT M$,A$
90   INPUT "WRITE ANOTHER RECORD (Y OR N)";D$
100 NEXT
110 CLOSE #1
999 END
```

Additional Programming Problems

1. You are to write a program that stores in a sequential file the name and birthday of the following four individuals:

Joe—August 12	Sally—March 1
Bob—June 4	Nan—April 15

2. Write a program that will access the file created in Problem 1 and print out its contents.
3. You have been asked by your boss to inventory all the parts in the following list. The list is in alphabetical order. Unfortunately, everything is stored numerically. To save time (imagine the list has ten thousand parts in it), you are to write a program that will accept the data, rearrange it numerically, and then write it to a sequential data file.

Part Number	Part
0142	Nut
1662	Bolt
2439	Screw
2841	Washer

4. Write a program that will print the following headings and access and print out the file created in Problem 3. The space under QUANTITY will be left blank and is to be filled in as inventory is physically taken.

PART #　　　　*PART*　　　　*QUANTITY*

5. Write a program that creates a random access relative file of the persons and data listed here. The program should allow you to write as many records as you want to any record position you want.

Name	City	State	Telephone Number
Denise Epke	Los Angeles	CA	846–3592
Bob Szymanski	Boston	MA	524–6800
Candy Streeter	Eugene	OR	345–9164

6. Write a program that will access the file created in Problem 5 and will allow you to randomly access any record desired.

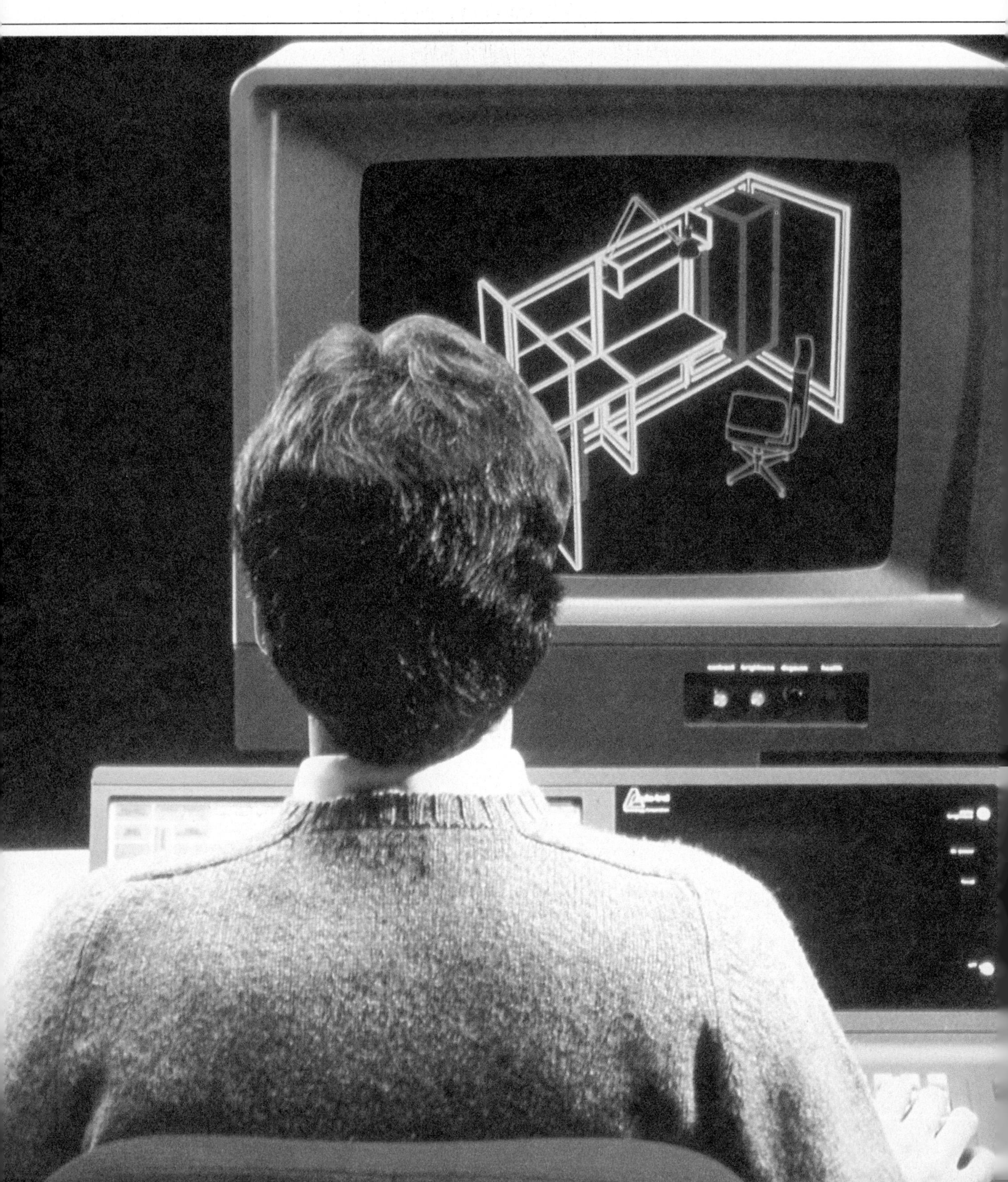

11 Matrix Commands

Outline

Objectives

After reading this chapter the student should be able to do the following:

- Understand and use the MAT READ and MAT PRINT commands.
- Understand and use the MAT command with math operations.

Overview

A matrix can be either a list or a table of data; essentially, the term **matrix** is just another name for a one- or two-dimensional array. Some implementations of the BASIC language have a set of matrix statements (nonstandard) that offer convenient, easy ways to carry out array operations. Unfortunately, many microcomputer systems do not include them in their basic compilers (none of ours do).

Matrix Statements

One key word in each matrix command is the word MAT. Table 11–1 shows typical MAT commands (X, Y, and Z are all matrices).

Matrix Input/Output

To read data into a matrix, we can use the MAT READ statement. The general format of the MAT READ statement follows:

line# MAT READ matrix name

Assume there exists a matrix X:

62	99	43
75	28	17

The following statements could be used to read this data into array X:

```
00010 DIM X(2,3)
00015 MAT READ X
00020 DATA 62,99,43,75,28,17
```

The MAT READ command causes the computer to read the data in a row order according to how it was dimensioned. That is, all of the first row is read into the matrix, then all of the second row, and so on. Another point to remember is that all the positions in the array must be filled when MAT commands are used. Otherwise, an "out of data" error message will result.

The MAT READ statement is equivalent to a READ within nested FOR/NEXT statements, as shown here:

Array Input with MAT Statement

```
00010 DIM X(2,3)
00015 MAT READ X
00020 DATA 62,99,43,75,28,17
00025 END
```

Array Input with Nested FOR and NEXT Statements

```
00010 DIM X(2,3)
00015 FOR I = 1 TO 2
00020   FOR J = 1 TO 3
00025     READ X(I,J)
00030   NEXT J
00035 NEXT I
00040 DATA 62,99,43,75,28,17
00045 END
```

Similarly, we can use a MAT INPUT statement to enter data from the terminal:

```
00010 DIM X(2,3)
00015 MAT INPUT X
```

Table 11–1 MATRIX STATEMENTS

Operation	BASIC Statement	Function	Array Manipulation
Dimension	`DIM X(2,2),Y(2,2),Z(2,2)`	Establish matrix size	$X = 2 \times 2$; $Y = 2 \times 2$; $Z = 2 \times 2$
Input/output	`MAT READ X`	Read data values into matrix X from DATA statements	$\mathbf{X}$ $\begin{vmatrix} 1 & 2 \\ -4 & 5 \end{vmatrix}$
	`MAT INPUT Y`	Enter data values into matrix Y from terminal	$\mathbf{Y}$ $\begin{vmatrix} 5 & 6 \\ 8 & 9 \end{vmatrix}$
	`MAT PRINT X,`	Print matrix X row by row	$\begin{matrix} 1 & 2 \\ -4 & 5 \end{matrix}$
Replacement	`MAT Z = X`	Assign matrix values on right side of equal sign to matrix on left side of equal sign	$\mathbf{Z} = \begin{vmatrix} 1 & 2 \\ -4 & 5 \end{vmatrix}$
Addition	`MAT Z = X + Y`	Sum X and Y, and place result in Z	$\underset{\mathbf{Z}}{\begin{vmatrix} 6 & 8 \\ 4 & 14 \end{vmatrix}} = \underset{\mathbf{X}}{\begin{vmatrix} 1 & 2 \\ -4 & 5 \end{vmatrix}} + \underset{\mathbf{Y}}{\begin{vmatrix} 5 & 6 \\ 4 & 5 \end{vmatrix}}$
Subtraction	`MAT Z = X - Y`	Subtract corresponding elements of Y from X and place result in Z	$\underset{\mathbf{Z}}{\begin{vmatrix} -4 & -4 \\ -12 & -4 \end{vmatrix}} = \underset{\mathbf{X}}{\begin{vmatrix} 1 & 2 \\ -4 & 5 \end{vmatrix}} - \underset{\mathbf{Y}}{\begin{vmatrix} 5 & 6 \\ 8 & 9 \end{vmatrix}}$
Multiplication	`MAT Z = X * Y`	Store products of X and Y in Z	$\underset{\mathbf{Z}}{\begin{vmatrix} 21 & 24 \\ 20 & 21 \end{vmatrix}} = \underset{\mathbf{X}}{\begin{vmatrix} 1 & 2 \\ -4 & 5 \end{vmatrix}} * \underset{\mathbf{Y}}{\begin{vmatrix} 5 & 6 \\ 8 & 9 \end{vmatrix}}$
Scalar multiplication	`MAT Z = (2) * X`	Multiply each element in X by 2 and place in Z	$\underset{\mathbf{Z}}{\begin{vmatrix} 2 & 4 \\ -8 & 10 \end{vmatrix}} = 2 * \underset{\mathbf{X}}{\begin{vmatrix} 1 & 2 \\ -4 & 5 \end{vmatrix}}$
Initialization	`MAT Z = ZER`	Initialize Z to zero	$\mathbf{Z}$ $\begin{vmatrix} 0 & 0 \\ 0 & 0 \end{vmatrix}$
	`MAT Z = CON`	Place 1s into Z	$\mathbf{Z}$ $\begin{vmatrix} 1 & 1 \\ 1 & 1 \end{vmatrix}$
Identity	`MAT Z = IDN`	Create the identity matrix	$\mathbf{Z}$ $\begin{vmatrix} 1 & 0 \\ 0 & 1 \end{vmatrix}$
Transposition	`MAT Z = TRN(X)`	Enter the transposition of X into Z	$\mathbf{Z}$ $\begin{vmatrix} 1 & -4 \\ 2 & 5 \end{vmatrix}$
Inversion	`MAT Z = INV(X)`	Enter the inverse of X into Z	$\mathbf{Z}$ $\begin{vmatrix} 0.038 & -0.15 \\ 0.031 & 0.08 \end{vmatrix}$

A MAT PRINT statement can be used to print out a matrix in row order. The MAT PRINT statement has the following general format:

line # MAT PRINT matrix name

Thus, the statement

```
00010 MAT PRINT X,
```

is equivalent to the following statements:

```
00010 FOR I = 1 TO 2
00015    FOR J = 1 TO 3
00020       PRINT X(I,J),
00025    NEXT J
00030    PRINT
00035 NEXT I
```

The following example illustrates the use of the MAT INPUT statement to enter data into a 3 × 3 matrix and the use of the MAT PRINT statement to get output

Figure 11–1 THE MAT INPUT STATEMENT

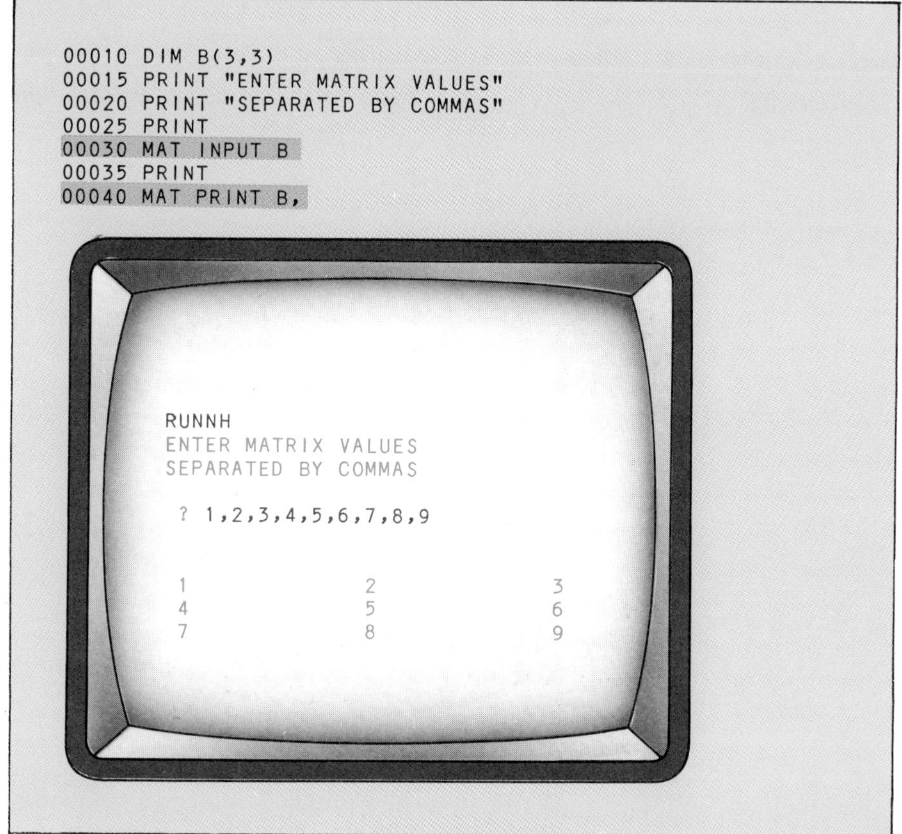

00010 DIM B(3,3)
00015 PRINT "ENTER MATRIX VALUES"
00020 PRINT "SEPARATED BY COMMAS"
00025 PRINT
00030 MAT INPUT B
00035 PRINT
00040 MAT PRINT B,
RUNNH
ENTER MATRIX VALUES
SEPARATED BY COMMAS
? 1,2,3,4,5,6,7,8,9
1 2 3
4 5 6
7 8 9

Notice that line 40 ends with a comma. If we omit the comma, the output looks like this:

```
1
2
3

4
5
6

7
8
9
```

Although the output is formatted differently, the matrix values are still printed in row order.

LEARNING CHECK

1. The term ________ is another name for a one- or two-dimensional array.
2. The ________ statement is used to read data into a matrix.
3. To enter data into a matrix from a terminal, the ________ statement is used.
4. The following statements are equivalent to what MAT statement?

```
10 FOR I = 1 TO 2
15   FOR J = 1 TO 3
20   PRINT Z(I,J),
25   NEXT I
30   PRINT
35 NEXT J
```

Answers

1. matrix
2. MAT READ
3. MAT INPUT
4. 10 MAT PRINT Z,

Matrix Math

Matrices can be added, subtracted, multiplied, and made equivalent.

Addition and Subtraction

Two matrices must have the same dimensions if they are to be added or subtracted. For example, the arrays below have the same number of rows (three) and the same number of columns (two):

```
00010 DIM B(3,2),A(3,2),C(3,2)
00015 MAT B = A + C
00020 MAT B = B -C
```

The corresponding elements of one matrix are added to (or subtracted from) another matrix. Notice that the same matrix can be referred to on both sides of the equal sign:

$$\underset{B}{\begin{vmatrix} 6 & 8 \\ 10 & 12 \\ 12.4 & 2 \end{vmatrix}} = \underset{A}{\begin{vmatrix} 5 & 6 \\ 7 & 8 \\ 3.4 & 2 \end{vmatrix}} + \underset{C}{\begin{vmatrix} 1 & 2 \\ 3 & 4 \\ 9 & 0 \end{vmatrix}}$$

$$\underset{B}{\begin{vmatrix} 5 & 6 \\ 7 & 8 \\ 3.4 & 2 \end{vmatrix}} = \underset{B}{\begin{vmatrix} 6 & 8 \\ 10 & 12 \\ 12.4 & 2 \end{vmatrix}} - \underset{C}{\begin{vmatrix} 1 & 2 \\ 3 & 4 \\ 9 & 0 \end{vmatrix}}$$

Matrix Multiplication

For two matrices to be multiplied, the number of columns of the first matrix must equal the number of rows of the second matrix. The resulting matrix will have the same number of rows as the first matrix and the same number columns as the second one:

```
00010 DIM B(3,3),E(3,2),D(2,3)
00015 MAT B = E * D
```

$$\underset{3 \times 3}{\overset{B}{\begin{vmatrix} ? & ? & ? \\ ? & ? & ? \\ ? & ? & ? \end{vmatrix}}} = \underset{3 \times 2}{\overset{E}{\begin{vmatrix} 5 & 6 \\ 7 & 8 \\ 9 & 10 \end{vmatrix}}} * \underset{2 \times 3}{\overset{D}{\begin{vmatrix} 1 & 2 & 3 \\ 4 & 5 & 6 \end{vmatrix}}}$$

The result is derived by addition of the products of the row elements of the first matrix times the column elements of the second matrix:

$$\overset{B}{\begin{vmatrix} 29 & 40 & 51 \\ 39 & 54 & 69 \\ 49 & 68 & 87 \end{vmatrix}} = \begin{vmatrix} (5*1)+(6*4) & (5*2)+(6*5) & (5*3)+(6*6) \\ (7*1)+(8*4) & (7*2)+(8*5) & (7*3)+(8*6) \\ (9*1)+(10*4) & (9*2)+(10*5) & (9*3)+(10*6) \end{vmatrix}$$

When using MAT commands, you can perform only one operation at a time. The following statement is invalid:

```
00020 MAT X = A * B + Y
```

Scalar Multiplication

A matrix can be multiplied by a **scalar** value (a constant, variable, or expression) enclosed in parentheses. For example,

```
00010 MAT E = (2) * E
```

$$\overset{E}{\begin{vmatrix} 10 & 12 \\ 14 & 16 \\ 18 & 20 \end{vmatrix}} = 2 * \overset{E}{\begin{vmatrix} 5 & 6 \\ 7 & 8 \\ 9 & 10 \end{vmatrix}}$$

Replacement

Replacement takes place when whatever is on the right side of the equal sign is placed into the matrix on the left side of the equal sign. The matrices must have the same dimensions, of course. For example,

```
00010 DIM A(2,4),B(2,4)
00015 MAT A = B
```

$$\overset{A}{\begin{vmatrix} 10 & 20 & 50 & 60 \\ 30 & 40 & 70 & 80 \end{vmatrix}} = \overset{B}{\begin{vmatrix} 10 & 20 & 50 & 60 \\ 30 & 40 & 70 & 80 \end{vmatrix}}$$

Initialization

It is often necessary to initialize variables to specific values. The same can be done with matrices.

Initializing to 0. The following MAT statement stores 0s in an array:

```
00015 DIM B(4,2)
00020 MAT B = ZER
```

$$\overset{B}{\begin{vmatrix} 0 & 0 \\ 0 & 0 \\ 0 & 0 \\ 0 & 0 \end{vmatrix}}$$

Initializing to 1. We also can use a MAT command to initialize all the elements of an array to 1:

```
00015 DIM J(2,4)
00020 MAT J = CON
```

J

$$\begin{vmatrix} 1 & 1 & 1 & 1 \\ 1 & 1 & 1 & 1 \end{vmatrix}$$

The Identity Matrix

The following statements create an identity (IDN) matrix:

```
00015 DIM Q(4,4)
00020 MAT Q = IDN
```

The diagonal of an identity matrix contains 1s; all other elements are 0s:

Q

$$\begin{vmatrix} 1 & 0 & 0 & 0 \\ 0 & 1 & 0 & 0 \\ 0 & 0 & 1 & 0 \\ 0 & 0 & 0 & 1 \end{vmatrix}$$

When the IDN function is used, the number of rows in the matrix must be equal to the number of columns.

Transportation

When a matrix is transposed, the rows of the old matrix become the columns of the new matrix. For example,

```
00010 MAT G = TRN(J)
```

If J looks like this:

$$\begin{matrix} 1 & 2 \\ 3 & 4 \\ 5 & 6 \\ 7 & 8 \end{matrix}$$

then the transposition of J looks like this:

$$\begin{matrix} 1 & 3 & 5 & 7 \\ 2 & 4 & 6 & 8 \end{matrix}$$

You must be careful that the dimensions of the matrix that will contain the transposed matrix values are the reverse of the dimensions of the matrix to be transposed. For example, J is a 4 × 2 matrix. therefore, G (which is to contain the transposition of J) must be a 2 × 4 matrix.

Inversion

One of the most powerful matrix commands is the inverse function. It often is used to solve simultaneous linear equations. The inverse of A usually is written A^{-1}. The usefulness of the inverse function comes from the fact that A multiplied by its inverse gives a result that is the identity matrix. (See "A Programming Problem" for an example of its use.)

LEARNING CHECK

1. To add or subtract two matrices, they must have ________.
2. The same matrix cannot be referred to on both sides of the equal sign.
   TRUE FALSE (Circle the correct answer.)
3. When multiplying two matrices, the resulting matrix will have the same number of ________ as the first matrix and the same number of ________ as the second one.
4. 10 MAT B = X + Y * Z is a valid MAT statement. TRUE FALSE (Circle the correct answer.)
5. Give the statements needed to create an identity matrix for a matrix with two rows and two columns.
6. ________ is the process whereby the rows of the old matrix become the columns of the new matrix.

Answers

1. the same dimensions
2. False
3. rows; columns
4. False
5. 10 DIM Q(2,2)
   20 MAT Q = IDN
6. Transposition

A Programming Problem

The Problem

We want to use MAT commands to solve two equations with two unknowns. This type of problem is very common in statistics, the sciences, engineering, and the area of business administration called operations research. Our method easily can be expanded for use with higher numbers of equations and unknowns.

In this example, we want to find the values X_1 and X_2 that simultaneously satisfy the following two equations:

$$1X_1 + 2X_2 = 5$$
$$3X_1 + 4X_2 = 6$$

Solution Design

If we looked at this problem in terms of matrices, we can analyze the two equations as follows:

$$A = \begin{vmatrix} 1 & 2 \\ 3 & 4 \end{vmatrix}$$

$$X = \begin{vmatrix} X_1 \\ X_2 \end{vmatrix}$$

$$B = \begin{vmatrix} 5 \\ 6 \end{vmatrix}$$

The resulting matrix math operations follow:

$$\begin{vmatrix} 1 & 2 \\ 3 & 4 \end{vmatrix} * \begin{vmatrix} X_1 \\ X_2 \end{vmatrix} = \begin{vmatrix} 5 \\ 6 \end{vmatrix}$$

In matrix notation, the two equations can be written as follows:

$$AX = B$$

We can use the inverse of matrix A to solve this problem in the following steps:

1. Multiply both sides by A^{-1} (the inverse of A):

$$A^{-1}AX = A^{-1}B$$

2. Notice that $A^{-1}A$ is just the identity matrix $\begin{vmatrix} 1 & 0 \\ 0 & 1 \end{vmatrix}$

$$IX = A^{-1}B$$

or

$$X = A^{-1}B$$

All we have to do to find the matrix X is to multiply matrix B by the inverse of matrix A.

The Program

Lines 105 and 110 of Figure 11–2 set the dimensions of the arrays (matrices) A, B, C, D, and X. Line 125 reads data into A. Line 145 prints A. Line

Figure 11-2 LINEAR EQUATIONS PROGRAM & FLOWCHART

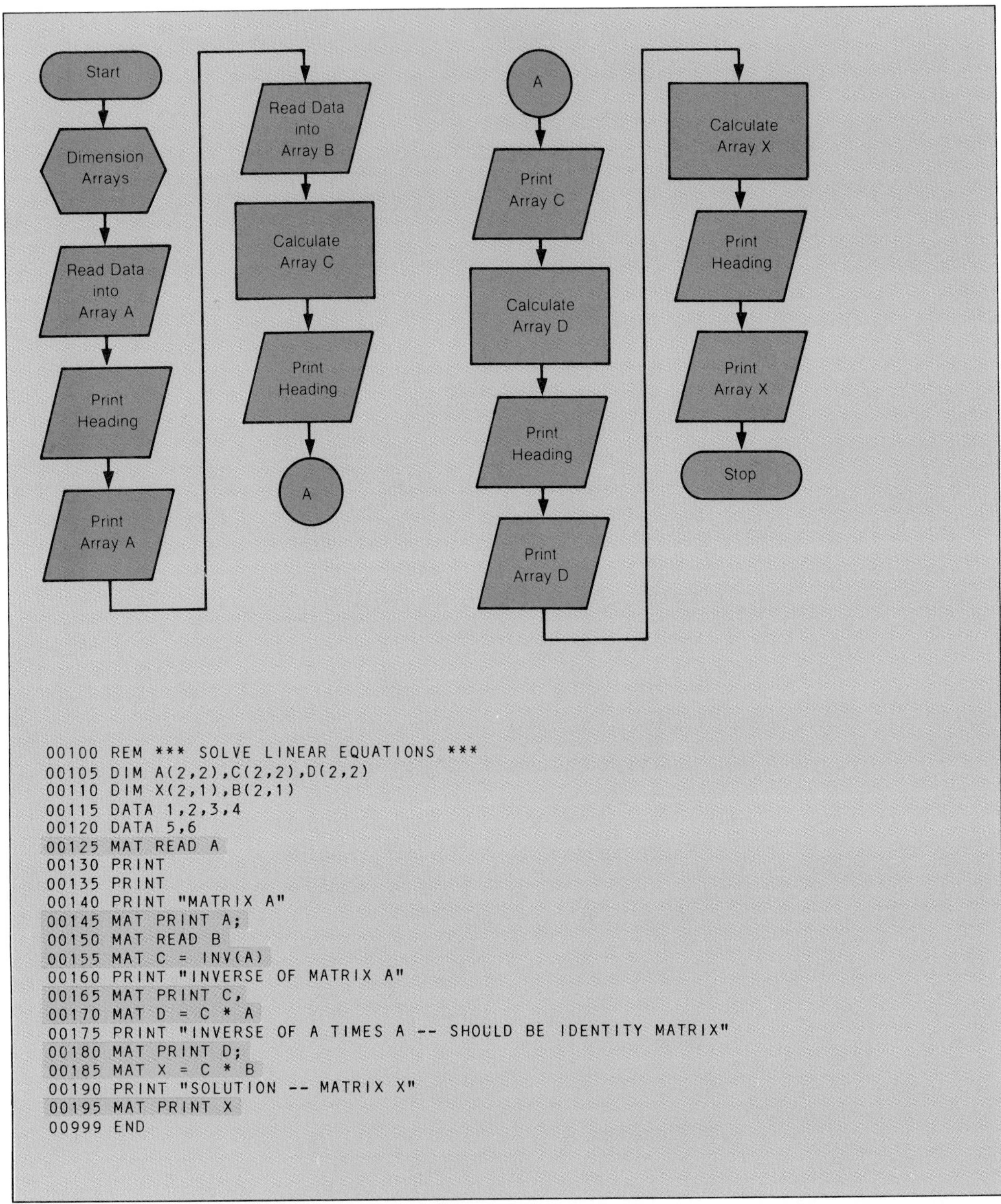


```
00100 REM *** SOLVE LINEAR EQUATIONS ***
00105 DIM A(2,2),C(2,2),D(2,2)
00110 DIM X(2,1),B(2,1)
00115 DATA 1,2,3,4
00120 DATA 5,6
00125 MAT READ A
00130 PRINT
00135 PRINT
00140 PRINT "MATRIX A"
00145 MAT PRINT A;
00150 MAT READ B
00155 MAT C = INV(A)
00160 PRINT "INVERSE OF MATRIX A"
00165 MAT PRINT C,
00170 MAT D = C * A
00175 PRINT "INVERSE OF A TIMES A -- SHOULD BE IDENTITY MATRIX"
00180 MAT PRINT D;
00185 MAT X = C * B
00190 PRINT "SOLUTION -- MATRIX X"
00195 MAT PRINT X
00999 END
```

Figure 11-2 *(continued)*

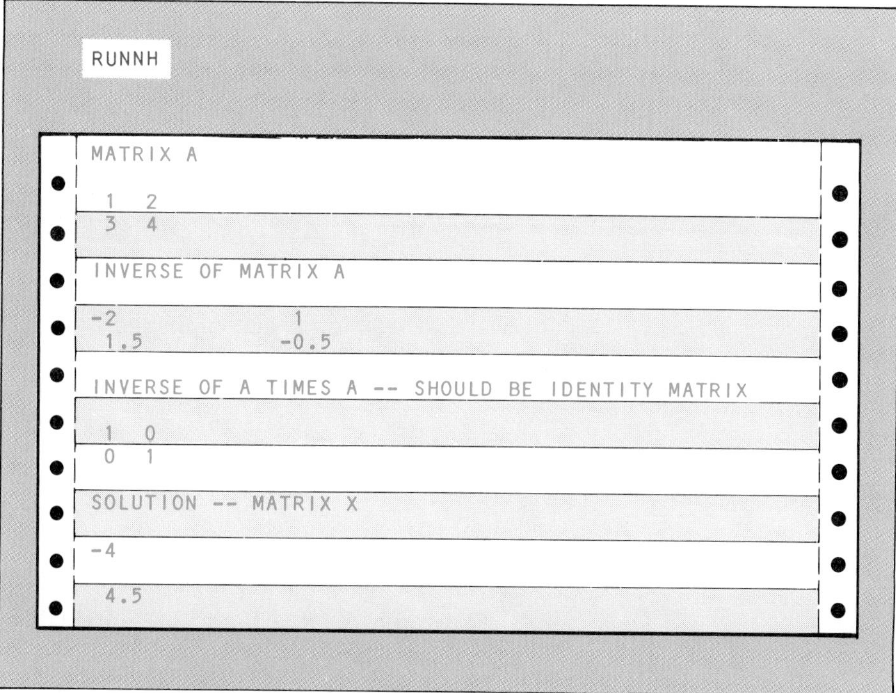

RUNNH
MATRIX A
1 2
3 4
INVERSE OF MATRIX A
-2 1
1.5 -0.5
INVERSE OF A TIMES A -- SHOULD BE IDENTITY MATRIX
1 0
0 1
SOLUTION -- MATRIX X
-4
4.5

150 reads data into B. Line 155 makes C the inverse of A. C is printed by line 165. (To better illustrate how the inverse works, lines 170 through 180 multiply A by its own inverse and print the result—the identity matrix.) Line 185 calculates the solution (two unknowns, X_1 and X_2) by multiplying B by the inverse of A. The solution is printed in line 195.

The output of the program displays matrix A, its inverse, and these two multiplied by each other (they do produce the identity matrix). The solution shows that $X_1 = -4$ and $X_2 = 4.5$. You can check this by putting these two values in the original equations and seeing that the numbers all work.

Summary

- Some BASIC compilers provide MAT statements to simplify array operations.
- The MAT READ and MAT PRINT statements read data and print data in row-by-row order.

- The MAT INPUT statement permits data to be entered into a matrix from the terminal.
- There are various MAT commands to concisely perform the math manipulations of addition, subtraction, multiplication, scalar multiplication, and replacement.
- The ZER function initializes a matrix to 0; the CON function initializes an array to 1.
- An identity matrix can be created by the use of the IDN function.
- The TRN function transposes a matrix.
- Matrix inversion is accomplished by the INV function.

Review Questions

1. What is a matrix?
2. What is the keyword used in all matrix commands?
3. How do MAT READ and MAT INPUT read in the data?
4. What statement will reserve space for a 3 × 4 matrix called G?
5. What statement will print the matrix G in matrix form?
6. What restriction is placed on the addition and subtraction of matrices?
7. How are matrices subtracted?
8. What restriction is placed on the multiplication of matrices?
9. If matrix A is 2 × 4 and B is 4 × 3, what are the dimensions of matrix C, which is A * B?
10. Explain how one matrix is multiplied by another.
11. What is a scalar value?
12. How do you multiply a matrix by a scalar?
13. What command initializes an array to 0?
14. What does the statement MAT A = CON do?
15. What is an identity matrix?
16. What restriction is placed on the dimensions of an identity matrix?
17. How do you create an identity matrix?
18. What is the transposition of a matrix?
19. What command is used to transpose a matrix?
20. What is the inverse of a matrix?
21. What command will invert the matrix X?
22. Why is the inverse of a matrix useful?

Debugging Exercises

Identify the following statements and program segments that contain errors, and debug them.

1.
```
00010 MAT READ X
00020 MAT PRINT X,
00030 DATA 10,20,30,40,50,60
```

2.
```
00010 DIM A(3,3)
00015 MAT READ A
00020 MAT PRINT A,
00025 DATA 7,1,9,6,3,8,2,4
```

3.
```
00010 DIM X(2,3),Y(2,3),Z(2,3)
00020 PRINT "INPUT MATRIX X"
00030 MAT INPUT A
00040 PRINT "INPUT MATRIX Y"
00050 MAT INPUT B
00060 LET Z = X + Y
00070 MAT PRINT Z,
```

4.
```
00010 DIM A(2,3),B(3,2),C(2,3)
00020 MAT READ A
00030 MAT READ B
00040 MAT C = A - B
00050 MAT PRINT C,
00060 DATA 1,2,3,4,5,6,7,8,9,10,11,12
```

5.
```
00010 DIM X(3,4),Y(4,3),Z(4,4)
00015 MAT INPUT X
00020 MAT INPUT Y
00025 MAT Z = X * Y
00030 MAT PRINT Z,
```

6.
```
00010 DIM A(4,3)
00015 MAT READ A
00020 MAT A = 5 * A
00025 MAT PRINT A,
00030 DATA 2,5,7,9,3,11,8,1,4,10,6,12
```

7.
```
00010 DIM X(1,3),Y(1,3)
00020 MAT X = ZER
00030 MAT Y = X
00040 MAT PRINT X,
00050 MAT PRINT Y,
```

8.
```
00010 DIM A(3,5)
00020 MAT A = ONE
00030 MAT PRINT A,
```

9.
```
00010 DIM X(2,3)
00015 MAT X = IDN
00020 MAT PRINT X,
```

10.
```
00010 DIM B(5,4)
00015 MAT INPUT B
00020 MAT B = TRN
00025 MAT PRINT B,
```

Additional Programming Problems

1. Write a program to explore the power of the matrix commands. Given the matrices A and B below, compute A + B, A − B, (2) * A, A * B, and B * A. Notice that A * B does not equal B * A.

$$A = \begin{vmatrix} 2 & 3 & 4 \\ 6 & 7 & 7 \\ 4 & 4 & 3 \end{vmatrix} \qquad B = \begin{vmatrix} 1 & 2 & 1 \\ 1 & 2 & 1 \\ 1 & 0 & 0 \end{vmatrix}$$

2. The White Snowmobile Company sells three models of snowmobiles (regular, super, and deluxe) in two colors (red and blue). The snowmobile sales for January and February are recorded here. Compute the total and average sales for each type of snowmobile.

JANUARY	Regular	Super	Deluxe
Red	3	5	2
Blue	1	4	1

FEBRUARY	Regular	Super	Deluxe
Red	7	2	3
Blue	4	1	6

3. Mr. Brown teaches an evening class in computer science. He decided to curve the grades at the end of the semester by adding five points to each test. Write a program to compute the new grades for Mr. Brown. The grades are now as follows:

Student	Test 1	Test 2	Test 3
Alice	70	65	73
Joe	81	79	74
Bob	93	95	89
Sue	87	83	85
Peg	54	63	70

4. An insurance company has the following income and expenses over a three-month period. Write a program that calculates the company's monthly profit. Also, determine the amount of cash to be reserved for

Christmas bonuses based on 10 percent of the monthly profit. (*Hint:* Use two 1 × 3 matrices.)

	October	November	December
Income	22,247	25,475	34,628
Expenses	17,753	19,091	23,152

5. Given the following matrix A, write a program to print A and to compute and print its transposition and inverse (A^{-1}). Then multiply A by A^{-1} and A^{-1} by A, and print the results. Can you explain these results?

$$A = \begin{vmatrix} 1 & 2 & 3 \\ -9 & 8 & 7 \\ -2 & 5 & -7 \end{vmatrix}$$

6. The demand for a product is given by the equation $100p - q = 300$. The supply of that same product is given by the equaiton $100p + q = 500$. In these equations, p stands for the price of the product, and q stands for the number of units demanded or supplied. Write a program to find p and q so that all products produced will be sold. That is, solve the simultaneous linear equations for p and q. (*Hint:* See "A Programming Problem" at the end of this chapter.)

APPENDIX A DEC System 2060

Outline

Hardware

Signing On

Saving and Loading Programs

Signing Off

Keyboard

Specialized Keys

Special Features

Hardware

The DECSYSTEM 2060 is a large minicomputer that can have up to several million bytes of addressable internal storage for programs—as opposed to tens of thousands of bytes in the microcomputers discussed here. The exact form of BASIC employed with the DECSYSTEM 2060 is called BASIC PLUS 2 by the manufacturer.

The detailed hardware description depends heavily on what CRT terminal is used with this computer. The one used here is the standard VT-100 terminal.

Signing On

The power switch (toggle variety) is on the lower left at the back of the terminal. If the terminal is linked directly to the computer, press the CONTROL and C keys at the same time. If the terminal is linked to the computer by telephone, dial the correct number. When you hear a constant high-pitched tone, place the telephone receiver in the modem; most modems have a light that comes on when the connection is made properly. Then press CONTROL-C.

A header will appear, followed by the symbol @:

```
TOPS-20 MONITOR 4(3247)
@
```

This is the prompt for the TOPS-20 MONITOR. (A **monitor** is the housekeeping program that controls the computer.) You must type LOGIN and an account identifier followed by a password. The password should be privileged information known only to those who need access to the programs in this particular account. For example, the programs for this manual were kept in an account called IACCT.SZYMANSKI; access to the account was controlled by the password BASIC. The screen looked like this after log-in:

```
@LOGIN IACCT.SZYMANSKI
```

The password did not appear on the screen because the monitor knows that any characters following the blank after an account identifier are not to be made public.

After the RETURN key is pressed, the computer responds with a header giving the date and time. Then the monitor prompt (@) is displayed. To use the BASIC language, just type BASIC. When the computer is prepared to accept BASIC commands, it responds READY. To write a program, type NEW; the computer asks for a name for the program:

```
READY
NEW
New program name--BOB.1

READY
```

If you hit RETURN without supplying a name, the computer will call the program NONAME. You can now proceed to type in your program.

Saving and Loading Programs

We assume this computer uses disks for auxiliary storage. To save a program named BOB.1, simply type SAVE BOB.1:

```
READY
SAVE BOB.1

READY
```

To load the program at a later time, type OLD after the computer responds READY. The computer will ask for the old program's name. Type BOB.1:

```
READY
OLD
Old file name--BOB.1

READY
```

After the computer again responds READY, you may run or list the program or perform editing operations on it.

Signing Off

If you are in BASIC, type BYE when you are finished. If you are in the system mode, type LOGOUT. After the computer acknowledges your message, turn the terminal off.

Keyboard

The DEC keyboard allows entry of all standard text control characters. The DEC keyboard also has some additional characters, such as ~ and ∧. By pressing the shift key, you can enter the upper symbol on those keys that have two symbols. To do this, hold down the shift key while hitting the key with the desired symbol. The shift key also can be used to produce uppercase letters when the CAPS LOCK key is in the up position. When the CAPS LOCK key is pressed down, all letters will be displayed in uppercase. To switch back to lowercase, press the CAPS LOCK key again.

The CNTRL key also is used along with other keys. By itself, this key does nothing. See your user's manual for the control characters created when CNTRL is pressed with particular keys.

Specialized Keys

The following keys have special functions. BASIC will perform a specified function when these are used rather than accept them as keyboard data.

Key	Function
RETURN	Carriage control; enters lines to the computer.
ESC	Escape key; saves the trouble of typing long filenames by allowing you to type in only enough characters so that the computer cannot confuse the filename with any other one in your directory, then pressing the ESC key will display the rest of the filename for you; indicates an end to what you are doing; displays guide words as hints about what information a DEC command needs.
DELETE	Eliminates the last character typed.
NO SCROLL	Stops the display at any time so that what is on the screen may be read before it goes off the top. Press it again to continue display.
TAB	Moves cursor to the beginning of the next eight-column field.
LINEFEED	Moves the cursor to the next line.
SET-UP	Sets margins.
BACKSPACE	Moves the cursor back one space.
BREAK	Stops program execution.
↑ ↓ ← →	Moves the cursor in the indicated direction.

Special Features

Each key has a repeat feature; when the key is held down for about one second, a stream of that character will be printed until you release the key. The DEC keyboard also has a numeric keypad similar to that of a calculator. The keys at the top of this numeric keypad (PF1, PF2, PF3, and PF4) can be programmed to perform specific functions.

APPENDIX B Apple 2 Plus

Outline

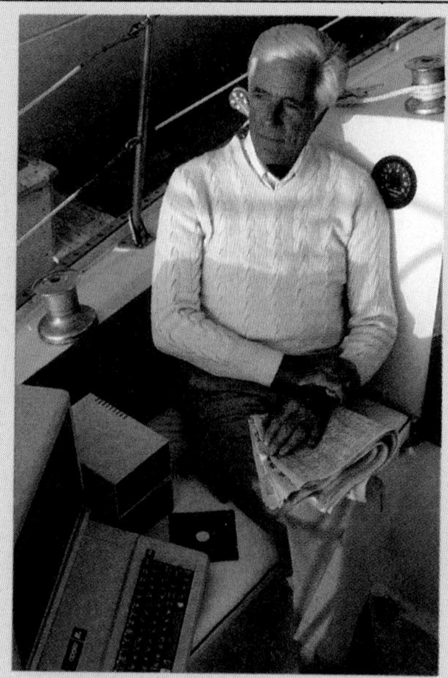

Hardware

Starting the Computer

Saving and Loading Programs

Cassette

Disk

Keyboard

Specialized Keys

Display Differences
Using the 80-Column Card

Hardware

The Apple II initially contains INTEGER BASIC. Since INTEGER BASIC lacks many important features of the ANSI standard, this discussion only refers to this computer once Applesoft floating-point BASIC has been loaded. The Apple II Plus computer automatically comes up in Applesoft.

Starting the Computer

The power switch is located on the left rear portion of the computer. Since an external monitor or CRT is required, you must remember to turn on power to this device also. If a disk drive is attached, it will whir and try to **boot** the disk-operating system (DOS), so be sure that a diskette is placed in the disk drive before the computer is turned on. (When the disk drive boots the DOS, it loads from a diskette the instructions that tell the computer how to manage the disk. This must be done before the computer can perform any disk-related tasks.) The computer "comes up" with floating-point BASIC, as indicated by the use of the] character as a prompt.

Saving and Loading Programs

Programs are commonly accessed from either cassette tape or disk on this system.

Cassette

To recall a program from a cassette tape into main memory, you must first position the tape to the beginning of the program. This means that you must keep a record of where programs are located on the tape. Next, push the PLAY button and pull out the earphone plug on the recorder until you can hear the tape sounds. When you hear a constant high-pitched tone, stop the recorder and plug the earphone jack back in. Then type LOAD, push the PLAY button, and hit RETURN. The program has been loaded when you hear a beep and the cursor appears on the screen. (The **cursor** is usually a flashing character, such as an underline or a block, that shows where the next typed character will appear on the screen.)

To store a program, position the tape to a blank area, type SAVE, push the PLAY and RECORD buttons simultaneously, and then press RETURN. Again, you will hear a beep, and the cursor will return when the program has been written to the tape.

Disk

The Apple has a convenient file-by-name catalog system for the DOS. To save an Applesoft program—for example, one named TEST 3—on disk, type the following:

```
SAVE TEST3
```

and press RETURN. To load the same program from disk, type this:

```
LOAD TEST3
```

and press RETURN. You then can run the program. Alternatively, you can type RUN TEST3 without loading it; this causes the DOS to both load and run the program.

Keyboard

The Apple II and Apple II Plus keyboards contain all the standard keyboard characters with the exception of lowercase letters. The Apple II and Apple II Plus only have an uppercase mode, so no lowercase letters can be entered. The shift key can be used to enter the upper symbol on those keys that contain two symbols. For example, to enter a *, hold down the shift key and hit the * key.

The CNTRL key does nothing by itself; when used along with other keys, however, it produces additional control characters. Check your reference manual to find the uses of these combinations.

Specialized Keys

When these keys are pressed, BASIC performs a specific function rather than accept them as keyboard data. The following keys have special functions:

Key	Function
RESET	Stops program execution.
RETURN	Enters the line.
ESC	Clears the screen; also is used with I(↑), J(←), K(→), and M(↓) for cursor movement.
REPT	When held down with another key, causes that character to be repeated.

Display Differences Using the 80–Column Card

Some of the Applesoft BASIC features presented in this book are affected by the use of the 80-column text card. These features include using commas to tab in a PRINT statement, and the TAB command.

Comma tabbing will not function properly for the second forty columns of an eighty-column display. One method to avoid this problem is to embed blank spaces within the quotes of the PRINT statement.

The TAB command also does not function as described when in eighty-column mode. The statement:

POKE 1403,<horizontal postition 0 to 79>

can be used when in eighty-column mode. For example, to tab over to column 67 when in eight-column mode type:

POKE 1403,67

Do not use the POKE command when in the forty-column mode.

APPENDIX C IBM Personal Computer

Outline

Hardware

Starting the Computer

Saving and Loading Programs

  Disk

Keyboard

Specialized Keys

Special Features

Hardware

The IBM Personal Computer contains an enhanced version of Microsoft BASIC. We will discuss the hardware configuration using disk only. Consult your documentation for cassette commands.

Starting the Computer

Place the diskette into drive A, the left-hand drive. Then turn the computer on. The power switch is located on the right rear of the machine. Do not forget to turn on the television monitor, too. When the computer is turned on, it will try to load the disk-operating system (DOS). (If no diskette has been placed into the disk drive, the computer will "come up" in Cassette BASIC.)

The IBM Personal Computer has three BASIC dialects: Cassette BASIC, Disk BASIC, and Advanced BASIC. For the purposes of this book, they are the same.

Once the DOS has been booted, or loaded, the computer asks for the date and time. If you don't want to enter the date and/or time, just hit the RETURN key after the prompt. The date and time prompts appear as follows:

```
Current date is Tue  1-01-1980
Enter new date:
Current time is  0:00:07.96
Enter new time:
```

After you have responded to the time prompt and pressed the carriage return, the computer responds with the following:

```
The IBM Personal Computer DOS
Version 1.10 (C)Copyright IBM Corp 1981, 1982

A>
```

The A> is the system prompt. Simply type BASIC and press the carriage return to load the disk BASIC translator, or type in BASIC A to load the Advanced BASIC translator. The BASIC prompt is OK. Now you are ready to start programming.

Saving and Loading Programs

Disk

The IBM has a convenient file-by-name catalog system for the DOS. To save a program (for example, one named TESTS), type the following:

```
SAVE "TESTS"
```

The name of the program should be less than or equal to eight characters. Do not embed any spaces. To load the same program from disk, type this:

```
LOAD "TESTS"
```

The ending quote (") is optional. You can then list and run the program.

Keyboard

The IBM keyboard allows entry of all standard characters. However, some special symbols are included that are not found on a regular typewriter, such as ∧, [, and]. The shift key on this keyboard is marked with the symbol . While holding down the shift key, you may enter the upper symbol on any key that has two symbols. The shift keys produce uppercase letters when used with the A through Z keys. The CAPS LOCK key will cause uppercase letters to be produced every time an A through Z key is hit. To switch back to lowercase, hit the CAPS LOCK key once again. In addition to the shift keys, the CNTRL and ALT keys may be used with many other keys to enter characters or perform specific functions (check your manual).

Specialized Keys

When pressing the following keys, BASIC will perform a specific function rather than accept them as keyboard data:

Key	Function
↵	Carriage return key; usually has to be pressed to enter information into the computer.
←	Backspace key (located above the carriage return key); backspaces and erases characters.
PRTSC	Print screen key; when pressed along with the shift key, causes whatever is on the screen to be printed on the printer.
HOME	Moves the cursor to the upper left corner and clears the screen.
↑	Moves cursor upward.
↓	Moves cursor downward.
←	(Located below the 4 on the numeric keypad) Moves the cursor to the left but does not erase.
→	Moves the cursor to the right.
END	Moves the cursor to the end of the logical line.
INS	Allows characters to be inserted into the statement at the current cursor position.

DEL	Deletes characters at the current cursor position.
ESC	Causes the entire logical line to be erased from the screen; the line is not passed to BASIC for processing.
⇥ ⇤	(Tab) Moves the cursor to the next tab stop. (Tab stops occur every eight characters.)

Special Features

The IBM keyboard has a function key section (F1 through F10) on the left side of the keyboard and a numeric keypad similar to a calculator keypad on the right, in addition to the regular typewriter area. The function keys can be set to automatically type any sequence of characters. Some already have been assigned frequently used commands but can be changed. Pressing the NUM LOCK key shifts the numeric keypad so that it can be used to get the numbers 0 through 9 and the decimal point. Pressing the NUM LOCK again returns the keypad to its cursor control mode.

APPENDIX D TRS-80

Outline

- Hardware
- Starting Model III
- Saving and Loading Programs
  - Cassette
  - Disk
- Keyboard
- Specialized Keys
- Special Features

Hardware

This discussion refers to the TRS-80 Model III with the Model III BASIC language. An older computer, the Model I with level II BASIC, is very similar to the Model III. The comments about BASIC programs here generally apply to either computer but do not deal with the level I BASIC language.

Starting Model III

The power is turned on by use of a rocker switch beneath the keyboard on the right side nearest the programmer. When the switch is turned on (consult your manual about the proper sequence if you use peripherals), the computer responds as follows:

```
CASS?
```

The computer is asking whether you want to use low speed (63 characters per second) or high speed (190 characters per second) for cassette tape communication. Respond by typing L and pressing the ENTER key, typing H and pressing the ENTER key, or simply pressing the ENTER key. The L and H indicated low speed and high speed, and the default is high speed.

Next, the computer displays the following:

```
MEMORY SIZE?
```

Simply pressing the RETURN key is the standard response unless you want to save some space in memory for machine language programs. Next, the computer displays this:

```
RADIO SHACK MODEL III BASIC
(C) 80 TANDY
READY
>
```

You now can begin using BASIC commands.

Saving and Loading Programs

Programs commonly are accessed from either cassette tape or disk on this system.

Cassette

The TRS-80 has a convenient file-by-name cataloging system. To save a program, do the following:

1. Position the tape to a blank area.
2. Type SAVE "program-name"; for example, SAVE "PROGRAM1".
3. Press the RECORD and PLAY buttons on the cassette.

To load a stored program, you need only type the following and hit the RETURN key:

```
CLOAD "program-name"
```

When the cassette PLAY button is pressed, the computer will search for the program. The names of the programs found during the search will be displayed on the screen. After the computer has found the desired program, it will load it into main memory.

Disk

To save a program (for example, PROGRAM1), just type the following:

```
SAVE "PROGRAM1"
```

and hit the ENTER button. To load the same program from disk, type this:

```
LOAD "PROGRAM1"
```

Keyboard

This keyboard allows entry of all standard text and control characters. By pressing the shift key, you can enter the upper symbol on those keys that contain two symbols. For example, to enter a $, hold down the shift key and hit $.

The TRS-80 has two modes of operation: CAPS and ULC (uppercase/lowercase). When the computer is started, the keyboard is in the CAPS mode; the A through Z keys will always produce uppercase letters. To switch to the ULC mode, press the shift key and 0. In this mode, the A through Z keys produce lowercase letters unless you press the shift key. The shift key and 0 also will switch back to the CAPS mode. The shift key can be used in combination with many other keys to produce additional control characters. Check your reference manual for the uses of these combinations.

Specialized Keys

In BASIC, the following keys have special functions. BASIC performs the specified function instead of accepting the items on these keys as keyboard data.

Key	Function
←	Backspaces and erases the last character typed.
→	Tabs to the next eight-column boundary.
↓	Line feeds.
↑	Causes BASIC to accept a bracket ([) used for exponentiation.
ENTER	Enters the line; BASIC will not interpret a line until you press ENTER.
CLEAR	Cancels the current line, erases the display, converts to sixty-four characters per line, and positions the cursor to the upper left corner ("home").

Special Features

Each key has a repeat feature; if you hold it down for about one second, that character will be repeated until you let up. The TRS-80 has a separate numeric keypad for convenient numeric entry. These keys are equivalent to their matching key on the standard keyboard section.

APPENDIX E PET/Commodore 64

Outline

Hardware

Starting the Computer

Saving and Loading Programs

Cassette

Disk

Keyboard

Specialized Keys

Special Features

Hardware

The PET 64 and Commodore 64 computers are made by the same manufacturer, Commodore Business Machines. For each number series, the two computers are nearly identical. For example, the PET 64 and the Commodore 64 differ only as follows:

- The PET 64 comes with a monitor, and the Commodore 64 does not.
- The Commodore 64 has color capabilities, and the PET 64 does not.

The following discussion will focus on the Commodore 64. However, the commands for saving and loading programs are identical on both machines.

Starting the Computer

The power switch is in back near the left corner underneath the body of the computer. When the power switch is turned on, you see something like this:

```
****COMMODORE 64 BASIC V2****
64K RAM SYSTEM 38911 BASIC BYTES FREE
READY
```

The first line tells which version of the BASIC language is available. The second line tells how much memory your computer has (64K in this example). The third line indicates that you can immediately begin typing in BASIC line numbers and statements.

Saving and Loading Programs

Programs are commonly accessed from either cassette tape or disk on this system.

Cassette

The Commodore 64 has a convenient file-by-name cataloging system. After typing in a program, you may want to save it on cassette. The SAVE command is used to save a program on tape in the following manner:

```
SAVE "program-name"
```

To save a program, position the tape to a blank area and type SAVE and the program name in quotes, for example,

```
SAVE "MASTER"
```

The program name can be up to sixteen characters long. After hitting the RETURN key, the computer responds with the following:

```
PRESS PLAY AND RECORD ON TAPE
```

You must then press the RECORD and PLAY buttons on the cassette. If you have more than one cassette tape drive, you may have to specify the device number; otherwise it will default to 1. For example, if you want to save MASTER on cassette tape drive 2, type the following and hit the RETURN key:

```
SAVE "MASTER",2
```

To load a stored program, you need only type LOAD and the program name (enclosed in quotes), for example,

```
LOAD "MASTER"
```

After hitting the RETURN key, the computer responds with the following:

```
PRESS PLAY ON TAPE #1
```

Then, when the cassette PLAY button is pressed, the computer will search for the named program. The names of other programs found during the search will be displayed on the screen. Therefore, the tape does not have to be positioned precisely for loading. The computer will tell you when it has found the desired program. To actually load the program, press the C= key. After the program is loaded, the screen will return to its normal state, and the READY prompt will reappear. Remember to specify the device number if you have more than one cassette drive.

An example—loading a program named PINBALL, the third one on a tape—is shown here:

```
LOAD "PINBALL"

PRESS PLAY ON TAPE #1
OK

SEARCHING FOR PINBALL
FOUND METRIC
FOUND DCLOCK
FOUND PINBALL
(Press C= key)
LOADING
READY
```

Disk

The Commodore 64 floppy disk system has a file-by-name catalog. After typing in a program, you may want to save it on disk. Saving programs on disk is similiar to saving programs on cassette; just type the following:

```
SAVE "program-name",8
```

The 8 tells the computer that you want the program saved to disk. After the RETURN key is pressed, the disk will start to turn, and the computer will respond with this:

```
SAVING "program-name"
OK
READY
```

For example, if you want to save a program called MASTER on disk, type the following:

```
SAVE "MASTER",8
```

To load a program from disk, you type the following:

```
LOAD "program-name",8
```

Here again, the 8 is the code for the disk, which lets the computer know you want the program loaded from the disk. After the RETURN key is pressed, the disk will start whirring, and the following will be displayed:

```
SEARCHING FOR "program-name"
LOADING

READY
```

For example, if you want to load a program called MASTER from disk, just type the following:

```
LOAD "MASTER",8
```

Keyboard

The keyboard has the characters of a standard typewriter keyboard, with the addition of the £ character on the upper right side. The shift key works like that on the standard typewriter. When in the uppercase/lowercase mode, the shift key will cause uppercase letters, or the top symbol on those keys with two symbols, to be entered. The shift and CNTRL keys may be used with other keys to produce additional control characters.

Function Keys

The following keys have special functions.

Key	Function
CRSR ⇧⇩	Moves the cursor downward; when used with the shift key, moves the cursor upward.
CRSR ⇦⇨	Moves the cursor to the right; when used with the shift key, moves the cursor to the left.
RETURN	Carriage control; enters the line or command.
INST DEL	Moves the cursor back a space, deleting the previous character typed; with the shift key, you may insert a character.
CLR HOME	Positions the cursor in the upper left corner of the screen ("home"); with the shift key, clears the screen and places the cursor in home position.
RESTORE	Restores the computer to its normal state.
RUN STOP	Stops execution of a BASIC program; with the shift key, allows you to automatically load a program from tape.

Special Features

The PET/Commodore 64 has a wide range of graphics keys for colors (on Commodore 64 only) and graphic symbols. Pressing the Commodore key C= or CNTRL key with other keys allows you to work with these graphics control characters.

The PET/Commodore 64 keyboard also has an additional set of four function keys on the right side of the keyboard. These can be programmed to handle a variety of functions.

Flowcharting Supplement

Outline

Problem Solving Using Computers

- Defining, Analyzing, and Understanding the Problem
- Preparing a Flowchart Defining the Problem Solution
- Writing the Computer Program
- Running, Debugging, and Testing the Computer Program

Flowchart Preparation

- Flowchart Symbols
- Logic Patterns
- Flowcharting Example: Temperature Conversion

Alternatives to Flowcharting

- Pseudocode
- Hierarchy Charts

Pros and Cons of Flowcharting

Common Program Logic Flowcharts

- Input/Output Using Counters
- Multiple Decisions
- Accumulating Subtotals and Totals
- Tables
- Merging Files
- Sorting

Problem Solving Using Computers

Problem solving using computers involves writing a computer program. Since the program is the focal point of computer-assisted problem solving, a five-step procedure can be used for the process of problem solving using computers. These five steps are as follows:

- Defining, analyzing, and understanding the problem.
- Design and document (flowchart) the solution
- Write and document the computer program.
- Submit the program to the computer.
- Running, debugging, and testing the computer program.

Defining, Analyzing, and Understanding the Problem

The initial step begins with recognizing that a problem does exist and that a computer can be used in the attempt to solve the problem. The defining, analyzing, and understanding of the problem, its causes, and its possible solutions is very critical to the remaining steps of the process. Once the problem has been clearly defined and analyzed, a solution is chosen, and Step 2 of the process is begun.

Design and Document (Flowchart) the Solution

Once the problem solution has been defined, a diagram depicting the necessary inputs, processes, and outputs needed to solve the problem is prepared. This diagram is better known as a *flowchart* and will be described in detail shortly.

Writing the Computer Program

The next step is to use the flowchart developed in Step 2 to write a computer program. This program can be written in numerous programming languages but will contain the logic flow of inputs, processes, and outputs described by the flowchart. The flowchart can represent a one-to-one correspondence to the statements of the computer program, or it can represent the general logic flow of the program. The one-to-one representation of flowchart to program is referred to as a *detail flowchart* or *microflowchart,* and the general program flow flowchart is referred to as a *modular flowchart* or *macroflowchart.*

Submit the Program to the Computer

This step requires sitting down at the terminal and typing the program into the computer. Once this is done we can move on to the final step; running, debugging and testing the computer program.

Running, Debugging, and Testing the Computer Program

The final step in the problem-solving process is to run the program written in Step 3. The program should be run, resolving the errors that may result (debugging), and then it should be tested to determine if the information created by the program is in fact correct. This is an important step, and care should be taken to test the program under as nearly actual conditions as possible.

Flowchart Preparation

Flowchart preparation can be a very important step in problem solving using computers, particulary if the individual preparing the flowchart is not the individual who will write the computer program. This situation arises on a regular basis in systems analysis and design. The systems analyst may prepare a flowchart describing the program to be written and then pass the flowchart to the computer programmer who will actually write the program. It is important, therefore, that a common set of symbols be used in preparing flowcharts.

Flowchart Symbols

The American National Standards Institute (ANSI) has adopted a set of flowcharting symbols that are used to depict the types of operations performed in a computer program. A basic subset of these symbols is shown in Figure F–1. The symbol ⬭ is referred to as the terminal symbol and represents the beginning and end of the program flowchart. The symbol ▱ is the input/output symbol and is used to describe the point at which data enter or are output by the program. The input mediums consist of such things as punched cards; CRT terminals; and secondary storage devices such as magnetic tape, magnetic disks, or magnetic drums. The output mediums can consist of printers, CRT terminals, or secondary storage devices. The symbol □, the process symbol, describes such operations as addition, subtraction, multiplication, and division. The symbol ◇ depicts a comparison or decision that can take one of two possible paths. One path

Figure F–1 FLOWCHART SYMBOLS

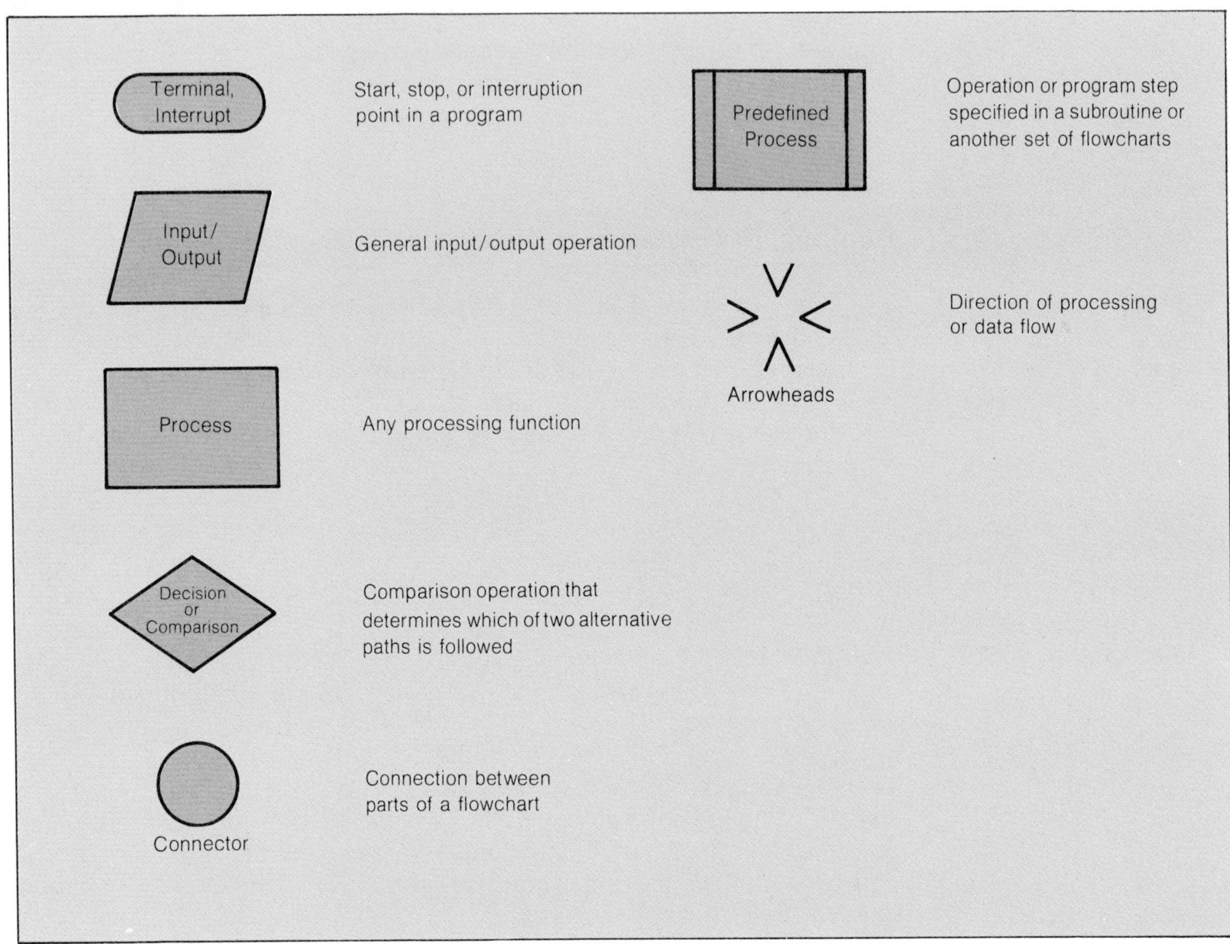

represents a comparison or decision that is true, and the other represent a comparison or decision that is false. The connector symbol, O, represents a connection between two points within the flowchart. The symbol ◫ represents a predefined process that describes a subroutine or another set of flowcharts. The arrowhead symbols, >V<Λ, simply represent the direction of the logic flow of the flowchart.

Logic Patterns

When writing flowcharts, four basic patterns of logic can be used. Figure F–2 uses the flowcharting symbols previously described to show these four basic logic patterns. The simple, or linear, sequence logic pattern describes the execution of the computer program statements as being one after the other in the sequence in which they were stored. The selection pattern uses the decision or comparison symbol to demonstrate the ability to conduct a test and then follow one of two possible paths based on the outcome of the test.

The loop, or repetition, pattern also uses the decision or comparison symbol. In this logic pattern, the test checks on the number of times the loop has been executed. Once the test is satisfied and the loop has been executed the correct number of times, the basic flow will advance beyond the loop. The branch, or link, logic pattern is used to skip a portion of a program based on the result of a decision or comparison. The GOTO statement or clause of many programming languages provides the branching mechanism.

These four basic program logic patterns can represent an entire program or a small segment of a program. It is also possible that all four logic pat-

Figure F–2 FOUR BASIC PROGRAM LOGIC PATTERNS

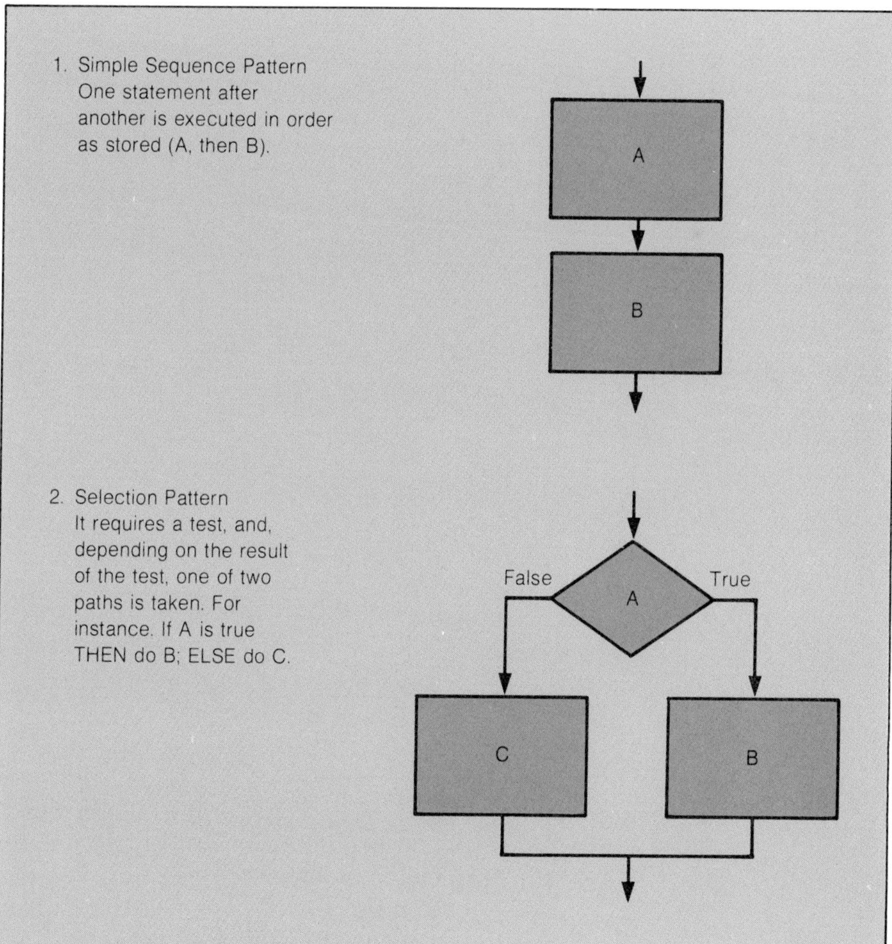

(Continued next page)

Figure F-2—*Continued*

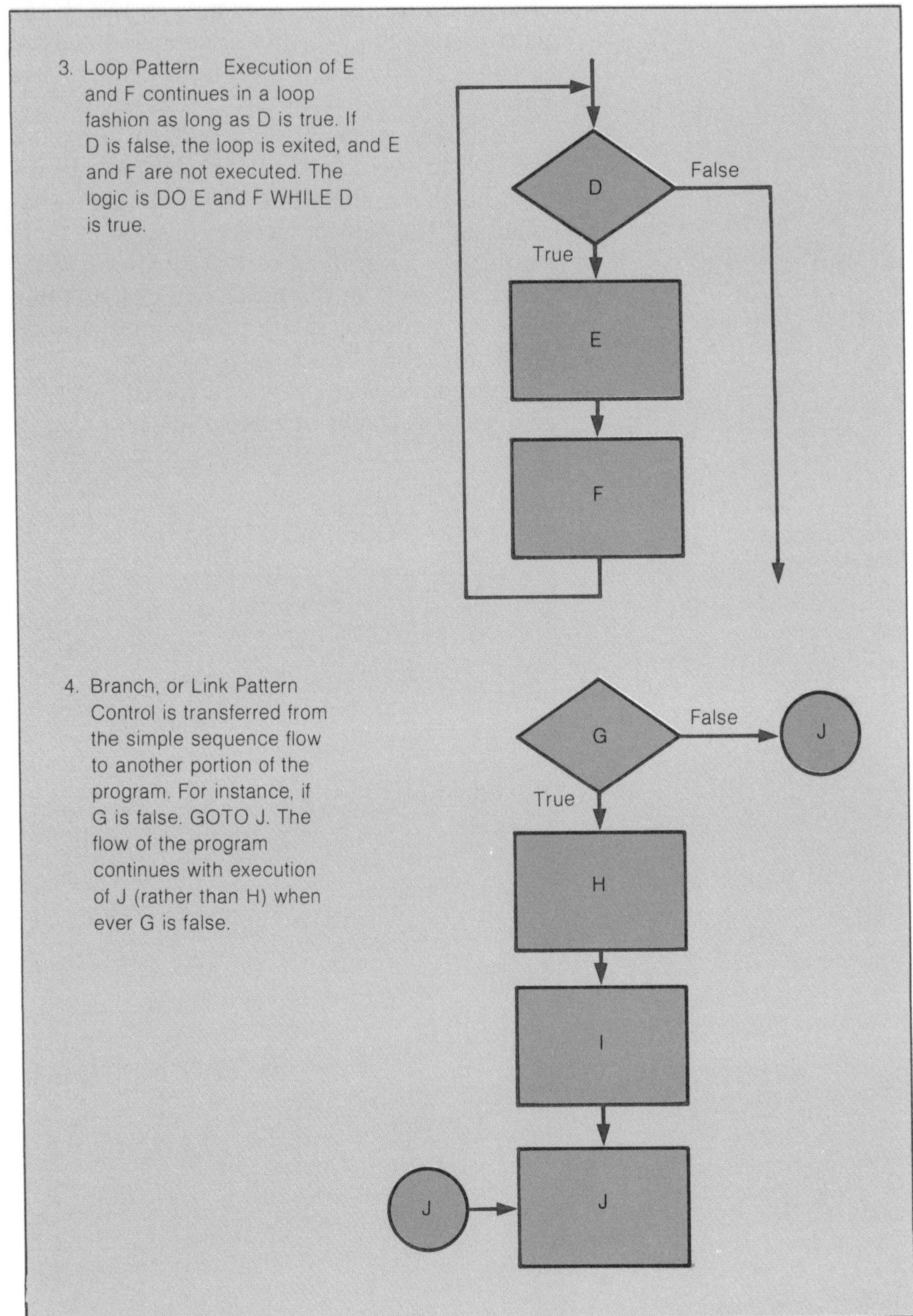
3. Loop Pattern Execution of E and F continues in a loop fashion as long as D is true. If D is false, the loop is exited, and E and F are not executed. The logic is DO E and F WHILE D is true.
D
False
True
E
F
4. Branch, or Link Pattern Control is transferred from the simple sequence flow to another portion of the program. For instance, if G is false. GOTO J. The flow of the program continues with execution of J (rather than H) when ever G is false.
G
False
J
True
H
I
J
J

terns could be contained in a single program. Although the number and syntax of the statements necessary to perform these logic patterns may vary from programming language to programming language, the basic logic patterns themselves will not vary.

Figure F-3 FLOWCHARTING EXAMPLE: TEMPERATURE CONVERSION

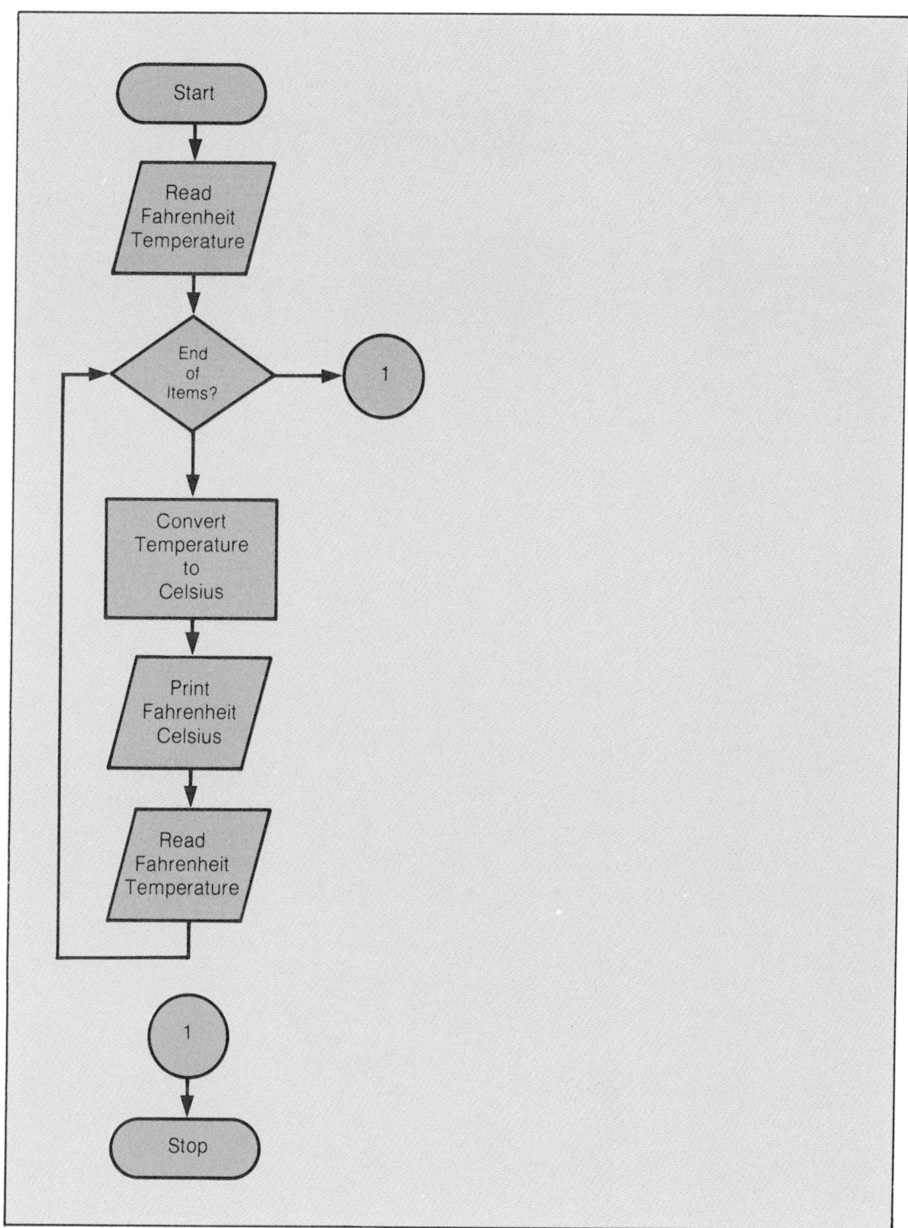

Flowcharting Example: Temperature Conversion

Figure F–3 demonstrates the use of flowcharting symbols and the loop logic pattern in the flowcharting of the logic flow to convert a Fahrenheit temperature to a Celsius temperature.

Figure F–4 PSEUDOCODE EXAMPLE: TEMPERATURE CONVERSION

```
Start.
Read Fahrenheit temperature to be converted.
Do until end of items.
Convert Fahrenheit temperature to Celsius.
Print Fahrenheit and Celsius temperatures.
Read Fahrenheit temperature to be converted.
End loop (no more data).
Stop.
```

Alternatives to Flowcharting

Recently, alternatives to describing the logic flow of a program have been gaining acceptance. Two of these alternatives, pseudocode and hierarchy charts, use English statements and rectangles to describe the logic patterns within the computer program.

Pseudocode

Pseudocode uses English statements to describe the logic of the program without being concerned with the syntax of a particular programming language. As with flowcharting, pseudocode and hierarchy charts can be used to represent the logic patterns in the program regardless of the programming language used. Figure F–4 demonstrates the use of pseudocode as it applies to the temperature conversion example.

Hierarchy Charts

Hierarchy charts use rectangles to portray the various levels of a program and the manner in which these levels interconnect. The charts are arranged from a top-down view. Lower levels are accessed from a process in the level above, and two processes on the same level cannot access each other. The temperature conversion example is illustrated in Figure F–5 using a hierarchy chart.

Pros and Cons of Flowcharting

Although flowcharts are an important tool in systems analysis and design, their popularity and use are declining. In the past, flowcharts have been an important piece of program documentation. They can serve as a valuable

Figure F-5 HIERARCHY CHART EXAMPLE: TEMPERATURE CONVERSION

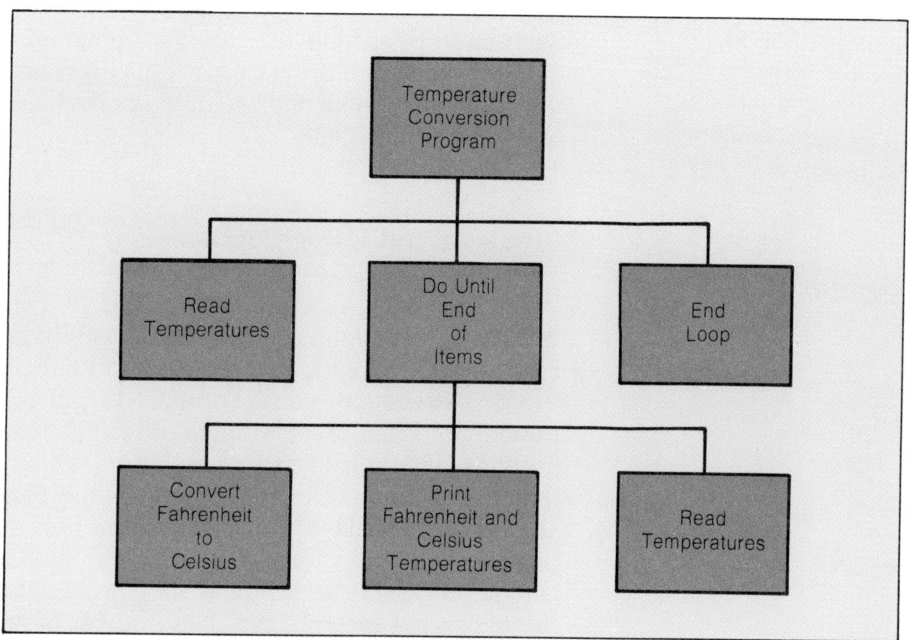

tool to a programmer in the maintenance of existing programs written by another person. However, because of the amount of time and effort necessary to prepare a flowchart when the program is written and to update the flowchart when the program is altered, the use of flowcharts has declined significantly.

Many professional programmers can write, debug, and test a program without ever writing a flowchart. Programmers address the problem of program maintenance without flowcharts by advocating commenting on programs within the program code itself. Those working on the program in the future then will have explanations of coding in the program via comments inserted directly into the program code.

Although flowcharting has lost favor in the professional programming environment, it can still serve as an invaluable tool in the education of programmers and systems analysts. By presenting a method of problem solving including the use of flowcharts, students of programming are forced to prepare a definite pattern of logic through a flowchart before writing the computer program. This type of problem-solving procedure then can act as the foundation of a logical problem-solving procedure.

The final section of this appendix will demonstrate the use of flowcharts and pseudocode in depicting the logic of six common logic problems frequently encountered in computer applications.

Common Program Logic Flowcharts

Each one of the following common program logic flowcharts uses one or more of the four basic logic patterns previously discussed. To understand the problems better, an example is provided for each, including a flowchart and pseudocode.

Input/Output Using Counters

When processing several input records, one method of detecting the end of the file is a counter. Each time an additional record is processed, the counter is incremented. When the counter equals the number of records in the file, execution stops. To effectively use a counter, the program can provide for input of the number of records to be processed. This allows the number of records to change each time the program is executed. To insure that the counter reflects the proper number of executions, the counter should be initialized to 0 prior to the first execution. This replaces any previously stored value.

The processing of customer statements is one example where the number of records may change. The number of current customers is inputted at the start of execution. Customer data will be read, and statements will be printed the specified number of times. Figure F–6 illustrates the basic logic for this process.

Multiple Decisions

Managers make decisions daily. Often, these decisions are based on several criteria. Just as often, these multiple criteria or decisions are answered through a computer program. Various answers are generated, depending on how many of the required criteria are met.

As an example, a used car dealer who operates several lots may wish to provide fast responses to customer inquiries concerning cars in stock. A master inventory listing is maintained for the cars on all lots. Inquiries can be made via a CRT for the required make, model, and year. The customer will obtain almost instantaneous results concerning the in-stock status and location of the car. This logic is shown in Figure F–7.

Accumulating Subtotals and Totals

Various subtotals and totals are needed in decision making. These are indicators of business activity. The subtotals may be categorized by department, item, account classification, or otherwise. The subtotals and totals are accumulated as records are read or as values are calculated.

Figure F–8 illustrates the logic for subtotaling various types of checking accounts in a bank's files. These may include minimum balance accounts,

Figure F–6 INPUT/OUTPUT USING COUNTERS

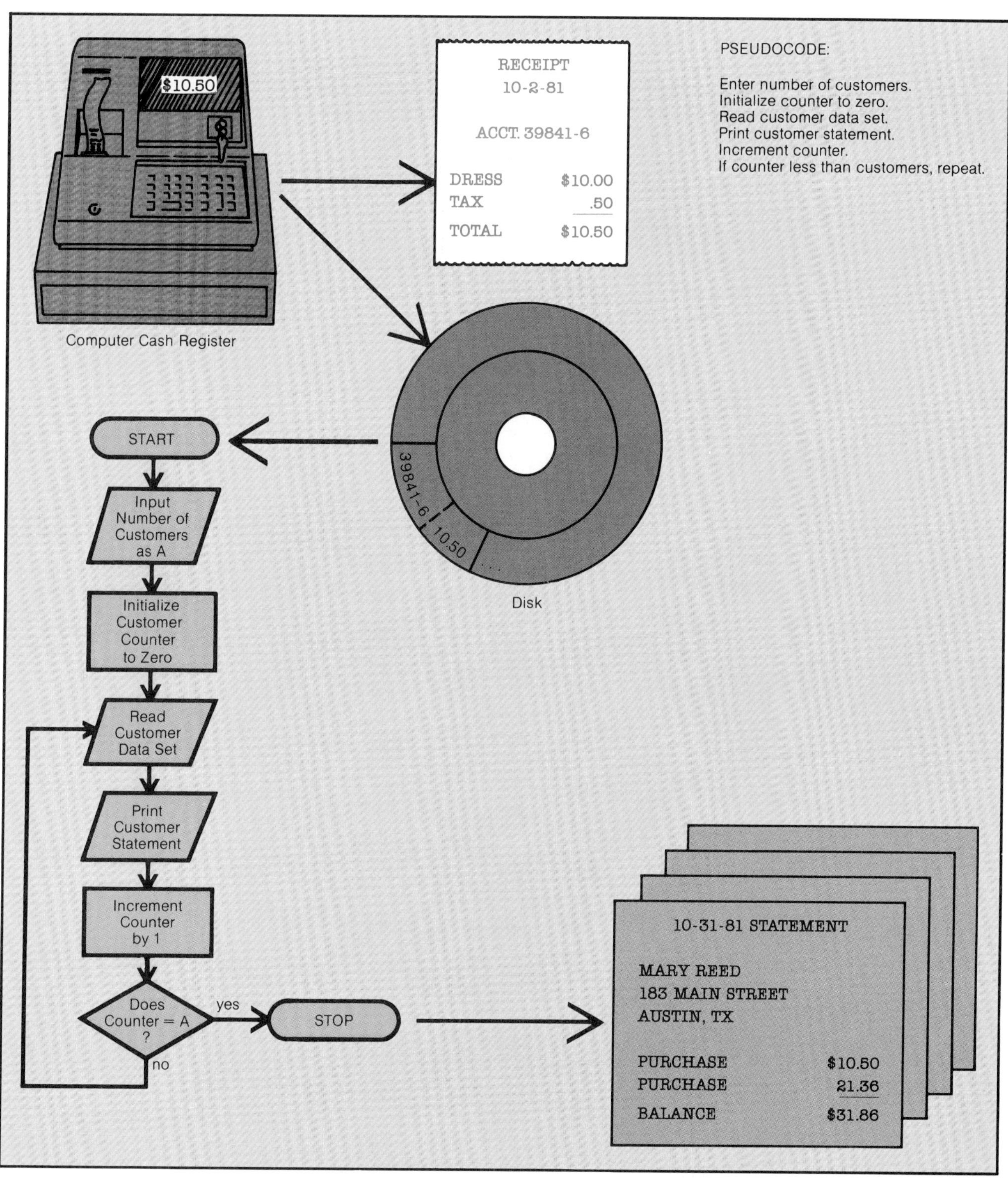

Figure F-7 MULTIPLE DECISIONS

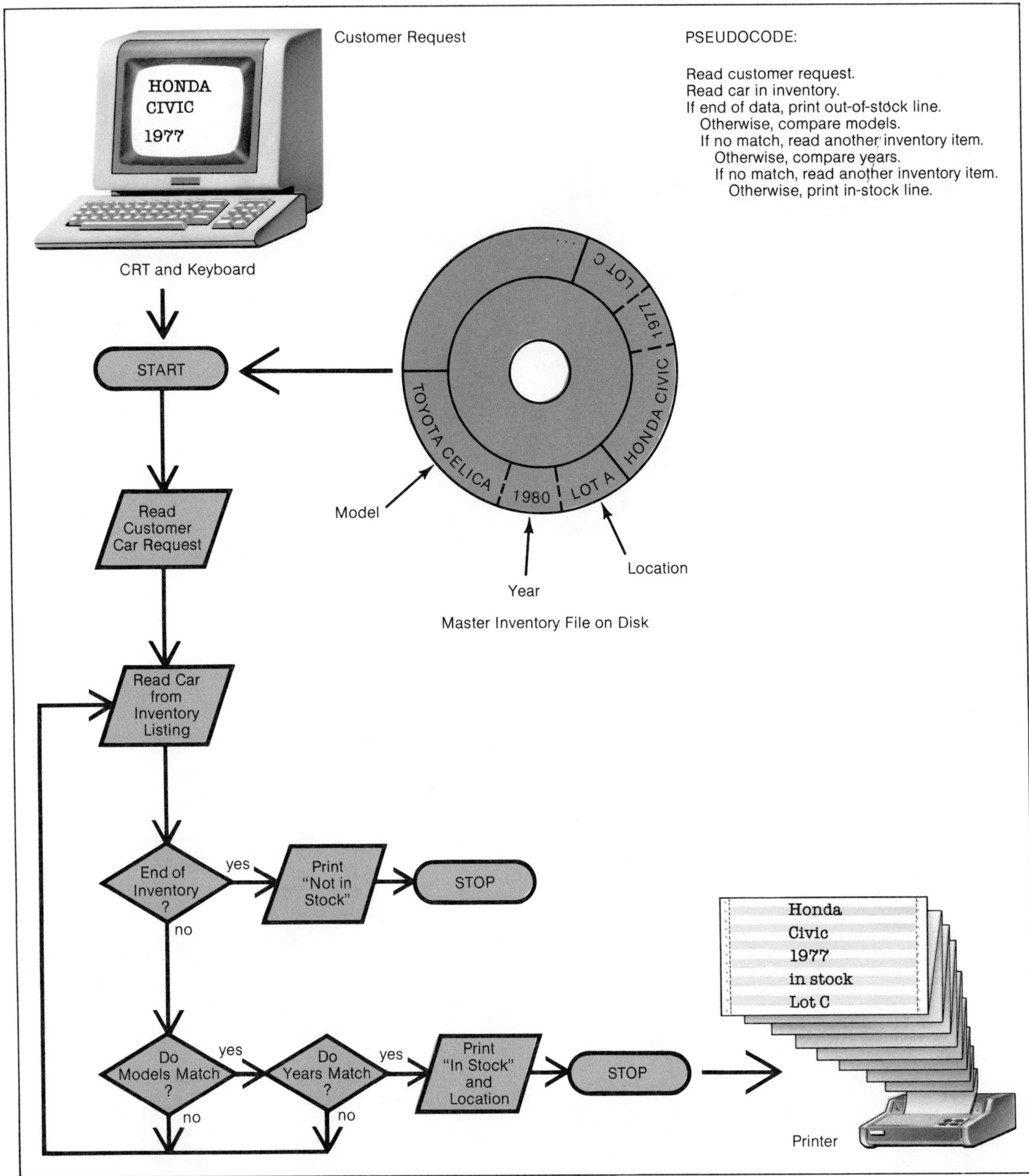

Customer Request
HONDA
CIVIC
1977
CRT and Keyboard
PSEUDOCODE:
Read customer request.
Read car in inventory.
If end of data, print out-of-stock line.
Otherwise, compare models.
If no match, read another inventory item.
Otherwise, compare years.
If no match, read another inventory item.
Otherwise, print in-stock line.
LOT C
1977
HONDA CIVIC
LOT A
1980
TOYOTA CELICA
Model
Year
Location
Master Inventory File on Disk
START
Read Customer Car Request
Read Car from Inventory Listing
End of Inventory ?
yes
no
Print "Not in Stock"
STOP
Do Models Match ?
yes
no
Do Years Match ?
yes
no
Print "In Stock" and Location
STOP
Honda
Civic
1977
in stock
Lot C
Printer

Figure F–8 ACCUMULATING SUBTOTALS AND TOTALS

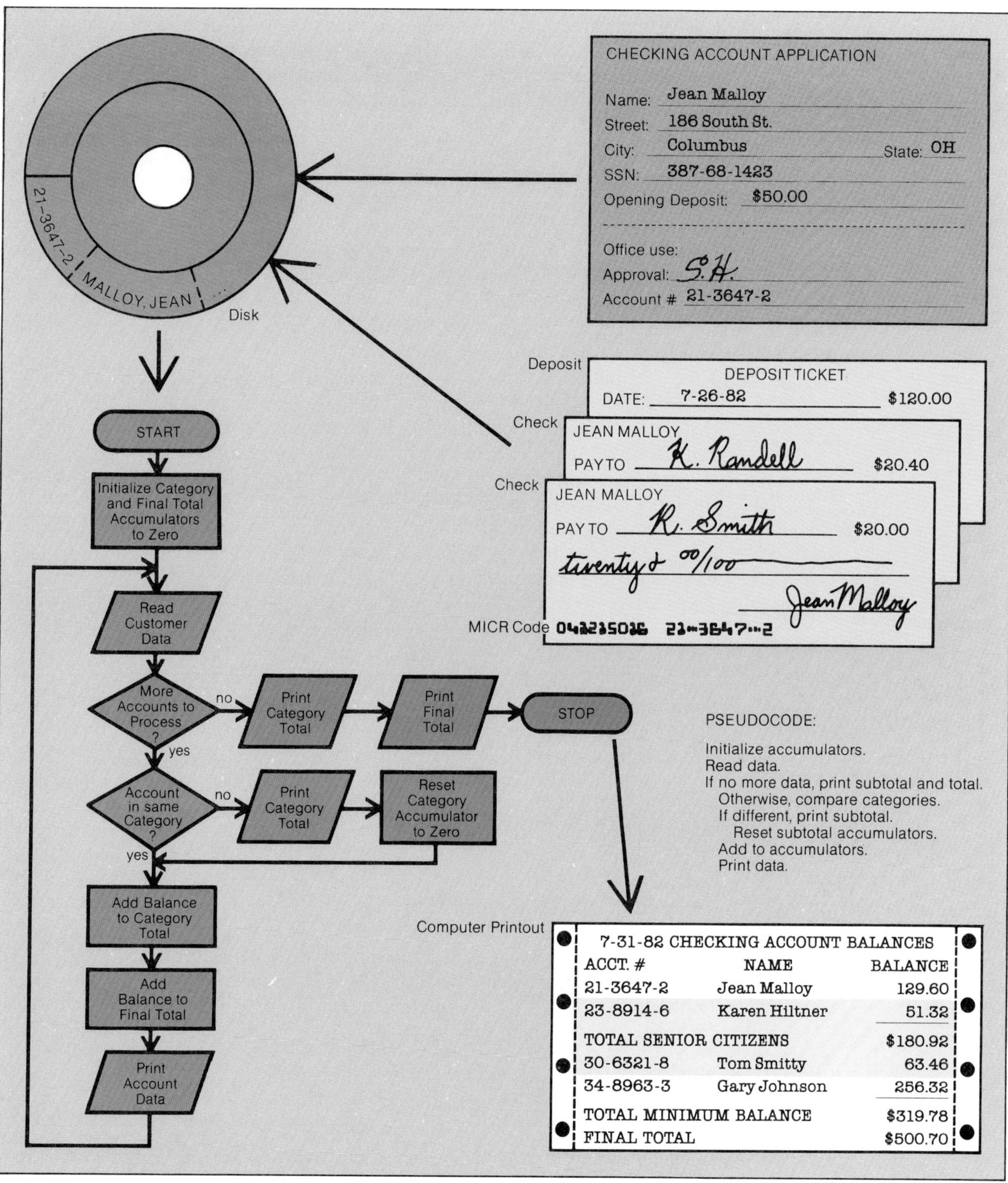

CHECKING ACCOUNT APPLICATION
Name: Jean Malloy
Street: 186 South St.
City: Columbus
State: OH
SSN: 387-68-1423
Opening Deposit: $50.00
Office use:
Approval: S.H.
Account # 21-3647-2
21-3647-2
MALLOY, JEAN
Disk
Deposit
DEPOSIT TICKET
DATE: 7-26-82
$120.00
Check
JEAN MALLOY
PAY TO K. Randell
$20.40
Check
JEAN MALLOY
PAY TO R. Smith
$20.00
twenty & 00/100
Jean Malloy
MICR Code
START
Initialize Category and Final Total Accumulators to Zero
Read Customer Data
More Accounts to Process ?
no
yes
Print Category Total
Print Final Total
STOP
Account in same Category ?
no
yes
Print Category Total
Reset Category Accumulator to Zero
Add Balance to Category Total
Add Balance to Final Total
Print Account Data
PSEUDOCODE:
Initialize accumulators.
Read data.
If no more data, print subtotal and total.
Otherwise, compare categories.
If different, print subtotal.
Reset subtotal accumulators.
Add to accumulators.
Print data.
Computer Printout
7-31-82 CHECKING ACCOUNT BALANCES
ACCT. # NAME BALANCE
21-3647-2 Jean Malloy 129.60
23-8914-6 Karen Hiltner 51.32
TOTAL SENIOR CITIZENS $180.92
30-6321-8 Tom Smitty 63.46
34-8963-3 Gary Johnson 256.32
TOTAL MINIMUM BALANCE $319.78
FINAL TOTAL $500.70

senior citizen accounts, corporate accounts, and others. Each type of account is identified with a different leading digit. Checking accounts are typically ordered by number. As each account balance is read, it is added to both the subtotal and total. When the end of a category is reached, the subtotal is recorded and reset to 0 to begin the next category. The total, however, is retained until all categories are completed.

Tables

In some business applications, it is more efficient to store data in a table than on each individual record. A code written on the record permits access to the table as needed during processing. When the stored values need to be changed, the changes are made directly to the table rather than to each record. The code on the record remains the same, and the new table value is accessed with that code.

For example, a wholesaler in Indiana may service retailers in all fifty states. A table is used that lists the freight charges for shipping to each of the states. These are identified on each shipping record by the two-letter state abbreviations. Figure F–9 illustrates the logic for generating freight statements using this table. At the start of the program, all the data from the table are read into arrays so that each data item is read only once. The state code from the shipping record is compared with the state codes in the array until the correct code is located. If the freight rates change at a later date, the table is changed rather than the numerous retailer records.

Merging Files

Some applications may routinely or periodically require the merging of files. This process combines two or more files into one larger file. If sequential files are used, one record is read from each file and the keys are compared. If the keys are ordered from lowest to highest, for example, the record with the lowest key is written to the new file. An additional record is read from one of the original files to replace the record that was transferred. Another comparison is then made. This process continues until all records from the original files have been transferred to the new file.

An automobile insurance company may merge a new customer file with a master file as often as daily. Figure F–10 shows the logic for this process, assuming the records are ordered sequentially by policy number. Depending on the circumstances, a hard copy of the new master file may or may not be generated. In this example, a new file is in computer-readable form for future processing.

Sorting

In many business applications, it is necessary to sort, or order, data sets alphabetically or numerically. This can occur when data is collected or

Figure F-9 TABLES

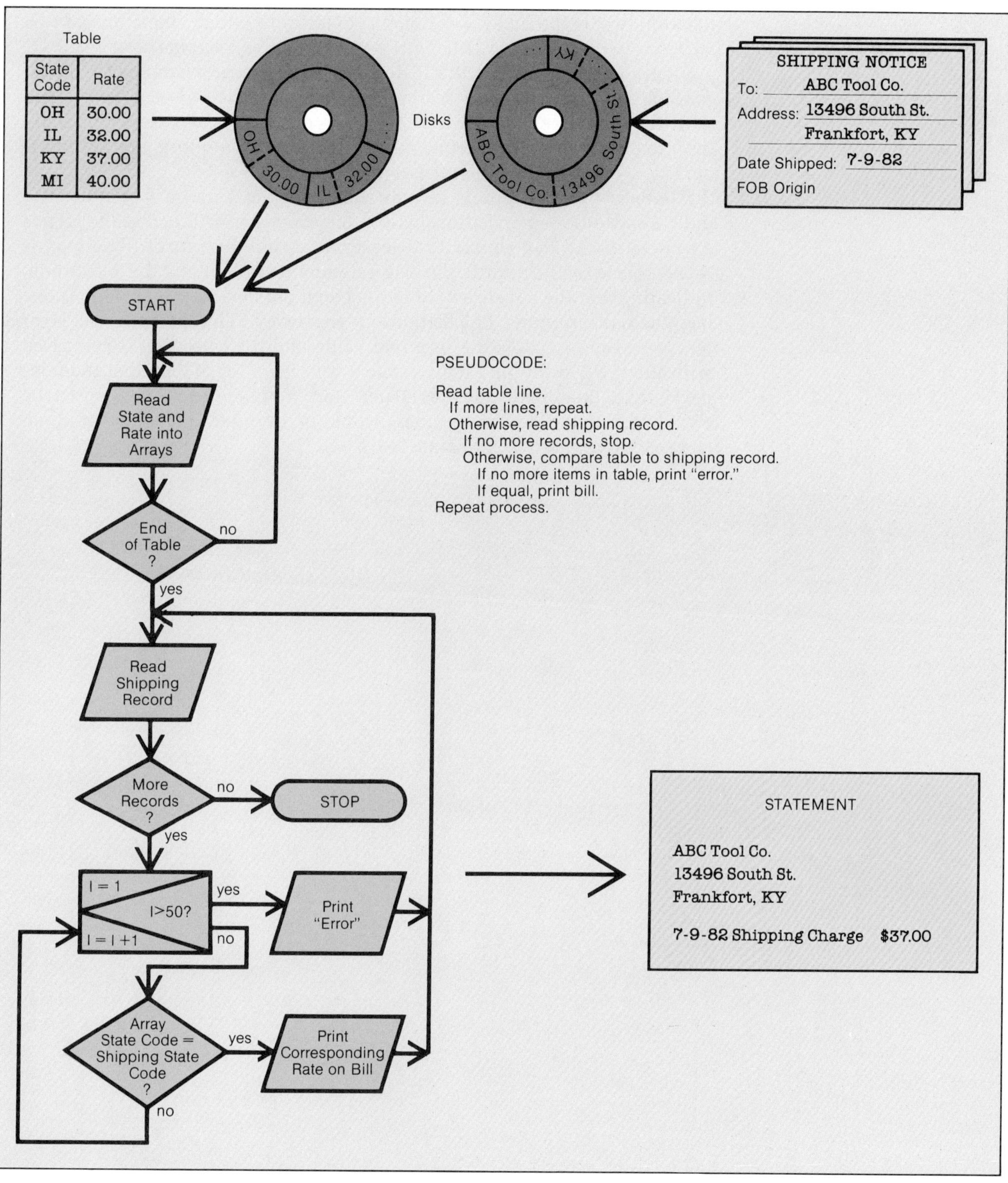

stored in an order different from that required for sequential file processing or printing reports. Arrays are used to sort the data, with comparisons made between the array locations to determine which items need to be switched within a given list. This is referred to as a *bubble sort.*

Figure F–11 illustrates the logic for sorting ten new employees by ascending employee number so that the new employee file can be merged with the master employee file. The new employee data were originally inputted as the applications were submitted and, therefore, are not in order.

There are several points to note when sorting. First, a flag is used to indicate whether any positions within the array are switched as the loop is executed. If the flag equals 1, at least one switch was made. The loop is repeatedly executed until the flag remains 0 throughout the execution, indicating that the data are in order. Second, the loop terminal value is one less than the number of positions in the array. This prevents an error message when I equals the terminal value and the I position is compared with the I + 1 position. Finally, when ordering a set of data that includes more than one field, such as name and number, each field must be switched. Otherwise, the numbers would be in order, but they would not correspond to the correct name.

Figure F-10 MERGING FILES

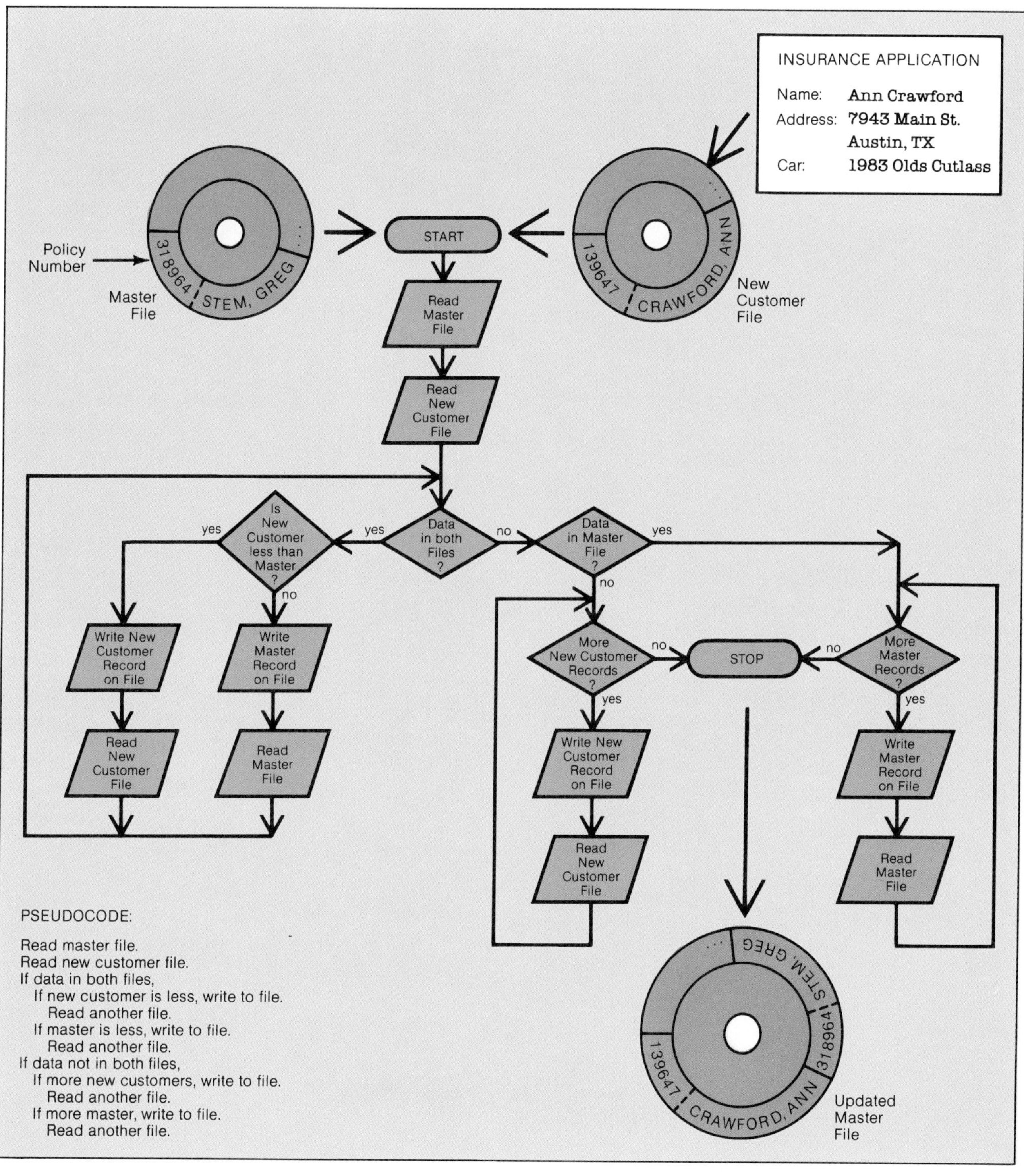

PSEUDOCODE:

Read master file.
Read new customer file.
If data in both files,
  If new customer is less, write to file.
    Read another file.
  If master is less, write to file.
    Read another file.
If data not in both files,
  If more new customers, write to file.
    Read another file.
  If more master, write to file.
    Read another file.

Figure F-11 SORTING

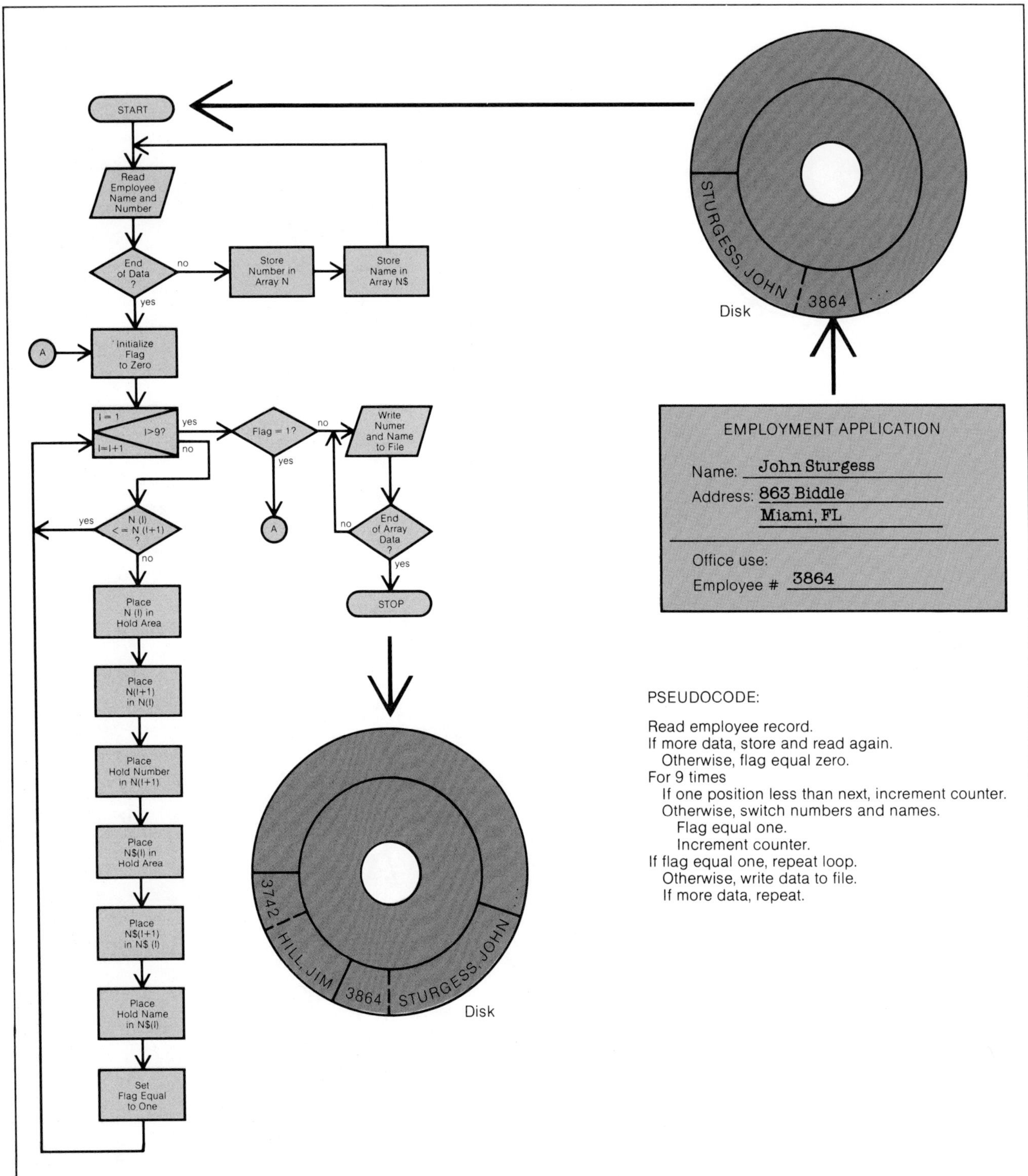

PSEUDOCODE:

Read employee record.
If more data, store and read again.
  Otherwise, flag equal zero.
For 9 times
  If one position less than next, increment counter.
  Otherwise, switch numbers and names.
    Flag equal one.
    Increment counter.
If flag equal one, repeat loop.
  Otherwise, write data to file.
  If more data, repeat.

INDEX

BASIC Reference Card

Complete BASIC Programming ■ Mandell

BASIC Language Commands

Command	Explanation	Example
CLOSE	Closes a file	100 CLOSE #1
DEF	Defines a function	10 DEF FNR(X) = 4 * 3.1416 * X∧2
DIM	Sets dimensions for arrays	20 DIM A(25)
END	Indicates the last statement in a program	999 END
FOR/NEXT	Sets up a loop	30 FOR I = 1 TO 5 . . . 70 NEXT I
GET	Reads a record from the file into a buffer	230 GET #1,RECORD 4
GOSUB/RETURN	Branches to a subroutine, then returns to the main line of the program	100 GOSUB 350 . . . 400 RETURN
GOTO	Signals unconditional transfer of control	15 GOTO 60
IF/THEN	Signals conditional transfer of control	200 IF N$ = "LAST" THEN 400
IF/THEN/ELSE	Signals conditional transfer of control	350 IF X = Y THEN PRINT "X = Y" ELSE PRINT "X<>Y"
INPUT	Allows data to be entered at the terminal	40 INPUT J$, A or 40 INPUT "NAME, AGE"; J$, 4
LET	Indicates an assignment statement	90 LET B = B + A
MAP	Establishes a buffer for file input and output	10 MAP BUFF 1 N$ = 20
MAT	Indicates a command for various matrix operations	400 MAT PRINT A
ON/GOTO	Signals a conditional transfer of control	10 ON J GOTO 40, 50, 60
OPEN	Creates or accesses a data file	10 OPEN "GRADES" AS FILE #2
PRINT	Displays or prints output	60 PRINT "TOM"
PRINT USING	Permits flexibility in formatting output; used with image statement	40 PRINT USING 90,B
PUT	Writes a new record from the buffer to the file	160 PUT #1,RECORD 12
READ/DATA	Reads data into variables from the data list	30 READ A,B,C 40 DATA 40,50,60
REM	Provides documentation	10 REM LOOP BEGINS
STOP	Stops execution of a program	75 STOP
TAB	Used in a PRINT statement to format output	80 PRINT TAB(5);N
UNTIL/NEXT	Sets up a loop	25 UNTIL C = 10 . . . 60 NEXT
WHILE/NEXT	Sets up a loop	80 WHILE A<X . . . 120 NEXT

BASIC String Functions

String Function	Operation	Example	Microcomputer Differences
string A$ + string B$	Concatenates joins two strings together	KUNG + FU is KUNGFU	None
LEN(string)	Finds the length of a string	If H$ is HELLO HOWARD, then LEN(H$) is 12	None
LEFT$(string,expression)	Returns the number of leftmost characters of a string specified by the expression	LEFT$("ABCDE",2) is AB	None
RIGHT$(string,expression)	Returns the rightmost characters of a string, starting with the character specified by the expression	RIGHT$("ABCDE",2) is BCDE	Finds last n characters of a given string RIGHT$("ABCDE",2)
MID$(string,expression 1,expression 2)	Starting with the character at expression 1, returns the number of characters specified by expression 2	MID$("ABCDE",3,2) is CD	None
ASCII(string)	Returns the ASCII code for the first character in the string	If A$ contains DOG, then ASCII(A$) is 68	Apple: ASC(string)
CHR$(expression)	Returns the string representation of the ASCII code of the expression	If CHR$(F$) > Z, then 20	None
VAL(expression)	Returns the numeric equivalent of the string expression	X = VAL(H$)	None
STR$(expression)	Converts a number to its string equivalent	STR$(123) is the string 123	None

System Commands

Command	Explanation	Microcomputer Differences
RUN	Executes program; output printed with header	No header
RUNNH	Same as RUN, but no header printed	Not applicable
LIST	Lists entire program with header	No header
LIST 100	Lists line 100 with header	No header
LIST—100	Lists all lines from beginning of program to line 100 with header	No header
LIST 100—	Lists all lines from line 100 to end of program with header	No header
LIST 100—150	Lists lines 100 through 150 inclusive with header	No header
LISTNH	Same as LIST, but no header printed	Not applicable
SAVE	Saves program in memory to auxiliary storage device	None
NEW	Clears memory	None
OLD	Loads specified program from auxiliary storage device into memory	LOAD

BASIC Arithmetic Functions

Function	Purpose	Microcomputer Differences	Function	Purpose	Microcomputer Differences
SIN(X)	Trigonometric sine function, X in radians	None	EXP(X)	e raised to the X power	None
COS(X)	Trigonometric cosine function, X in radians	None	SQR(X)	Square root of X	None
TAN(X)	Trigonometric tangent function, X in radians	None	INT(X)	Greatest integer less than X	None
ATN(X)	Trigonometric arc tangent function, X in radians	None	SGN(X)	Sign of X	None
LOG(X)	Natural logarithm function	None	ABS(X)	Absolute value of X	None
			RND	Random number between 0 and 1	Apple, TRS-80, PET/Commodore 64: RND function requires an argument, RND(X)